Viella History, Art and Humanities Collection
3

Antonín Kalous

Late Medieval Papal Legation

Between the Councils and the Reformation

viella

First edition: november 2017
ISBN 978-88-6728-942-4

The preparation and publication of this work was supported by the GAČR project Prelates on the road: Cultural and social contacts of late medieval Europe, reg. no. 13-01279S; and by the Faculty of Arts, Palacký University, Olomouc.

viella
libreria editrice
via delle Alpi, 32
I-00198 ROMA
tel. 06 84 17 758
fax 06 85 35 39 60
www.viella.it

Contents

Introduction 7

1. Theory and practice 17
  1.1. Typology and terminology 19
  1.2. The sources 39
    1.2.1. An example: Sources for the legation of Angelo Pecchinoli 49

2. Rights and powers 55
  2.1. The authority of the legates 55
    2.1.1. Judicial authority 63
    2.1.2. Benefices and papal reserved powers 67
    2.1.3. Dispensations 68
  2.2. Faculties 69
    2.2.1. Benefices 76
    2.2.2. Indulgences and other graces 77
    2.2.3. Apostolic Penitentiary 79
    2.2.4. Specific cases 87
  2.3. Geographical and temporal limits of the legation 90

3. *Modus operandi* 103
  3.1. Ceremonial 103
    3.1.1. Rome 105
    3.1.2. Outside Rome 112
  3.2. On the road 124
    3.2.1. Travelling 125
    3.2.2. The retinue 129
  3.3. Financing a legation 135
    3.3.1. Procuration 135
    3.3.2. Central payments 137
    3.3.3. The salary of the legate 139
    3.3.4. The salary of the nuncio 144
    3.3.5. Further resources 146

4. Politics and diplomacy 149
4.1. Papal legates and the crusades 150
4.1.1. Papal legates and the Hussite crusade 151
4.1.2. The Ottoman crusades 158
4.2. *Angeli Pacis* 167
4.2.1. International and internal conflicts 169
4.2.2. Communication 186
4.3. Church politics and policy 188
4.3.1. Outside Rome 189
4.3.2. Rome 199
4.4. Acceptance of legates 208

Concluding remarks 213

Bibliography 217

Index 247

Introduction

> The Roman Pontifex is placed over the peoples and kingdoms, but because he cannot personally travel in all individual regions and cannot administer the solicitude of pastoral care over the herd entrusted to him, it is sometimes necessary owing to the servitude put upon him to send his legates to diverse lands of the world, as the need emerges, who correct errors, difficulties transform to simplicities and serve the peoples entrusted to them with the growth of salvation (*Extrav. comm. 1.1.un.*).

> You have come, dearest father, whom we expected in our sorrows, you have come with the celestial gifts to bless all the people of good will (*Staré letopisy české*).

These two little quotations bring us to a topic that has never been forgotten and that often became crucial to treatments of European medieval history, but not so often central to the historical research. The first quote comes from a constitution *Super gentes* of Pope John XXII that asserted the absolute respect for the papal legates in all regions under the authority of the Roman papacy. The latter is the glorious triumphal antiphon *Advenisti desiderabilis*, which was sung by the Prague burghers to greet Cardinal Juan Carvajal, papal legate *de latere*, in 1448. The first quote demonstrates the intention of the papacy to clearly promote the ecclesiastical and papal authority even in areas outside the scope of actual power of the pope. The latter exemplifies the results of such an attitude: even though Juan Carvajal arrived in Utraquist Prague and even though he was later criticised and even derided, he represented the pope in his judicial as well as spiritual capacity and as such his position was not questioned, but accepted by all with high expectations.

Papal legates constitute one of the means of central papal government that evolved throughout the High Middle Ages, at the time of the reform of the Church and its institutions and administration. The reference in *Super gentes* to the "injunction" of Jeremiah (Jer 1:10) puts the legates in the context of reasoning for the general papal authority.[1] The pope was no longer just one of the bishops of the universal episcopal body, but the uncontested head of the Church and

1. Jer 1:10 (Vulgate), *ecce constitui te hodie super gentes et super regna ut evellas et destruas et disperdas et dissipes et aedifices et plantes*; Extrav. comm. 1.1.un. (Friedberg, ed., *Corpus*, vol. 2, col. 1237), *Super gentes et regna Romanus Pontifex a Domino constitutus, quum personaliter singulas regiones circuire non possit, nec circa gregem sibi creditum curam pastoralis sollicitudinis exercere…*; cf. for the use of Jeremiah, Rennie, "The 'Injunction of Jeremiah'".

representative of Christ on Earth. In the eleventh century, the popes had two most crucial points on their agenda: to gain ground against the secular power and to consolidate the leading position within the Church itself.[2] Even if in the first point the popes were successful only partially and temporarily, the other part of the programme was quite clearly implemented. The reform papacy of the twelfth century with the help of the gradually codified canon law managed to cement this claim, which only intensified during the twelfth and thirteenth centuries. Although the superiority of the spiritual power over the secular one was still contested and questioned, the papal primacy became a matter of fact confirmed by the canon law that developed in the two centuries. The struggles at the start of the fourteenth century brought a downfall of the papal power; nevertheless, the Avignon papacy consolidated the 'papal monarchy' through administrative and financial government and centralisation. The schism and conciliar theories most notably postponed the developments, which resulted in the renovated papacy's stress on reinforcing the pope's leadership of the institutionalised Church.

The period of the fifteenth century was, then, filled with the renewed efforts of the popes to restore the prominent role in the Church that was shattered by the Councils. The long fifteenth century was understood by (especially) Church historians as the period from the 1370s to 1520s, but not all the institutions functioned the same throughout this period.[3] The period can be distinguished further into smaller parts with dividing point in 1417 and 1449. The election of the new pope in 1417 brought some changes, but definitely did not mean that the pope prevailed. On 25 April 1449, the Council of Basel dissolved itself in Lausanne where eighteen days before the last conciliar pope Felix V abdicated.[4] After the 1440s, the conciliar thoughts lost ground and the achievements of Pope Eugenius IV, the fruits of which were garnered by his successor Nicholas V, confirmed the supreme role of the pope again.[5] This book will focus mostly on the period that can be characterised by the success of the popes against the Council and other central institutions of the Church. By the beginning of the sixteenth century, the position of the popes was strengthened within the general Church as well as at the Curia against the College of Cardinals, which could not act independently. The 1520s then brought not only the spread of the German Reformation and the *sacco di Roma*, but also the reforms of the Curia, which also changed the system of papal representation including the role of legates *de latere*.[6] The conciliar and the reformation periods,

2. Cushing, *Reform and the Papacy*; Morris, *Papal Monarchy.*

3. Van Engen, "Multiple Options"; cf. for example Rapp, *L'Église*; recently e.g. Decaluwe, *A Successful Defeat*; Müller, ed., *Das Ende*; Dendorfer and Märtl, eds., *Nach dem Basler Konzil*; Christianson, Izbicki and Bellitto, eds., *The Church.*

4. Cf. Gießmann, *Der letzte Gegenpapst*; Stieber, ed., *Concilium Basiliense*, p. 1157.

5. On conciliarism see at least, Tierney, *The Foundations*; and also Stump, *The Reforms*; Black, *Council and Commune*; idem, *Church, State and Community*; Oakley, *The Conciliarist Tradition.* On conciliar attempts in the second half of the fifteenth and early sixteenth centuries see Thomson, *Popes and Princes*, pp. 13-28.

6. On the papacy in the fifteenth century see, Thomson, *Popes and Princes*; Pellegrini, *Il papato*; Setton, *The Papacy*, vol. 2. On legates Marco Pellegrini remarked that "le legazioni cardinalizie non scomparvero, ma divennero più rare e furono riservate a circostanze di particolare delicatezza", Pellegrini, "Il sacro collegio cardinalizio", p. 325.

however, are excluded so that the system of papal legations may be described and analysed in the form that belonged to the period in between.

Popes of the Middle Ages developed and maintained a system of government of the Church that was based on canon law, the papal plenitude of power and the distribution of that power. There is a long history of the development of papal power and the fifteenth century built on that, including the struggle against the Council.[7] Various parts of the Papal Curia developed over the few centuries since the Gregorian Reform and further adjustments were introduced during the following centuries. Legates were installed as one of the basic instruments of the papal government, with a powerful reach outside Rome. The system of legatine representation evolved by legal practice that was incorporated in the compilations and handbooks of canon law. Pope Gregory VII sent out many legates and only after his period, the system received its form that lasted for the rest of the Middle Ages. Canon law then differentiated between three types of legates, i.e. *legati de latere*, *legati missi* and *legati nati.* The legate became a direct representative of the pope, who received part of the papal plenitude of power (*plenitudo potestatis*); the legate *de latere* became an alter-ego of the vicar of Christ with the highest possible authority. In later years, legates *de latere* became crucial for the entire system, whereas the other two categories were slowly disappearing from usage. The period between the beginnings of the definitions in the canon law in the twelfth century and the changes of the sixteenth century seems to have been standardised by the canon law. However, it kept changing according to current needs.

The second half of the fifteenth century is a period when popes again manifested their power even more by sending cardinals – legates *de latere* as their crucial representatives.[8] After the crisis of the fourteenth century, legates were dispatched from Rome with renewed efforts and intensity. Popes of the period had one powerful tool for strengthening their position and it was the crusade, which was propagated by all the pontiffs of the period and directed against the advancing Ottoman Turks in the Balkans. In addition, there were three basic values to the crusade: the crusade itself, organising peace among Christian princes (or states in general) for the crusade and increasing the authority of whoever proposes the idea of the holy war. These values brought about the negotiations for peace among Italians as well as among Christian states beyond the Alps.[9] The Renaissance papacy looked for ways

7. On papal government, Ullmann, *The Growth*; Weinfurter, ed., *Päpstliche Herrschaft* and other general works.

8. On cardinals in the later Middle Ages most recently, Dendorfer and Lützelschwab, eds., *Geschichte des Kardinalats*; iidem, eds., *Die Kardinäle*; Richardson, *Reclaiming Rome*; see also, Thomson, *Popes and Princes*, p. 57-77; Hallman, *Italian Cardinals*; Chambers, *Renaissance Cardinals.* Otherwise, a vast body of literature exists, which cannot be recounted here; from the point of canon law see at least Kuttner, "Cardinalis", with additions in idem, *The History of Ideas.*

9. Setton, *The Papacy*, vol. 2; and from the vast new literature cf. at least, Housley, *The Later Crusades*; idem, *Religious Warfare in Europe*; idem, *Crusading and the Ottoman Threat*; idem, ed., *Crusading in the Fifteenth Century*; idem, ed., *The Crusade in the Fifteenth Century*; idem, ed., *Reconfiguring the Fifteenth-Century Crusade*; Pellegrini, *Le crociate*; idem, *Guerra santa*; idem, *La crociata*; Weber, *Lutter contre les Turcs.*

of updating the system of medieval papal representation not only in relation to the organisation of the crusades, but also in respect to the renewal of papal power and administration within the Church. Popes tried to innovate the concept of legates *de latere* and utilise them as representatives of the Roman Curia with the highest authority. Pius II, for example, sent no less than twenty-four legations during his pontificate and employed many more other papal envoys.[10] Such a development seems to be absolutely clear. However, where does the office of legates *de latere* fit within the system of papal administration? How are they accepted within the Church? How do they fit into the local Church system? Is there any relation to the new trends in spirituality in the fifteenth century? Did the legates follow the general rules designed earlier or is the fifteenth century specific?

Answers need to be sought to all of these questions, even though they will not be final, as the research still goes on. The structure of the Roman Curia, as presented by historians, is defined by individual offices and tribunals. Papal legates do not usually find a place in the general description of the structure, even though their authority has the same origin: they are not regarded as a standard office within this system. However, the fact that legates and nuncios regularly visited all parts of Europe with more or less standardised powers and authority makes them an integral part of that arrangement. Although they were not traditionally described as part of the system, recently, even in general overviews of medieval papacy, historians have recognised their role within the organism of papal administration, usually in relation to the College of Cardinals and the cardinals' role outside Rome.[11] Clearly, legates were not a stable office within the Curia, but they often replaced the decisions of the Curia with their entrusted powers. Functionally, they could figure as one of the institutions that derived their authority from the papal plenitude of power as other offices of the Curia did.

Moreover, the position of legates in the fifteenth century is specific in their mobility and the response of the office to the necessities of the new era. In his highly inspirational essay, John Van Engen pointed out several tendencies within the late medieval Church. Basic intellectual events and processes, for example, "shifted decisively to local forces" as opposed to the centralising powers of the previous period. Various regions gave rise to new religious impulses and spiritual trends.[12] Papal legates, then, constituted the long arm of papal authority that could solve the problems on the spot, when the central power could not reach the place that easily. The successor of St Peter could solve various problems by means of papal legates even down to the parish level. Changes in piety and ecclesiastical life in the fifteenth century were connected to the changes in legal awareness even in the point of spirituality. Canon law gave limits to the behaviour of Christian believers, but then the system of dispensations and licences allowed for adjustments.[13] These graces were published by the Curia (and most importantly

10. Cf. Lesage, *La titulature*, p. 214.

11. Cf. e.g. Frenz, *Das Papsttum*, pp. 205-208; Whalen, *The Medieval Papacy*, p. 115; and as a chapter by Harald Müller in Sisson and Larson, eds., *A Companion*, pp. 199-219.

12. Van Engen, "Multiple Options", p. 263.

13. *Ibid.*, pp. 272-275.

the Apostolic Penitentiary), but legates usually carried faculties that allowed them to do the same, as shown for example by Ludwig Schmugge and dispensations of illegitimacy.[14] A similar situation prevailed in the question of indulgences, which began to be extremely popular in the late medieval period. Papal legates were able to publish indulgence letters and even more crucially the confessional letters to enable believers to have their sins absolved in the region even in cases that would otherwise require travelling to Rome. The involvement of legates in the local Church is therefore absolutely crucial and when it lasted for a longer time, the local dioceses could have been substantially influenced.

Legates were also political and diplomatic envoys of the Roman pontiff, so their position could have changed following the tasks and negotiations they had to lead. They built not only on the status of the pope in the field of international relations in the later Middle Ages, but also from the spiritual authority and popes' efforts to become peace-makers and arbiters of international politics. It is impossible, then, to separate the legates' political, diplomatic, ecclesiastical and spiritual authority, as they were all interlinked and built on one other. Thus, the meaning and significance of legates (and especially legates *de latere* or envoys with similar powers) are central to the government of the Church, and thus the interest of historians.

Research on papal legates is vast, as can be stated about almost any field of medieval studies by now. Papal legates feature in books and studies on national political histories, as they crucially influenced political developments; they are part of the history of the papacy and of the Church or canon law and more specifically papal diplomacy. However, closer interest in the specialised study of papal diplomacy has been very much focused on the period of the high Middle Ages, namely the eleventh to thirteenth centuries (in relation to the reform of the papacy and the development of canon law), and early modern times, namely the sixteenth and seventeenth centuries (in relation to the papal nunciatures).[15] Studies and research in general are not that frequent for other periods, even though their number grows every year. The period researched in this book has – apart from two or three attempts – never been studied in a concise manner, editions are few as are historical studies.[16] In 2007, Birgit Studt was even sceptical in terms of mapping and creating an overview of individual legations of the fifteenth century.[17] As for systematic study of the fifteenth-century legations, not all that much research has been carried out either. There are a number of studies on individual legates and individual legations in certain regions, but studies that try to describe the system are few. This was the reason why at the German Historical Institute in Rome Ludwig Schmugge organised a

14. Schmugge, *Kirche, Kinder, Karrieren*, pp. 47-63.

15. Cf. at least, Koller, ed., *Kurie und Politik*.

16. Cf. Petersohn, ed., *Diplomatische Berichte*, p. 9; Studt, "Anspruch und Wirklichkeit", p. 85.

17. *Ibid.*, "Ein Zensus aller Legationen des 15. Jahrhunderts wird wohl angesichts der ungleichen Editionslage der kurialen Überlieferung für die einzelnen europäischen Länder noch lange ein Desiderat bleiben".

one-day conference ten years ago on the topic of papal legates in the fifteenth century (*Die Delegation der* plenitudo potestatis? *Päpstliche Legaten im 15. Jahrhundert*).

Werner Maleczek was the first one to attempt to evaluate the system and activities of legates in the fourteenth and fifteenth centuries in general. His 2003 study offered an excellent overview of the problem in the context of the period.[18] Birgit Studt, then, provided insight into the problem in a shorter study on the legates' diplomatic activities in the first half of the fifteenth century.[19] Since then, my book on the legates of the second half of the fifteenth and early sixteenth centuries was published in 2010, which gave an analysis of the system of papal legations in the period and a list of legates and nuncios in the region of Central Europe in 1447-1527. The current volume is a substantially updated version of the first part of the book that focused on the system itself.[20] Two years later, the excellent doctoral dissertation of Wolfgang Untergehrer was written that, in its systematic part, revealed the functioning of legates and nuncios in the second half of the fifteenth century. Building on the research for *Repertorium Germanicum*, the second part gave a detailed overview of legates and nuncios to Germany in 1447-1484 with available sources.[21] Long before that, Franz Wasner focused on papal legates in his seminal study on the legatine ceremonial in the fifteenth century.[22]

The fifteenth-century situation was described before, however, as part of larger treatments of papal diplomacy.[23] In a fundamental book, *Histoire de la Répresentation Diplomatique du Saint Siège des origines à l'aube du XIXe siècle*, Pierre Blet delivered the basic narrative of the development of papal diplomacy throughout the Middle Ages up to the nineteenth century.[24] He might have built on a German study that tried to provide an overview of the growth of papal diplomacy, namely the work of Knut Walf, who published *Die Entwicklung des päpstlichen Gesandtschaftswesens in dem Zeitabschnitt zwischen Dekretalenrecht und Wiener Kongress (1159-1815)* in 1966.[25] While both Walf and Blet based their analyses on legal sources, Blet used more actual documents of individual legations, even though for the fifteenth century Blet's account also remains quite basic. Both of them could have relied on previous research, especially in France, where several enquiries focused on the fifteenth century legates and nuncios, including P. Richard's and Georges-L. Lesage's studies published in 1905-1906 and 1941.[26] Also of importance is the work of Bernard Barbiche, who was their

18. Maleczek, "Die päpstliche Legaten".
19. Studt, "Anspruch und Wirklichkeit".
20. Kalous, *Plenitudo potestatis.*
21. Ungergehrer, *Die päpstlichen nuntii und legati.*
22. Wasner, "Fifteenth-Century Texts".
23. Some general works, Wynen, *Die päpstliche Diplomatie*; Feldkamp, *La diplomazia pontificia.*
24. Blet, *Histoire.*
25. Walf, *Die Entwicklung.*
26. Richard, "Origines: Nonces"; idem, "Origines: Débuts"; Lesage, "La titulature"; idem, "Note".

follower in research on papal legates in France.[27] There is no need to list here even more studies; the point is that even though the topic is not so very popular among historians, it has received a fair degree of attention (in the study of individuals or specific details), although there are only few substantial systematic treatments.

In four bigger chapters this volume tries to at least hint at the complexity of the problem of late-medieval papal legation. The first section of chapter one addresses the tricky question of terminology, which is closely related to the typology of papal legates and nuncios of the late medieval period. The generic term 'legate' that was often used by contemporary sources as well as historical studies, may bring further problems, when speaking about its legal consequences. Legates were divided into several categories according to their ranks and nuncios completed the picture with even more nuances. The sources that are used for this study are at least to some extent typologically evaluated in the following section. By definition, the sources that may be utilised for the study of papal legates are extremely widespread all over the continent. Naturally, a number of them can be found in the papal centre, but local sources then may be almost anywhere, which necessarily limited the approach to a selected region, here most importantly the area of Central Europe (i.e. Germany, Hungary, Bohemia and Poland), an area that often appeared united in legatine mandates.

The second chapter of the book intends to introduce the authority and powers of the late medieval legates. These originated in the authority of the pope himself, as the papal plenitude of power was transferred to these envoys in all matters of the Church, which gave them a special position even over the local bishops, as the argumentation stemmed from the idea of the pope as *iudex omnium*, a universal judge within the Church. Judicial powers that were inherent in the title of a legate were accompanied by powers related to conferral of benefices and granting dispensations and absolutions to individuals. These powers innate to the legatine office were enhanced with special mandates that granted the legates powers even in cases that were strictly reserved to the Papal Curia. Such mandates contained matters associated with benefices, indulgences and most significantly with the activities of the Apostolic Penitentiary. Thus, legates could even be viewed as small travelling 'curias', that brought the chances of receiving dispensations, absolutions and licences in the cases of petitions that normally had to be dealt with in Rome. In this respect, legates *de latere* brought to their province not only judicial authority as such, but also a number of 'celestial gifts', as it was remarked by contemporary sources. A travelling legate could even represent a blessing for the region, as he eased the way to salvation. These powers, however, had a clear limitation, as most of them were limited to the territory of the legatine province that had to be defined in the general mandate of the legation. Legates in general could wield their powers in regions that were allotted to them and even entering and leaving had special rules that influenced the authority of the legate.

27. Barbiche, *Bulla, Legatus, Nuntius.*

When travelling is mentioned, chapter three focuses on *modus operandi*, i.e. the conditions of the legations themselves. As high church and papal representatives, legates left Rome on a ceremonial occasion that in a way confirmed their status. From the consistory in the papal palace to the gates of the City, the remaining cardinals and members of the Curia accompanied them to pay them respect and show the dignity of the cardinal legates. In the late fifteenth and early sixteenth centuries these departures from Rome, as well as entries to Rome after the legation ended, were highly formalised and even had a shape of a constitutive ritual. Once departed, the cardinal's status changed; once he crossed the border of the City and was accepted in the consistory after the legation, he regained his position in the College of Cardinals. The legate was expected, however, to proceed according to ceremonial advices even when travelling outside of Rome, and especially in his legatine province. Meeting secular rulers, entering main cities of the province, travelling in general or taking part in various ceremonies had clear rules that could not be transgressed. Legates as travellers, however, did not differ much from other people on the road: they had to face the same dangers and perils and solve the same problems. However, the question of financing the legation also comes to attention. While up to the fourteenth century it was often the legatine province itself that financed (through procurations) the legation, in the fifteenth century payments from the Apostolic Chamber were introduced. A stable salary for the legate was established, which really tested the financial potential of the Chamber. The last section of the third chapter then attempts to reveal the nuances of the economic background of the legations.

The last part of the volume focuses on tasks and assignments associated with the diplomatic and political relevance of the legates. First and foremost, in the fifteenth century, it was the crusades that needed to be addressed by legates *de latere* or other papal envoys. In the post-conciliar period, popes tried to organise crusades predominantly against the Ottoman Turks and being connected to the crusade only enhanced the legates' authority. A holy war served as a justification for almost any action that was done in its name or in connection with making the war possible. In secular matters, however, legates had further tasks, which entailed diplomatic negotiations and talks. They had to make use of all their abilities as peace-makers, but some jobs seemed to be impossible even for cardinals. Often, political disagreements within the region – and the second section of chapter four is mostly related to the above-mentioned area of Central Europe, as local sources and local situations were described, explained and analysed – proved too much even for the papal diplomacy. Nevertheless, concrete situations elucidate the procedure and even the attempts of secular rulers to negotiate about the person of a legate or nuncio. They were, however, involved not only in political and diplomatic matters, but most crucially in the administrative and organisational matters of the Church. Even though the innate power of the legates did not extend over bishops, they were often commissioned to solve problems of local churches ranging from organisation of local synods and reforming the local Church and monasteries, to deciphering complicated problems of contested bishoprics and disobedient or imprisoned bishops. Church politics had its impact not only in the provinces, but also in Rome, where the process of selection of individual legates could be followed and analysed. The final section then deals with the acceptance of legates *in partibus:* some sources even allow us to grasp how they were received not only by the secular rulers or by bishops, but also by ordinary believers. All their powers than contribute to their image in the regions, which they visited.

The topic of this book is approached from general European perspective, even though most of the situations and individual legations are taken from the context of Central Europe. When available, various other sources were utilised so that the image is balanced. However, the system of legation did not change from place to place or from region to region but worked the same in fifteenth century England or Poland. This volume makes an effort to elucidate one crucial but sometimes forgotten part of European political, ecclesiastical, spiritual and social history. It is a result of a longer period of study of the topic, which started roughly ten years ago with the support of the Grant Agency of the Czech Republic (Grantová agentura České republiky). Institutional support for such a research, which required studies at the Vatican, Rome and Venice, but also other places especially throughout Central Europe, was indispensable and I am thankful that I was able to make use of such aid. My thanks, first of all, belong to the Grant Agency of the Czech Republic, as the current volume represents one of the results of a research project funded by the agency, Prelates on the Road: Cultural and Social Contacts of Late Medieval Europe (2013-2016), which I worked on together with my colleague Jan Stejskal. The research was also facilitated by the Czech Historical Institute in Rome (Istituto storico ceco di Roma), which enabled my stays in Rome, and naturally by the Department of History at the Faculty of Arts of Palacký University in Olomouc, my current employer. Both of these institutions provided a helpful and creative environment, for which my thanks cannot be exaggerated. The Faculty of Arts even supported the publication of this volume. Many thanks have to go to colleagues in many places and institutions, whom I was meeting in the archives and libraries (especially in the Vatican Secret Archives and the Vatican Apostolic Library), at conferences and lectures at various places and institutions over the last four or five years (Rome, London, Paris, Budapest, Prague, Munich, Brno, Debrecen, Bochum, Olomouc, Đakovo and Poděbrady) and with whom we frequently corresponded. I would like to express my thanks to a number of colleagues and friends who helped me in my study with advice and inspiration or commented on various stages and parts of my research. To name at least some of them, I would like to thank Zdeňka Hledíková, Ludwig Schmugge, János M. Bak, Gábor Klaniczay, Letizia Pellegrini, Paweł Kras, Marek Kowalski, Alena Pazderová, Jan Hrdina, Jadranka Neralić, Tamás Fedeles, Krzysztof Ożóg, Miri Rubin, Norman Housley, Nelson Minnich, Gergely Kiss, Katalin Szende; Libuše Hrabová, Martin Elbel, Jan Stejskal, Jana Oppeltová, Tomáš Parma, Radmila Prchal Pavlíčková, Hana Ferencová and other Olomouc colleagues and friends as well as other Czech historians during the fruitful evening meetings at the Czech Historical Institute in Rome. My special thanks have to go to David Livingstone from Olomouc, who helped improving my English, to Marco Pellegrini who took the burden of reading the text before its publication together with other readers of the text for the publisher, as well as to Andrea Settis Frugoni and Francesca Ortalli, who were the most helpful editors in the publishing house of Viella. Last but not least my heartiest thanks belong to my family, especially Julie, Daniel and Eva. The book is dedicated to my brothers.

1. Theory and practice

The reform of the Church in the eleventh and twelfth centuries decisively influenced the development of the papacy as an institution as well as the entire Church. The Gregorian reform initiated a process that led to the final acceptance of the pope as head of the Church, even though the nature of the authority was still to be decided: was it to be the spiritual heart of western Christianity or an administrative and legal centre? After the first impetuses of the reform papacy, two tendencies competed – one directed towards asceticism and strict following of Christ, the other being more priestly based on a looser interpretation of the New Testament and an emphasis on the educational and even judicial role. As is well known, the conflict with the Empire brought the need for a stronger papacy in secular matters and although the inclination of the popes toward an administrative role brought a spiritual reaction in society, the general tendency remained linked to the legal definition of the Church and the papacy.[1] Although Bernard of Clairvaux strongly supported the ascetic line of the papacy, political and institutional developments held sway over the Church developments of the mid-twelfth century.[2]

The institutional development of the Church inevitably meant the rise of papal canon law, most notably in Gratian's *Decretum.* As demonstrated by Anders Winroth, the period of the first half of the twelfth century brought innovations and meant the advance of papal judicial immunity.[3] Although Gratian systematised the papal letters, decrees and mandates, the later collections showed even more systematic treatments, beginning with *Compilatio prima* of Bernard of Pavia and leading to *Liber extra, Liber sextus* and the *Extravagantes.*[4] Canon law naturally

1. Cf. Barraclough, *Medieval Papacy*; Schimmelpfennig, *The Papacy*; Whalen, *The Medieval Papacy*; and other overviews. For the period also Morris, *The Papal Monarchy*; Ryan, *The Religious Roles*; Robinson, *The Papacy*; idem, "The institutions".

2. White, "The Gregorian Ideal"; for White's approach see Paul, "A Weberian medievalist"; cf. also Robinson, "Reform and the church".

3. Winroth, *The Making.*

4. An overview, Brundage, *Medieval Canon Law*; and recently the series *History of Medieval Canon Law*, esp. vol. 6, Hartmann and Pennington, eds., *The History*. For the later period, most crucially the website, Pennington and Donahue, *Bio-Bibliographical Guide*; cf. also Pennington, *Popes, Canonists and Texts*; and Bertram, ed., *Stagnation oder Fortbildung?* The collections published by Friedberg, ed., *Corpus*, 2 parts; idem, ed., *Quinque compilationes.*

established the basic guidelines for papal legates, who began to be an indispensable part of the Church government in the eleventh century. Although Gratian did not write about the legates specifically, a number of references might be found in the *Decretum* as well as in the writings of decretists, who commented on the collection.[5] The following compilations of canon law, however, gave specific attention to the functioning of the legation. One of the oldest papal decretals in this direction is *Cum non ignoretis*, which clearly identified legatine powers in relation to the power of bishops and was incorporated into the first compilations and the *Liber extra* of Gregory IX, where it formed the basis of the title *De officio legati*.[6]

The decretals of canon law originally published by individual popes (Alexander III, Celestine III, Innocent III and Gregory IX for *Liber extra*; Innocent IV, Clement IV and Boniface VIII for *Liber sextus*; and John XXII for the *Extravagantes communes*) set the powers of legates *de latere* and other papal representatives. Much more, however, could be found in the works of many canonists of the period, of decretalists who commented on these texts as well as created their own treatises (e.g. Johannes Teutonicus, Goffredus of Trani, Innocent IV, Bernard of Montmirat (Abbas antiquus), Bernard of Parma, Henricus de Segusio (Hostiensis) and most crucially Guillaume Durand).[7] After the classical canon law period, later canonists wrote their treatises on papal legates, who needed to be defined in increasing details and also in response to the new legal and social developments. In the fourteenth century, Johannes Andreae and Baldus de Ubaldis also focused on legatine activities and powers (and both of them glossed the *Speculum legatorum* of Durand).[8] There were also a number of canonists later, whose treatises were collected in the *Tractatus universi iuris* in 1584 (Andrea Barbazza, Nicolas Bohier, Pietro Andrea Gambaro, Jean Bruneau and Gonzalo García de Villadiego),[9] and others, whose works are still in manuscripts (Antonio Roselli and Dionysius Ryckel de Leeuwis).[10]

The fact that the papacy developed as a legal and administrative institution during the reform period also made it necessary for the legates to be – in general – governed by stipulations of canon law. The legates (usually cardinals, who closely cooperated with the pope in their legations), filled a gap in papal government as an extended arm of papal authority. For that purpose, however, not only the law, but also the custom and practice were crucial. These, however, are much more difficult to evaluate as historians must enter less clearly defined fields of documents related to the individual legations as well as the customary regulations of ceremonial and ritual. As will be clear, the terminology and typology of papal envoys had consequences for both these areas.

5. Figueira, *The Canon Law*, pp. 10-120; Pennington, "Johannes Teutonicus"

6. *Ibid.*, 185; cf. 1 Comp. 1.22.1.; X 1.30.1.

7. The works on legates based on canon law, Ruess, *Die rechtliche Stellung*, pp. 64-236; Paro, *The Right of Papal Legation*; Walf, *Die Entwicklung*, pp. 12-55; and in a most detailed way Figueira, *The Canon Law* (and see his studies in the bibliography).

8. Durantis, *Speculum iudiciale*; Johannes Andreae, *Novella*, pp. 93-96.

9. *Tractatus universi iuris*, vol. 13/2, fol. 131v-282v.

10. Cf. Pennington and Donahue, *Bio-Bibliographical Guide.*

1.1. *Typology and terminology*

In principle, the papal representatives were defined and differentiated both in canon law and in practice. The terminology of the legatine system of the Middle Ages may seem too complex and problematic, inaccurate or obscured, but relevant sources prove that this is not the case. Documents published by the Papal Curia are usually clear as to what they mean and the terminology is distinctly identifiable and discernible. The unofficial (or rather non-curial) documents and sources tend to use, in contrast, certain terms in a very general way not paying sufficient attention to the legal connotations. Non-curial sources, consequently, might seem imprecise or inconsistent in using the terms, particularly when it comes to the use of the term legate, *legatus*. The differences in legatine terminology have sparked academic discussion and historians have tried to study the problem on the basis of canon-law sources as well as other curial documents and occasionally using sources of a local provenance.[11]

For the period prior to the classical canon law, scholars had to deal with extremely loose terminology, which was not really established in the legal procedures of the period. Historians have described three categories: apostolic vicar, papal *apocrisarius* and *legatus ad causam*. The last category was further divided by Kriston R. Rennie into three sub-categories: papal nuncio (*nuncius*), defenders of the Church (*defensores ecclesiae)* and *legati vagantes*, a category that was devised by the author himself referring "primarily to Christian missionaries"; these were called *Missionslegaten* by Karl Ruess.[12] The term legate (*legatus*) comes from Roman law, the terminology of which was used throughout the Middle Ages and incorporated into canon law as well as elsewhere.[13] The definition of this term changed several times. Up until the mid-eleventh century the term was used as *legatus ad causam*, i.e. one of the three basic categories of papal representatives, as mentioned above. The term itself was not utilised all that much in the period itself, but seems to be convenient for historians when describing the actual activity of this kind of papal envoys. Kriston R. Rennie defined the term as useful for "a common purpose for identifying a group of papal representatives whose mandates, duties, and responsibilities set them apart from the apostolic vicars and *apocrisarii* of their time, and whose impermanent commissioning distinguishes them more explicitly from the later general legate (*legatus generalis*)".[14] Karl Ruess referred to them as

11. A wide range of literature is available on this issue, most often seeking out agreement on the basis of canon law and with some using actual sources of real legations, cf. for example, Ruess, *Die rechtliche Stellung*; Walf, *Die Entwicklung*; Blet, *Histoire*; Figueira, *The Canon Law*; Barbiche, "Les 'diplomates' pontificaux"; cf. also idem, *Bulla, Legatus, Nuntius*; Untergehrer, *Die päpstlichen nuntii und legati.*

12. Ruess, *Die rechtliche Stellung*, pp. 4-63; Schmutz, *The Foundations*, pp. 110-158; Rennie, *The Foundations*, pp. 37-87, quote p. 66.

13. Perrin, "Legatus, the Lawyers"; idem, "'Legatus' in Medieval Roman Law"; Figueira, "Decretalists"; for the dependence of canon on Roman law cf. Stein, *Roman Law*, pp. 49-52; Kuttner, "The Revival", 299-323; Nörr, "Institutional Foundations", pp. 324-338; for legates in Roman law cf. Berger, *Encyclopedic Dictionary*, p. 539.

14. Rennie, *The Foundations*, pp. 65-66.

"die nichtständigen Legaten", and Richard A. Schmutz as "occasional legates". No narrower definition within the then system of papal representation has appeared; the position of the individual categories of legates was defined by practice itself.[15]

The terminology was not yet standardised, because not only canon law, but also the offices themselves were not consistently structured. In addition, a key term of the later legatine system, *legatus a/de latere*, was only used on an occasional basis prior to the ninth century. The popes of the second half of the century, however, used it more often, but it is only defined clearly with the swift development of canon law and canonical practice two centuries later, in the second half of the eleventh century.[16]

The transitional period of Gregorian reform was analysed by Richard Antone Schmutz, who focused specifically on the discrimination between the three basic categories of papal representatives up until the pontificate of Gregory VII.[17] It may seem as if he treated the same period as Rennie, and to some extent, this is the case, however, unlike Rennie, he placed an emphasis on the pontificate of Gregory himself. The three early categories of the "pre-Hildebrandine institution of papal representation", namely the *vicarius*, the *apocrisarius* and the *legatus ad causam* were described by Rennie as well. Schmutz followed the changes into the "post-Hildebrandine" system of papal representation with the basic distinction of categories of legates, nuncios and judge-delegates. This stage differentiated between general and special legates: both being legates with the mandate powers pertaining to the office, but differing in terms of jurisdiction. The *legati generales* had general jurisdiction in all ecclesiastical matters within the province, while the *legati speciales*, in contrast, had to have causes assigned and clearly defined.[18] More than fifty years ago, Schmutz criticised the inaccuracy of the then modern literature, in which no one substantially treated the distinction between the individual categories of papal representatives. In his view, the studies, which dealt with legates in general, also lacked precision. He tried to explain the differences within the full range of papal representation, whereas the earlier studies treated predominantly the papal legates and sometimes even mixed them with nuncios and judge-delegates. In cases of doubt as to which category the individual representatives belonged to, Schmutz had a clear solution as to reading the legatine mandates "for identifying the legate, whether he exercised a general or special authority." As a second step, the activity of the legates may help in the case of missing mandates. Schmutz, however, warned against relying on the terminology of medieval scribes, who were "seldom consistent in their use of terms".[19] This statement was often picked up and contested by later literature, e.g. Clifford Ian Kyer and Robert C. Figueira.

15. For the description of the system of the legatine system Ruess, *Die rechtliche Stellung*, pp. 4-63; Schmutz, *The Foundations*, pp. 110-158; idem, "Medieval Papal Representatives", p. 446; and most recently Rennie, *The Foundations*, pp. 37-87.

16. Rennie, *The Foundations*, pp. 163, 170-174.

17. Schmutz, *The Foundations*; cf. also idem, "Medieval Papal Representatives".

18. Idem, *The Foundations*, pp. 188, 213.

19. Idem, "Medieval Papal Representatives", p. 456.

Kyer dedicated his doctoral dissertation to a detailed study of curial sources with the intention of proving inaccurate the conclusions of his predecessor. For Kyer, two key questions were missing in the treatment of Schmutz: which authors were inconsistent in differentiating between the legates and nuncios, and when the authors deemed it necessary to differentiate. Kyer believed, on the basis of contemporary sources, that for the period of 1245-1378, the terms were used differently by various writers.[20] He drew a distinction between their usage on several levels. First, it is important to demonstrate the difference between the generic and specific usage of the terms: the term *legatus* (and *nuncius*) might denote any envoy or ambassador (*quicumque ab alio missus est*),[21] and thus the word is used in other treatises that do not exclusively write about papal diplomacy.[22] The first conclusion by Kyer is consequently that a historian must first identify in what sense the terms are applied, either generic or specific, and if it is specific then a differentiation has to be made between papal and other representatives.[23] In agreement with Kyer, Figueira also criticised Schmutz's image of the inconsistency of medieval scribes and emphasised that scribes only represented the intentions of their superiors and that the term *nuncius* has not been sufficiently researched.[24]

The system of legatine representation was more clearly defined in the developing canon law, even though the practice was still more important. Canon law created the definitions on the basis of practice and (to some extent) the Roman law, not only in terms of terminology, but also as concerns the authority and powers of a legate. During the period of the reform of the Church (perhaps as early as the pontificate of Leo IX, but most significantly from the pontificate of Gregory VII), the number of legates grew considerably, their activity increased and their authority and powers were defined more clearly. The first mandates, which gave the legates full powers in representing the pope, appeared in this period.[25] In general, the period of the second half of the eleventh century is viewed by historians as a turning point in the functioning of the papal legates, as they were increasingly becoming a tool for the papal centralization policy and for the later creation of a "papal monarchy". The principles of the new government of the Church consisted of a number of elements that contributed to its fast development in the eleventh and twelfth centuries. Apart from the cardinals (and extensively non-Roman cardinals), there were "other equally significant extensions of governance … in the development in three age-old traditions: councils, legates and canon law, all of which were vital in extending papal authority and the papal promotion of reform".[26] Legates then appeared as

20. Kyer, "*Legatus* and *nuncius*", pp. 473-477; idem, *The Papal Legate*, pp. 4-20.

21. Idem, "*Legatus* and *nuncius*", p. 474, he quotes Duranti, *Speculum iuris*, lib. 1, rubrica *De legato*, §1.1 (Durantis, *Speculum iudiciale*, p. 29).

22. Cf. Hrabar, ed., *De legatis*; Behrens, "Treatises"; Fubini, "L'ambasciatore"; Schwinges and Wriedt, eds., *Gesandtschafts- und Botenwesen*; Lazzarini, *Communication and Conflict*; Andretta, Péquignot and Waquet, eds., *De l'ambassadeur.*

23. Kyer, "*Legatus* and *nuncius*", p. 474.

24. Figueira, "The Classification", pp. 212-213.

25. Schmutz, "Medieval Papal Representatives", pp. 446-447.

26. Cushing, *Reform*, p. 83; similarly see the standard analysis of Robinson, *The Papacy*, pp. 146-178.

legati apostolice sedis and could be categorised as general (*legati generales*) and special legates (*legati speciales*).[27] Gratian's *Decretum* as well as the decretists did not define, however, the term *legatus* very clearly. As Robert C. Figueira put it, "in *Decretum* the term *legatus* often denotes persons other than papal legates, or is (at the very least) used in such a vague manner as to allow no categorical judgment".[28] The work of the thirteenth-century popes and the decretalists, however, offers a more "sophisticated classification systems for types of papal legates". Even if the systems presented by *Liber extra* and the decretalists are not completely consistent, they point to the three-fold division and classification of legates that is clearly defined later in *Liber sextus*.[29]

Another change, thus, came with the progress of the reform of the Church and the afore-mentioned standardization of canon law predominantly in the two collections of decretals, the *Liber extra* and *Liber sextus*. The legatine system had developed over the previous two centuries.[30] Based on practice, the latter collection codified the typological division of the legates. There were three categories of the legatine office; these types were legally defined and their authority differed in terms of the powers and limitations to the office. The basic categories, in later terminology, are: *legatus a/de latere*, *legatus missus* and *legatus natus*. The *Liber sextus* defines them in different terms, but the diversification is quite clear. They are defined as legates *praetextu suarum ecclesiarum* (i.e. *legati nati*), those who are sent (*missi*) and cardinals, by Innocent III called *fratres nostri* (*a latere*).[31] This division was stabilized in the second half of the thirteenth century and in principle (with some corrections and changes) functioned up until the later Middle Ages. The renowned French canonist of the thirteenth century, Guillaume Durand, used this division for his *Speculum iudiciale*. The rubric *De legato* used the terms *legati laterales*, *constituti* (or *missi*) and *nati*.[32] This terminology, then, became standardised for the rest of the Middle Ages and created a clear division among the ranks of papal envoys.[33]

27. Ruess, *Die rechtliche Stellung*, pp. 115-117; Perrin, "Legatus, the Lawyers", pp. 464-465; Schmutz, *The Foundations*, pp. 159-233; idem, "Medieval Papal Representatives", pp. 447-452; Kyer, *The Papal Legate*, pp. 24-25; Figueira, *The Canon Law*, p. 114.

28. Idem, "The Classification", p. 213; cf. also Figueira's dissertation, idem, *The Canon Law*, pp. 10-14 (about Gratian and decretists on legates see *ibid.*, pp. 10-120).

29. Idem, "The Classification", quote on p. 214. Cf. also the actual collections X 1.30 and VI 1.15 and also idem, *The Canon Law* and his other works (in bibliography), esp. idem, "'Legatus apostolice sedis'".

30. For the older period, see – apart from a number of older studies, especially German dissertations (evaluated in Schmutz, *The Foundations*, pp. 10-41; listed also in Maleczek, "Die päpstlichen Legaten", pp. 35-36, n. 5) – the newer studies of Kriston R. Rennie, Claudia Zey, Blake Beattie and collected volumes, e.g. Alberzoni and Zey, eds., *Legati e delegati papali*; Herbers, López Alsina and Engel, eds., *Das begrenzte Papsttum*.

31. VI 1.15.1; cf. for example, Walf, *Die Entwicklung*, pp. 12-14, 18-19, 30-31; Schmutz, "Medieval Papal Representatives", pp. 453-454.

32. Durantis, *Speculum iudiciale*, p. 31 (rubr. *De legato*, §3).

33. See in general, Queller, *The Office*, pp. 65-68; Feldkamp, *La diplomazia pontificia*, pp. 34-39.

To complete the picture, it is worth mentioning two other categories of papal representatives, although neither of them will be treated in exhaustive detail. Apart from various types of legates, there were additional papal envoys that were used in this period. Most importantly there were the judge-delegates (*iudices delegati*).[34] Their powers and authority followed the same concept, namely the legal precondition that the pope had jurisdictional power over the entire Church. The basic difference, which will be mentioned here, as the judge-delegates will be set aside, was the fact that judge-delegates had specific legal cases assigned to them, whereas the legates had general jurisdictional powers. The obligations and individual commissions were given by the pope and could not even be changed by the legates *de latere* on their legation.[35] The description and definition of the authority inherent in the office of judge-delegate was always given in the collections of canon law as well as in the glosses and commentaries of decretalists, often being more extensive than the definitions of the legates themselves.[36] Even if judge-delegates also appear in the later Middle Ages, the height of their activity may be linked with the twelfth and thirteenth centuries. Thereafter, they were not so often dispatched from Rome but rather named from among the local clergy.

Another special form of papal representatives defined in canon law in the thirteenth century were the representatives of the legates and judge-delegates, namely the *subdelegati*. A subdelegation was primarily created in judicial matters so that the subdelegates could sit at courts and hear the cases which fell under the jurisdiction of the legate or judge-delegate. Their authority was derived from the legate (or judge-delegate) directly and not from the pope, although the head of Christendom was the ultimate source of it. It is significant that in case of appeals the cause was supposed to be treated by the legate, if he was still in office, and not by the Papal Curia.[37]

The post-classical period of canon law development brought about certain changes and alterations to the system of papal legation, its typology and consequently its terminology. The fourteenth and fifteenth centuries constitute a period that was, as concerns papal legates, not so extensively studied by historians as the immediately preceding one. According to Kyer, the years 1243-1378 brought substantial modifications to papal representation; he has explained the lesser interest in these changes on the side of historians with the above-mentioned confusion in using the terms *legatus* and *nuntius* in the medieval sources themselves. The terms did not change, but the utilization of the existing categories of legates, nuncios or judge-delegates had transformed.

34. About judge-delegates, see Schmutz, *The Foundations*, pp. 98-109; Pavloff, *Papal Judge Delegates*; for a great overview of also general matters of judge-delegates see Sayers, *Papal Judges Delegate*.

35. Figueira, "Subdelegation", pp. 56-57; cf. X 1.30.2.

36. X 1.29; VI 1.14; Clem. 1.8; Durantis, *Speculum iudiciale*, pp. 9-29 (rubr. *De iudice delegati*).

37. In detail on subdelegation, see Figueira, "Subdelegation"; also Pavloff, *Papal Judge Delegates*, pp. 21-24, 41-44.

Cardinals, or *legati de latere*, became the most prominent among the legates; not only in terms of their powers and authority, which had always been the case, but in terms of numbers and activity. The other two categories, *legati missi* and *nati*, gradually fell out of usage or lost their original significance. *Legati missi* were no longer papal chaplains, which used to be typical (the last one to be created legate was Gaufridus de Bellomonte in 1265, sent as a legate to Lombardy). Almost all the non-cardinal legates were bishops or archbishops. The position of *legatus natus*, a legate who was crucial for spreading the papal influence outside Rome as a stable legate in the province, was still claimed by a number of archbishops because of the prestige of their metropolitan churches. The office disappeared, however, and the term became an empty title, Kyer explained, making use of primarily curial sources.[38] Exceptions were possible. It was only in the second half of the fourteenth century, for example, that the archbishop of Prague (the bishopric was promoted to an archbishopric as late as 1344) acquired the title of *legatus natus.* Unlike his colleagues, he exercised his legatine powers in the legatine province, which was composed not only of his archdiocese, but also the bishoprics of Regensburg, Bamberg and Meissen. The powers and obligations included visitation, legislation and jurisdiction with the archbishop continuing to employ them until at least 1396.[39] Kyer noted that a number of non-cardinal legates "were employed in the less accessible reaches of Christendom, such as Hungary, the Eastern Empire, and the Holy Land".[40]

Major changes in the activities of legates were introduced in the fourteenth century and by the Avignon papacy. This was a period that was substantially studied by Clifford Ian Kyer, who – still in response to Schmutz – drew attention to the question of distinguishing "between official documents emanating from the Papal Curia and unofficial accounts, such as biographies, chronicles and the like": and not surprisingly, mostly the latter sources "used *legatus* and *nuntius* interchangeably".[41] Kyer consequently focused on the curial sources and found an apparent diversification in the usage of the terms. It often happened that the terms were not used at all (mostly before the pontificate of Boniface VIII), but when they were used, then it was according to the powers of the envoy. For his period, Kyer found the curial sources, as well as the sources that came out of the envoy's chancery, absolutely consistent.[42] The office of a legate or nuncio had legal significance and consequences in terms of status in the required ceremonial as well as financial matters. The financing of cardinals and consequently of papal legations (which will be treated later in detail) was dependent on whether or not the cardinal had a legatine status. According to the papal ceremonial of the period, most often attributed to Giacomo Stefaneschi, a cardinal who became a legate ceased to participate in the income of the chamber of the college of cardinals, whereas a nuncio could hold on to his claims to the

38. Kyer, *The Papal Legate*, pp. 27-28, 36.
39. Hledíková, "Die Prager Erzbischöfe".
40. Kyer, *The Papal Legate*, p. 28.
41. Kyer, "*Legatus* and *nuncius*", p. 474.
42. *Ibid.*, p. 476.

income.[43] Stefaneschi designed his ceremonial for both legates and nuncios, but in appropriate places differentiated between the two offices.[44] Even the pope himself, in this case Clement VI in 1342, wrote that a "legate has great pre-eminence over the nuncio, and not whatever legate, but a legate *a latere*".[45] Thus, it is clearly of great importance to distinguish between the rank of the legates and nuncios within the official documents and especially within the offices of the Papal Curia, which were responsible for the ceremonial and finance.

The Avignon popes brought in the nuncios as crucial representatives of the pope, even cardinals were sent as nuncios of the pope, which brings further concerns about the role of the two ranks of papal representatives. According to Kyer, legates were sent more often to regions such as Italy, the eastern Mediterranean, some to Hungary and Castile, with the number of legatine missions dropping significantly and being incomparable with that of the thirteenth century. The legates who were destined to go to Italy, the papal states and the city of Rome were, in contrast, of the highest rank with their missions lasting for a long period of time starting with the legation of Bertrand de Deux and continuing most importantly with the great legation of cardinal Gil Albornoz. Peter Partner went even so far as to ascribe to the legates the powers of "vice-pope" or calling them a "satrap-legate".[46] Nuncios, on the other hand, were much more numerous and sent to all regions including those that did not receive any legate (like England, Germany or France). Nuncios, who were employed by the popes were not only low ranking clergy, but there were also cardinals or archbishops, who took part in the non-legatine missions.[47] Nuncios were not a new office, but the term began to have a new content. In Roman law the term *nuntius* designated a messenger, who was employed as a medium through which declarations could be made with the same validity as made by letter.[48] In general, a medieval nuncio was an envoy who carried a message and carried out the will of his master, whereas a legate (in general a procurator) was an ambassador who could decide matters in his master's name.[49] The term was

43. *Ibid.*; Dykmans, ed., *Le cérémonial papal*, vol. 2, p. 500. Cf. also Lützelschwab, *Flectat cardinales*, pp. 134-135.

44. Dykmans, ed., *Le cérémonial papal*, vol. 2, pp. 245-247, 495-502.

45. Quoted in Lützelschwab, *Flectat cardinales*, p. 134, "Et ideo iste tantam habuit celsitudinem ut legatus, qui habet magnam preeminentiam supra nuncium et non quicumque legatus, sed legatus a latere".

46. Partner, *The Lands*, pp. 327-365, quote on p. 332; cf. also Lützelschwab, *Flectat cardinales*, pp. 231-319, on Bertrand de Deux pp. 270-297, which includes an analysis of the pope's address at the return of the legate, which (despite the not very successful legation of Cardinal Bertrand) defines very clearly what a good legate should be (pp. 288-297); cf. in general also Rollo-Koster, *Avignon*, pp. 89-93; Beattie, "The Cardinals"; Willershausen, *Die Päpste*, pp. 349-369.

47. Kyer, *The Papal Legate*, pp. 27-31.

48. Berger, *Encyclopedic Dictionary*, p. 602.

49. The general theory of representation in diplomacy is described by Queller, *The Office*, pp. 6-10, cf. also pp. 3-25; idem, "Thirteenth-Century Diplomatic Envoys"; Schmutz, "Medieval Papal Representatives", p. 458.

used throughout the Middle Ages and in secular or papal representation. For the latter, the term was used for an "agent adaptable for such representational purposes as bargaining, negotiating, persuading, investigating, expounding and gathering information; he was to be believed and trusted; he was well-informed as to his master's will; capable and industrious".[50] Originally, a nuncio was not a term for a specific category or rank of clearly defined papal representative; it was a messenger and the term utilized by others outside the papal context.

This rank was more precisely defined only in the fourteenth century.[51] Nuncios now appeared with more powers than their predecessors used to have. Legates hold the powers and authority that belonged to them by the nature of the office, whereas nuncios only had mandated authority, the *iurisdictio ordinaria* and *iurisdictio mandata* in terms of jurisdiction. It is in this period, however, that nuncios were also sent with the full power of a legate *de latere*. Kyer has drawn attention to the work of the celebrated canonist Egidius de Bellamera (Gilles Bellemère), who was the bishop of Avignon and was involved in diplomatic missions to France in the late fourteenth century. In his commentary on the *Extravagantes communes*, namely the first titulus *De consuetudine*, which contains only one decretal *Super gentes* that deals with the legates, Egidius made mention of the fact that it was a long-established custom that not legates but rather nuncios, with the fullness of power of the legates, were sent to France.[52] The decretal itself speaks of the dignity of the legates and that they should be accepted by everyone, under the penalty of *ipso facto* excommunication. An innovation in this case is that together with the legates, nuncios are mentioned as well, which did not occur in either *Liber extra* or *Liber sextus*.[53] What also supports this idea of highly ranking nuncios is the term *solemnus nuncius* which appears in this period in the writings of Petrarch and in the documents published by the Papal Curia, as well as the term *apostolice sedis nuncius*, which appeared occasionally in the thirteenth and more often in the fourteenth century.[54]

Each period brought with it changes to the system of papal representation. The greatest one came about at the beginning of the sixteenth century with the introduction of the permanent nunciature. The fifteenth century also adjusted, however, the system to the needs of the day, as will be made clear from this volume.[55] The office of the legate *de latere* seems to have been revived in

50. Idem, *The Foundations*, pp. 87-98, quote on p. 98.

51. Kyer, "*Legatus* and *nuncius*"; idem, *The Papal Legate*, pp. 37-66.

52. Idem, "*Legatus* and *nuncius*", pp. 37-38; cf. BAV, Vat. lat. 6351, fol. 77va, "Iam a longis temporibus servatum est, quod ad regnum Francie legati apostolici destinari non solent, licet nuncii cum legatorum plenitudine potestatis ibi quandoque destinentur. Et hoc propter dominum Bonifacium, qui propter rigores quos contra regem Francie tenuit multa scandala passus fuit".

53. That only in the part on excommunication, Extrav. comm. 1.1.un (Friedberg, ed., *Corpus*, pt. 2, col. 1237): "Qui vero de cetero super praedictis dictos legatos aut etiam nuncios, quos ad quascunque partes pro causis quibuslibet sedes ipsa transmiserit, praesumpserint impedire, ipso facto sententiam excommunicationis incurrant".

54. Kyer, *The Papal Legate*, pp. 39-45; for Petrarch see Lützelschwab, *Flectat cardinales*, p. 134.

55. An excellent overview of the development is also the dissertation of Wolfgang Untergehrer, *Die päpstlichen nuntii und legati*, written in 2012.

comparison with what the Avignon papacy experienced. Legates *de latere* were sent to all the regions once again, cardinals played the decisive role here and the system was influenced by crucial moments in the history of the papacy, including the Great Schism, the Councils and – most importantly for this study – the revival of papal power in the post-conciliar period. What is significant for this period is that as for legates the *legati de latere* prevailed and the role of the other two categories of legates diminished. The title of *legatus natus* was mostly given to high ranking archbishops, often primates of their countries, as of the twelfth century. Even prior to the fifteenth century, as mentioned earlier, the office lost its purpose and significance. In Central Europe, for example, there were still two metropolitan churches to which the position of the *legatus natus* was linked. The activities of the archbishops were, however, not related to this office and the expression became only a part of their general titulature without any genuine authority and powers. Although the archbishop of Esztergom Dionysius Szécsi bore this title, he was also created legate *de latere* for Hungary. In order to have a legate in place the pope could not merely use the old title of *natus*, but instead needed to create a legate *de latere.* One notable exception of the fourteenth century was the archbishop of Prague, who actively exercised the office of *legatus natus* after 1365, only to disappear from the sources as such a legate after 1396. The title is once again only a phrase in the intitulation. Moreover, the archbishopric of Prague was vacant between the years 1431-1561, so there was no such office-holder for Prague any longer.[56] The other category of legatine representatives, *legatus missus*, followed the same track and such titles appear for the last time at the beginning of the second half of the fifteenth century. The general tendency to leave out the title grew stronger during the pontificates of Pius II and Paul II,[57] although individuals who called themselves with such a title can still be found. These included, for example, Domenico Dominici in 1464 or Rudolf of Rüdesheim in 1466.[58] The single title of *legatus missus* appeared in 1466, while other examples indicate that the term itself – as the examples show – was accompanied by the specification *cum potestate legati de latere* (which will be treated in detail later). Although it disappeared in the official documents of the Papal Curia, it continued to occur only in the charters published by the individual legates.

56. Hledíková, "Die Prager Erzbischöfe".

57. Lesage, "La titulature", pp. 215-216; idem, "Note", p. 244.

58. MNL Budapest, OL DF 45080 (16 Mar 1464), "Dominicus dei et apostolice sedis gratia episcopus Torcellanus sanctissimi domini nostri pape referendarius et eiusdem ac sedis predicte cum potestate legati de latere in terris et dominiis serenissimi domini imperatoris ac quendam aliorum Germanie principum et dominorum legatus missus…"; NA Prague, fond ŘF, charter no. 37 (15 Jul 1466), "Nos Rudolphus, dei gracia episcopus Lavantinus, sedis apostolice et sanctissimi domini nostri domini Pauli divina prudencia pape secundi ad Almanie et regni Bohemie partes legatus missus"; SOkA Jihlava, Archiv města Jihlavy, Charters, inv. no. 184 (8 May 1469), *cum potestate legati de latere legatus missus* (for Rudolf). The legates *de latere* referred to themselves at times as *legatus de latere electus confirmatus et missus*, but this has nothing to do with the canonical term *legatus missus.*

The writings of the canonists of the fifteenth century are not yet so thoroughly researched, the canon law, however, had remained the same and that which developed in the thirteenth and early fourteenth centuries was kept. The treatises on cardinals and legates usually mention the traditional division of the legates into three categories, *de latere*, *missus* and *natus*. The canonists Andrea Barbazza (Andreas Barbatius), Gonzalo (Gundisalvus) García de Villadiego, Jean Bruneau (Ioannes Brunellus), Nicolas Bohier (Boerius), Pietro Andrea Gambaro (Gambarus) and Martinus Garatus Laudensis wrote treatises on legates *de latere*, or on legates in general; Garatus also on legates as envoys of secular lords, even though he wrote other treatises on cardinals, where he discussed legates *de latere* as well.[59] They mostly refer to the classical collections of canon and Roman law, to Guillaume Durand and glosses; in terms of terminology and typology, they follow classical canon law (and primarily focus on legates *de latere*), although Gonzalo García de Villadiego specifically writes also about the nuncios. He even posed a question as to whether a non-cardinal legate should be called a legate or a nuncio as well. Although the practice was quite clear at the end of the fifteenth century when he wrote, he answered that the non-cardinal legate might be called a legate all the same, taking into account the legal tradition as opposed to practice.[60]

Legate *de latere* was clearly defined both in canon law and in practice. There was (and to some extent still is) confusion concerning nuncios. Most of the problems can be revealed in comparison of the two terms, legates and nuncios. The term *solemnus nuntius* does not appear any longer in the second half of the fifteenth century. There were instead other high-ranking nuncios with the title of *nuncius cum potestate legati de latere*. The legate and the nuncio were clearly differentiated and here the words of Pietro Griffi might help, who in the early sixteenth century defined that legates are all judges, they have ordinary jurisdiction and are sent to govern a province. The nuncios, in contrast, are sent for when in need of special negotiations even if they are cardinals.[61] The distinction

59. These treatises are printed in *Tractatus universi iuris*, vol. 13/2, fol. 131v-282v; the volume contains also treatises on cardinals that often mention legates *de latere*; for an overview with some rubrics see Hrabar, ed., *De legatis*, pp. 42-64, 79-86; see also Behrens, "Treatises"; most recently see, Gardi, "Parole di negoziatori?", pp. 206-214; on Garatus, see Baumgärtner, *Martinus Garatus*.

60. *Tractatus universi iuris*, vol. 13/2, fol. 258v, "Tertio quaero, quot sunt species legatorum, dicas quod tres, quidam enim dicuntur legati de latere, alii legati nati, alii legati missi, pro quo text. capit. excommunica. de officio lega. & eodem titulo, capitulo primo, lib sexto, & quoniam istud nomen est omnibus tribus commune, si fiat simpliciter mentio de legato in aliqua dispositione, comprehenditur nedum legatus de latere, sed etiam legatus natus, & missus, ut voluit glos. capituli statutum. de rescriptis. lib. sexto, in principio, & capitulo privilegium. de verborum significationibus, libro sexto. Ex quo deciditur unum de quo alias vidi dubitari, missus fuit quidam prothonotarius ad quandam provintiam a sede apostolica legatus cum amplissimis facultatibus, ipse faciebat se appellari legatum, erant tamen, qui sibi detrahebant dicentes, quod cum non esset de latere legatus deberet se appellare nuncius sedis apostolicae, & non legatum, sed per praedicta convincitur istos evidenter errasse".

61. Monaco, *Il De officio collectoris*, pp. 268-269, Neminem igitur latere existimo, eos qui ad tractanda pontificum et Apostolice Sedis negotia destinantur nusquam a sacris canonibus ac etiam raro a Curie stilo oratores vel ambassiatores appellari. Sed quos mittit Romana Sedes, si

is clear, the simple nuncio is a messenger with no general powers linked to his office, he is not a judge in the province and he does not possess any jurisdiction. The nuncio, who has the power of the legate *de latere* is treated differently, however. Two basic inherent powers are linked to the office of the legate *de latere*, namely the jurisdiction and possibility to confer the benefices. There was no certainty concerning these powers in the sources, as for example Gonzalo García de Villadiego demonstrated in his treatise stating that the practice allowed non-cardinal legates with the power of legates *de latere* to confer benefices, even though it was contrary to the law.[62] The actual documents of the legations of nuncios *cum potestate legati de latere* reveal that they could confer benefices and even take judgements, which means they actually possessed the office of legation.[63] There still exists, however, only a limited number of studies that would deal with the legal position of the nuncios *cum potestate legati de latere.*[64]

The office of a legation (*officium legationis*) was given to the legates *de latere* and to nuncios *cum potestate legati de latere.* Although this is clear in the case of cardinal legates, nuncios with the power of legate use this terminology as well.[65] All the documents related to Angelo Pecchinoli, a nuncio *cum potestate legati de latere* to Hungary, write about *legatio*: this appears in papal documents,[66] in reports about Angelo as well as in charters published by himself[67] and in letters to those who communicated with him in the province.[68] One case reveals the difference between the nuncios with powers of a legate and simple nuncios. Francesco Petrucci, sent to France in June 1478, was a simple nuncio (*nuncius et orator*) and in his case the term *commissio* is used. The scribe, who entered the bulls in the Vatican registers, made a mistake twice using automatically

modo ad aliquam provinciam gubernandam regendamve mittantur et Sancte Romane Ecclesie cardinales sint, hos de stilo legatos de latere, si vero fuerint prelati minores, eos simpliciter legatos appellat. Et ii omnes iudices sunt habentque ordinariam iurisdictionem, licet ex vi proprietateque vocabuli, quicumque missus sit dici possit legatus ... Ast ubi non ad provinciam administrandam, sed specialiter ad negotia cum principibus tractanda aliquem miserit, hunc nuncium appellat, ut plurimum, legatum perraro, cum secundum premissam significationem nuncii, qui a pontifice mittuntur pro ambassiata, ut ita loquar, improprie legati dicerentur. Invaluitque adeo hic stilus ut, nedum quos eadem Sedes ad alios destinaverit, verum etiam eos quos principes ad eandem miserint frequenter nuncios et non legatos pontifex nominet ... Quod procedit et observatur non solum cum per Sedem predictam mittuntur ad principes prelati inferiores sed etiam quando mitterentur cardinales; nam hoc casu non legati sed nuncii appellantur ...".

62. *Tractatus universi iuris*, vol. 13/2, fol. 264rv.

63. Cf. Bartolomeo Maraschi (ASV, Reg. Vat. 655, fol. 36rv); but also Angelo Pecchinoli, Orso Orsini and others metioned later in the text.

64. The best might be Untergehrer, *Die päpstlichen nuntii und legati*, pp. 146-163.

65. Cf. Untergehrer, *Die päpstlichen nuntii und legati*, pp. 146-150.

66. ASV, Cam. Ap., Div. Cam. 46, fol. 188v.

67. ASV, Misc., Arm. II 56, fol. 178r; MNL Budapest, OL DL 105524; NA Prague, ŘF, no. 74 (www.monasterium.net); Archiwum Państwowe Poznań, Akta Braci Czeskich (1507) 1557-1817 (1961), sygn. 47 (microfilm Nr. 0-76628), p. 152 (my thanks for this reference go to Ota Halama).

68. BMV, sign. Lat. X 175 (=3622), fol. 145r-146r (Agostino Luciani); AS Venezia, Collezione Podocataro, busta 5, no. 263 (Frederick III to the Pope; he uses the terms *onus legacionis* and *munus legacionis*).

the word *legatio*, which was then crossed out and replaced with *commissio.*[69] Legation was then strictly limited to those with legatine powers.

The non-cardinal legates would be called *legati missi* or in the fourteenth century more often nuncios or solemn nuncios. There was, however, still a difference between the general understanding of the legate and the nuncio, as the nuncio should not possess the jurisdiction and possibility of dealing with the benefices. The term *legatus missus* began to change in the fifteenth century. The new supplement *cum potestate legati de latere* or *cum plena legationis officio* was crucial in this sense.[70] This means that the non-legatine envoys were called *nuncii* rather than *legati missi*, but had special powers that were usually possessed by the legates *de latere.* In local sources, however, nuncios with such powers were often termed legates. The sources that stem from the practice of the Papal Curia are quite precise, a tendency that was observed by other scholars (e.g. Kyer in his differentiation between legates and nuncios in the fourteenth century).[71] The reasons for sending nuncios with powers of legates *de latere* will be treated later; it is crucial to realize, however, that the system was again adjusted to the needs of the Church and the papacy at the time.

It became a rule in the fifteenth century that cardinals were sent as legates *de latere*, and the nuncios were then prelates of lower rank. It is at this time that the cardinals identified with legates *de latere* and cardinals accepted the attire that previously belonged to the legates. The original rule that a legate *de latere* could only be a cardinal was changed to the rule that a cardinal was legate *de latere.* This was also the case in 1518 when four legates *de latere* were created, but all of them explicitly *sine facultatibus*, which means their commission was not primarily directed towards the spiritual government of their legatine provinces, but rather to negotiations and diplomacy. They still held, in all probability, the powers in spiritual and jurisdictional matters that belonged to them because of the legatine office, but did not have any special mandates that would confer to them powers reserved for the pope.[72] Several months later, for political reasons,

69. ASV, Reg. Vat. 679, fol. 173r; Wolfgang Untergehrer also noticed this case.

70. Cf. Barbiche, in "Les 'diplomates' pontificaux", pp. 361-364; Untergehrer, *Die päpstlichen nuntii und legati*, pp. 150-163.

71. Kyer, "*Legatus* and *nuncius*".

72. ASV, Arch. Concist., Acta Vicecanc., vol. 2, fol. 67v (26 Feb 1518), "Sanctissimus dominus noster exposuit, quę tractata fuerunt in congregationibus habitis super expedicione contra Turchas, de responsis principum super huiusmodi re, et de resolutione publicandi indutias inter principes christianos, decernendi processiones, missas et ieiunium. Et quod sua sanctitas cum reverendissimis dominis cardinalibus et toto clero Romano et curia ad beatam Mariam super Minervam ire decreverat ad placandam Dei iram, insuper fuit factum verbum de legatis mittendis ad reges et principes christianos sine tamen facultatibus, et lecta fuerunt summaria litterarum et instructiones principum, videlicet cesaris, christianissimi et catholici"; fol. 69r (3 Mar 1518), "Creavit quattuor legatos de latere mittendos ad principes christianos pro sanctissima expeditione contra Turchas, videlicet reverendissimos dominos Laurentium tt. Sancti Thome in Parione presbiterum cardinalem de Campegio ad serenissimum regem Anglię [Lorenzo Campeggi], Egidium tt. sancti Matthei presbiterum cardinalem ad serenissimum regem catholicum [Egidio di Viterbo], Alexandrum sancti Eustachii diaconum cardinalem de Farnesio ad Maximilianum in imperatorem electum [Alessandro Farnese], Bernardum sancte Marie Importicu diaconum cardinalem Bibienna ad

the *collegati* were created for England and Germany, an also they were without faculties.[73] One can only speculate as to whether they might have been called solemn nuncios in the fourteenth century.

Even if the local sources would often refer to the nuncios as legates *cum potestate legati de latere*, the inhabitants of the provinces (or at least the learned ones) did know the difference between these kinds of nuncios and legates *de latere*. The cardinal legate had much higher authority and not only in jurisdiction and spiritual matters, but also in informal and symbolic authority – thanks to his cardinalate as well as the direct impersonalization of the Pope. The title *nuncius cum potestate legati de latere* appeared for the first time at the end of the fourteenth century, in connection with Cardinal Pedro de Luna, who was not created legate *de latere* directly. As cardinal, however, he held a number of powers that were denied to non-cardinal envoys.[74] As for these, non-cardinal nuncios with the power of legates *de latere* emerged initially in the early 1440s still under Eugenius IV, namely in the person of the archbishop of Florence Bartolomeo Zabarella as nuncio to France (1440),[75] and the archbishop of Milan Enrico Rampini to Milan, Germany and England (1445).[76] Wolfgang Untergehrer then spoke about a transitional period for the competences and titulature of the non-cardinal envoys.[77]

Wrocław in Silesia, which was part of the Kingdom of Bohemia, was, for example, always a centre for the organisation of the anti-Hussite struggle. Legates and other representatives of the Pope were present during the Hussite wars, but also afterwards during the 1450s and 1460s at the time of the negotiations with the Utraquists and King George of Poděbrady, first governor and then king of Bohemia. At the beginning of January 1464, the burghers of Wrocław wrote to Pope Pius II and tried to persuade him to send a legate with a higher authority, a cardinal, despite the fact that Girolamo Lando, *nuncius et orator cum potestate legati de latere*, was present in the city.[78] Such a cardinal legate, in this case Cardinal Marco

regem christianissimum [Bernardo Dovizi da Bibbiena] et omnes sine facultatibus"; fol. 74v (26 Apr 1518), "Creavit reverendissimum dominum Tho[mam]. tt. sancti Sixti presbiterum cardinalem legatum de latere ad Maximilianum in imperatorem electum in Germania et ad regem Datię in loco reverendissimi domini cardinalis de Farnesio, qui infirmitate detentus non potuit munus legationis implere et sine facultatibus". Grassi, *Il diario*, p. 63 mentioned their creation, but left aside their being without the faculties.

73. ASV, Arch. Concist., Acta Vicecanc., vol. 2, fol. 77r (17 May 1518), "Creatio Collegatorum. Creavit reverendissimos dominos collegatos, videlicet dominos Thomam tt. sanctę Cicilię presbiterum cardinalem Eboracensem [Thomas Wolsey] in Anglia et Mattheum sancti Angeli diaconum cardinalem Gurcensem [Matheus Lang] in Germania sine facultatibus et quod eorum legatio cesset, cessante illorum dominorum legatorum a latere sue sanctitatis missorum". The creation of these collegates had obviously political reasons, cf. Thomson, *Popes and Princes*, p. 75.

74. Barbiche, "Les 'diplomates' pontificaux", p. 365; Untergehrer, *Die päpstlichen nuntii und legati*, p. 156.

75. Blet, *Histoire*, p. 168; Barbiche, "Les 'diplomates' pontificaux", p. 363.

76. Untergehrer, *Die päpstlichen nuntii und legati*, p. 156.

77. *Ibid.*, pp. 150-160.

78. Markgraf, ed., *Politische Correspondenz*, vol. 2, pp. 26-27, no. 205, "... Unum tamen scimus omnino esse necessarium..., quod vestra sanctitas que sic itura est huc mittat

Barbo, arrived in Wrocław in 1472 and was hailed by Peter Eschenloer, the city scribe and chronicler, as a prelate who had never been seen in the city before.[79]

A few examples might illustrate the problems with the nomenclature and the terminology of nuncios in the second half of the fifteenth century. The above-mentioned archbishop of Crete, Girolamo Lando, was on three missions to Central Europe: 1459-1460 as *nuntius et orator*; 1461-1464 and 1464-1465 as *orator cum potestate legati de latere.* He was called *noster et apostolice sedis nuncius atque orator* by the pope in a breve to the King of Poland in 1459. When addressed together with his colleague Francesco da Toledo, they were called *nuncii et oratores nostri.* When the two of them published letters, they titled themselves *sancte sedis apostolice ac sanctissimi in Christo patris et domini, domini Pii divina providentia pape secundi nuncii et oratores ad infrascripta specialiter missi et deputati*[80] and elsewhere *sanctissimi domini nostri pape oratores.*[81] It may seem evident that he was with the powers of the legates *de latere* only with the other two missions, however, in a breve which was published on 16 September 1459, he received a special faculty which authorized him to act with the power of the legate *de latere* to be able to better achieve what he was commissioned to do.[82] Two questions can be followed here: first, the nuncio was given this faculty by the Pope with a breve, a letter and not with a proper bull; second, a breve published on the same date and sent to the King of Poland does not state anything about the power of the legate *de latere.* This would widen the scope of possible uncertainty as for the actual titles and commissions. However, after this date, he entitled himself in his letters with the attribute *cum potestate legati de latere.*[83] All the three commissions of Girolamo Lando were therefore with the title of nuncios *cum potestate legati de latere,*

unum ex reverendissimis dominis cardinalibus plenissima potestate preditum. Hec quidem metuendissima dignitas et auctoritas pusillanimes animaret christianos et terrorem faceret hereticis, ut a bellis repellerentur …".

79. Eschenloer, *Geschichte*, p. 903, "… vnd vormols hatte nymant einen sulchen prelaten zu Breslow gesehen".

80. Theiner, ed., *Vetera monumenta Poloniae*, vol. 2, p. 120, no. 165 (16 Sep 1459), "… Misimus ad Regnum Boemie Venerabilem fratrem Ieronimum Archiepiscopum Cretensem nostrum et apostolice sedis ad concordandos inter se ibidem dissidentes nuncium atque oratorem …"; p. 121, no. 166 (20 Sep 1459); p. 122, no. 168 (13 Jan 1460).

81. Palacky, ed., *Urkundliche Beiträge zur Geschichte Böhmens*, p. 196, no. 202 (17 Nov 1459).

82. ASV, Arm. XXXIX 9, fol. 81v, "Archiepiscopo Cretensi. Cum fraternitatem tuam ad Boemie et Polonie regna necnon ad dominia dilectorum filiorum magistri et fratrum ordinis beate Marie Teutonicorum nostrum et apostolice sedis nuncium et oratorem ad concordandum inter se dissidentes duxerimus destinandum, volentes illa tibi concedere, per que ampliori cum facultate commissionem tibi datam valeas exequi eidem tue fraternitati in regnis et dominiis antedictis dumtaxat durante commissione huiusmodi potestatem legati de latere presencium tenore concedimus".

83. Cf. for example NA Prague, ŘP, no. 133 (3 Jan 1460), "Hieronymus dei et apostolice sedis gratia archiepiscopus Creten. sanctissimi in Christo patris et domini nostri domini Pii divina providentia pape secundi in regnis Bohemi et Polonie ac terris Slesie et Prusie cum potestate legati de latere nuntius et orator".

the first one, however, only from a certain point and *durante commissione.* Moreover, he had signed one letter to the city council of Olomouc in 1463 as *legatus, etc.* He consequently accepted the generic term legate, perhaps for a better understanding of his position in the region.[84]

The title of *legatus missus* appeared in a similar context as late as the 1460s. The bishop of Lavant and later of Wrocław, Rudolf of Rüdesheim, called himself *legatus missus, cum potestate legati de latere legatus missus*, or *legatus missus specialier deputatus* in his own letters and in German letters then *bebstlicher legat etc.*, or *ausgesanndter legat etc.*[85] It also has to be observed in his particular case when and how he acquired the powers of the legate *de latere.* After he was transferred from the bishopric of Lavant to Wrocław, he was also confirmed as nuncio *cum potestate legati de latere*;[86] and then again by another bull which was transcribed by Peter Eschenloer, the scribe of Wrocław.[87] He was, however, still called only *noster et apostolice sedis nuncius* by Pope Paul II when he had been holding the *cum potestate legati de latere* commission for two years.[88] It should be mentioned that even the local environment paid attention to his legatine title, as a contemporary formulary of the Wrocław Dominicans entitled him *Reverendissimo in Christo patri ac domino domino Rudolpho Vratislaviensi episcopo necnon sacrosancte sedis apostolice in regno Bohemie, Polonie etc. cum potestate legati de latere legato.*[89] Central Europe was visited at that same time by Domenico Dominici, who entitled himself *legatus missus cum potestate legati de latere* as well.[90] Lorenzo Roverella, another nuncio, who was active in Central Europe in this period was called *orator cum potestate legati de latere* or *cum potestate legati de latere nuncius et orator noster* in papal letters in 1470,[91] and in his own letters of the same year, he used the title *cum plena potestate legati de latere dicti domini nostri pape legatus specialiter deputatus.*[92] In 1476, a year before he was created

84. SOkA Olomouc, fond: AMO, Charters, inv. no. 240 (3 Jul 1463). Similarly, Ladislaus Geréb, who was entitled *legatus cum potestate legati de latere* in the mandates, signed a letter (MNL Budapest, OL, DL 62925; 24 May 1486) as "Ladislaus Gereb episcopus Transsilvan. apostolice sedis legatus etc.".

85. SOkA Olomouc, fond: AMO, Charters, inv. no. 263 (24 Apr 1467), 264 (26 Apr 1467), 267 (16 Jul 1467), German letters, inv. no. 269 (25 Aug 1467); SOkA Jihlava, fond: Archiv města Jihlavy, inv. no. 184 (8 May 1469); Palacky, ed., *Urkundliche Beiträge zur Geschichte Böhmens*, p. 342, no. 324 (8 Mar 1465); HHStA Vienna, fond: St. Paul, OSB, sign. 1465 III 04 (www.monasterium.net; 17 Mar 2017).

86. Theiner, ed., *Vetera monumenta Poloniae*, vol. 2, pp. 158-159, no. 195 (27 Apr 1467).

87. Markgraf, ed., *Politische Correspondenz*, vol. 2, pp. 233-236, no. 365.

88. ASV, Reg. Vat. 531, fol. 290r (22 Apr 1469).

89. Dragoun, *Soupis*, p. 315.

90. MNL Budapest, OL DL 45080 (16 Mar 1464).

91. ASV, Arm. XXXIX 12, fol. 65r (1470; Fraknói, ed., *Mathiae Corvini Hungariae regis Epistolae*, pp. 81-82, no. 61; Theiner, ed., *Vetera monumenta Hungariae*, vol. 2, p. 415, no. 590), fol. 70r (28 Dec 1470); fol. 72v (28 Dec 1470).

92. MNL Budapest, OL DL 17005 (17 May 1470); similarly, NA Prague, ŘF 45 (2 Jan 1470), "Laurentius dei et apostolice sedis gracia episcopus Ferrariensis, sanctissimi domini nostri pape referendarius et datarius eiusdemque ac dicte sedis per universam Germaniam et

cardinal, Gabriele Rangoni entitled himself *apostolice sedis cum plenitudine potestatis legati de latere legatus*,[93] Angelo Pecchinoli, who is always referred to in papal bulls as *nuncius et orator cum potestate legati de latere*,[94] entitled himself *cum plena potestate legati de latere sedis apostolice legatus* in his letters.[95] Orso Orsini, who was sent to Central Europe in 1493-1495 called himself *apostolice sedis necnon sanctissimi domini nostri pape cum plena potestate legati de latere legatus*,[96] but in an official bull published by the Papal Chancery, the title is *noster et apostolice sedis nuncius cum potestate legati de latere*.[97] Angelo Geraldini as *nuntius et commissarius cum plena potestate legati de latere* was only *orator noster* in papal bulls in a papal breve, both published by Sixtus IV.[98]

Numerous examples of the last paragraph demonstrate the variability of the terminology of papal envoys. The original bulls of the mandates given to the envoys at the start of their missions were sometimes insufficient and additional commissions might change the picture. In the case of the nuncios *cum potestate legati de latere*, the terminology was not so clearly established and terms such as *legatus* or *orator* appear in that context. What should be observed, however, is the fact that there exists a clear-cut division between the legates *de latere* and the other non-cardinal envoys, usually bishops, nuncios *cum potestate legati de latere*, even though there were various terms involved such as *legatus*, *legatus missus*, *nuncius et orator* and *orator*. When in use, the term *legatus* for these non-cardinal envoys was used by the chancery of the envoy himself, even though there are also instances when the Papal Curia published documents with such terms, as in the case of Ladislaus Geréb, who was called *legatus cum potestate legati de latere*.[99]

The question arises as to whether there were other connotations to these titles and their usage by the envoys themselves. Janusz Smołucha believed that the fact that Girolamo Lando called himself *legatus*, even though in curial sources he is always *nuncius et orator*, indicated his personal ambitions. He supposedly even longed for the cardinalate.[100] This possibility cannot be ruled

regnum Hungarie singulasque ipsorum patrias, provincias, civitates, terras, oppida, castra, villas atque loca cum potestate legati de latere ab eodem domino nostro pape legatus specialiter deputatus"; NA Prague, ŘP 140 (22 Jun 1471), "cum plena potestate legati de latere legatus apostolicus" (both letters at www.monasterium.net, 17 Mar 2017).

93. MNL Budapest, OL DL 17835 (18 Jul 1476)

94. ASV, Reg. Vat. 734, fol. 228v-242r (1 Sep 1488).

95. For example, MNL Budapest, OL DL 63338 (4 Oct 1489); NA Prague, ŘF, inv. no. 74 (31 Jul 1489).

96. For example, MNL Budapest, OL DL 20188 (2 Jun 1494).

97. ASV, Reg. Vat. 779, fol. 42v (18 Oct 1493).

98. Storm, ed., *Diplomatarium norvegicum*, vol. 17, pp. 1090, 1093; ASV, Arm. XXXIX 16, fol. 16r. In the breve addressed to a papal collector, it might be a generic term for an envoy.

99. Theiner, ed., *Vetera monumenta Hungariae*, vol. 2, p. 500, no. 688 (8 Nov 1484); ASV, Arm. XXXIX 19, fol. 26rv (7 Oct 1485); in the registers of supplics, he was called *apostolice sedis cum potestate legati de latere nuncius generalis*, cf. Lukcsics, ed., *Monumenta*, vol. 3, p. 301, no. 450 (24 Apr 1486).

100. Smołucha, *Polityka kurii rzymskiej*, pp. 239, 321; cf. also Urbánek, *České dějiny*, vol. 3/4, p. 633. Cf. the career of Girolamo Lando as Patriarch of Constantinople, Mureşan, "Girolamo Lando".

out, however, in light of all the other examples, the situation is not all that special as many other envoys called themselves legates. What is crucial is that they did not assume the higher title of legates *de latere*, but simply interchanged the terms *nuncius* and *legatus*. Therefore, either it is the general ambition of such envoys (Smołucha also ascribed such a longing to Rudolf of Rüdesheim), or – which is much more probable – the terms could be interchanged, because by the second half of the fifteenth century there was a clear-cut difference between the legates *de latere* and the non-cardinal envoys with the powers of the legates *de latere*. As concerns the terminology, there is no general rule written down by the instructions of the nuncios and they never state what term should be used. The above-mentioned treatise by Gonzalo García determined that the non-cardinal envoys might still be called legates and not merely nuncios.[101] The term *legatus* might bring a higher prestige. On the other hand it was also a generic term for papal envoys outside the legal framework; in discussions, they would be addressed as *domine legate*, as some of the reports of Bartolomeo Maraschi and Angelo Pecchinoli show.

The title of *legatus de latere* was naturally forbidden to all such nuncios *cum potestate legati de latere*. Cases of contrary behaviour, however, can be traced in contemporary sources. One such nuncio was Francesco Coppini, bishop of Terni, who was sent as nuncio to England. His powers were later enhanced to *nuncius et commissarius cum potestate legati de latere*, which he might have considered as equivalent to legate *de latere*. This is what his activities would seem to indicate as he had a legatine cross carried in front of him (a privilege that only belonged to a legate *de latere*). He also granted dispensations that he was not entitled to, and was later accused of simony and publishing illegal excommunications. He was very active in organising the Crusades and in English and French politics. His political involvement and negotiations were expressly refused, however, by Pope Pius II, Coppini was tried in Rome, deprived of all ecclesiastical ranks and became a Benedictine monk.[102] Similarly, Alexander Numai assumed illegally certain powers he was not entitled to. He was sent to Germany as a nuncio and orator in 1474 and stayed at the court of Emperor Frederick III or in other places beyond the Alps until his death in 1483.[103] He was first informed that he should come back by a messenger from the Pope.[104] Then, he was officially called back and all his faculties were revoked (in a general revocation of faculties for all the legates and nuncios), because he reportedly transgressed the terms of his commission. Later, following appeals from Frederick III, his position was restored, but first only as a *privatus orator*

101. *Tractatus universi iuris*, vol. 13/2, fol. 258v.

102. Harvey, *England, Rome and the Papacy*, pp. 195-206; Lesage, "La titulature", 219-220; cf. also *Pii Secundi Pontificis Maximi Commentarii*, pp. 183-184, 505-506.

103. On Numai in more detail, Erfle, *Alexander Numai*; for the extant papal letters see Opll, "Das Archiv".

104. AS Roma, Collezione acquisiti e doni, b. 27, n. 1, fol. 63v (5 March 1477), "Remittimus ad te dilectum filium Petrum Paulum capellanum tuum, a quo de reditu tuo et de aliis rebus nostram voluntatem intelliges".

without any faculties, only for his faculties to finally be restored to him and even enhanced.[105] When responding to the imperial envoy in Rome, Andrea Jamometić, the Pope even explained that the nuncio was criticised by many at the Curia as well as elsewhere for using faculties he did not have or using those he had immodestly. Some princes even claimed he served as a mercenary in an army, which cannot be matched with papal dignity. For these reasons Alexander was recalled, but the Pope wanted to believe the Emperor rather than others and put him back in place at the imperial court only advising him to use the faculties modestly.[106] A year later, despite the fact that many archbishops and bishops, nuncios and collectors were recalled, the faculties of Alexander Numai, once abolished, were confirmed as well as his deeds.[107] When getting back to the beginning of the problem, the May general revocation of all the faculties of legates and nuncios did not hold for Luka Tolentić, bishop of Šibenik and nuncio *cum potestate legati de latere* in Burgundy.[108] These cases only confirm, what was stated earlier: the crucial difference among the papal diplomats were

105. Schlecht, *Andrea Zamometić*, pp. 26, 29. Chmel, *Actenstücke*, vol. 3, p. 446, no. 14 (14 May 1477), "... Nuper rationabilibus respectibus moti; reuocauimus omnes et singulas facultates, legatis: Oratoribus: et nuntijs nostris concessas: quod tibi significamus, volentes et mandantes vt facultatibus tibi concessis, nullo pacto utaris"; p. 447, no. 15 (30 May 1477), "... Nam facultates omnes quibuscunque concessas, bonis de causis et respectibus reuocauimus"; p. 447, no. 16 (20 Dec 1477), "... Vt complaceamus ... Friderico Romanorum Imperatori ..., qui nobis hac in parte instantes supplicauit, contentemur ut istic remaneas, tanquam priuatus orator: et nullas habeas facultates: cum omnes reuocauerimus: et pacem potius quam discordiarum causam inter christianos Principes desideremus Reliquum est: ut aduertens et sollicitus sis, in omnibus rebus que ad honorem huius sancte sedis pertineant"; p. 447, no. 17 (13 Jan 1478), was supposed to deliver the cardinal's hat to Gabriele Rangoni; p. 448, no. 18 (15 Mar 1478), "Fuit apud nos venerabilis frater Archiepiscopus Craynen. Orator Imperialis (Andrea Jamometić), qui ... rogauit nos plurimum, vt facultates semel concessas tibi restituere vellemus. Nos etsi omnes reuocauerimus et multa ad nos de fraternitate tua perferrentur tum ab Italicis tum a Germanis, quod facultatibus utebaris, quae non habebas, et ijs quas habebas immodeste utebaris, adeo vt propter honorem nostrum et tuum te reuocare necesse fuerit. Contemplatione tamen maiestatis sue contenti sumus eas tibi restituere, et ita per presentes tibi restituimus, quacunque reuocatione non obstante. In quibus tamen ea moderatione utaris, vt nulla ad nos querela perferatur, sed potius te eas restrixisse quam ampliasse uidearis. Quid ad postulata maiestati sue respondeamus, putamus te uisurum ..." (instructions for the imperial envoy in Rome Andrea Jamometić, see Schlecht, *Andrea Zamometić*, pp. 6*-11*, the problem of Alexander was also mentioned); p. 448, no. 19 (17 Mar 1478), two days later he acquired further faculties for publishing indulgences. Sixtus IV later communicated with Alexander as with any other nuncio, sent instructions, etc., pp. 449-465, passim. As concerns the use of the faculties, when they were abolished, but the nuncios did not know yet, the Pope confirmed all the acts, pp. 453-454, no. 42 (6 Oct 1478), "Significauit nobis nuper tua fraternitas: quod cum nos facultates Legatis et nuncijs nostris traditas reuocauerimus atque suspenderimus: nihilominus dum huiusmodi suspensio atque reuocatio ad notitiam tuam non prouenisset, facultates tibi a nobis traditas et concessas exercuisti. flagitas igitur ea omnia per te gesta eo tempore quo nihil de reuocatione predicta ad aures tuas peruenerat a nobis confirmari. Quare ea omnia confirmamus et plenarie firmitatis robur habere tenore presentium decernimus".

106. Bachmann, ed., *Urkundliche Nachträge*, pp. 448-449.

107. ASV, Reg. Vat. 679, fol. 129v-131v.

108. AS Roma, Collezione acquisiti e doni, b. 27, n. 1, fol. 162v-163r (two briefs, 10 May 1477).

between the legates *de latere* who were cardinals and the non-cardinal envoys, who could enjoy special privileges and faculties, but never reached the dignity and authority of the legates *de latere*, whose office was defined by canon law and who also based their position on being cardinals.

Another two tendencies might define the changes in the system of papal diplomacy at the end of the period covered in this book. One significant change was linked to the revolutionary transformations of diplomacy in general. Medieval diplomacy was based on embassies and ambassadors who usually fulfilled their tasks and returned to their lord. Only during the fifteenth century (even though the first instances come from the previous century), did a new kind of diplomacy arise which became the basis for diplomacy of modern times, namely resident ambassadors and permanent representation of sovereigns in other courts. The greatest boom and expansion of this system of diplomacy could be attested to for the princely courts in Italy of the second half of the fifteenth century with the institutionalisation of the Italian League.[109] Papal diplomacy transformed along the same lines: the nuncios gradually became permanent representatives of the popes in individual countries or at individual princely courts. The first indications of such a development can be observed as early as the second half of the fifteenth century. A well-known example is Luka Tolentić, who spent almost twenty years in the Burgundian court.[110] Similarly, some of the above-mentioned legates and nuncios stayed on their missions for a longer period of time and became agents of papal policy in the region with more than one task. In a similar fashion as Luka Tolentić, they reported back to Rome with a number of written accounts of their doings. These were systematically preserved for a later period of the sixteenth century; at the end of the fifteenth century, only some reports survived in occasional contexts, the most well-known being the *Collezione Podocataro* of Venice.[111]

Another trend in papal diplomacy at the beginning of the sixteenth century stemmed from general trends in papal administration, namely the involvement of lay people in papal service.[112] Changes in diplomatic service made it even more possible than before. The nuncios did not have to be prelates, but were predominantly diplomats in political matters rather than representatives of the Pope in spiritual and ecclesiastical ones. As nuncios, they did not have any faculties and certainly no jurisdictional powers. They were political and diplomatic servants of the Pope.[113] One such example might be the very active papal nuncio of the 1520s Giovanni Antonio Buglio barone di Burgio. He spent several years

109. Queller, *The Office*; Mattingly, "The First Resident Embassies"; idem, *Renaissance Diplomacy*; Ilardi, "Fifteenth-Century Diplomatic Documents"; Fubini, "L'ambasciatore nel XV secolo"; changing the perspective slightly and showing there was no linear progress from medieval ambassadors to resident embassies, see Lazzarini, *Communication and Conflict*; see also Margaroli, *Diplomazia*; Pillinini, *Il sistema*.

110. Blet, *Histoire*, pp. 183-185; some of his reports published in Ljubić, ed., *Dispacci*, pp. 12-48.

111. A new catalogue (unfortunately, with many mistakes), De Poli, *Inventario*.

112. Partner, *The Pope's Men*.

113. Walf, *Die Entwicklung*, pp. 76-85.

on missions in Central Europe, despite having a wife and four children; he thus never entered the ecclesiastical status. His powers were consequently adjusted, for example receiving bulls with indulgences announced in connection with the Crusade. He was, however, to hand them over to the archbishops of Esztergom and Gniezno or the legate *de latere* Cardinal Lorenzo Campeggi, who was present in Austria, for them to make them public.[114] The fact that the nuncio would not have any holy orders (and this was not a rule) did not have to be known to everyone. Sigismund the Old, the King of Poland, addressed Antonio Burgio in 1523 as *reverendissime in Christo pater* or *vestra reverendissima paternitas*, which were titles reserved for prelates, in these forms usually cardinals.[115] This fact, then, only confirms the original thesis, that the local sources may often have been inaccurate and that even the contemporaries (apart from the members of the Papal Chancery and Curia) might have been confused.

Nuncios, however, were not only lay diplomats. The early sixteenth century brought another tendency for dismissing the title of nuncio *cum potestate legati de latere* again, which had been so very popular in the second half of the fifteenth century. Zaccaria Ferreri, who was active in 1519-1520 for example, was called by the Pope and the Papal Curia only *nuntius* or *nuntius et orator*, even though he was a bishop and had a considerable number of faculties.[116] His extensive powers even resulted in him being called *legatus* in local sources, for example, by the King of Poland, and he himself called his mission a *legatio*.[117] It may be speculated that a few years earlier, he would have been called nuncio *cum potestate legati de latere*. The last such cases appear in 1510 in the personality of Achille Grassi (to Germany, Hungary and Poland), in 1516 with Roberto Latino Orsini (to Hungary), who, however, never left for his mission, Lodovico Canossa in 1514-1517 and Esteban Gabriel Merino as late as 1522-1523 (to France).[118] Thus, the innovation of the fifteenth century disappeared in the early years of the century that followed.

The system of papal representation was very complicated and although canonically defined, it still evolved according to current needs. This is crucial to realize, as the content of the individual terms may have differed throughout the centuries. The position of the legates *de latere* did not change much, as it clearly stemmed from the codifications of the canon law. The rest, however, was very flexible and the period of classical canon law may be evidently distinguished from the period of the Avignon papacy and the papal schism as well as from

114. Wojtyska, ed., *Acta*, vol. 2, pp. 153-155, no. 4 (18 Jul 1524).

115. *Acta Tomiciana*, vol. 6, p. 314, no. 285 (as I use the edition, the explanation might also be an inconsistency on the part of the editors).

116. Wojtyska, *Acta*, vol. 1, 197-198; Wojtyska, ed., *Acta*, vol. 2, pp. V-VI; Smołucha, *Papiestwo a Polska*, pp. 178-180.

117. Wojtyska, ed., *Acta*, vol. 2, p. 12, no. 6; cf. p. 129, no. 52, "Reverendissimo domino Zachariae, episcopo Gardensi, sanctae sedis apostolicae oratori et legati …"; p. 132, no. 54 (31 Aug 1522), "… dum legationem sarmaticam agerem …".

118. Kalous, *Plenitudo potestatis*, pp. 366-368, 371; Barbiche, *Bulla, Legatus, Nuncius*, pp. 282, 283.

the fifteenth century and the post-conciliar period that led to the most substantial changes to the system of papal representation.

The crucial personalities within the system were still the legates *de latere*, who were cardinal legates, and those of the highest rank. Unlike the thirteenth and mostly fourteenth centuries, when cardinals could be named nuncios as well, it became a rule in this period that cardinals were always created legates *de latere*. Their position was not only codified in canon law, but also modified by the special mandates, the faculties that were given to all of them and by adjustments to their powers and privileges. Both the offices – the cardinals and papal legates *de latere* – were connected permanently. The nuncios *cum potestate legati de latere* had almost equal powers and privileges on a lower level. The authority given to them was smaller, however, and limited mostly in terms of ceremonial, which in the case of legates *de latere* drew on the general papal ceremonial of the period. Certain constituent parts of it were withheld from the nuncios. They were endowed, in contrast, with special mandates and faculties just like the cardinal legates, and were given a province to govern in spiritual matters and to exert jurisdiction. The even lower rank of papal representation can be exemplified by nuncios, orators and the like, who had very limited powers and usually were sent with clear tasks for negotiations. Only occasionally, were they endowed with faculties, which – when they themselves were not consecrated as bishops – were transmitted to the local ordinaries. Moreover, there would be a number of messengers, couriers and envoys of lesser importance, who were used also by the legates or nuncios themselves. Furthermore, the legates then created their own commissaries or delegates. In the system of papal diplomacy, sometimes the judge-delegates (*iudices delegati*) are mentioned, but their authority was mandated to specific judicial causes and they otherwise did not really represent the pope as such, but rather his judicial authority in singular cases. They do not belong to the system of papal diplomacy.

The most well researched modification or even revolution in papal diplomacy were the changes of the first half of the sixteenth century. Papal legates *de latere* remained in the system, of course, but their legations and activities were adapted. They were not dispatched from the Curia as often as in the second half of the fifteenth century. The principal activity of political negotiations was taken over by the permanent nuncios. The title of nuncio *cum potestate legati de latere* disappeared and even if the nuncio was allotted a province to govern, he was not given the above-mentioned title. The general development of papal policy meant involvement in political matters and a nuncio became an emblematic expression for a papal representative in (early) modern Europe. Although the revolution of the sixteenth century that was institutionalized by the Council of Trent was extremely significant, it is important to realize that the system of papal representation was not stable between its definition in the thirteenth century and this period. This can be illustrated in the fifteenth century.

1.2. *The sources*

It may seem useful to have a closer look at the sources for the study of the legates, as these may be not only sources used for event history, but also documents that constituted the basis of the power of legates and defined them as such. The origin of the new understanding of the office was clearly delineated in the thirteenth century. A number of sources and a number of types of sources have already been mentioned above. These sources are scattered all over Europe, as – for obvious reasons – the office of the legates was not limited to a specific place. To give it a more precise framework, it is possible to differentiate the sources according to their provenance into three basic categories. First, there were the documents that were produced by the Papal Curia; second, the documents that came from the activity of the legates themselves, and finally, external documents that were produced by other chanceries or individuals.

The first category is the most obvious one, namely the sources that emanate from the popes and the Curia who provided the legates with their powers. As concerns general documents that shaped legations, we must first turn to canon law, which was defined (to some extent) in Gratian's *Decretum* and (much more) in other collections promulgated by the popes (*Liber extra*, *Liber sextus*, *Extravagantes communes*) and often discussed the problems of legates as representatives and envoys of the popes.[119] These collections represent canon law of the twelfth to early fourteenth centuries, which, however, was modified and explained by later commentators. Guillaume Durand wrote in the thirteenth century his *opus magnum* entitled *Speculum iudiciale.* The rubric *De legato* formed together with the following rubric *De dispensationibus* the treatise *Speculum legatorum*, the most detailed account of the legal context of legates.[120]

Canonists of the fifteenth and early sixteenth centuries also took interest in the legates, usually in connection with the cardinals as such.[121] Treatises on legates of Andrea Barbazza, Nicolas Bohier, Pietro Andrea Gambaro, Jean Bruneau and Gonzalo García de Villadiego were printed in the second part of the thirteenth volume of *Tractatus universi iuris* in 1584 in Venice together with other treatises on cardinals in general.[122] These treatises introduce the types of legates and papal envoys in general, specify their powers and privileges and focus on the individual questions and problems of the legates and their activities. These will not be introduced in detail, but some of their comments appear when dealing with specific topics. Furthermore, Wolfgang Untergehrer included in his treatment the work of Giovanni Bertachini, whose *Repertorium utriusque iuris* had in the form of an encyclopedia clear definitions of the envoys under the items *legatus* and *nuncius.*[123] Although a detailed discussion does appear

119. Friedberg, ed., *Corpus*, 2 parts.

120. Durantis, *Speculum iudiciale*, pp. 29-98.

121. An indispensable overview of the canonists, which is still developing, can be found in the *Bio-Bibliographical Guide to Medieval and Early Modern Jurists*, compiled by Kenneth Pennington (found at http://legalhistorysources.com) and updated by Charles Donahue at http://amesfoundation.law.harvard.edu/BioBibCanonists (accessed 29 May 2017).

122. *Tractatus universi iuris*, vol. 13/2, fol. 131v-258r, treatises on cardinals appear on fol. 57v-131v. From the point of view of diplomacy, they are listed in Hrabar, ed., *De legatis*, pp. 31-86, including a number of treatises on secular envoys.

123. Untergehrer, *Die päpstlichen nuntii und legati*, pp. 103-106.

in all these treatises, they seem to comment more on canon law as opposed to designing the actual practice of individual legations.

The normative sources of canon law may be complemented with other normative sources that stem from the liturgical usage of the Curia. Popes had special ceremonial books that defined the ways of liturgy and non-liturgical ceremonies of the Curia: processions, order of celebrations, posts of dignity, etc. They were still more precisely regulated by the authors of such books and based on the *Ordo Romanus*, most crucially *Ordo Romanus XIV*, which is described as the work of many authors, but most often attributed to Cardinal Giacomo Stefaneschi.[124] Out of these sources, which will be used later, the books of the papal masters of ceremonies prove to be most elucidating and crucial for all such ceremonial operations (Agostino Patrizi Piccolomini, Johannes Burckard, Paride Grassi).

When one proceeds to documents related to single legations, the faculties (*facultates*) are the most significant, after the general definitions of the canon law, for analysis of the legates' authority and their activities.[125] In the faculties, legates were endowed with powers for their legation predominantly in ecclesiastical matters (jurisdictional or spiritual), but the faculties also had the potential for political negotiations. The spiritual instruments could be used as tools for solving political problems or for placing pressure on opponents (excommunication, interdict, etc.). The faculties were published as *litterae* and were usually preserved as copies in the Vatican registers (*Registri Vaticani*); only rarely did political matters appear among other faculties in the registers in *brevia sub plumbo*, a special category of papal breve, which, however, from the point of view of the papal diplomatics belongs among the *litterae clausae.*[126] Usually, a *bulla legationis* was found among these faculties, this being a bull that contained the general authorization for the legation, the reasons for the legation itself and the definition of the legatine province. Additional bulls that appear in the registers are various recommendation letters or credentials (required only for nuncios, never for legates *de latere*).[127] The rest are usually the actual faculties, which authorised legates to take various steps or gave them powers in matters reserved only for the Pope. Such faculties began to appear in the thirteenth century and their number for the individual legates grew from that time. These faculties were either published in one larger bull, or were more often published as singular bulls for each faculty. It was typical for a legate to have some twenty to forty faculties, however, there were cases when the faculties could reach even greater numbers. Cardinal Ottobuono Fieschi, later Pope Hadrian V, was sent to England and the German provinces of Mainz, Trier and Cologne with no less than seventy faculties. Similarly, Cardinal Gui de Boulogne received some seventy faculties in 1348 for his legation in Hungary, Lombardy and some other church provinces and dioceses.[128] An example from the

124. Dykmans, ed., *Le cérémonial papal*, vol. 2; Schimmelpfennig, *Die Zeremonienbücher.*
125. Maleczek, "Die päpstlichen Legaten", pp. 43-46.
126. Frenz, *Papsturkunden*, pp. 23-30.
127. Cf. later the chapter on faculties.
128. Ruess, *Die rechtliche Stellung*, pp. 120-126; Maleczek, "Die päpstlichen Legaten", p. 43; on the legation Ottobuono Fieschi, see also Ollendiek, *Die päpstlichen Legaten*, pp. 69-82.

later period might be Cardinal Giovanni d'Aragona, who was sent to Hungary, Bohemia and Poland in 1479 with some seventy-five bulls.[129]

When it came to practical ways of solving their tasks, the legates and nuncios were given instructions to follow. These complement the faculties and are an indispensable part of their diplomatic activities. The instructions generally ordered or recommended legates as to what to do and how to do it, how to behave and how to proceed in negotiations, where to begin their legation when their legatine province was larger and encompassed more princely courts. In the Papal Chancery, the instructions were transcribed into manuscripts that contained a collection of such texts only from the time of the pontificate of Pope Sixtus IV and which are preserved in manuscripts dating from the later sixteenth century.[130] At times, the instructions could contain directions on the usage of the above-mentioned faculties, which might have been conditioned by specific political or church-political situations. The actual use of the faculties was up to the decision of the individual papal legate and the clearly defined context.

There is, for example, an illustrative case of Cardinal Marco Barbo who was active as papal legate *de latere* in Central Europe in 1472-1474 and had a faculty that enabled him to confirm King Matthias Corvinus as King of Bohemia.[131] This was within the framework of the struggle for the Kingdom of Bohemia between King Matthias of Hungary and the Jagiellonians represented by King Casimir of Poland and his son Wladislas, the elected King of Bohemia in 1471. The instructions added that Marco Barbo could only use the faculty if all the peace negotiations failed. The decision was left to the prudence of the legate himself.[132] Both the faculty and the instructions were published after only three months of his legation, so both were additional and reacted to the political developments in his legatine province as well as – in all probability – to his reports. The instructions could also order the legates and nuncios to coordinate their activities between themselves, when there were more papal representatives in the region, and even to meet in Rome before they set out for their respective provinces. The nuncio to the Emperor was instructed, for example, to meet and consult those who were destined to go to the Kings of Hungary and Poland.[133]

129. ASV, Reg. Vat. 680, fol. 167r-259r.

130. Cf. ASV, Misc., Arm. II (e.g. vols. 7, 20, 30, 53, 56); BAV, Vat. lat. 13451, 13454; DHI Roma, Minucciana, ms. 14; an overview of the instructions of the "nuncios" of Sixtus IV in Schlecht, *Andrea Zamometić*, pp. 148-170; a number of them are published by various source publications (e.g. Theiner, Artner, Valentinelli, Bachmann, Teleki, see bibliography).

131. ASV, Reg. Vat. 680, fol. 84r-85r (14 May 1472).

132. ASV, Misc., Arm. II 30, fol. 42r (20 May 1472), "Quo ad tertium capitulum de confirmatione electionis factae regis Hungariae, expediatur bulla in bona forma, et mittatur ad legatum; illa tamen utatur pendente tractatu concordiae, nisi viderit eandem confirmationem utilem et necessariam ad pacem melius et celerius consequendam, eodem vero tractatu iam omisso et pacis nulla remanente spe, tunc poterit uti illa facultate, et dictam electionem confirmare, prout melius expedire suae prudentiae videbitur".

133. ASV, Misc., Arm. II 30, fol. 53r (1476), instructions for Luka Tolentić, bishop of Šibenik, "Procurabitis cum aliis nunciis mittendis ad regem Hungariae et Poloniae, antequam discedant, habere bonam intelligentiam, et invicem convenire hic Romae, ut si alioquin occurrat, quod aliquis indigeat ope alterius, invicem impartiantur et suffragetur unus alteri".

As it was just mentioned in the case of Marco Barbo, the legates and nuncios could receive additional faculties and instructions when they were present in their legatine provinces. Communication between the Papal Curia and the legate and further orders could also be conveyed by the papal briefs. The scope of the papal briefs, reserved for political matters only up until the mid-fifteenth century, was enlarged in the second half of the century and legally binding documents in spiritual matters may be found as well.[134] The conditions of the legation could have been changed and modified, when the briefs contained further faculties or instructions. The communication was transmitted by papal couriers (*cursores*), who could even have the obligation to deliver more such documents and letters to various addressees, as Cardinal Bessarion pointed out when he received a papal brief on his legation at the Emperor from a papal courier, who then left to deliver letters to others.[135] Most often, however, briefs were used for simple communication with the legates in the form of a letter. In both usages, the briefs are extremely valuable for the researcher as they elucidate the actual course and functioning of individual legations. As an example, the briefs addressed to papal nuncio *cum potestate legati de latere* Bartolomeo Maraschi, might be mentioned. The nuncio was re-called from his legation by a brief in the beginning of January 1485.[136] In contrast, another brief published as late as 29 September 1485 prolonged by five years all the privileges and concessions granted by the nuncio to churches and other corporations and granted perpetual validity in the case of individuals.[137] The conditions of the legation were modified several times by simple briefs, short isolated letters that change the validity of many acts of the nuncio.

The three categories, *facultates*, *instructiones* and *brevia*, the addressees of which were usually the legates themselves, are the basic documents that emanated from the Papal Chancery and formed the legations as such. The briefs, then, were often addressed to others as well, namely the sovereigns and other prelates and these rather elucidate and explain than shape the legations. They might contain credentials, which were sent directly to such addressees and when the mission of a papal representative was supposed to have a larger scope there might have been a large number of those, as in the case of the papal commissary and nuncio Bartolomeo da Camerino in 1482-1483. His task was to negotiate the Crusade, its financial backing and other papal matters in the regions of Austria,

134. Frenz, *Papsturkunden*, pp. 35-38.

135. Mohler, *Kardinal Bessarion*, vol. 3, pp. 499-500, no. 45 (Aug 1460), "Applicuit ultimus cursor vestrae beatitudinis sexta praesentis cum brevibus apostolicis ad principes convocatoriis. Quae maiestati imperiali et domino Gurcensi dirigebantur, illemet praesentavit. Quod vero domino Saltzburgensi scribebatur, ego misi per alium nuntium cum litteris meis, quibus eum multis precibus oro, ut attenta propinquitate vellet venire personaliter. Cursor vadit ad alios. Breve autem ad mihi scriptum et cum debita reverentia suscepi et cum magna iucunditate legi, cum viderim, quod tanta clementia tantaque suavitate verborum vestra pietas erga servulum suum utatur".

136. ASV, Arm. XXXIX 18, fol. 91r (3 Jan 1485; ed. Kalous, *Plenitudo potestatis*, pp. 333-334).

137. ASV, Arm. XXXIX 19, fol. 18rv (29 Sep 1485; ed. Kalous, *Plenitudo potestatis*, p. 334).

Bavaria and Poland, with no less than thirty-two briefs related to his mission sent to local rulers, bishops and worldly officials.[138]

There are a number of other documentary sources of the curia that may be related to the legates. The previous ones are crucial for communication and definition of the position of the legates and nuncios, while from the other sources one learns about the financial dispositions of individual legations, the reception of letters or events related to the presence of the legates in Rome or at the Papal Curia in general. Only a short typological description will follow.

The records of the Apostolic Chamber are filled with references to individual papal legates and nuncios. In the series of the *Introitus et Exitus*, not only the income of the legates, the salary given from the central sources, is documented, but also special payments to the legates as in the case of Cardinal Oliviero Carafa, who was to organise the papal fleet in 1472 and for this task received from the Chamber almost 70,000 florins.[139] A special case consisted of the accounts of the fund for financing the Crusade where the money was drawn from the revenues of the alum monopoly at Tolfa. Special payments to legates and nuncios involved in crusading may be found in the *Depositeria generale della crociata*.[140] The records of the Apostolic Chamber, however, are not only accounts. The registers of contracts, concessions, reports and other documents entitled *Diversa cameralia*, also show the financial details of the legations. In relation to legates and nuncios, there are contracts concerning the amount of money paid as a salary, or – more often – contracts between the legate and the Chamber, as a debtor who needs to pay further money to fulfil the original financial claims of the legate, this being the case of Cardinals Marco Barbo and Pietro Isvalies mentioned later.[141]

Although there are normative sources on the ceremonial of the papal legates in Rome, these could be complemented by the documentary sources of the Roman diaries of the above-mentioned papal masters of ceremonies. For this period, the works of Agostino Patrizi Piccolomini, Johannes Burckard and Paride Grassi are the most fruitful ones. These can be supplemented by the official records or diaries of the Papal Consistory, where the information is conveyed in the form of short concise texts or entries;[142] the *Acta vicecancellarii* were recorded in the same way.[143] Among other more non-official documents, the collections of letters of cardinals might be mentioned. These are usually quite informative as concerns the course of the legations or the role of the legates at the Curia. For the period of the second half of the fifteenth century, for example, the collections of Cardinal Giacomo Ammannati Piccolomini

138. ASV, Arm. XXXIX 15, fol. 115r-120r, 129rv (some of them ed. Kalous, *Plenitudo potestatis*, pp. 303-306).

139. ASV, Cam. Ap., Intr. et Ex. 487, fol. 163r-183v passim.

140. AS Roma, Camerale I, Depositeria della crociata (1463-1490), vols. 1233-1237.

141. ASV, Cam. Ap., Div. Cam.; see chapter three, § 3.3.

142. ASV, Arm. XXXI 52 (largely, but not in its entirety, published by Eubel, *Hierarchia catholica*, vol. 2, pp. 26-48).

143. ASV, Arch. Concist., Acta Vicecanc. 2, 3 (cf. Eubel, *Hierarchia catholica*, vol. 2; Eubel and Schmitz-Kallenberg, *Hierarchia catholica*, vol. 3).

or Cardinal Marco Barbo are very special.[144] The variety of sources is extremely wide in this context, as papal legates were the highest representatives of the popes and the Curia and thus needed to communicate frequently with the centre.

The documents published by the individual legates themselves are also fairly diverse as concerns the form and addressees, the greatest issue being that they are dispersed in a vast number of archives and libraries. Two legations of the fourteenth and fifteenth centuries might serve as illustrative examples of the great variety and number of sources. As Werner Maleczek has remarked, the most crucial are in this sense the collections of sources related to the legation of Cardinals Gentile da Montefiore in Hungary (1307-1311) and Nicholas of Cusa in Germany (1451-1452).[145]

Crucial importance should be given to those texts which were sent by the legates back to the Curia. These are the relations (*relationes*) with which the legates informed the Pope and the Curia about the progress of their legations and the fulfilment of their tasks. Instructions might even mention the obligation to inform the Pope and the central offices, as in the case of the papal nuncio Mariano Bartolini.[146] It is attested by the above-mentioned sources that his relations were read in the Consistory, when they arrived.[147] The relations of the second half of the fifteenth and early sixteenth centuries usually do not have any standardized format, they are not regular and most importantly not well preserved. They are only preserved on a greater scale in the end of the fifteenth century, when some of them were transcribed in a number of manuscripts. The greatest change, however, comes about only with the standardization of the position of the nuncios in the first half of the sixteenth century. The preservation of the relations is much better and becomes part of the system of papal nunciatures of the modern age. A number of the older ones are preserved in the manuscripts of the instructions, as in the case of the three relations of Bartolomeo Maraschi, a papal nuncio *cum potestate legati de latere* in Central Europe in 1483-1485.[148] The most fruitful collection, however, in this sense are the manuscripts of the *Collezione Podocataro* which are held in the *Marciana*, the National Library of Venice. In this collection and some

144. Ammannati Piccolomini, *Lettere*; Paschini, ed., *Il carteggio.*

145. Maleczek, "Die päpstlichen Legaten", p. 37; for Gentile, Pór, ed., *Acta legationis*; for Nicholas, Meuthen, ed., *Acta Cusana.*

146. ASV, Misc., Arm. II 30, fol. 176v (22 Feb 1504), "De his autem, quae egeris, aut afficere speras, et de statui illarum rerum, ut de omnibus, qua evenire contingent, ad nos diligenter scribere curato". Concerning relations in the later Middle Ages, see Maleczek, "Die päpstlichen Legaten", pp. 63-67.

147. ASV, Arch. Concist., Acta Misc. 6, fol. 128rv (18 Apr 1505), "Deinde fuit lectum exemplum literarum domini Mariani de Bertholinis auditoris rotę nuntii apostolici apud cesaream maiestatem sub datum sexta Aprilis…"; ASV, Arm. XXXIX, vol. 22, fol. 58v-59r (14 May 1504), "Dilecte fili salutem et apostolicam benedictionem. Binas literas tuas accepimus alteras sextadecima alterasque recentiores erant XXII mensis Aprilis Auguste data. In primis scribis te iterum auditum a regia celsitudine… In secundis significas, responsum tibi XXI.a eiusdem mensis datum esse et ipsum regem de nobis honorificentissime et pientissime fuisse locutum …"

148. ASV, Misc. II, vol. 7, fol. 228r-248v; vol. 20, fol. 49r-58v; vol. 56, fol. 347r-358r.

other manuscripts of the *Marciana*, one may find a number of reports of legates and nuncios of the 1470s-1490s, such as Baldassare Turini da Pescia, Lodovico Agnelli, Antonio Grassi, Alexander Numai, Giuliano della Rovere, Orso Orsini, Angelo Geraldini, Bartolomeo Maraschi, Raymund Peraudi, Antonio Flores, Leonello Chieregato and Angelo Pecchinoli.[149] Some reports are even published, as in the case of Angelo Geraldini, Luka Tolentić and Leonello Chieregato.[150]

The reports appear in other manuscripts very selectively and not systematically. Such relations were most often sent to the Curia, but could also be delivered in the form of a speech at the return of the legate to Rome and his acceptance at the Consistory. For example, Cardinal Marco Barbo returned from his legation to Central Europe and Germany in 1474. Cardinal Giacomo Ammannati Piccolomini reported in a letter to Cardinal Theodor Paleologos that on 15 November 1474 Cardinal Marco had a presentation in the Consistory and "his speech about the lengthy peregrination lasted almost two hours" and included a description of all his deeds from his departure from Rome to his return.[151] A part of such a general relation, which, however, is much more detailed than anything that could, as a speech, last for only two hours in total, can be found in a manuscript related to the activities of Marco Barbo, which also contains a number of his letters.[152] The later relations reflect the changes in the system of papal representation and are organized in a much more systematic way. The most illustrative of these are the reports of the papal nuncio Antonio Burgio and his colleague, the papal legate *de latere* Cardinal Lorenzo Campeggi.[153] The reports are relatively frequent and regular and like the reports from Italian nuncios, describe his activities and the general developments of the political, ecclesiastical and military aspects of the region, in this case Hungary. These reports are very well preserved and, moreover, the *Acta vicecancellarii* reported on the individual sessions of the Consistory when the relations were read in front of the Pope and the cardinals. The letters of Antonio Burgio from 1526 informed on the advance of the Ottomans and the military preparations of the Hungarians and, on average, the letters from Hungary reached the Curia after three weeks.[154] The reports, then, were crucial for the decision-making process at the Curia.

149. BMV, Lat. X 174 (=3621), Lat. X 175 (=3622), Lat. X 176 (=3623), Lat. X 177 (=3624), Lat. X 178 (=3625), Lat. XIV 99 (=4278), Lat. XIV 100 (=4279). Cf. Valentinelli, ed., *Regesten*; De Poli, *Inventario.*

150. Petersohn, ed., *Diplomatische Berichte*; Ljubić, ed., *Dispacci*; Paschini, *Leonello Chieregato*, pp. 53-110.

151. Ammannati Piccolomini, *Lettere*, vol. 3, pp. 1890-1891, no. 767 (15 Nov 1474), "Hodie cardinalis Sancti Marci Marcus nomine, qui triginta mensibus legatus Apostolicae Sedis abfuerat, in senatu de rebus in provincia gestis ex consuetudine rettulit. Longa fuit diuturnae peregrinationis oratio, horis ferme duabus sine intermissione continuata ..."

152. BAV, Vat. lat. 5641, fol. 201r-208v (ed. Kalous, *Plenitudo potestatis*, pp. 264-284).

153. ASV, Segr. Stato, Germania 53 (Campeggi), 55 (Burgio); Fraknói, ed., *Relationes oratorum*; Theiner, ed., *Vetera monumenta Hungariae*, vol. 2, pp. 676-808, published partially; Wojtyska, ed., *Acta*, vol. 2, pp. 149-224.

154. ASV, Arch. Concist., Acta Vicecanc., vol. 3, fol. 109r-121r, passim (ed. Kalous, "Elfeledett források", pp. 616-621; Tusor and Nemes, eds., *Consistorialia documenta pontificia*, pp. 59-70).

In a way, the diaries written by the legates themselves or by the members of their retinue were in the form of a report. Of particular interest are those composed by the above-mentioned masters of ceremonies, namely Agostino Patrizi Piccolomini for the legation of Francesco Todeschini Piccolomini in 1471 to Regensburg,[155] and Johannes Burckard for the legation of Bernardin Carvajal to the King of the Romans in 1496.[156] An informer among the followers of Cardinal Juan Carvajal wrote a report on the events of his legation to Prague in 1448.[157] These extended reports might have served as commemorative writings, but also as the bases for the later oral reports of the legates, when they arrived back to Rome and to some extent might even have replaced the relations in the form of letters sent by other legates to the Curia.

Naturally, the reports and letters were not the only documents that were published by the legates and their chanceries. They published a vast number of charters and letters addressed to the inhabitants of their legatine provinces. These sources contribute to an understanding of their missions and an analysis of their activities in the regions. They also constitute, however, the most significant heuristic problem, as such sources are dispersed around the entire legatine province in present-day archives and libraries and published in a variety of editions. Charters of this kind are only found in one place when the registers of the legates were preserved, which is extremely rare for the fifteenth and early sixteenth centuries. Only the registers of Cardinals Juan Carvajal and Bessarion have partially survived.[158] From among the legatine charters, the confessional letters (*litterae confessionales*, i.e. charters that would allow the addressee to select a confessor and also receive absolutions in cases reserved for the Papal Curia) may be singled out as the most common ones. Others would be indulgence letters for churches and other institutions, which would enable the church to distribute indulgences to individuals upon certain special occasions or for financial or manual help involving reconstruction, etc. Moreover, as these charters – especially the confessional letters – were so common and formalized, they were later printed and vast number of copies of such letters survive in local archives. The most common ones were published, at the end of the fifteenth century, by the papal nuncio Raymund Peraudi, but there are letters published by others, such as Cardinals Pietro Isvalies and Tamás Bakóc.[159]

155. *Deutsche Reichstagsakten*, vol. 8, pt. 2, pp. 459-473, 650-691, 939-943 and the rest edited in Frank Rutger Hausmann, *Giovanni Antonio Campano: Erläuterungen und Ergänzungen zu seinen Briefen*, Freiburg im Breisgau (PhD dissertation), 1968, pp. 533-575, as quoted by *Deutsche Reichstagsakten.*

156. Celani, ed., *Johannis Burckardi Liber*, vol. 1, pp. 615-644; Thuasne, ed., *Johannis Burchardi Diarium*, vol. 2, pp. 291-334.

157. Emler, ed., *Fontes*, vol. 7, pp. 48-53; Gómez Canedo, *Don Juan*, pp. 303-311.

158. Maleczek, "Die päpstlichen Legaten", pp. 59-60.

159. Peraudi's printed confessional letters are preserved in many archives, cf. e.g. NA Prague, ŘF, charter no. 123 (2 Jul 1490; ed. Kalous, *Plenitudo potestatis*, pp. 338-340); SOkA Olomouc, Archiv města Olomouce, Sbírka listin, inv. no. 320 (28 Jul 1489); SOkA Znojmo, Archiv města Znojma, Listiny, sign. 154 (7 Jul 1489); NA Prague, ŘM, inv. no. 1194 (14 Apr 1490); cf. Housley, "Indulgences"; Kühne, "Raimund Peraudi"; for Isvalies, BAV, Vat. lat. 3922, fol. 305rv (ed. Kalous, *Plenitudo potestatis*, pp. 358-360); VK Olomouc, sign. 39012 (bound

Among other powers, the legate held jurisdictional authority in his province, thus, the legate's chancery also produced documents related to lawsuits and tribunal court acts. These were preserved, for example, from the judicial proceedings of Cardinal Gentile da Montefiore in his legation in Hungary in 1307-1311,[160] but also from other legates (and nuncios with the powers of the legates) who produced a number of documents related to court proceedings.[161] When legates exercised their powers in a local church, they published many more types of documents. Thus, charters related to the reform of monasteries and the organisation of the ecclesiastical life of the diocese, communication with the bishop, etc. The last case might be exemplified by the Bishop of Olomouc Prothasius (Tas) of Boskovice. Originally, he ranked among the supporters of King George of Bohemia, but after the King was proclaimed a heretic by Pope Paul II, the legates and nuncios in the region placed pressure on the bishop to leave his secular master, in which they finally succeeded.[162]

As it is apparent, the legates and nuncios represented the Pope not only in church and ecclesiastical matters, but also as diplomatic envoys and political agents in their provinces. They published letters and communicated with local rulers, influenced local political events or informed about them. Their activities ranked from Crusade to peace-making, they influenced or at least observed royal elections and nobility negotiations, they were present at royal courts and performed rituals of political importance and they used ecclesiastical censures to achieve political goals. At all these occasions, they produced sources of varying forms from letters and charters to accounts and liturgical orders. These are singular matters, that are typologically varied and will be treated at appropriate places.

The third basic category of sources that may be employed to study the late medieval legations is even more diverse than the previous one. These are all the other sources that were published by a third party, i.e. by someone else than the Papal Curia or the legate's chancery. Here, any categorization is impossible, so it is only useful to mention in general the most fruitful types of sources. For every region this would be specific. There are a number of detailed chronicles written by locals or by Italian historians for later medieval Central Europe. For Poland, for example, the chronicle of Jan Długosz, for Silesia and Wrocław, in particular, the two chronicles of Peter Eschenloer, the Latin and the more detailed German one. These are extremely valuable as Jan Długosz had direct access to the King of Poland, and Peter Eschenloer represented the city, which had most contacts with the papacy in this period, especially due to the fight against the Hussites

to an early print); Biblioteka Jagiellońska Kraków, sign. Cim. 34; Moravská zemská knihovna Brno, sign. ST3-0108.046; MNL Budapest, OL DL 22544, 36087, 46599, 60895, 66756, 93699; for Bakóc, Borsa, "Bakócz Tamás nyomtatott"; idem, "Bakócz Tamás újabb nyomtatott"; Fekete Nagy, Kenéz, Solymosi and Érszegi, eds., *Monumenta rusticorum*, pp. 54-55, no. 7.

160. Pór, ed., *Acta legationis*, pp. XXXVI-XLI; cf. Maleczek, "Die päpstlichen Legaten", pp. 56-57.

161. For Hungary, for example, in great numbers listed by Bónis, *Szentszéki regeszták.*

162. Kalous, "Služba Boskovických"; idem, "Boskovice urai"; idem, "Bohemians and Moravians".

and King George of Bohemia. For Hungary, due to the representation policy of Matthias Corvinus, historians are fortunate to have more chronicles, namely those of the two Italians Antonio Bonfini and Pietro Ransano, but also local one by János Thuróczi. For Bohemia and Moravia, there are a number of manuscripts of a collection of annalistic entries gathered first by František Palacký and entitled *Staré letopisy české* (Old Czech Annals) and for the later period the chronicle of Bartoš Písař (Bartoš the Scribe). All these might be used for the detailed accounts of the activities of the legates, but naturally, they are all ideologically and politically biased. The chronicle of Peter Eschenloer had, however, the benefits of having a number of original documents transcribed in the text itself.[163]

For local diplomatic sources, there are a number of collection of letters and charters, some of which are based on chancery collections of medieval origin, others are collections prepared by modern historians. As modern editions they are extremely useful for research.[164] The city registers of important cities, local songs or diaries make a valuable supplement to all the sources. These, however, are like the sources published by the legates themselves, scattered over the whole of Europe and thereby illustrating the roles of papal diplomacy. The papal envoys were sent all around Europe as an instrument of papal administration and government of the Church, control of Christian society and the influence of political matters of the period.

1.2.1. *An example: Sources for the legation of Angelo Pecchinoli*

To illustrate the situation of the sources for individual legations, the sources available for the legation of Angelo Pecchinoli, Bishop of Orte and Cività Castellana, who served as nuncio *cum potestate legati de latere* to the court of King Matthias Corvinus in 1488-1490, can be analysed. His legation was limited to the countries where King Matthias ruled, meaning the Kingdom of Hungary and Croatia and all the subjugated lands and the Kingdom of Bohemia (effectively the lands of Moravia, Silesia and Lusatias). Austria is not mentioned in the documents, even though Matthias Corvinus resided at this time in Buda and in Vienna intermittently. Angelo's legation can be treated as illustrative in the point of sources, as they stemmed from various curial offices as well as from himself.[165]

First of all, there is a set of twelve bulls preserved in the Vatican registers, which were partially edited by Augustin Theiner. To obtain the full image of the

163. *Joannis Dlugossii Annales*; Eschenloer, *Historia*; idem, *Geschichte*; Bonfinis, *Rerum Ungaricarum Decades*; Ransanus, *Epithoma*; Thurocz, *Chronica*; Palacký, ed., *Staří letopisové*; Šimek, ed., *Staré letopisy*; Šimek and Kaňák, eds., *Staré letopisy*; Šimák, *Fontes*, vol. 6.

164. *Fontes rerum austriacarum*; *Scriptores rerum silesiacarum*; *Mátyás király levelei*; *Monumenta Vaticana Hungariae*; *Acta Tomiciana*; *Archiv český* etc.

165. This chapter is a shortened version of a study that will appear in a volume edited by Adinel Ciprian Dincă based on a conference *Bullaria, Monumenta, Repertoria: Editing Late Medieval Documentary Texts preserved in the Vatican and Roman Archives* on 2-4 June 2016 in Cluj-Napoca. Currently, I am preparing an edition of the documents related to Angelo Pecchinoli's legation.

legation, historians have to study the registers, as the editions are usually only selective, due to the high number of documents.[166] These documents include the general commission as *bulla legationis* and a general recommendation as the credentials of the nuncio to all Christians. Additional documents that clearly establish the tasks of the nuncio are instructions and in the case of Angelo, there are two sets of them. The first instructions were published upon the nuncio's departure from Rome and planned his activities after he arrived in his province. In this case, the text is not dated, but naturally was written sometime around the departure of the nuncio or when the faculties were given to him.[167] The second set of instructions reacted to the first report of the nuncio and further specified what was expected from him and elaborated on the plan of action.[168] The document is again preserved in this case without a date, which, however, might be complemented from a brief of Pope Innocent VIII to Angelo sent on 26 March 1489.[169] Both the texts were not preserved as originals, but in the volumes copied in the sixteenth century by the Papal Chancery in sets of instructions for legates and nuncios of Sixtus IV and the following popes. What might be considered remarkable, however, is the preserved concept of the second set of instructions, which can be found in a manuscript that contains a number of letters and other documents linked to the activities of Cardinal Marco Barbo. He had been a legate to the region in 1472-1474 and his experience was highly valued at the Curia. Thus, he might have been involved (or at least interested) in the process of composing the instructions.[170] This conjecture can even be supported by the fact that the very same manuscript contains a copy of the first report of Angelo sent to Cardinal Marco directly with an accompanying letter, to which the second set of instructions reacted.[171]

Correspondence between the nuncio and the papal centre constituted the third part of the control and transmission of tasks and charges to the representative of the Pope. One can observe a number of papal briefs that were addressed to Angelo

166. ASV, Reg. Vat. 734, fol. 228v-242r (1 Sep 1488); Theiner, ed., *Vetera monumenta Hungariae*, vol. 2, pp. 515-521, nos. 711-717.

167. ASV, Misc., Arm. II 7, fol. 492r-508v; 30, fol. 93r-100r; 53, fol. 128r-140v; 56, fol. 153r-170v (s.d.; around 1 Sep 1488); Teleki, ed., *Hunyadiak kora*, vol. 12, pp. 417-432, no. 780; Artner, ed., *"Magyarország"*, pp. 134-137, no. 113 (selectively).

168. ASV, Misc., Arm. II 7, fol. 519r-529v; 20, fol. 123r-130r; 30, fol. 105r-109v; 56, fol. 193r-202v; BMV, Lat. IX 42 (=3483), fol. 59v-65r; DHI, Roma, Minucciana, ms. 14, fol. 191v-206r (s.d.; [26 Mar 1489]); Theiner, ed., *Vetera monumenta Hungariae*, vol. 2, pp. 530-534, no. 719, Artner, ed., *"Magyarország"*, pp. 140-142, no. 118 (selectively).

169. AS Venezia, Coll. Podocataro, busta 2, no. 513/34, fol. 13r, "Episcopo Ortan. oratori nostro. Venerabilis frater etc. Accepimus litteras tuas et responsiones per te prudenter factas carissimo in Christo filio nostro Mathie Hungarie regi illustri, legimus omnia diligenter et accurate singula consideravimus. Commendamus plenum studium et diligentiam tuam, quibus in rebus istis uteris et respondemus tibi ad plenum sicuti introclusis instructionibus videbis. Expones omnia prefato regi, cui breve credentiale in personam tuam dirigimus, quod illi reddes, et solita prudentia et diligentia cuncta curabis".

170. BAV, Vat. lat. 5641, fol. 96r-99v.

171. BAV, Vat. lat. 5641, fol. 237v-247v.

or otherwise related to his mission. First, before the legation even began some of the briefs were directed towards King Matthias Corvinus,[172] others to Angelo himself in relation to his diocese in Italy.[173] These letters ensure that the diocese is prepared for the bishop's longer absence (even though this was a diocese that was traditionally held by curial bishops) and the king for a new legate/nuncio in his court. Still before Angelo left Rome, three more briefs were addressed to him that contained faculties of absolutions to Hungarian bishops who had become involved in bloodshed while acting against robbers and highwaymen and to a bishop who wanted to enter a religious order.[174] Additional direct briefs to Angelo are related to the sending of instructions (as mentioned above), to his diocese once again and to further faculties.[175] Other correspondence in both directions is between the Pope and the kings and other potentates or prelates of the region, who came into contact with the nuncio (ten letters in total).

Reports of the nuncio can be regarded as part of correspondence. Angelo Pecchinoli's reports have the luck of being largely preserved in the above-mentioned *Collezione Podocataro* housed in Venice. The manuscripts of the *Marciana* contain twelve of his reports (one of them is also in the manuscript of Marco Barbo of the Vatican Library)[176] and one further report can be traced to a sixteenth century manuscript where it was included among copies of legatine instructions.[177] As the latter one was preserved in the Vatican archives, it was edited by Augustin Theiner,[178] the rest, however, remains in a manuscript form (apart from the selective publication of excerpts from two of the reports),[179] and have been studied in detail only by Vilmos Fraknói.[180] Two reports were sent from Vienna, the rest from Buda on 30 January, 17 April, 15 May, 1 and 25 June (in one letter), 18 September, 15 October, 3 and 27 November and 26

172. ASV, Arm. XXXIX 20, fol. 404v-405r (6 Aug 1488), the pope sends a nuncio to solve a long-standing problem of the bishopric of Olomouc, "... Quemadmodum etiam latius nostra ex parte communicabit cum maiestate tua nuncius noster propediem ad te destinandus". Cf. also the concept in ASV, Arm. XL 1, fol. 75r; another brief (almost the same) in ASV, Arm. XXXIX 20, fol. 542rv (concept in ASV, Instr. Misc. 4151) (11 Aug 1488).

173. ASV, Arm. XXXIX 20, fol. 455v-456r (26 Aug 1488), Angelo should make a visitation to two cities of his diocese, namely Sant'Oreste and Ponzano Romano before he left for Central Europe, "Venerabilis frater salutem etc. Ne forte ecclesie tue Civitatis Castellan. ex absentia tua, cum te ad regna Hungarie pro nonnullis nostris et sedis apostolice negociis impresentiarum mittamus, preiudicium generetur, volumus, ut inter eundum oppida Horestis et Ponzani, que de dioc. Castellan. esse asseris pro tuo iure episcopali visites et alia facias, que ad prefatum visitationis officium de iure spectant et pertinent ..."; fol. 458v (26 Aug 1488).

174. ASV, Arm. XXIX 20, fol. 460v-462r (26 Aug 1488).

175. ASV, Arm. XXXIX 21, fol. 166rv, 423v-424v.

176. BMV, Lat. X 174 (=3621), fol. 97r-97v; Lat. X 175 (=3622), fol. 110v-113r, 113v-114v, 116r-117v, 118r-120v, 121r-122v, 123r, 124r-125r, 127r-136v, 138r-146v; Lat. X 178 (=3625), fol. 167r-168v; Lat. XIV 99 (=4278), f. 16r-22r.

177. ASV, Misc., Arm. II 56, fol. 170v-191v; only the beginning of the report may be found in ASV, Misc., Arm. VI 39, fol. 145r-146v.

178. Theiner, ed., *Vetera monumenta Hungariae*, vol. 2, pp. 521-530, no. 718.

179. Lukcsics, ed., *Monumenta*, vol. 3, pp. 312-313, no. 464; pp. 314-315, no. 467.

180. Fraknói, "Pecchinoli Angelo".

December 1489 and 6 January, 6 April, 24 June and 18 and 24 July (in one letter) 1490. The letters were not sent on a regular basis, but even then larger time spans between some of them might indicate that there could have been more letters sent. Angelo even responded to allegations by the Pope that he did not write enough or not frequently enough. His response is, as in the case of the first report, which he sent relatively late after his arrival to the region, that the King should be held responsible. He even described him as morose due to his illness. Additionally, Angelo mentioned on 26 December 1489 that he had three messengers on the way with letters to the Pope.[181] An enciphered letter sent after the death of King Matthias reveals that the nuncio sent more reports than those that survived up until today: for the time between the death of the King (6 April) and this letter (24 June), Angelo recorded four different messengers that were sent with his reports.[182]

Information is lacking on the legation of Angelo Pecchinoli when it comes to the accounts of the Papal Chamber, which usually listed the payments to individual legates *de latere.* Cardinals seem to be present in the accounts much more often than the non-cardinal nuncios with the powers of the legate *de latere.* These accounts will be utilized later, here, however, we can make use of the special registers of the Chamber which are called in the Vatican Archives *Diversa cameralia.* The Chamber calculated the nuncio's salary and the Pope even specified that he could receive more than the usual pay, if he collected his money from the revenues of the archbishopric church of Kalocsa. These documents, however, cannot indicate what the result was and whether Angelo was able to acquire the money from Kalocsa or from the central budget.[183]

The above-mentioned sources, mostly found among the collections representing the central administration of the Church, constitute a solid ground, a body of documents, for a detailed study of Angelo Pecchinoli's legation. There are, however, additional sources that elucidate further events of the legation and the activities of the nuncio. The local archives of the countries Pecchinoli visited might produce such documents. This part of the research, naturally, is the most problematic one, as there is a huge number of relevant archives and archival collections. These are not only central archives, but also various city archives or archives of ecclesiastical institutions such as bishoprics, chapters and monasteries. As an illustration only a few will be mentioned.

There are singular documents or individual cases. Angelo assumed the same power as a legate *de latere* and thus performed similar legal acts. He wielded jurisdictional power in the province, reformed monasteries, dealt with benefices as even if this was questionable in legal literature, in practice nuncios with powers of a legate *de latere* had such an authority. The large-scale reform of all religious orders (mostly concerned, however, with Benedictines) was published by King Matthias Corvinus "assistente nobis reverendissimo in Christo patre domino

181. BMV, Lat. X 178 (=3625), fol. 168v; cf. Lat. X 175 (=3622), fol. 136v; BAV, Vat. lat. 5641, fol. 237v, 248r.

182. BMV, Lat. X 174 (=3621), fol. 97r.

183. ASV, Cam. Ap., Div. Cam. 46, 188v, 195rv.

Angelo episcopo Ortensi sancte sedis apostolice cum plena potestate legati de latere ad predicta regna legato".[184] This crucial document for the relationship between the King and the monastic orders demonstrates the close cooperation between the sovereign and the nuncio in the region.[185] The jurisdiction of the nuncio may be illustrated with the documents related to the judicial processes run in the kingdom under the authority of Angelo. There was a protracted dispute between the city council of Bardejov and Georgius Swarcz, a citizen of Košice, concerning certain vineyards. The documents are mostly preserved in the archives of the town of Bardejov in Slovakia,[186] but a letter of the city council to the nuncio also appears in the National Archives of Hungary. The citizens of Bardejov wanted to take the case from the jurisdictional authority of the nuncio to their ordinary court, i.e. the judgement of the *magister tavernicorum* (Hung. *tárnokmester*).[187] There also appears, in contrast, a document where the nuncio himself rejects jurisdiction over a case, which he clearly described as pertaining to the secular court rather than to his ecclesiastical jurisdiction.[188] The jurisdiction of the nuncio might have been delegated to a commissary, as in the case of Doctor Johannes Lopecz[189] or Johannes de Milei.[190]

Other acts of the nuncio include indulgences or other graces distributed within his legatine province. The Franciscan friary of Kusály (present-day Coşeiu in Romania) obtained a license to grant indulgences to visitors to the church (on certain feast days) or those who helped with keeping up the church.[191] The Franciscans in Bohemia and Moravia were ordered to reside in friaries (old or new) in the regions of heretics, so that they were able to impact them and bring them back to Catholicism. In order to do so, they had a faculty to accept the heretics back to the bosom of the Church and absolve them from all sins.[192] At the very start of his legation, Angelo Pecchinoli gave the faculty to the administrator Georg von Niederaltaich to award a dispensation from *defectus natalium* to Silvester Koldrer, a scholar of the diocese of Passau.[193] The nuncio also allowed the priests of the chapel in Slavkov (in Moravia) to organise a procession on the feast of Corpus Christi. A transcription of the

184. MNL Budapest, OL DF 207956 (3 Nov 1489; ed. Pongrácz and Rezner, eds., *A pannonhalmi főapátság története*, pp. 540-542, no. 87).

185. Cf. Kubinyi, *Főpapok*, p. 247.

186. Iványi, *Bártfa*, pp. 401-411, nos. 2724, 2726, 2734, 2746, 2763, 2767, 2768, 2775, 2777, 2792-2794, 2796, 2798.

187. MNL Budapest, OL DL 46140 (8 Jun 1490).

188. MNL Budapest, OL DL 56234 (26 Oct 1489).

189. MNL Budapest, OL DL 90200 (31 Mar 1489).

190. MNL Budapest, OL DL 102244 (24 Apr 1490). Cf. further Bónis, *Szentszéki regeszták*, pp. 470-473.

191. MNL Budapest, OL DL 105524 (20 May 1489; ed. Kalous, *Plenitudo potestatis*, pp. 350-351).

192. NA Prague, ŘF (Řád Františkáni), no. 74 (31 Jul 1489).

193. Munich, Bayerisches Hauptstaatsarchiv, fond Kloster Niederaltaich Urkunden (790-1801), no. 1042 (31 Dec 1488) (www.monasterium.net); cf. also no. 1041a insert in 1044 (23 Jun 1489)

charter, accompanied by a Czech translation, might be found in the archives of the Unity of Brethren.[194]

Such a list of sources might still be enlarged, as can be illustrated with the case of Nicholas of Cusa, whose *Acta* cover over 1500 documents related to his mission in Germany in 1451-1452.[195] For the individual legates and nuncios, however, this means years of heuristic research in local archives and libraries. Even though these documents are difficult to collect and compile, they are necessary complementary material to the curial sources so that we can rightly evaluate the individual legations.

194. Archiwum Państwowe Poznań, Akta Braci Czeskich (1507) 1557-1817 (1961), sygn. 47 (microfilm Nr. 0-76628), pag. 151-158 (I am indebted to Ota Halama for sharing the results of his research).

195. Meuthen, ed., *Acta Cusana.*

2. Rights and powers

2.1. *The authority of the legates*

The papal legates carried their authority which stemmed from the authority of the Pope himself and which was clearly defined by canon law, especially in the collections of papal decretals, *Liber extra* of Gregory IX, *Liber sextus* of Boniface VIII and *Extravagantes communes.* Legates were systematically discussed and dealt with by canonists, commentators of canon law, decretists and especially decretalists as mentioned above. The authority of the legates lied in the jurisdiction that was granted to them and that they could exercise in their legatine provinces. In this sense, they intruded upon the jurisdiction of the local bishop and interfered with the local administration of the Church. As direct representatives of the Pope they acquired their powers and authority straight from the Pope and became instruments of papal centralising policy from the eleventh century onwards. Thus, the legates could also have become unwanted and unwelcome visitors in the local dioceses. Apart from the jurisdiction itself, legates were endowed with powers over conferring and other administration of benefices within their legatine province, as well as powers to preside over synods, grant dispensations in certain cases or use ecclesiastical penalties. The decretals defined only part of the powers conferred to the principal representatives of the Pope. Canonists then defined all the nuances of the legatine rights.

From the eleventh and twelfth centuries, the jurisdictional supremacy of the papacy was clearly stressed with the papal premise of plenitude of power, *plenitudo potestatis*, within the Church. This Latin formula "served to invoke, express, and justify the papacy's most exalted claims to jurisdiction over the Church and even over the secular world".[1] And this was naturally crucial for the legates, as their power derived directly from the Pope's authority. Post-Gregorian papacy finally inclined towards being an administrative and legal organisation rather than the spiritual centre of Christendom. In the twelfth and thirteenth centuries, the Pope's authority was even supported by the new title of vicar of Christ (*vicarius Christi*), which had been officially used since the twelfth century and unmistakeably

1. Benson, "Plenitudo potestatis", p. 196; number of studies on *plenitudo potestatis*, cf. Rivière, "In partem sollicitudinis..."; Watt, *The Theory*, pp. 75-105; Pennington, *Pope and Bishops*, esp. pp. 43-74; idem, "The Canonists".

confirmed the pontiff as the head of the Catholic Church.[2] From there the Pope accepted the authority and jurisdiction over the entire universal Church, which was defined by the plenitude of power. This formula has its origin in the letter of Pope Leo I to Anastasius, Bishop of Thessaloniki, and there it reflected the ideas of the Pope (Bishop of Rome) that all the jurisdictional power within the Church was entrusted to him. Pope Leo then transferred part of his power to bishops, who were called "to share part of solicitude, but not to the fullness of power".[3]

One of the greatest canonists to become Pope was Sinibaldo Fieschi, Pope Innocent IV, who as one of the many canonist popes confirmed the legal and jurisdictional position of the Apostolic See. As theoretician of papal power, he used all these terms in his writings. The term *vicarius Christi* denotes the office of the Pope, bishop of Rome; the term *plenitudo potestatis* then describes the jurisdiction that was given to the Pope over the whole of Christendom; "both had their terms of reference in a concept of a single united Christian society over which the vicar of Christ exercised authority".[4] The Pope as the holder of the office of vicar of Christ was the highest monarch in medieval society; *plenitudo potestatis* (following the Profession of Faith of the Second Council of Lyons in 1274) expressed the idea that the Pope held the "supreme monarchical jurisdictional authority" and that "all other ecclesiastical powers derived their jurisdiction from the Roman Church".[5]

In the treatment of the canonical concepts of *vicarius Christi* and *plenitudo potestatis*, scholars put in relation the fullness of power of the Pope and a further step of the canonists in this argumentation, namely the fact that the Pope, bishop of Rome, was considered to be the judge ordinary over all Christians (*iudex ordinarius omnium*). The ordinary judge (*iudex ordinarius*) is a judge who holds his authority and jurisdiction from the power of his office, *ex officio*, and not as a delegated judge. Within the structure of the Church, every bishop was a judge ordinary of his diocese, but following the discussion of the canonists, it was also the Pope, who was an ordinary judge over all, i.e. in all the dioceses of Christendom.[6] Although any detailed analysis of these canonical concepts must be relegated to specialised literature, it is, however, crucial to realize the profound significance of them for legatine representation of the Pope.[7] These concepts were clearly valid not only for the classical period of canon law of the twelfth and thirteenth centuries, but also for the later period, when they, however, lost some impact in the popes' temporal supremacy. Nevertheless, the

2. Paravicini Bagliani, *The Pope's Body*, pp. 58-59.

3. Quoted by many authors, e.g. Watt, *The Theory*, pp. 76-77; Robinson, "Church and papacy", p. 282; Shogimen, *Ockham*, p. 160; the letter is published in Migne, *Patrologia latina*, vol. 54, col. 671-672.

4. Watt, *The Theory*, p. 71.

5. *Ibid.*, pp. 75-6.

6. *Ibid.*, pp. 92-97; cf. Morris, *The Papal Monarchy*, pp. 205-210; Shogimen, *Ockham*, pp. 156-184.

7. Watt, *The Theory*, pp. 75-105; Robinson, "Church and papacy", pp. 277-288; idem, "The institutions", passim; Shogimen, *Ockham*, passim.

jurisdictional power of the popes survived, even though it was occasionally challenged by secular rulers or other structures of the Church.[8]

Later treatises on papal power and the power of the Church in general also contain the same concepts, which then accompany the theories of papal power throughout the Middle Ages. For example, Giles of Rome, who supported Pope Boniface VIII in his struggle with Philip IV, King of France, closed his treatise *De ecclesiastica potestate*, completed about 1300, with a discussion on papal power and *plenitudo potestatis*. Following the hierocratic concepts of Pope Boniface, he focussed on the conflict between the secular and spiritual powers and demonstrated why the Pope possessed the supreme secular power (the largest part of the treatise), but discussed the position of the Pope within the Church as well. The Pope's power is defined as the highest power, the Pope as supreme judge who cannot be judged by anyone, as already incorporated in the final recension of *Decretum Gratiani*. (Here, chapters: *Quod Summus Pontifex est tante potencie quod est ille spiritualis homo qui iudicat omnia et ipse a nemine iudicatur*; *Quod Summus Pontifex est tante potencie quod ipse est illa potestas sublimis cui omnis anima debet esse subiecta*), the last chapter then proved that *plenitudo potestatis* has no limits (*Quod in Ecclesia est tanta potestatis plenitudo quod eius posse est sine pondere, numero et mensura*). Giles of Rome attributed *plenitudo potestatis* to the Pope as something natural: the Pope can do all legal operations within the limits of the law, but is also able to transgress the law thanks to the fullness of power. This is why jurisdictional authority over all is ascribed to the Pope. Giles even argued:

> Therefore, just as, in God, there is fullness of power absolutely, since God can do whatever any agent can do, and whatever He can do by means of any agents He can do without those agents, so the Supreme Pontiff has fullness of power to such an extent as there is power in the Church, since whatever any ecclesiastic can do the Supreme Pontiff can do. Hence, he is said to be the ordinary judge everywhere.

The Pope, in the argumentation of Giles of Rome, was not only the judge over all, but also a legislator, the law-giver of the entire Church.[9]

Fourteenth-century treatises concerning the power of the Pope are numerous; only a few examples will be sufficient to illustrate the matter. Two decades after Giles of Rome, Guillaume de Pierre Godin, a French cardinal created by Clement V, wrote his *De causa immediata ecclesiastice potestatis* (around 1318). He himself acted as a papal legate *de latere* in Spain. His treatise focused less on the secular rule of the Pope, but more on the problem of papal *plenitudo potestatis* and the papal jurisdiction over the entire Church. Cardinal Guillaume claimed that *plenitudo potestatis* belongs to the Roman Church and thus to the Pope, with which it surpasses all the local churches. The reason behind this is also the fact that the power is given to the Pope not by the Church, but by Christ himself.[10] Also here, the author believes that the Pope can judge everyone and that the power of

8. Thomson, *Popes and Princes*, pp. 181-200. Cf. also Tierney, *The Foundations*.
9. Dyson, ed., *Giles of Rome*, pp. 4-16, 360-396; part 3, chapter 9 (pp. 360-370).
10. McGready, *The Theory*, p. 195.

ordinary judges is obtained only through the Pope. Similarly, papal legate is an ordinary judge in his legatine province, because it was also the legate to whom such power was conferred by the Pope.[11] This concept was, however, not universal and there were scholars who did not agree with such an interpretation. Most prominent among these scholars of the early fourteenth century was William Ockham, who did not believe the papal authority was correctly defined and even – in reaction to the teachings and constitutions of John XXII and Benedict XII – wrote about papal heresy. For him, the will of the Pope could not be the source of Christian doctrine, as Benedict XII decreed. Ockham then criticised the necessity of papal monarchy and its foundations in papal usage of *plenitudo potestatis*.[12] In contrast, this concept was also transferred to the secular environment, predominantly in Italy and later also to other parts of western Christendom. Crucial in this respect was Baldo degli Ubaldi, a commentator on both canon and civil law, who brought this concept to the sphere of civil law and whose conclusions were criticized by his followers in the fifteenth century.[13]

Listing further treatises that have analysed, documented, supported or discredited the fullness of power of the popes in the Church context would be possible, but not necessary. The situation of the fifteenth century was radically changed by the papal schism and the fast development of conciliar theories.[14] After the conflict between Pope Eugenius IV and the Council of Basel, the Pope was able to enforce his authority once again and confirm it with the help of the council transferred to Ferrara and Florence, and the terms *vicarius Christi*, *plena potestas* and others.[15] Conciliar theories and ideas on limitations of papal power were, however, still present in fifteenth-century thought, even though Pope Pius II with his bull *Execrabilis* limited the power of the council and cancelled the possibility of appealing to the council. The popes of the post-conciliar period clearly defended their power within the Church. When the "schismatic" cardinals, together with the King of France, called a new council to

11. *Ibid.*, pp. 250-251, 350-351.

12. In detail Shogimen, *Ockham*, pp. 156-184; cf. also Tierney, *Origins*, pp. 205-237.

13. Cf. Black, *Absolutism*, pp. 8-35. Cf. also Vallerani, ed., *Tecniche*; Rizzi, "'Plenitudo potestatis'".

14. Vast literature on conciliarism, e.g. classic studies by Brian Tierney (Tierney, *The Foundations*), Anthony Black (Black, *Council and Commune*; idem, "The conciliar movement"; idem, *Church, State and Community*), who sees the theories of conciliarism in a political context; further e.g. Horst, *Autorität*, with an analysis of treatises on the power of the pope and the council; recently and from the side of the Church, Christianson, Izbicki and Bellitto, eds., *The Church*; see also Oakley, *The Conciliarist Tradition*; Decaluwe, *A Successful Defeat*.

15. Cf. Stieber, Lauritzen, Uhlich and Suermann, eds., *Concilium Ferrariense–Florentinum – Romanum*, p. 1217, Sessio VI (6 Jul 1439), "Item diffinimus sanctam apostolicam sedem et romanum pontificem in universum orbem tenere primatum, et ipsum pontificem romanum successorem esse beati Petri principis apostolorum et verum Christi vicarium totiusque ecclesie caput et omnium christianorum patrem ac doctorem existere, et ipsi in beato Petro pascendi, regendi ac gubernandi universalem ecclesiam a domino nostro Iesu Christo plenam potestatem traditam esse, quemadmodum etiam in gestis ycumenicorum conciliorum et in sacris canonibus continetur".

Pisa in 1511, Pope Julius II reacted by calling the papal council to Lateran. This situation then entailed new discussions concerning the power of the council and the Pope. Conciliarism was still to some degree present, but in practice papacy and papalism were victorious.[16]

New treatises on papal power in relation to the council emerged in this period: for example, just before the publication of the bull *Execrabilis* the Bishop of Torcello Domenico Dominici, who was also active as legate in Germany in 1463-1464, wrote his *De potestate pape et termino eius* (1456). The treatise itself falls into five parts: first, the relation of the Pope to the universal Church; second, papal power and bishops; third, papal power and cardinals; fourth, papal authority in relation to secular powers; and fifth, papal authority in relation to the papacy as an institution. Following the discussion of the fourteenth century, Dominici understood the Pope as *vicarius Christi* with *plenitudo potestatis* who was *iudex ordinarius omnium.* With the fullness of power the Pope can make dispensations of anything.[17] Another treatise from the beginning of the sixteenth century, published in 1504, was written by a Strasbourg scholar, public notary and canonist Johannes Hug. In his treatise *Quadruvium ecclesie*, which was among others dedicated to the papal legate Cardinal Raymund Peraudi, he discussed the four states of prelates, namely the Pope, the bishop, parish priests and the Emperor. The Pope holds *plenitudo potestatis*, the souls of all Christians are entrusted to him, all laws are locked in his mind and with the fullness of power the Pope can dispense anything.[18]

The number of treatises on papal power is naturally much higher than what can be introduced here. General outlines, however, are clear from this little exposition, which serves only as a reminder of the origins of papal jurisdictional power within western Christendom. Since the time of Gratian and the first canonists, the basis of papal authority did not change much. Of crucial importance are the concepts of papal government and jurisdiction over all Christians (*plenitudo potestatis* and *iudex ordinarius omnium*) and sharing this office with bishops *in partem sollicitudinis.*[19] Papal legates then acquired their authority only on the basis of papal power and derived everything from the Pope, who created them.

16. Thomson, *Popes and Princes*, pp. 3-28; Watanabe, "Pope Eugenius IV"; Burns, "Angelo da Vallambrosa"; Izbicki, "Papalist Reaction". Cf. also Stinger, *The Renaissance*, esp. pp. 83-155.

17. Smolinsky, ed., *Domenico de' Domenichi*, an edition with a detailed analysis (without part three which was not preserved); on Dominici, idem, "Dominici, Domenico".

18. Hug, *Quadruvium*, fol. XI-XIIII; fol. XV, "Sed est advertendum quod omnes episcopi sunt sub papa. Et eorum auctoritas est semi plena ipsos quoque vocat fratres. Et in partem sollicitudinis sunt vocati. Et non in plenitudinem potestatis. II. q. VI. c. Decreto et c. qui se scit [C. 2 q. 6 c. 12]"; see about Hug, Graf, "Der Straßburger Gelehrte".

19. On papal power in detail, Tierney, *Origins*, for mid-twelfth to fourteenth centuries, when the theory formed, Tierney, *The Foundations*, pp. 21-140; in relation to canon law, Shogimen, "The Relationship"; and see also, Shogimen, *Ockham*, pp. 156-231 for the first half of the fourteenth century. Gratian in many places, e.g. decree C. 2 q. 6 c. 12, or dictum C. 9 q. 3 (quoted by Watt, *The Theory*, p. 77). In relation to legates, see Figueira, *The Canon Law*, pp. 196-229. Cf. Winroth, *The Making*, for judicial immunity, p. 194.

The second principal source of the authority of papal legates was Roman law, which appeared in canon law in higher frequency since the twelfth century and to which canonists referred more often. They treated canonical concepts on the basis of civil, Roman law; for example, they compared institutions and offices and their powers with Roman offices. As for Roman law, crucial terms here are *iurisdictio*, *imperium* and the terminology of office.[20] Canonists of the thirteenth century attempted to link institutions of canon law to Roman institutions. This was the reason for comparing of offices, replacing terminology and demonstrating the relationship between papal legates and individual Roman offices. Most often, papal legates appeared to be linked to proconsuls, as their authority and government of a certain province had many similarities; they were, however, compared to other institutions as well: *praeses provinciae (legatus Augusti pro praetore)*, *senator*, *preafectus praetorio*, *praefectus urbis*, *praetor*, *rector provinciae*, *legati*. However, the last Roman office, *legatus*, did not have much in common with legates of the medieval period.[21]

John W. Perrin dedicated much space to the terms *iurisdictio* and *imperium*, their varieties and the possibility of delegating them. In order to do so he took into consideration not only Roman law itself (*Corpus Iuris Civilis*), but also the later legists, especially the Gloss of Accursius (1185-1263). Perrin introduced the system of jurisdiction in Roman law and hinted at the special situation of the late empire: "the emperor, as holder of *imperium* and therefore *iurisdictio*, could assume first instance jurisdiction in any matter, whether civil or criminal" (the civil and criminal procedure was not as strictly separated as in the classical period). Moreover, he could delegate his jurisdiction. These elements of Roman law were then passed down to the Middle Ages in the Justinianian compilations.[22] Accursius then, glossing *Corpus Iuris Civilis*, divided general jurisdiction into several categories (*species*), namely voluntary jurisdiction (*voluntaria*) for those who agree with the process, and contentious (*contentiosa*) for administering justice to unwilling persons; jurisdiction can consequently be ordinary (*ordinaria*) and delegated (*delegata*); the third category of jurisdiction is then the rule (*imperium*). What is crucial for the legatine authority and jurisdiction is the distinction between ordinary and delegated jurisdiction. Ordinary jurisdiction comes from the power of the office and can be delegated, but only in certain cases. Delegated jurisdiction, in contrast, cannot be in Roman law further delegated; in medieval canon law subdelegation in special cases was possible.[23] Similarly, Robert C. Figueira analysed the system of Roman law in

20. See, Perrin, "Legatus, the Lawyers"; idem, "'Legatus' in Medieval Roman Law"; Figueira, "Decretalists". Perrin was the first to study closely the relationship between Roman law and medieval papal legates; he also hinted at the fact that Ruess compared legates and proconsuls, but saw in canonist references to Roman law only an "academic fancy" (Perrin, "Legatus, the Lawyers", p. 469; Ruess, *Die rechtliche Stellung*, p. 1).

21. Figueira, "Decretalists", pp. 119-124; cf. Roman terms, Berger, *Encyclopedic Dictionary*, pp. 653 (*proconsul*), 646 (*praeses*), 694-695 (*senator*), 643-644 (*praefectus praetorio*), 644 (*praefectus urbis*), 647 (*praetor*), 669 (*rector provinciae*), 539 (*legatus*). – cf. also Perrin, "Legatus, the Lawyers"; idem, "'Legatus' in Medieval Roman Law".

22. Idem, "Legatus, the Lawyers", pp. 470-472, quote p. 471.

23. Idem, "'Legatus' in Medieval Roman Law", pp. 476-483; *iurisdictio (imperium)* is further divided in *imperium mixtum*, *imperium merum*, *coercio modica* and actual, simple *iurisdictio*. Only

terms of jurisdiction. He explained the concept of delegated jurisdiction (*iurisdictio delegata*), which was personal and restricted to a singular case and mandated jurisdiction (*iurisdictio mandata*), in which case the person that was given such jurisdiction represented the juridical instance of the mandator (appeals then went to the mandator's superior) and could not be further transferred by the mandatee. The third category of jurisdiction was *imperium*, i.e. the power that represented ordinary jurisdiction (*iurisdictio ordinaria*). These concepts differed according to various types of offices in Roman law. For the canonists, the medieval papal legate possessed all these three types of jurisdiction, for he held ordinary jurisdiction by the power of his legatine office and mandated as well as delegated the jurisdiction given to him by the Pope. Unlike the Romans, however, canonists did not decline legates the right to transfer the jurisdiction further (by delegating or mandating) to their delegates, deputies or commissaries.[24]

Although the origins of legatine power can be traced within the discussions of Roman law offices and the papal position within the Church, its ultimate source was the Pope. He shared his powers with the offices of the Roman Curia, which performed a number of decisions in his name without him even seeing the problem. Similarly, the legates were part of the office and participated in the power of the Pope. As mentioned above, the basis is defined in the collections of canon law, most significantly in *Liber extra* of Gregory IX, *Liber sextus* of Boniface VIII and *Extravagantes communes*.

The *Decretales Gregorii IX*, or *Liber extra* systematically treated various topics of canon law and under the title *De officio legati* of book one it focused on the basic characteristics of a legate.[25] The ten chapters of the title can be summarized as follows: 1. the legate can judge in the first instance;[26] 2. the legate cannot interfere in cases when a delegated judge is appointed by the Pope;[27] 3. the legate cannot transfer bishops without a special mandate;[28] 4. the legate cannot subordinate one diocese to another one, he cannot join two bishoprics or divide one, he can absolve those excommunicated for violence against clerics;[29] 5. as soon as the legate handed over the case to the Pope, he ceased to be its judge;[30] 6. the legate *de latere* can confer a vacant benefice, even if the patronage right belongs to another cleric;[31] 7. the legate can administer jurisdiction in all the places

the simple *iurisdictio*, whereas *imperium merum* (the most crucial cases) and *imperium mixtum* (less serious cases), which belonged to the office, could not be delegated. *Coercio modica* was associated with simple *iurisdictio*. On subdelegation in canon law, see Figueira, "Subdelegation".

24. Idem, "Decretalists", pp. 125-129; cf. Berger, *Encyclopedic Dictionary*, p. 524.

25. X 1.30.1-10 (Friedberg, ed., *Corpus*, pt. 2, col. 183-186). In general, cf. Figueira, *The Canon Law*.

26. Cf. Pennington, "Johannes Teutonicus", pp. 185-188.

27. Cf. Figueira, "'Legatus apostolice sedis'", pp. 558; idem, "Papal Reserved Powers", pp. 193-194; idem, "Subdelegation", p. 57.

28. Cf. idem, "Papal Reserved Powers", p. 192.

29. Cf. idem, "Decretalists", p. 127; idem, "Papal Reserved Powers", p. 192-193, 195.

30. Cf. idem, "'Legatus apostolice sedis'", pp. 552-558.

31. Cf. Pennington, "Johannes Teutonicus", pp. 189-193; Figueira, "Papal Reserved Powers", p. 202.

of his province;[32] 8. if a legate *de latere* is present in the province, a lesser legate ends his office;[33] 9. a legate, who is not legate *de latere*, cannot absolve cases of excommunication for violence against clerics outside his province, *legatus natus* cannot do it at all;[34] 10. statutes published by the legate are valid even after the legate left his province, the power of his delegates, however, ends, if the process did not start before his departure.[35] The decretals of *Liber sextus* (in the same structure, under title *De officio legati* of book one) contain further specifications of the powers and details concerning the system of legatine representation.[36] The five chapters cover the following: 1. cardinal legates (*de latere*) can confer benefices, other legates cannot do it without a special mandate;[37] 2. the legate holds ordinary jurisdiction and that is why his office does not end with the death of the Pope;[38] 3. after the end of legation, reservations made by the legate in his legatine province are not valid any longer, if the benefice was not occupied; 4. legates cannot reserve or confer cathedral benefices or give the right to anyone to confer the benefice after receiving resignation; 5. conferral of a benefice is not valid, if the previous benefice held by the applicant is not mentioned. One more decretal of the *Extravagantes communes* dealt with legates and the source of their power. Under the title *De consuetudine* of book one, the decretal *Super gentes* of Pope John XXII[39] decreed that legates should be freely allowed to travel in their province and that those who hinder them are *ipso facto* excommunicated and countries ruled by them are put under an interdict.

As mentioned above, canon law further defined the powers of legates through the work of the canonist, who commented on these decretals. The most crucial, and to some extent founding work, was that of Guillaume Durand, who – as part of a larger *Speculum iudiciale* – wrote a treatise on papal legates *Speculum legatorum.* Durand dedicated the first part or his tract (*De legato*) to the powers of papal legates, what privileges and rights belonged to the office, what was the legate's judicial authority and what right he had with conferral of benefices. The other part (*De dispensationibus*) was more general, but also focused on the legatine powers in terms of spiritual benefits bestowed on the inhabitants of the province or others.[40] All the other canonists, who dealt with the subject and were mentioned above, moved along the same lines: after defining the office of the legate, kinds of legates, their powers belonging to the office, they focused mainly on the jurisdictional authority and the conferral of benefices. The treatises often consist of a huge number of chapters and cases that specify the situational context of wielding legatine power.

32. Cf. idem, "The Medieval Papal Legate", pp. 80-92.
33. Cf. Schmutz, "Medieval Papal Representatives", p. 453.
34. Cf. Figueira, "Papal Reserved Powers", pp. 193, 198; idem, "The Medieval Papal Legate", pp. 92-95.
35. Cf. idem, "Subdelegation", pp. 58-60.
36. VI 1.15.1-5 (Friedberg, ed., *Corpus*, pt. 2, col. 983-985).
37. Cf. Schmutz, "Medieval Papal Representatives", p. 453.
38. Cf. *Ibid.*, p. 454; Figueira, "Decretalists", p. 121.
39. Extravag. comm. 1.1.un (Friedberg, ed., *Corpus*, pt. 2, col. 1237).
40. Durantis, *Speculum iudiciale*, pp. 29-98; cf. Kyer, "The Legation".

2.1.1. *Judicial authority*

The first decretal that newly defined the legatine office and defined legates' powers and authority within the local church was the decretal of Alexander III *Cum non ignoretis*, which was in all probability published during the first year of Alexander's pontificate (1159). In a letter addressed to the suffragans of Richard, Archbishop of Canterbury, the Pope informed the bishops that Richard had the right to act as a tribunal of primary jurisdiction. As Archbishop and Primate of England he could hear appeals, but as legate he exercised judicial power of the first instance in other dioceses than his own.[41] The legate assumed the judicial power of the Pope within his legatine province, i.e. he judged in the first instance in all local dioceses. This meant an infringement of the rights and authority of local bishops. As shown by Kenneth Pennington, the decretal created an opposition with bishops and some canonists, especially Johannes Teutonicus, who after a short career in Bologna returned to Germany and became provost of the cathedral chapter of Halberstadt. As a canon law expert, then, he rather represented ideas of local bishops than those of the papal centre; his conclusions, however, were not shared by any other canonist of the thirteenth century. It is clear from the later developments that even if it was accepted in the thirteenth century, the decretal was not actually popular and the Council of Trent abolished it at its twenty-fourth session; primary jurisdiction belonged to local bishops.[42] However, for the High and Later Middle Ages, the judicial power of the bishops could be appropriated by direct representatives of the Pope.

The judicial powers of the legates could provoke not only the local Church, but also local sovereigns. In England, for example, King Henry VIII when learning about the nomination of Lorenzo Campeggi as legate *de latere* to England in 1518 reportedly said that: "it was not the rule of this realm to admit legates *de latere.* If, however, he had nothing else except to treat against the Turks he would admit him." Later, Thomas Wolsey joined him as collegate and exercised strong powers.[43] The case of the Kingdom of Hungary even more clearly illustrates the problem. The King of Hungary held patronage right over the Hungarian Church.[44] Another right, or *libertas regni*, was the right to initiate

41. X 1.30.1 (= 1 Comp 1.22.1) (Friedberg, ed., *Corpus*, pt. 2, col. 183); cf. Pennington, "Johannes Teutonicus", p. 185.

42. Pennington, "Johannes Teutonicus", pp. 183-188; Walf, *Die Entwicklung*, p. 104. Cf. Ganzer, ed., *Concilium Tridentinum*, pp. 146-147, Sessio XXIV, canon XX, "Causae omnes ad forum ecclesiasticum quomodolibet pertinentes, etiam si beneficiales sint, in prima instantia coram ordinariis locorum dumtaxat cognoscantur atque omnino, saltem infra biennium a die motae litis, terminentur; ... Legati quoque, etiam de latere, nuntii, gubernatores ecclesiastici aut alii, quarumcumque facultatum vigore, non solum episcopos in praedictis causis impedire, aut aliquo modo eorum iurisdictionem iis praeripere aut turbare non praesumant, sed nec etiam contra clericos aliasve personas ecclesiasticas, nisi episcopo prius requisito eoque negligente, procedant; alias eorum processus ordinationesve nullius momenti sint, atque ad damni satisfactionem partibus illati teneantur".

43. Brewer, ed., *Letters and papers*, pp. 1247-1248, no. 4034. Cf. Fletcher, *Cardinal Wolsey*, p. 58.

44. Mályusz, *Das Konstanzer Konzil*; Erdő, "The Papacy and the Kingdom of Hungary"; Tusor, *The Papal Consistories*, pp. 35-60.

all lawsuits in Hungary and not elsewhere, as would be the case with citing inhabitants of Hungary before the Roman Curia.[45] Such claims were made in the decrees promulgated at the land diets in 1440, 1445, 1447, 1471 and 1481.[46] During the first years of the reign of King Wladislas II (Cz. Vladislav, Hung. Ulászló), an innovation was introduced by the Hungarian land diets: the legatine powers were mentioned and even criticized. By the 1492 decree, all the citations and summoning in various lawsuits to the Roman Curia and "when a legate of the Pope comes to this kingdom of Hungary, into his presence" were to cease immediately.[47] Consequently, in the kingdom of Hungary, where the liberty of the kingdom forbade the papal jurisdiction in the first instance, the legatine powers in such matters were also to be dismissed. In 1495, the decree specifically named Orso Orsini, a nuncio with the power of legate *de latere* in Hungary and bishop of Teano: all the cases, which were judged by him, should be brought back to the ordinary judges.[48] This happened, for example, in the diocese of Veszprém, where all the cases that were heard by Orso Orsini appeared before the local bishop.[49]

45. On the discussion of forbidding even the appeal, see Erdő, "The Papacy and the Kingdom of Hungary", pp. 67-68.

46. See the law articles: 1440:4, 1445:16, 1447:33, 1471:19, 1481:17, cf. *Decreta Regni Hungariae 1301-1457* and *Decreta Regni Hungariae 1458-1490.*

47. Law article 1492:45, see *Decreta Regni Mediaevalis Hungariae*, vol. 4, pp. 22-25, "Item quia nonnulli clerici et alterius condicionis plerique homines, tam nobiles, quam et ignobiles in curiam Romanam, vel dum aliquis legatorum sumpmi pontificis in hoc regnum Hungarie missus introiret, in eius presenciam incolas huius regni, presertim simpliciores, exquisitis quibusdam occasionibus, interdum eciam calumpniosis, in curiam Romanam vel presenciam ipsius legati citare et eos lite mediante, magis ac magis urgentes et vexantes ad solucionem alicuius sumpme compellere, sicque suam vitam criminose nonnumquam per phas et nephas alere et sustentare consueverunt, propterea, ut talium sceleratorum lucro gaudencium illicitus questus et via calumpniandi cesset in posterum, per barones, proceres et communitatem tocius regni huius ordinatum est et statutum, quod deinceps nullus omnio hominum quempiam racione alicuius negocii in curiam Romanam aut presenciam cuiusvis legati citare presumpmat, nisi prius coram suo ordinario diocesano, archiepiscopo vel episcopo, aut eius vicario in causam convenire et cum eo iuridice procedere, tandemque dum aliqua parcium iusticiam sibi vel denegatam, aut alias se indebite aggravari et condempnari sentiret, causam huiusmodi in curiam Romanam aut presenciam ipsius legati per viam appellacionis et non aliter provocare deducereque et prosequi possit atque valeat. Contrarium autem facientes debita pena puniantur".

48. 1495:10, see *Decreta Regni Mediaevalis Hungariae*, vol. 4, pp. 60-61, "Item ad articulum quadragesimum quintum istud additum est: Quod sicut de appellacionibus ad curiam Romanam et legatos ibidem sanctitum est, ita quoque de dominis archiepiscopis in hoc regno existentibus is articulus intelligatur: Quod scilicet nullus omnino hominum per simplicem querelam, nisi per viam appellacionis de dioecesi aliquorum dominorum prelatorum causam suam in presenciam eorundem deducere possit. Hoc quoque non pretermisso, quod si quipiam prescriptum articulum simul cum presentibus transgredi ausi fuerint, tales ab accione sua et acquisicione decidant et insuper in quadraginta florenis auri per comitem vel vicecomitem et iudices nobilium irremissibiliter exigendis contra partem adversam pro expensis convincantur, si tantas res habuerint, alioquin in persona detineantur et usque debitam emendam castigentur. Cause vero, que nunc in presencia reverendissimi domini Ursi de Ursinis legati verterentur, ipsi actores in presenciam iudicis eorum ordinarii tales causas eorum reducere teneantur".

49. Lukcsics, ed., *Monumenta*, vol. 4, pp. 56-57.

Limiting the power of legates in case of primary jurisdiction could also be seen in the decisions of the kings of Hungary to nominate them as local bishops. They would then prefer being linked to their diocese and would judge with the episcopal authority. This was done several times under King Matthias Corvinus or King Wladislas, while nuncios or legates, Gabriele Rangoni, Baldassare Turini, Giovanni d'Aragona, and Pietro Isvalies accepted some Hungarian bishoprics.[50] The jurisdictional authority of such a legate outside his diocese was, however, not entirely clear; sometimes problems emerged, as in the case of Ladislaus Geréb, who as Bishop of Transylvania was created legate *cum potestate legati de latere* in 1484. András Kubinyi believed the main reason for asking for a legate, who was a bishop in the country was limiting the legatine judicial power. His judicial decisions were criticised by the land diet in 1488, when the Hungarian estates accused him of misusing the system of papal jurisdiction.[51] He was accused of similar misbehaviour even earlier. In April 1486 a supplication arrived in Rome, in which Ladislaus de Cepha, a burgher of Buda, wanted to receive justice in his case. He divorced his wife convicted of adultery, and the dowry was supposed to remain in his possession. Ladislaus Geréb appropriated it, however, and the other Ladislaus, a burgher of Buda, wanted to have the solution corrected.[52] The legate also delegated his judicial power to his commissary and *auditor causarum* Christian, who judged a number of cases, including those whose process was initiated by Cardinal Giovanni d'Aragona, active as legate in Hungary in 1479-1480 and 1483-1484.[53]

The authorization of Ladislaus Geréb ended with the arrival of another nuncio *cum potestate legati de latere* to the country, Angelo Pecchinoli, Bishop of Orte.[54] Pecchinoli also judged a number of cases in his province,[55] but in some cases his judgement or cognizance of the case was rejected by the litigants who wanted to transfer the case to another court. After a number of letters between the nuncio and the city of Bardejov, related to a dispute of the city council and a burgher of Košice about a vineyard, the city council claimed the case belonged to their ordinary judge, namely the *magister tavernicorum*.[56] In another case,

50. Kubinyi, *Főpapok*, p. 82.

51. Idem, *Matthias*, pp. 125-126.

52. Lukcsics, ed., *Monumenta*, vol. 3, pp. 300-301, no. 450.

53. Cf. Bónis, *Szentszéki regeszták*, pp. 457-465; and for example MNL Budapest, OL DL 102636 (12 Jan 1486).

54. ASV, Arm. II 56, fol. 162v-163r.

55. Bónis, *Szentszéki regeszták*, pp. 470-473.

56. MNL Budapest, OL DL 46140 (8 Jun 1490), "... Vestram idcirco reverendissimam paternitatem humiliter et summopere exorantes, quatenus eadem dignetur nos ab huiusmodi gravaminibus sua commissione mediante erga ipsos executores fienda presertim in hiis sacris temporibus, gratiose absolutos habere, et in ipsam causam inter nos et Georgium Swarcz vertentem se non intramittere, cum eadem non sit duarum tamen privatarum personarum, sed tocius civitatis uti vestra reverendissima paternitas ex testimonio litterarum nostrarum nuper in facto emanatarum nostrarum nuper in facto emanatarum clarius intelligere potuit, non infringente libertatibus et privilegiis nostris verum eandem remittere ad ordinarium iudicem nostrum magistrum thavernicorum, quod erga vestram reverendissimam paternitatem deluta cum obedientia super deservire curabimus ..."; cf. Iványi, *Bártfa*, pp. 401-411; and here § 1.2.1.

when Angelo Pecchinoli was approached by certain nobles of the county of Szatmár, he responded that the case actually belonged to a secular court rather than his spiritual jurisdiction.[57] The clash between secular and spiritual jurisdiction was also observed some sixteen years earlier. In 1473, Cardinal legate Marco Barbo was to make decisions in the case of the Tolštejn castle in northern Bohemia and its adjoining villages, which had been put under an interdict. The Dukes of Saxony, the owners of the castle at the time, questioned the legate's authority, as the dispute was of a secular nature and thus did not belong to the legate's jurisdiction. Such an argumentation, however, could be countered by the fact that the origin of the dispute lay in a conflict with George of Poděbrady, King of Bohemia, who was excommunicated and treated as a heretic and who expropriated the original owner (Albrecht Berka of Dubá) and confiscated the castle.[58] Even if legatine jurisdiction followed clearly definitions of canon law, there could appear cases, when the authority was unclear or even disputed by individual litigants and needed to be negotiated.

I started this little subchapter with England and the situation of the twelfth century. The topic may well be illustrated by the situation of the English Church a few centuries later. The most influential figure of the kingdom was at the beginning of the sixteenth century Thomas Wolsey, lord chancellor and Archbishop of York. In 1518, thanks to political pressure on the pope, Wolsey (like Matheus Lang in Germany) obtained the position of a legate *de latere* (in curial sources entitled *collegati*, as they both joined the earlier created legates for England, Lorenzo Campeggi, and for Germany, Tommaso De Vio). As cardinal from 1515 and papal legate from 1518, Thomas Wolsey became the most influential person in the English Church, even surpassing the Archbishop of Canterbury. With a series of requests, he finally managed to secure the confirmation of his legatine power even after Lorenzo Campeggi left England and later even for life. With legatine powers he could hear cases at his legatine tribunal, but also, for example, dissolve the clerical assembly at St. Paul's that was convoked by the Archbishop of Canterbury and start his own at Westminster. The infringement of the local bishops' privileges and powers even led to some of them buying back "their episcopal rights in order to avoid future legatine interference in [their] dioceses".[59] Naturally, then, such non-standard solutions could only lead to the above mentioned abolition of the legatine judicial powers in respect to bishops and their dioceses at the Council of Trent.

57. A letter (18 May 1489) inserted in another one, MNL Budapest, OL DL 56234 (26 Oct 1489), "… Tamen ex proposicione actionis in libello deducte, causam ipsam non nostrum spirituale sed vestrum seculare iudicium concernere agnovimus, premissis igitur et aliis de causibus animum nostrum monere, premissam causam in vestri provinciam deliberacioni et examini, vestris duximus transmittere et trasmissimus, eosdemque nobiles et laicos ab instantia nostri iudicii et observacionibus terminorum duximus esse absolvere et absoluimus, harum nostrarum vigore et testimonio litterarum mediante …"

58. BAV, Vat. lat. 5641, fol. 215rv (22 Mar 1473; ed. Kalous, *Plenitudo potestatis*, pp. 259-262).

59. Fletcher, *Cardinal Wolsey*, pp. 57-58, 64-65, 89-90, 94, and quote on p. 107.

2.1.2. *Benefices and papal reserved powers*

Legatine authority was defined against the diocesan structures of the church on the one hand and against papal power on the other. Clear limits were set to a legate's power, even when he represented the Pope in the fullness of his power. The papal reserved powers were soon defined within canon law to specify what cases were strictly limited to the decision of the Pope. In such cases, papal authority could not be replaced by the legatine one. Most significantly, this limitation concerned benefices, namely those of a higher rank, bishops and cathedral benefices. Among the decretals of *Liber extra* on the power of legates, two specifically discuss the case of Cinthius, cardinal of St Laurence in Lucina, on a legation in Sicily in 1199-1200. Cardinal Cinthius attempted to transfer the bishop of Troia to the vacant archbishopric of Palermo. On learning about this translation, Pope Innocent III disagreed with the act in principle and criticized Cinthius in two letters, which became part of the *Liber extra* (X 1.30.3,4). The Pope confirmed, however, the validity of the result taking into account the position of the bishop as the chancellor of the Kingdom of Sicily and the significance of his personality. Then, even if the result was confirmed, the situation itself could not be regarded as a standard procedure.[60]

What does this event serve to illustrate? The decretals of Pope Innocent III state very clearly that Cinthius transgressed his powers. Despite the fact that he held the office of a legate, the general commission did not give him the right to transfer a bishop to the archbishopric. For such a legal act the legate would need not only the general commission of the legatine office, but also a special mandate that would allow him to enlarge his powers concerning the cases limited to the decision of the Pope himself. A special mandate (or delegation of powers in a certain case) was considered higher than the general commission. This was also the case for papal representatives with a lower status. A decretal of Pope Celestin III clearly stated that if a delegated judge began to judge a case for which he had a commission, the legate *de latere*, even if in general he was of a higher rank, could not take it over, as "mandatum speciale derogat generali".[61]

If a special mandate was needed for certain cases, it seems crucial to know what these cases were. Robert Figueira consequently remarked that a "special category of 'reserved powers', that is, powers normally reserved to papal judgment alone and not transferable by any grant of general legation," had to be created (the most well-known list of such powers being the *Dictatus pape* of Pope Gregory VII). Figueira also created lists of such reserved powers on the basis of the discussion of individual canonists in the twelfth and thirteenth centuries. His lists are virtual, however, as no single decretist or decretalist listed all the cases. Nevertheless, these are instances and situations that were generally agreed to be limited to papal judgment.[62] The legates received special mandates for a number

60. Figueira, "Papal Reserved Powers", pp. 192-193; the rights to transfer bishops in *Liber extra* esp. X 1.7, cf. especially X 1.7.2 and 4.

61. X 1.30.2; cf. also Figueira, "Papal Reserved Powers", pp. 193-194.

62. *Ibid.*, pp. 194-195; the attitude of canonists, pp. 196-204; a list of reserved powers by decretalists, pp. 206-210, and by decretists idem, *The Canon Law*, pp. 493-495.

of the acts they were then able to perform; such mandates are known as faculties (*facultates*) and to some extent defined the legation. In the period of the later Middle Ages, these were quite common: usually, legates *de latere* or nuncios *cum potestate legati de latere* acquired such faculties in special cases or some part of the Pope's powers was handed over to the legates.

The administration of the benefices belonged to the Pope, who could then delegate his power either to the institutions of the local church, or to his legates. The decretals of the *Liber extra* are mostly concerned with the higher benefices, namely with the office of a bishop. Only one of the decretals (X 1.30.6) deals with the benefices, as the legate *de latere* can confer any vacant benefice, whose patron is a cleric, thus taking over the general power of the Pope. This measure may again infer substantially into the rights of the local bishop, similarly as the decretal concerning the judicial authority of the legate. Although Innocent III asserted that legates did not violate any rights of the local bishops, Johannes Teutonicus nevertheless insisted in the early thirteenth century that to be able to take over the *ius presentandi*, the legates must have acquired a special mandate.[63] The *Liber sextus* concentrated on benefices and legatine power much more than *Liber extra.* After defining that only legates *de latere* can confer benefices without a special mandate (VI 1.15.1), the decretals limit the legatine powers to dealing with the benefices (VI 1.15.3-5). The duration of reservations ceased to be valid after the legation ended; cathedral, collegiate and conventual churches are excluded from the legatine decisions; and that legates may validly confer benefices to multiple benefice holders only when the previous benefice is mentioned. These decretals reveal a certain development, as legates acquired power over almost all benefices, but this seemed to be too wide and conflicting with the power of the local church.

2.1.3. *Dispensations*

Guillaume Durand inserted in his *Speculum iudiciale* a treatise that he wrote about papal legates, *Speculum legatorum*, which encompassed two rubrics, namely *De legato* and *De dispensationibus.* The part on dispensations is a general overview of dispensations, their origins and types, and of irregularities that could be dispensed. After listing the irregularities, Durand defined which of them might be dispensed by a bishop and adds a much shorter list for a legate *de latere.* This is an extension, however, as legates may grant dispensations in the same cases as bishops. Their power to grant dispensations is passed on to them with the general mandate of the legation.[64] Durand added one irregularity that could be dispensed by legates, namely in the case of *ubi pater* dispensations, when a priest's son wanted to hold the same benefice as his father. Such petitions were normally handled by the Apostolic Penitentiary, but form only a small fraction of the illegitimacy petitions.[65]

63. Pennington, "Johannes Teutonicus", pp. 189-190; in general cf. Landau, *Jus Patronatus*, pp. 155-170.

64. Durantis, *Speculum iudiciale*, pp. 82-83.

65. *Ibid.*, 82; cf. Schmugge, *Kirche, Kinder, Karrieren* pp. 162-165; Salonen and Schmugge, *A Sip*, pp. 58-59.

Later canonists of the fifteenth century also dealt with dispensations in relation to the legates and created long lists of situations that could have been treated by them and conditions under which dispensations could have been awarded. They usually registered the views of older canonists, who often disagreed on individual points.[66] Apart from dispensations, canonists wrote about absolutions in certain contexts, especially about the power of the legate *de latere* to absolve excommunications incurred on people *ipso facto*, i.e. with the illegal act itself – and that not only in the legatine province itself, but legates had this power within universal Christendom.[67]

Listing all the cases of absolutions and dispensations would be very difficult. It is crucial to realise, however, that such acts were possible: the legates carried the highest authority of the pope, had judicial powers, could confer and deal with lower benefices in general and also had powers related to the spiritual matters and *forum internum*, the matters of conscience. Most of such matters, which relate to the activity of the Apostolic Penitentiary, appeared listed in the faculties and special mandates of individual legates and individual legations.

2.2. *Faculties*

Apart from the general commission of a legation, *facultates* defined the powers of a legate. These special mandates endowed the legates with the exceptional rights and privileges that formed their legation, be they a concession of papal reserved powers or other rights that enabled them to act outside the framework of the usual powers of a legate *de latere.* The number of faculties grew continuously from the thirteenth century onwards. The faculties could be given to cardinal-legates, i.e. legates *de latere*, or to other papal representatives with a comparable (but lesser) status, nuncios *cum potestate legati de latere.* Due to the spiritual character of some of the faculties, the bearers of them needed to be consecrated bishops in order to be able to use them. To understand the naming of representatives from the other point of view, it was usual that nuncios with extensive faculties bore the title of nuncios *cum potestate legati de latere.*

It is true, however, that the system changed at the start of the sixteenth century and that there were even some papal representatives with the title of *nuncius*, who had at their disposal a larger number of faculties. Zaccaria Ferreri,[68] for example, who was named apostolic nuncio to the King of Poland, Grandmaster of the Teutonic Knights and Grand Duke of Muscovy in 1519, had a large number of faculties, but could not boast of the attribute *cum potestate legati*

66. Especially the treatises of Pietro Andrea Gambaro and Gonzalo García de Villadiego (and to some extent of Nicolas Bohier) contain detailed analyses of previous canon law in various questions, *Tractatus universi iuris*, vol. 13/2, passim.

67. X 1.30.9, for the cases of violence against clerics (Friedberg, ed., *Corpus*, pt. 2, col. 186); Figueira, "The Medieval Papal Legate", pp. 78-80, 101-102; cf. also §2.3. in this chapter.

68. On Zaccaria Ferreri, Stöve, "Ferreri".

de latere. Ferreri came to the service of the Curia at the end of the first decade of the sixteenth century. He then joined the French side, however, which together with the "schismatic" cardinals organised a council in Pisa (*conciliabulum*). As a learned doctor of theology and *utriusque iuris*, he published and dedicated to Cardinal Bernardin Carvajal the acts and decrees of the Councils of Constance and Basel in 1511 in Milan. As with others, he was excommunicated and only during the pontificate of Pope Leo X was finally pardoned and, after becoming a bishop in 1518, could be used as a papal diplomat. He had been given powers that were usually linked with the office of a legate *de latere* (jurisdiction, power over benefices, indulgences, etc.) as well as additional faculties as special mandates typically awarded to the legates. The faculties are in some sense unusual, as they contain matters and powers normally given to the legates in their general commission. As Ferreri was "just" a nuncio, these also had to be specified: he received a faculty to judge in the first instance all the cases belonging to the church jurisdiction. Other faculties, then, were comparable to those of legates *de latere.*[69] Although the King of Poland expressly asked for the extension of the faculties to Poland, originally only valid for Lithuania and Muscovy, the nuncio's usage of them was criticized among the Poles as well as the way of collecting large sums of money.[70]

This short exposition of the activity and faculties of Zaccaria Ferreri presents a case of a nuncio with faculties in a period when the system began to change. Even during the fifteenth century, however, simple nuncios (often called *nuncius et orator*) could have faculties at their disposal. Their status was lower, however, than that of the nuncios with the power of legate *de latere* and most often they acquired faculties related to their political activities. Some of them, however, still wielded a larger number of faculties in spiritual matters. In February 1479, Gentile da Spoleto, bishop of Anagni, was dispatched as nuncio to Germany and given a larger number of faculties.[71] A few months ealier, in June 1478, Francesco Petrucci, papal prothonotary and *decretorum doctor*, was also given a larger number of faculties for his mission to France. His case demonstrates that not being a bishop did not disqualify him from using such faculties.[72] The highest number of faculties was obviously given to legates *de latere* and to nuncios with the power of legates *de latere*.

69. Wojtyska, ed., *Acta*, vol. 2, pp. 19-29, no. 11 (1 Nov 1519), "… matrimoniales, beneficiales et alias spirituales ac profanas causas quaslibet, ad forum ecclesiasticum quomodolibet pertinentes, tam primae instantiae, quam appellationum quarumlibet, a quibuscumque iudicibus ordinariis et delegatis, etiam per nos et Sedem Apostolicam praedictam deputatis et ad nos et sedem eandem, seu quoscumque alios iudices interpositarum et pro tempore interponendarum, etiam similiter et de plano, per te vel alium, seu alios, audiendi, cognoscendi, seu pertractandi ac aliis iudicialiter audiendas, cognoscendas et fine debito terminandas et delegandas, illasque etiam, si per nos vel alios auctoritate apostolica delegatae forent, seu aliter etiam quomodocumque penderent; et cum tibi placuerit et iustum fieri videbitur, ad te advocandi et aliis committendi".

70. Wojtyska, ed., *Acta*, vol. 2, p. IX.

71. ASV, Reg. Vat. 679, fol. 158r-164v.

72. ASV, Reg. Vat. 679, fol. 170r-176r.

What were, however, the typical faculties and documents acquired by a legate *de latere* during the fifteenth century? What did they usually cover? As the faculties defined the legation, they were carefully recorded in the registers by the Papal Chancery and were often re-used for other legates. There are a huge number of them preserved in the Vatican Registers among other bulls published by the Chancery. Bearing in mind that usually every legate received tens of faculties, let us examine two volumes of the Vatican Registers that were specifically created under Pope Sixtus IV to hold faculties of legates,[73] with introducing examples from other cases, other legates or nuncios under other popes. As mentioned above, the special mandates could be conceded to the legates in a form of one large charter or individual letters for each mandate, i.e. each *facultas*.

The documents of these two registers come from the entire pontificate of Pope Sixtus IV and are addressed to legates *de latere* and nuncios with the powers of the legates *de latere*. The power of cardinal legates is clearly defined by canon law and the short attribute *cum potestate legati de latere* brought the nuncios into the same position. Unlike simple nuncios, those *cum potestate legati de latere* held the office of a legation, which means they could wield legatine powers just like cardinals who were legates *de latere*. This can be illustrated by the case of Nicolò Sandonnini, bishop of Modena, who was dispatched from the Curia as *nuncius et commissarius cum potestate legati de latere* to France, Brittany, Burgundy and Savoy to organize the crusade against the Ottoman Turks in 1476. It is explicitly stated that Pope Sixtus IV conceded the "office of full legation" to him, which means he could acquire all the powers normal legates *de latere* would have.[74]

Among the charters entered in the Vatican registers, there was usually a single document that can be called *bulla legationis*, which defined the position of the legate, defined his legatine province and in general published the reasons for his mission. The *arenga* of the charter in general characterized the significance of the legation and its *narratio* mentioned the actual reasons and grounds for the legation itself. In the case of Cardinal Marco Barbo, a legate *de latere* to Germany, Hungary, Bohemia and Poland in 1472-1474, the actual reasons for his mission, mentioned in his *bulla legationis*, were manifold. The bull mentioned troubles with the Ottoman expansion and the fall of the isle of Euboia and the city of Negroponte, the incursions of the Ottoman Turks into the territories of Emperor Frederick III, and the struggles over the Crown of Bohemia between the Kings of Hungary and Poland, which hindered the usage of Central European forces for the fight for Christendom, i.e. against the Ottomans. As the Pope could not personally take part in the affairs, Cardinal Marco was sent to the region (described in detail) as an "angel of peace". Similarly, the Pope even stated in

73. ASV, Reg. Vat. 679, 680.

74. ASV, Reg. Vat. 679, fol. 20r-21r (7 May 1476), "... de venerabilium fratrum nostrorum consilio nostrum et apostolice sedis nuncium cum plena potestate legati de latere et commisso tibi plene legacionis huiusmodi officio destinamus iniungentes tibi in regno ducatibus et nacione civitatibus terris et locis eisdem inter ecclesiasticos et mundanos unos ac alios cuiuscunque condicionis status et preeminencie fuerint agas tractas et ordines, que ad laudem dei sedis eiusdem honorem et rei publice christianorum huiusmodi defencionem tuicionem pacem et eciam illarum parcium commodum salutem et tranquillitatem quomodolibet pertinebunt".

the bull that he dispatched a number of additional legates for the same cause all over Europe. Marco Barbo received the faculty to preach the crusade and distribute plenary indulgence for taking part in the crusade or supporting it with financial donations. He could also collect tithes from ecclesiastical institutions within the boundaries of his legatine province.[75] Apart from the directives on the crusade, the bull of the legation provided with its reasoning a legitimisation for the dispatching of the legate.

The *bulla legationis* for Cardinal Marco Barbo is quite extensive, written on eight pages in the registers. The key part of it, however, is one sentence that in a declaratory form publishes the fact that the cardinal was named legate to the region:

> ... therefore we directed the eyes of our mind to your foresightedness (*circumspectio*), whom we have known as provident in actions and attested with experience in our arduous tasks and the business of the Roman Church, as well as prominent in the letters and learning of the doctrine, and in the same foresightedness we place a special trust in Lord that you will see to fulfilling those things, that we will have entrusted to you, with unyielding and watchful zeal and diligence to the glory of the omnipotent God and the honour of the apostolic see and ours, as well as the salvation of ordinary Christian peoples, and we send [you] as an angel of peace and legate *de latere* of us and the apostolic see to *Alamania* and the whole of Germany, as well as the universal and individual provinces, cities, lands and places of the same Germany subjugated to the Holy Roman Empire, as well as the Kingdoms of Hungary and Poland.[76]

The lengthy explanations and legitimations of the legation then need not be repeated in other faculties, where other forms and verbs were used and the fact of the dispatching of a legate was only recalled in the introduction:

> As we send you at present to the nation of *Alamania* and the whole of Germany, as well as the universal and individual provinces, cities, lands and places of the same Germany subjugated to the Holy Roman Empire, as well as the Kingdoms of Hungary and Poland, for several arduous tasks of the universal Church and our business as our legate *de latere*

75. ASV, Reg. Vat. 680, fol. 37r-40v (Theiner, ed., *Vetera monumenta Hungariae*, vol. 2, pp. 428-431).

76. ASV, Reg. Vat. 680, fol. 38rv (Theiner, ed., *Vetera monumenta Hungariae*, vol. 2, p. 429), "Et cum nos ad huiusmodi necessitates explicandas, regesque, principes, potentatus, communitates et dominia hortandum, requirendum et monendum, ut semotis quibusvis dissidiis huic sancto operi vacent ac se ad reprimendum ipsius perfide Turchorum gentis elatos conatus actingant, personaliter progredi non valeamus, ad huiusmodi presentes necessitates, quas et maiores in foribus et prope futuras, nisi protinus obvietur, cernimus, declarandas de venerabilium fratrum nostrorum sancte Romane ecclesie cardinalium consilio nonnullos ex eis legatos de latere ad diversas mundi partes regnaque et dominia transmittendos duximus. Igitur ad circumspectionem tuam, quam in agendis preditam et in arduis nostris ac Romane ecclesie negociis experientia comprobatam ac licterarum et scientiarum doctrinis eminentem cognovimus, direximus oculos nostre mentis, de eadem circumspectione sumentes in domino fiduciam specialem, quod ea, que tibi duxerimus commitenda, ad laudem omnipotentis dei et sedis apostolice ac nostrum honorem necnon communem christiani populi salutem cura ac diligentia pervigili adimplere curabis, ad Alamanie ac totius Germanie necnon universas et singulas provincias, civitates, terras et loca eiusdem Germanie, sacro Romano imperio subiecta, necnon Hungarie et Polonie regna, tamquam pacis angelum nostrum et apostolice sedis legatum de latere transmittimus".

> and of the apostolic see as angel of peace by the advice of our brothers, the cardinals of the Holy Roman Church, we want to concede to you ...[77]

The general commission of the legation is only mentioned in the following faculties. The form of the bull would then also include the actual declaratory commissioning of the specific faculty, which would conclude the entire bull. It may have read, "we concede to you the full and unimpeded faculty by the authority of the present [bull]."[78] And only the formula of the date would follow.

As texts, the faculties were extremely formalised, which gave the chancery the possibility to easily copy what was needed from previous legations. Taking the example of one of the volumes of the Vatican registers, we can read the faculties of Cardinal Marco Barbo, who left the City in 1472. Seven years later, two other legates were sent to the region, Cardinal Ausias Despuig (Auxias de Podio) as legate *de latere* to Germany and the Holy Roman Emperor, and Cardinal Giovanni d'Aragona, brother-in-law of King Matthias Corvinus as a legate *de latere* to the same king. Even if both of the legates' faculties were transcribed as sets of documents in the registers, Cardinal Ausias had only twelve of them, whereas Cardinal Giovanni d'Aragona had seventy-five. Most of the faculties of Ausias Despuig are to be found among the faculties of Marco Barbo, as can be read under no less than thirty-three of them: "Similar faculty for Auxias, cardinal priest of Santa Sabina, legate of the apostolic see to the parts of Alamania and Germany only, under the date in Rome at Saint Peter's on 7 May 1479" or "Duplicated for Auxias...".[79] Thus, previous faculties could have been used as a form for the subsequent legations and the registers as a kind of formulary used by the chancery.

Also in 1479, the *bulle legationis* for the legates de latere comprise similar components as the one for Marco Barbo. They mention the crusade in the most prominent position and introduce certain faculties related to it that were conceded to the legate, e.g. preaching the crusade, distributing plenary indulgences, collecting money for the crusade, etc. The organisation of the crusade was a central reason for sending out the legates to the region of Central Europe, but also for all legates to Europe in general.[80] Even the bulls of the general commission of legates sent to other parts of Europe find it necessary to mention the Ottoman danger and the activities for the alleviation and relief of the eastern regions.[81]

77. ASV, Reg. Vat. 680, fol. 42r, "... Cum te ad nationem Alamanie ac totius Germanie necnon universas et singulas provincias, civitates, terras et loca eiusdem Germanie sacro Romano imperio subiecta ac Hungarie et Polonie regna pro nonnullis arduis universalis ecclesie ac nostris negociis legatum nostrum de latere tanquam pacis angelum de fratrum nostrorum sancte Romane ecclesie cardinalium consilio presentialiter destinemus, nos volentes illa tibi concedere ...".

78. ASV, Reg. Vat. 680, fol. 42v, "... plenam et liberam concedimus auctoritate presentium facultatem".

79. E.g. ASV, Reg. Vat. 680, fol. 34r, 43v.

80. Bulls for Ausias Despuig and Giovanni d'Aragona, ASV, Reg. Vat. 680, fol. 151r-152r, 167r-170r.

81. Cf. for example Giuliano della Rovere to France in 1475, ASV, Reg. Vat. 680, fol. 89r-90v; and in 1481, fol. 268r-270r

The *bulle legationis* were not the only ones which defined, however, the general standards of the legation itself. There could have been other letters that clearly stated the extension of the legation to other regions, as in the case of Cardinal Marco Barbo and the other above-mentioned legates. As will be discussed later in the section on the geographical scope of the legation, the power of the faculties could have been extended to the places the legate passed through, adjacent places to the province, or even to a specific diocese in possession of the legate, as in the case of Marco Barbo again, whose powers were extended to the Patriarchate of Aquileia.[82] The legation could have been extended not only in a geographical sense, but also in relation to individual persons, as shown by a faculty conceded to Ausias Despuig. With this faculty, he was entitled to use all the graces, concessions and indults for his collaborators during and within the borders of his legation.[83] The power of the legates could have been extended, not only in spatial or personal terms, but also in terms of changing legal restrictions and limitations. Thus, for example, Giovanni d'Aragona was also entitled to judge cases, which were already assigned to papal delegated judges. In this sense, the canonical requirement of *Liber extra* (X 1.30.2), that a legate cannot interfere in cases with an appointed delegated judge, was altered.[84] Legates could have

82. ASV, Reg. Vat. 680, fol. 61v-62r (18 Feb 1472).

83. ASV, Reg., Vat. 680, fol. 153r (7 May 1479), "Nos igitur volentes ea tibi concedere per que te prelatis et personis tuis obsequiis inter essentibus assiduis valeas reddere graciosum circumspectioni tue, ut cum prelatis ac quibuscumque familiaribus tuis continuis commensalibus aliisque personis tue legacioni assistentibus presentibus et futuris sub legacione tua huiusmodi non comprehensis omnibus et singulis per nos tibi concessis facultatibus uti ac quascumque gracias, concessiones et indulta et quecumque alia in eisdem contenta et specificata cuilibet ex prelatis personis et familiaribus eisdem elargiri in omnibus et per omnia perinde ac si infra limites tue legacionis huiusmodi comprehensi forent libere et licite valeas tenore presencium auctoritate apostolica concedimus facultatem".

84. ASV, Reg. Vat. 680, fol. 206v-207v, "Nos volentes tuam honorare personam, ut per honorem tibi exhibitum huiusmodi legationis offitium eo efficatius exequi valeas, quo maiori per nos fueris auctoritate munitus, circumspectioni tue quascumque causas ecclesiasticas benefitiales et prophanas civiles et criminales et mixtas ac quascumque alias cuiuscumque qualitatis existant, inter quascumque personas ecclesiasticas vel seculares infra limites tue legationis pro tempore constitutas per viam simplicis querele vel appellationis etiam a delegatis vel subdelegatis a sede apostolica seu eius auctoritate deputatis seu alius quovismodo interposite etiam iam motas seu inchoatas aut in futuris legationi huiusmodi durante movendas etiam simpliciter et de plano summarie sine strepitu et figura iuditii sola facti veritate inspecta etiam terminis substantialibus minime aut unico contextu servatis, prout tibi visum fuerit per te audiendi, cognoscendi, decidendi et fine debito terminandi cum omnibus et singulis earum independentiis, incidentiis, emergentiis et connexis. Et cum potestate citandi ad partes et sub penis sententiis et censuris alius prout tibi videbitur inhibendi et quantus opus sit adversus quecumque fatalia etiam ad unum vel duos aut plures annos lapsa restituendi illasque a quibuscumque iudicibus ordinariis et extra ordinariis etiam auctoritate sedis predictis delegatis et subdelegatis advocandi, necnon causas et quascumque huiusmodi sub eisdem potestate modo et forma audiendi, cognoscendi, decidendi et fine debito terminandi aliis delegandi seu committendi sentencias in illis latis executioni debite demandandi et demandari fatiendi, contradictores quoslibet et rebelles per censuram ecclesiasticam et alia iuris remedia appellatione postposita compescendi invocato ad hoc, si opus fuerit, auxilio brachii secularis. Testes autem, qui fuerint nominati, si se gracia odio vel timore subtraxerint censura

acquired other faculties, which modified their legation, or which were rather personalised to them and to their associates. They could have been given, for example, judicial immunity for all the participants, colleagues and servants at the legation, which meant all cases and processes against the associates of the legates were stopped for the time of the legation.[85] Similarly, these could be granted the opportunity to keep all the privileges and graces as if they stayed at the Curia, as a faculty for Cardinal Roderigo Borja, a legate *de latere* to Spain, shows.[86]

Documents that appear in the registers in relation to the legation in general account for typologically one more letter with universal validity. The nuncios *cum potestate legati de latere* were given *littere passus*, or a general recommendation (credentials) that was addressed to all, *universis et singulis*, who would read the letter, and asked them to assist to the nuncio.[87] This indicates the nuncios (and even those with the power of a legate *de latere*) were rather treated as diplomatic agents, who were given special powers, whereas the legates *de latere* themselves, who could show the honour and dignity of cardinalate, had those powers inherent in the office and did not need to receive an extra letter of credentials.[88] Moreover, it became part of the oath of an archbishop to assist and support the papal legate. Even if this oath is mentioned mostly in relation to the financial support of the train of the legate, it also meant accepting and respecting the legate of the Pope. In 1079, the Patriarch of Aquileia swore an oath to Pope Gregory VII, which later became a standard oath of an archbishop and to some respect also of a bishop.[89]

With most of the documents, then, the Pope conceded some reserved powers to the legate himself that could be used within the framework of his legation. These faculties form several thematic groups including benefices, indulgences, spiritual graces normally in the power of the Apostolic Penitentiary, other graces and faculties that specified the general powers of a legate (reforms, visitations,

simili appellatione postposita cessante veritati testimonium perhiberi compellendi omniaque et singula premissa et in eis ac circa ea quomodolibet oportuna per te vel alium seu alios fatiendi et exequendi plenam et liberam auctoritate apostolica tenore presentium concedimus facultatem. Non obstantibus etiam felicis recordationis Bonifatii pape octavi predecessoris nostri illis presertim, quibus cavetur, ne quis extra suam civitatem vel diocesim nisi in certis exceptis casibus in illis ultra unam dietem a fine sue diocesis ad iuditium evocetur, seu ne iudices a sede apostolica deputati alicui extra civitatem vel diocesim, in quibus deputati fuerant vices suas committere presumant et de duabus dietis in consilio generali, necnon apostolicis constitutionibus et ordinationibus ceterisque contrariis quibuscumque. Aut si personis prefatis vel quibusvis aliis communiter vel divisim ab eadem sit sede indultum, quod interdici, suspendi vel excommunicari aut extra vel ultra certa loca ad iudicium evocari non possint, per litteras apostolicas non fatientes plenam et expressam ac de verbo ad verbum de indulto huiusmodi mentionem".

85. ASV, Reg. Vat. 680, fol. 148r-149r, 214v-215v.

86. ASV, Reg. Vat. 680, fol. 1rv.

87. E.g. ASV, Reg. Vat. 518, fol. 164r (Domenico Dominici); Reg. Vat. 519, fol. 78v (Lorenzo Roverella); Reg. Vat. 679, fol. 7v-8r (Niccolò Sandonnino), fol. 138rv (Luka Tolentić), fol. 170rv (Francesco Petrucci); Reg. Vat. 734, fol. 231rv (Angelo Pecchinoli).

88. Cf. for example, Andrea Barbatia, *De cardinalibus legatis a latere*, in *Tractatus universi iuris*, vol. 13/2, fol. 132r-133r, who provides a long list of references to decretals and decretalists on this issue, quoting *Liber sextus*, Guillaume Durand and many others.

89. Robinson, "The institutions", p. 406.

jurisdiction) that was inherent in the office. The last category, which is specific to every single legate or nuncio, included faculties and powers to deal with single political or church-political matters. All the faculties formed a clear framework for the powers of the legate and for his legation and complemented the powers inherent in the general commission and the office of the legate.

2.2.1. *Benefices*

Working with benefices constituted one of the crucial parts of the activities of a legate *de latere.* As mentioned above, a number of powers were handed over to the legate as a direct representative of the Pope and were inherent in the office. The faculties that the legate acquired upon leaving the City and setting out on his mission, could have been specific to individual benefices or rather general, which were more common within the sets of faculties for the individual legates.

Faculties could entitle the legate to confer specific types of benefices, such as for example *beneficia reservata*, benefices the conferral of which was strictly reserved to the papal decision. Athough Cardinal Marco Barbo received a faculty to decide at the appeal in the case of conferral of benefices that were not reserved to the Papal Curia, he obtained another faculty during his legation, which authorized him to confer benefices in the Kingdoms of Bohemia, Poland and Hungary that were reserved to the Pope. Furthermore, from the start of his legation he was entitled to confer benefices vacated for whatever reason (illegally conferred, vacated by death, etc.). All these three faculties were also copied to Cardinal Ausias Despuig.[90] The case of Cardinal Giovanni d'Aragona indicates faculties that were very typical among the cardinal legates. Other faculties could permit, for example, the legate to confer benefices to his own colleagues or servants at the legation (in this instance including the reserved benefices). Another faculty entitled the legate to confer to the same people benefices that were vacated by a resignation, which the legate himself could accept (and this also in the case of Cardinal Ausias or Cardinal Giuliano della Rovere),[91] and to these benefices one has to also include those vacated by a promotion, *per promotionem* (or similarly to Cardinal Giuliano).[92] Giovanni d'Aragona could even unite (*uniendi*, *anectendi vel inconportandi*) benefices, this being a special faculty for dealing with the administration of the local church.[93] A large number of similar faculties can be found among the documents published for the legates as they were sent out from the Curia and these only illustrate the possibilities of the legatine authority in

90. ASV, Reg. Vat. 680, fol. 59v-60r (18 Feb 1472), fol. 81rv (8 Jun 1473); fol. 46r-47v (18 Feb 1472).

91. ASV, Reg. Vat. 680, fol. 170r-172r; fol. 204v; fol. 212v-214r; fol. 234v-238v (all 1 Jun 1479); the case of Ausias, fol. 156r-159v (7 May 1479); for Giuliano, fol. 109r-112r, 112r-114r (both 20 Feb 1475).

92. ASV, Reg. Vat. 680, fol. 221r-224r (1 Jun 1479); for Giuliano, fol. 105r-106v (20 Feb 1475).

93. ASV, Reg. Vat. 680, fol. 254v-257r (1 Jun 1479).

terms of benefices. Papal reserved powers remained untouched, however, in the case of episcopal sees, as none of the faculties affected the bishop's office or similar benefices (*dignitates maiores post pontificales*).

2.2.2. *Indulgences and other graces*

The above-mentioned faculties primarily had an impact on the organisation and administration of the local church and on clergy. There were, however, many more faculties that affected common members of the Church, common lay believers. For simplicity's sake, one could say that legates were small curias that could distribute spiritual graces derived from the power of the Pope. Two large categories, then, must be brought forth, namely indulgences and graces related to the Apostolic Penitentiary. As concerns indulgences,[94] legates were entitled to grant such graces by the power of their office. It was a common practice (reported in the legatine ceremonial) that legates *de latere* could publish indulgences when celebrating the solemn mass after their arrival in their province.[95] Nevertheless, special mandates were also granted to legates to have further authority in terms of indulgences.

Marco Barbo and Ausias Despuig, for example, had the right to publish three-year indulgences at their solemn mass.[96] Apart from this, however, they should have the possibility to publish one-year indulgences after the Holy Mass celebrated upon their arrival in their legatine province (as mentioned also by the legatine ceremonial) and they were conceded the faculty to publish indulgences for the contribution (physical as well as financial) to the reconstruction of churches, hospitals, bridges and other religious sites.[97] A later nuncio with the power of legate

94. Cf. Swanson, ed., *Promisory Notes*; Shaffern, *The Penitents' Treasury*; and most recently for the fifteenth and early sixteenth centuries Rehberg, ed., *Ablasskampagnen.*

95. Wasner, "Fifteenth-Century Texts", pp. 311, 315, 328-329, 335, 346.

96. ASV, Reg. Vat. 680, fol. 54rv (18 Feb 1472), "Nos optantes ut spiritualium largitione munerum incolas et habitatores partium earundem reddas deo et sedi predicte plus devotas circumspectioni tue, ut tua huiusmodi legatione durante quoscienscumque et ubicumque in dictis partibus solemniter missarum solemnia celebraveris, tres annos vel per alium, quem duxeris eligendum coram te solemniter celebrare, seceris aut parlamentum tenueris vel aliquam civitatem sive locum insignem pro prima vice et cum processione solemniter intraveris omnibus vere penitentibus et confessis ibidem presentibus auctoritate apostolica unum annum de iniunctis eis penitenciis relaxare plenam et liberam tenore presentium concedimus facultatem".

97. ASV, Reg. Vat. 680, fol. 48v (18 Feb 1472), "Nos volentes ut partium predictarum incole quanto spiritualium munerum pociora dona sibi provenire spexerint tanto ad pietatis opera propensius annuentur circumspectioni tue presentium auctoritate concedimus, ut omnibus vere penitentibus et confessis, qui ad constructionem et reparationem ecclesiarum necnon hospitalium et poncium ac aliorum piorum locorum sustentationem quoque infirmorum aut pauperum hospitalium eorundem manus porrexerint adiuctrices et eas devote visitaverint annuatim unum annum de iniunctis eis penitenciis misericorditer tua legatione durante relaxare possis licteris tuis super huiusmodi indulgenciis per te concedendis post decem annos a dat[o] ipsarum litterarum computandos minime valituris, volumus autem, quod si alias visitantibus huiusmodi ecclesias sive hospitalia seu ad fabricam et reparationem ipsarum manus porrigentibus adiuctrices aut alias inibi pias elemosinas erogantibus aliqua indulgencia in perpetuum vel ad certum tempus tempore huiusmodi concessionis, quam facies, nundum elapsum duratura auctoritate apostolica concessa fiunt concessiones, quas eis vigore presentium facies nullius existant roboris".

de latere, Bartolomeo Maraschi published such indulgences for the reconstruction of a church in Fürstenfeld in Styria, as the town was completely destroyed by the armies of King Matthias Corvinus in 1483. He visited the place in person and reported on the destruction of the town in one of his relations to Rome and one can imagine that upon such an occasion he was either asked or moved himself to publish such indulgences for the support of the local community.[98] Giovanni d'Aragona obtained a faculty to publish ten-year and seven-year indulgences on significant holidays in whatever church was in his province.[99] Apart from these, there were indulgences related to the organisation of crusades usually permitted in the general bull of the legation together with the obligation to preach the crusade. In this period, almost all legates were conceded this faculty to publish such plenary indulgences *in articulo mortis*, i.e. when the grantees died on the crusade.[100]

In relation to these there are a number of confessional privileges, *littere confessionales*, published by legates and nuncios or their commissioners. These entitled the addressees to choose the confessor who could grant them absolution even in cases reserved to the Pope (or Papal Curia) and remission of sins for contribution to a crusade. The most numerous ones were printed by Raymund Peraudi, active as papal nuncio *cum potestate legati de latere* in Central Europe in 1488-1491, or other instances of the Ottoman crusading activity.[101] There was also Cardinal Pietro Isvalies, who printed his confessional letters. In contrast to Raymund Peraudi, however, who had his letters printed on Italian parchments,

98. NA Prague, fond ŘM (Maltese Knights), Komenda Fürstenfeld, no. 2089 (12 Oct 1483); report in ASV, Misc., Arm. II 56, fol. 349r-358r (Oct 1483), here fol. 349rv (ed. Kalous, *Plenitudo potestatis*, pp. 320-329; from a different manuscript by Katona, ed., *Historia critica*, vol. 9, pp. 500-517).

99. ASV, Reg. Vat. 680, fol. 228r, "… et omni studio saluti animarum christifidelium quantum cum deo possumus providere, eosque ad pia caritatis opera exercenda, ut illorum participes efficiantur indulgentiarum muneribus inducere satagamus, tibi omnibus et singulis christifidelibus utriusque sexus, qui ecclesias cathedrales etiam metropolitanas vel collegiatas seu parrochiales aut monasteria ordinum quorumcumque seu hospitalia infra limites tue legationis constituta in omnibus festivitatibus per te singulis eorum deputandis devote visitaverint et pias inibi elemosinas erogaverint, decem annos et totidem quadragenas aut minus prout tibi videbitur, qui vero cappellas, altaria et alia pia loca etiam confraternitatum aut alias, ubi tibi videbitur in similibus festivitatibus visitaverint et manus ibidem adiutrices porrexerint, seu similes elemosinas erogaverint, septem annos et totidem quadragenas seu etiam minus de iniunctis eis penitenciis in domino misericorditer relaxandi, tuis super inde conficiendis litteris imperpetuum valituris plenam et liberam auctoritate apostolica tenore presentium concedimus facultatem".

100. Cf. for example, ASV, Reg. Vat. 680, fol. 39r (Marco Barbo), "Insuper cruciatam contra eosdem Turchos predicandi et ab aliis predicari faciendi et crucesignatis contra eosdem Turchos pugnantibus vel ad id contribuentibus non solum semel in vita, sed eciam in mortis articulo iuxta ordinationem tue circumspectionis, ut indulgentiam plenariam consequantur concedendi, precipiendi quoque in virtute sancte obediencie et sub excommunicationis late sentencie pena quibuscumque idoneis verbi dei predicatoribus secularibus seu cuiuscumque ordinis regularibus, ut fideles excitare et inflammare debeant ad huiusmodi insolentes ausus vi et armis reprimendos et ut suis iuribus ac facultatibus occurrant ad commune periculum propinquius repellendum".

101. Cf. Housley, "Indulgences"; Kühne, "Raimund Peraudi"; idem, "Magdeburg und der Ablass"; and numerous letters of Peraudi in central-European archives.

he had these printed in local printers' shops, e.g. in Olomouc. One of them then came ready with his letters from Italy, the other had them printed locally.[102] In several cases, confessional letters can be found in relation to the crusade against the Hussite King of Bohemia George. Unlike the previous letters, all of these are hand-written and published by nuncio Lorenzo Roverella or his commissaries.[103] For lay believers, opportunities such as these were extremely important, as they could obtain absolutions in cases when they could not be absolved by their local priests. Thus, by contributing to the crusade, they could save themselves long, dangerous and financially demanding travels to the Curia in Rome. The legates and nuncios, then, delegated the power of minor penitentiaries who heard confessions in the Lateran or at St Peter's in Rome to whatever confessors in their province who would be shown the *littere confessionales*. The powers normally entrusted to the Apostolic Penitentiary but also conceded to legates were much wider.

2.2.3. *Apostolic Penitentiary*

A large portion of legatine authority that was handed over by faculties concerned benefits and graces that were normally entrusted to the decision of the Apostolic Penitentiary. As one of the curial tribunals it dealt with the *forum internum* or the matters of conscience.[104] The legates could assume the authority of the Sacred Penitentiary and would publish dispensations, absolutions or licenses in cases normally dealt with by the office. The popes delegated their reserved powers to a Roman office and tribunal and at the same time to legates, who travelled all throughout Christendom. They thus spread the opportunity for believers to receive spiritual benefits, normally acquired in Rome, in their own province, *in partibus*.

The Apostolic Penitentiary, which was researched at the end of the nineteenth century by Emil Göller, but most importantly since 1983, when the archives of the office were opened to historians, had numerous tasks.[105] The office divided its cases into six rubrics in the registers, so that typologically similar cases were dealt with together. These rubrics then illustrate what the powers of the legates were, when they were entrusted the powers of the Penitentiary. The rubrics are as follows: first, *de matrimonialibus*, in which cases of canonical restrictions to marriage and matrimony were administered by publishing dispensations and absolutions. Second, *de diversis formis*, which was a very wide category. It contained absolutions from various ecclesiastical penalties, such as excommunications, be they excommunications *a iure* (*ipso facto*) or *ab homine*; absolutions and dispensations related to various violent deeds of clerics; monastic matters (e.g. transfer from one monastery or monastic order to another

102. Cf. chapter one, § 1.2., with references to examples of printed confessional letters.

103. E.g. MNL Budapest, OL DL 16820 (17 Mar 1469), DL 17005 (17 May 1470), DL 88508 (25 Jul 1470).

104. Cf. Christianson, Izbicki and Bellitto, eds., *The Church.*

105. On penitentiary a basic short account, Salonen, "The Curia: The Apostolic Penitentiary"; cf. however, more importantly, Salonen and Schmugge, *A Sip*; Salonen, *The Penitentiary*; Schmugge, Hersperger and Wiggenhauser, *Die Supplikenregister*; Jaritz, Jørgensen and Salonen, eds., *... et usque ad ultimum terrae.*

– sometimes solved as licenses); performance of the priestly office in the state of excommunication (or in the presence of the excommunicated, in the times of an interdict); simony; blasphemy (violence against clerics, violation or defilement of churches or other sacred places, or of the Eucharist, abuse of the Holy Mass); local excommunication; violation of an oath or a vow; or other less common cases, such as violation of celibacy, heresy, contact with unbelievers. Licenses were given to people who for legitimate reasons wanted or needed to proceed in conflict with canonical prescriptions, such as matters related to fasting during the Lent period, pilgrimage or study, but also licenses for establishing a portable altar, a license to take part in, or – for priests – celebrate a Holy Mass during an interdict. Third, the *de declaratoriis* category handled declarations for clerics, who wanted to be ordained and needed a certification that they did not commit a murder, when such a suspicion existed, or for lay people that they were not members of religious orders, even though they spent some time in a monastery, and for those, who wanted to annul their marriage. Fourth, *de defectu natalium* and *de uberiori* are often treated together as categories that dealt with cases of illegitimate origin. Dispensations were published in three different situations: a dispensation for those of illegitimate birth who wanted to be ordained and hold a benefice with the *cura animarum*, a dispensation for those who wanted to hold two or three such benefices, and a dispensation for those, who wanted to hold the same benefice as their father (*ubi pater*). Fifth, *de promotis et promovendis* meant dispensations for those whose condition was in contradiction with the restrictions of canon law as for advancing to Holy Orders or other offices, e.g. dispensations for *defectus etatis* (canonical restrictions of age to various ordinations), or *defectus corporis* (canonical restrictions in case of physical defects of the candidate, such as problems with eyes, a missing finger, etc.), and *defectus sciencie* (for cases when the candidate did not attain the education requested for an ordination). Finally, *de confessionalibus*, which was a category for those who wanted to obtain a confessional letter, which entitled them to confess to a personal confessor and receive absolutions in cases reserved to the Papal Curia.[106]

In practically all the cases, legates had at their disposal faculties, which contained some of the powers of the Apostolic Penitentiary. Cardinals Marco Barbo, Ausias Despuig, Giovanni d'Aragona and Jean Balue, for example, had a faculty, which gave them the powers of the major penitentiary (*penitentiarius maior*), that is the cardinal penitentiary, the head of the Penitentiary office.[107] Similarly, Marco

106. An overview of the powers of the Apostolic Penitentiary and its documents, Salonen, "The Curia: The Apostolic Penitentiary", pp. 267-271; Salonen and Schmugge, *A Sip*, pp. 17-68; Schmugge, Hersperger and Wiggenhauser, *Die Supplikenregister*, pp. 68-217.

107. ASV, Reg. Vat. 680, fol. 60v, for Marco Barbo (copied for Ausias), "Nos volentes ea tibi concedere, per que animarum Christi fidelium saluti possis salubriter providere, circumspectioni tue cum omnibus quibuscumque personis infra terminos tue legationis consistentibus in illis casibus, in quibus maior penitentiarius noster in Romana curia de speciali commissione dispensare potest et etiam super maiori irregularitate exinde contracta dispensandi et declarandi in eisdem casibus, in quibus idem penitenciarius potest declarare et absolvendi quascumque personas tue legationis ab omnibus casibus, in quibus minores penitenciarii in Romana curia predicta residentes possunt absolvere iniunctis personis ipsis

Barbo was permitted to elect two priests, who would give absolutions which normally fell under the competence of minor penitentiaries (*penitenciarii minori*) in St Peter's basilica in Rome, which means they could absolve all the cases reserved to the Papal Curia.[108] The Venetian cardinal, like others, also received additional faculties, which defined the individual cases in which he could provide graces commonly handled by the cardinal penitentiary. If one follows the categorization of the penitentiary office, the first concerns matrimonial matters. Legates could obtain faculties to grant dispensations to those who wanted to get married and were related by blood line (*consanguinitas*), by another marriage (*affinitas*), or were spiritual relatives (*cognatio spiritualis*) in the third or fourth degree. Marco Barbo could grant absolutions, if the applicants were already married, and dispensations to validate their marriage or simply dispensations for those who only intended to get married. For both degrees, the cardinal legate could choose one hundred people eligible for such absolutions and dispensations. Additionally, he was conceded a faculty to grant these graces without any limitation.[109] Such faculties were among

pro modo culpe penitencia salutari et aliis, qui de iure fuerit, indulgenda plenam et liberam tenore presentium concedimus facultatem"; fol. 183rv (1 Jun 1479), fol. 206rv (1 Jan 1479) for Giovanni d'Aragona; fol. 400v-401r (8 Oct 1483) for Jean Balue.

108. ASV, Reg. Vat. 680, fol. 62rv (also for Ausias), "Nos volentes ea tibi concedere, per que animarum saluti providere valeas, ut ad devotionem sancte Romane ecclesie atque nostram ferventius personas illarum partium excitare possis, tibi in locis quibuscumque tue legationis ubi te residere personaliter dumtaxat et non alibi contigerit, pro ipsius residentie tue tempore duos, si expediens fueris, probatos scientia, moribus et virtute conspicuos probateque consciencie viros in sacerdocio constitutos primarios et confessores, qui volentium sibi confiteri peccata sua confessiones audiant diligenter et confessos in forma ecclesie consueta ab eorum partis in illis casibus, in quibus minores penitenciarii nostri in basilica principis apostolorum de urbe deputati possunt casibus sedi apostolice vel nobis reservatis omnino exceptis iniunctis eis pro modo culpe penitencia salutari et aliis, que de iure fuerint iniungenda auctoritate nostra tua legatione durante, absolvant eligendi et deputandi tenore presentium concedimus facultatem".

109. ASV, Reg. Vat. 680, fol. 43rv (18 Feb 1472), "Nos tuam honorare personam volentes, ut per honorem tibi exhibitum in huiusmodi officio eo utilius proficere valeas, quo fueris per nos maiori auctoritate munitus, circumspectioni tue auctoritate nostra hac vice dumtaxat tua legacione durante cum centum, quibus tibi videbitur, personis, que tertio et quarto consanguinitatis et affinitatis gradu se invicem actingunt ex certis racionabilibus causis desiderant matrimonialiter copulari, aut que ignorantes vel scientes se huiusmodi gradu commaritos invicem matrimonium contraxerint et consummaverint ac prolem exinde susceperint cum illis videlicet, qui contrahere desideraverint, ut impedimento, quod ex huiusmodi consanguinitate vel affinitate provenit non obstante matrimonium inter se contrahere cum illis vero, qui ignorantes, ut in contracto matrimonio remanere, alios vero ab excommunicationis sentencia, quam propter premissa incurrerint, absolvedi ac cum ipsis eis prius ab invicem ad tempus, de qui tibi videbitur, separatis, ut matrimonium de novo contrahere et in contracto remanere libere et licite. Valeant dummodo mulieres ipse propter hoc rapte non fuerint dispensandi et prolem inde susceptam et suscipiendam legitimam decernandi plenam et liberam auctoritate apostolica concedimus tenore presentium facultatem"; fol. 85r-86r (21 Jan 1473), "Nos cupientes ut votis personarum quarumlibet infra metas tue legationis consistentium, in his presertim, que animarum salutem religionis propagationis ac divini cultus augumentum concernunt et ad pacem ac quietem eorum sedatis scandalis tendere dinoscuntur annuere et erga illas te gratiosum reddere valeas, circumspectioni tue racionabilibus, de quibus tibi videbitur, subsistentibus causis cum quibusvis personis infra limites tue legationis consistentibus, que ignorantes si tertio consanguinitatis vel affinitatis gradibus fore coniunctos matrimonia invicem contraxissent, ut in sic per eos contractis

the most common and were conceded to legates *de latere* as well as to the nuncios with the power of legates. The matrimonial cases also included those that dealt with a challenge to public moral chastity (*impedimentum publicae honestatis iustitiae*). These concerned a certain form of relationship (or kinship), as no one could marry a person who was closely related to their former fiancé or fiancée.[110] Such dispensations belonged to the authority of the Apostolic Penitentiary and could also be found among the faculties of legates in relation to dispensations for cases of relatives and of illegitimate birth.[111] Cases related to legatine authority over matrimonial cases also included divorce, as shown by Cardinal Pietro Isvalies, who initiated divorce proceedings for one Margaret and her husband Christopher in Olomouc in 1501.[112]

Cases, which fell under the category of *de diversis formis*, were also very common among the faculties published for legates. They could grant certain graces by the power of their office, as mentioned earlier, and others by the power of special mandates. Dispensations and absolutions could be granted, for example, to members of religious orders, who illegally left their monasteries and wanted to be received back.[113] Other faculties of Cardinal Marco Barbo contained absolutions from simony (the revenues of the benefice, which was conferred with simony, should serve in the fight against the Ottomans);[114] absolutions to those who suffered excommunication while celebrating Holy

matrimoniis remanere et cum his, que invicem, ut prefertur, coniuncte desiderant, matrimonialiter coppulari, ut matrimonium inter se contrahere, et in illo, postquam contractum fuerit, remanere libere et licite valeant, susceptam et suscipiendam prolem ex huiusmodi matrimoniis legitimam nuntiando dispensandi ... auctoritate apostolica tenore presentium concedimus facultatem".

110. Salonen and Schmugge, *A Sip*, p. 23.

111. E.g. ASV, Reg. Vat. 549, fol. 75v (7 Jun 1483), "Et cum quibuscunque hinc inde quarto aut mixtim tertio et quarto consanguinitatis et affinitatis gradibus et spirituali cognatione coniunctis ac impedimento publice honestatis impeditis, etiam qui per adulterium invicem se polluerunt, ut inter se matrimonialiter copulati et in contractis per eos forsan matrimoniis etiam scienter cum contrahentium eorundem ab excessu et censuris ac penis propterea incursis absoluti remanere, prolem susceptam et suscipiendam exinde legitimam decernendo".

112. SOkA Olomouc, fond: AMO, Sbírka listin, inv. no. 385 (30 Apr 1501).

113. ASV, Reg. Vat. 680, fol. 53v-54r (18 Feb 1472), "... et sicut accepimus plurime regulares et religiose persone, a quarum oculis domini timore abcessit abitu seu ordinis, de relicto ad seculum redierunt et in eo vagari dicantur in animarum suarum periculum et scandalum plurimorum. Nos de tua circumspectione gerentes in domino seduciam pleniorem tibi regulares et religiosos eosdem partium predictarum postquam eos ad claustrum et eorum ordines ac monasteria revocaveris, ut tenentur, absolvendi ab excommunicationum et aliis sentenciis censuris et penis, quas propterea dimittendo ipsorum habitus et apostatando incurrerunt ac cum eis super irregularitate per eos premissorum ocasione contracta ipsis prius ad tempus, de quo tibi videbitur, a suorum ordinum excussione suspensis ab ac iniuncta ipsis pro modo culpe penitentia salutari et aliis, que de iure fuerint iniungenda quodque quecumque beneficia ecclesiastica et officia regularia per sui ordinis proffessores solita gubernari, si eis alias canonice conferantur aut eligantur vel affirmantur, ad illa recipere et retinere libere et licite valeant auctoritae apostolica dispensandi plenam et liberam tenore presentium concedimus facultatem".

114. ASV, Reg. Vat. 680, fol. 50v-52r, "Proviso quod fructus beneficiorum ipsorum et alia ex eis indebite precepta seu male detenta vel indebite ocupata per personas ipsas, prout eisdem personis est possibile, vel pars aliquam expedicione adversus nefandissimos Turchos tuo arbitrio convertantur et eciam exponantur".

Mass during an interdict;[115] absolutions to priests who owed money to the Church (from annats, etc. on condition that the outstanding amount was sent to the reconstruction of basilicas of Rome);[116] and absolutions from crusading vows.[117] Cardinal Giovanni d'Aragona had, furthermore, faculties for absolutions of heretics[118] and absolutions in the case of blasphemy.[119] Cardinal Giovanni, as well as Cardinal Ausias Despuig, received a faculty to grant absolutions for cases when Christians visited forbidden countries of unbelievers and engaged in commerce with them without licence, especially dealing in arms and foods (*arma et victualia*).[120] The political dimension of such faculties might be illustrated by a faculty for Marco Barbo who granted an absolution to the Knights of the Virgin Mary of Germans (or Teutonic Knights) from their feudal oath to King Casimir IV of Poland so that they could fight for the Crown of Bohemia on the side of King Matthias Corvinus.[121] In this category, the legates could also distribute licences, especially those for establishing a portable altar (used for example by Cardinal Juan Carvajal in 1458).[122] The legate himself

115. ASV, Reg. Vat. 680, fol. 54v-55r.

116. ASV, Reg. Vat. 680, fol. 56v-57r, "Ita tamen quod personne (*sic*) predicte, quibus fiet remissio fructuum male preceptorum, prout tibi vel illi, cui id commiseris, videbitur expedire partem fructum eorundem pro reparatione basilicarum et aliarum ecclesiarum alme urbis efficaciter refondere teneantur".

117. ASV, Reg. Vat. 680, fol. 61r (18 Feb 1472), "et sicut accepimus nonnulli infra metas huiusmodi legationis tue constituti votum sancte cruciate emiserunt, qui ad presens valitudinarii et a deo senes et iuribus depressi sunt, quod illud observare ac deo reddere minime possunt, nos volentes illa tibi concedere, per que animarum suarum saluti valeas salubriter providere, circumspectioni tue legatione tua huiusmodi durante votum predictum, quod ut prefertur commode adimplere nequiverit relaxandi, dummodo hii, qui votum ipsum emiserint, de bonis eorum in expeditionem contra perfidissimos et truculentissimos Turchos contribuant, secundum quod tibi iuxta personarum exigenciam videbitur convenire, plenam et liberam auctoritate apostolica tenore presentium concedimus facultatem".

118. ASV, Reg. Vat. 680, fol. 175v (1 Jun 1479), "Circumspectioni tue omnes et singulas personas tam ecclesiasticas quam scolares, qui a catholice fidei et sancte matris ecclesie documentis deviaverunt seu deviantes in heresim quomodolibet lapse fuerint et propterea excommunicationis et alias sententias censuras et penas ecclesiasticas vel scolares per quoscumque iudices ordinarios vel delegatos etiam apostolicos aut inquisitores heretice pravitatis lactas inflictas et promulgatas incurrerint postquam ad veram et catolicam fidem redierint ac errores suos abiuraverint nec non hoc a te humiliter petierint illas ab huiusmodi sententiis et penis ac excessibus auctoritate nostra absolvendi in forma ecclesie consueta iniunctis personis ipsis pro modo culpe penitentia salutari ac quod talia de cetero non commuttent nec ea, commictentibus prebeant auxilium consilium vel favorem et cum personis ecclesiasticis super irregularitate, si quam sic ligate etc. Missas et alia divina officia celebrando vel illis se immiscendo contraxerint dispensandi auctoritate apostolica tenore presentium liberam et plenam concedimus facultatem".

119. ASV, Reg. Vat. 680, fol. 210v-211r.

120. ASV, Reg. Vat. 680, fol. 155r-156r, fol. 243r-245r.

121. ASV, Reg. Vat. 680, fol. 69r-70v (two documents; the first one edited by Theiner, ed., *Vetera monumenta Hungariae*, vol. 2, pp. 433-434, no. 614).

122. ASV, Reg. Vat. 680, fol. 49rv, fol. 62v-63r, fol. 203r. Cf. MNL Budapest, OL DL 15219 (9 Mar 1458) for the actual usage of such a faculty by Juan Carvajal, who allowed Counts John and Sigismund of St George and Pezinok (Pösing) to choose a confessor who could change their

could celebrate the Holy Mass and take part in it, even in territories affected by an interdict.[123] Legates were conceded faculties to grant licences to students so that they could remain absent from their benefices and receive revenues to be able to support themselves during their studies. Marco Barbo could grant such licences for seven years and Giovanni d'Aragona for five.[124] Giovanni could also grant licences for pilgrimages to distant pilgrimage sites, in this case to the Holy Land to visit the Holy Sepulchre.[125] In this respect, licences for changing a vow (*commutatio votis*) to visit various pilgrimage sites could also have been granted, as can be seen in the above-mentioned case of Cardinal Juan Carvajal. This overview, which could be easily expanded, reveals that in this category legates were conceded most of the powers of the Apostolic Penitentiary.

Further faculties were granted to legates in other categories as well, even though legates could not publish declaratory letters, declarations in the *de declaratoriis* category. In questions of illegitimate birth and conferral of benefices, legates often had faculties to grant dispensations (and also these faculties could have been limited to a certain number of applicants),[126] and they could have also handled cases of underage applicants for ecclesiastical orders or applicants with physical defects, i.e. cases that came under the category *de promotis et promovendis*.[127] Finally, also in the *de confessionalibus* category, legates acquired faculties, as in the case of Marco Barbo, which enabled them to award licences to choose a confessor.[128]

A number of other examples of such faculties for other legates could be listed. This overview demonstrates, however, a general tendency which is extremely significant. Papal legates were not only a threat to the authority of a local bishop, but also a travelling curia or travelling penitentiary where indulgences and various graces and spiritual benefits, dispensations, absolutions and licences could have been gained, which otherwise were available only in Rome. Among the faculties, the highest number of them were related to the powers and activities of the Apostolic Penitentiary. The Pope then transferred his authority to the legates in the same way he transferred it to this office.[129]

vows of pilgrimage to the Holy Land, to the thresholds of St Peter or to St James to other pious deeds and apart from that they received a licence to establish and use a portable altar.

123. ASV, Reg. Vat. 680, fol. 50rv.

124. ASV, Reg. Vat. 680, fol. 58r-59r, 228v-229r.

125. ASV, Reg. Vat. 680, fol. 184r.

126. ASV, Reg. Vat. 680, fol. 42rv, 53rv; 734, fol. 240v.

127. ASV, Reg. Vat. 680, fol. 34rv, 43v-44r.

128. ASV, Reg. Vat. 680, fol. 42r-43r.

129. It should be mentioned that such absolutions and dispensations could have been conceded not only to legates or nuncios with the power of legates, but also to diocesan bishops, as could be shown in a number of cases. These faculties could have been limited (sometimes even to one case only) and conceded at the request of nuncios, who could not wield the episcopal powers needed for some of the faculties. Cf. for Johann Beckensloer, archbishop of Esztergom and Uriel Górka, bishop of Poznań, ASV, Arm. XXXIX 15, fol. 118v (10 Dec 1482), "Dedimus alias tibi facultatem concedendi plenarias indulgentias porrigentibus manus adiutrices ad defensionem fidei catholice, prout latius in aliis nostris litteris continetur, et ut ex dictis indulgentiis uberior fructus pro tam sancto incepto proveniat, ultra alias, quas habest

Legatine involvement in the power of the penitentiary may even be observed in the documents of the office itself, namely in the registers of the original supplications or petitions.[130] When asking for a further dispensation in the same matter, these petitions must have mentioned all the previous dispensations. Thus, when such dispensations were granted by legates, the references appear in the registers and indirectly present the activity of the legates in this issue. However, most of it remains hidden in the local context, as dispensations were granted in a number of cases, when further dispensations were not needed or not possible and thus they could not appear in the penitentiary registers.[131] Legates and their dispensations appeared in various categories, most often in *de uberiori*, *de diversis formis*, *de promotis et promovendis*, and sometimes in *de declaratoriis*.

Legatine dispensations in terms of illegitimate birth were relatively common, as those who asked for such a dispensation could still ask for more in terms of acquiring further benefices or even benefices, where their fathers served.[132] It is apparent that the legatine dispensations are not mentioned in the *de defectu natalium* category, as these would be the first dispensations the applicants needed. Further dispensations are listed in the registers with proper reference to the previous grace in the *de uberiori* or *de promotis et promovendis* categories. Dispensations of Cardinal Francesco Todeschini Piccolomini are still mentioned, for example, after ten or fourteen years,[133] as late as 1489 a dispensation of Cardinal Nicholas of Cusa, who was active in Germany in 1451-1452 and 1455, is recorded in the registers.[134] In that same year an applicant from the diocese of Augsburg referred to a dispensation of the first degree which he obtained from nuncio Lorenzo Roverella, which must have been in 1468, when Roverella actively worked in the area.[135] A certain Johannes Duyn of the diocese of Liège acquired a dispensation of second degree from a nuncio, but asked the penitentiary office for further dispensation to be able to hold more benefices.[136] These are only a few examples taken from the registers of Pope

etiam tibi facultates ex certa scientia nostra per presentes elargimur, ut licent tibi ex illicito cohitu natos legitimare, et cum illis, qui natalium defectus patiuntur, dispensare ad honores eos reducere omnemque ab eis infamiam abolere ac etiam ad quoscunque actus legitimos et ad cuiuslibet ordinis promotionem habilitare ac legitimare etiam quoad forum contentiosum, ita quod taliter a te vigore presentium habilitati et legitimati omnibus privilegiis et prorogativis honoris et promotionis uti et potiri valeant, prout quilibet legitime natus potitur et gaudet"; for Sixtus of Tannberg, bishop of Freising, ASV, Arm. XXXIX 15, fol. 116v-117r (7 Dec 1482), an absolution and dispensation for only one matrimonial case, conceded at the request of nuncio Bartolomeo da Camerino.

130. For Germany and adjacent countries cf. *Repertorium poenitentiariae Germanicum.*

131. Cf. Schmugge, *Kirche, Kinder, Karrieren*, p. 57.

132. Ludwig Schmugge dedicated much space to these dispensations in *ibid.*, pp. 47-57, in the penitentiary registers, pp. 57-63.

133. *Ibid.*, p. 59; *Repertorium poenitentiariae Germanicum*, vol. 7, p. 586, no. 3846 (26 Jan 1485).

134. *Ibid.*, p. 612, no. 4018 (15 Oct 1489).

135. *Ibid.*, p. 613, no. 4019 (31 Oct 1489).

136. *Ibid.*, pp. 603-604, no. 3980 (16 May 1488).

Innocent VIII. They nevertheless clearly illustrate the functioning of the system, where such dispensations worked the same over the entire period in question.

Other cases were usually more complicated and belonged to the other above mentioned categories. The same pontificate can provide additional examples. A certain Henricus Locher of the diocese of Chur promised during his illness that if he was restored to health, he would enter a monastery within a year. When he recovered from his infirmity, he did not want to fulfil his vow and from a nuncio *cum potestate legati de latere* obtained the possibility to postpone the actual fulfilment of his promise. He later still did not want to go ahead with the vow and, at the age of fifty-three, asked for another change.[137] In Kirchberg, diocese of Mainz, nuncio Alexander Numai allowed the villagers to use dairy products during the fasting period (with the exception of Lent); due to their poverty, the parish asked the penitentiary office for further alleviation. The new supplication contained a reference to the nuncio's dispensation, who saw their poverty with his own eyes.[138] Such a distribution of licenses could work very easily: the villagers could have asked the nuncio for it when he passed through their village. This would prove that the villagers or the local priest did have a certain legal knowledge or at least awareness or that they could make use of the services of an agent with such a knowledge.

Further examples would only illustrate what has already been said. When the system required further dispensations, the previous ones had to be listed. Certain cases even show, however, that the legatine dispensations might have been regarded as not having the same power as dispensations obtained directly from the penitentiary office, i.e. directly from the Curia. For example, in 1517 a certain Ludovicus Schenck from the diocese of Mainz, who served "in the wars between the King of France and the lord of Frisia as a mercenary, but did not kill anyone," was absolved from these deeds by a legate and obtained an ecclesiastical benefice. *Pro maiori firmitate*, he asked the apostolic see for an absolution from the accusations of homicide and a dispensation from irregularity.[139] Similarly, a certain Johannes Czerstede, once inflicted a bleeding wound to the head of a cleric and was absolved from the excommunication sentence by a legate. His brother Brandanus, however, himself a cleric, asked for another absolution from the penitentiary office *pro maiori cautela*, to be certain and to be able to bury his

137. *Ibid.*, p. 226, no. 1723 (26 Oct 1486), "… postmodum vero valetudine recuperata non habens votum gratum a quodam nuntio sedis apostolice in partibus illis cum potestate legati de latere deputato se ad hoc ab eadem sede specialem per quasdam eius litteras facultatem habere dicentem et ex certis causis tunc expressis usque ad certum tempus tunc expressum votum adimplere non teneretur sibi indulgeri obtinuit …".

138. *Ibid.*, p. 318, no. 2172 (17 Sep 1490), "… quod nuper reverendus Alexander episcopus Forolivien., tunc Sixti IV. pape et sedis apostolice in Germania cum plena potestate legati de latere nuntius, de sterilitate et penuria nutrimentorum dicte parochie fidedignorum testimonio sufficienter informatus ac etiam oculari experientia, dum illas partes per legationes suas perlustraretur inductus, prefatis exponentibus pauperibus dicte parochie, ut omnibus et singulis diebus lacticiniis ab ecclesia prohibitis uti valeant, licentiam concessit quadragesimalibus dumtaxat diebus exceptis …".

139. *Repertorium poenitentiariae Germanicum*, vol. 10, p. 163, no. 855 (26 Dec 1517).

brother's body in the proper way according to the rules of the Church.[140] Even more problematic was the case of a certain Wilhelmus, a priest in Siebenborn in the diocese of Trier. He had wounded a priest of the same diocese and since this was a bloody wound, incurred excommunication from which he was absolved by a legate. Not certain about the validity, he asked the local bishop to grant him absolution and still in doubt after that even addressed the apostolic see.[141] These must be regarded as exceptional cases, as usually no such doubt can be found. Legates were as much a "well of grace" as the Apostolic Penitentiary itself.

2.2.4. *Specific cases*

Apart from matters related to the general organisation and administration of the Church and to various graces, legates were endowed with powers that belonged to the Pope but had a different significance and were part of the papal authority outside this sphere.

Legates had at their disposal faculties which granted them powers to award absolutions and dispensations normally given by other offices of the Papal Curia or by the Pope himself. They could grant licences to hold two incompatible benefices, i.e. two benefices with the care of the souls. Legates were also conceded authority to make visitations and reforms of cathedral churches,[142] or monasteries, chapters, universities and similar ecclesiastical institutions.[143] They could also have special powers to allow the transfer of holy relics. Even though such faculties, as far as I know, cannot be found in the Vatican registers, a letter from papal legate Cardinal Tommaso De Vio is preserved, which granted permission to transfer the relics of St Margaret. They were originally kept on Hare's Island (*insula leporum*, present day Margaret's Island, *Margit sziget*, in Budapest) on the Danube, but were placed elsewhere due to the threat of frequent floods.[144]

Legates were also often given authority over the datary (*dataria*) at the Curia, which was responsible for the sale of offices in the Curia.[145] Legates could create or name public notaries – the faculties even contained the form of the oath taken by them upon their naming; as in other cases, this faculty used to be limited by the number of applicants.[146] Similarly, legates could confer additional papal offices

140. *Ibid.*, p. 174, no. 901 (22 Apr 1518).

141. *Repertorium poenitentiariae Germanicum*, vol. 7, no. 2196 (3 Jan 1491).

142. ASV, Reg. Vat. 680, fol. 152rv.

143. ASV, Reg. Vat. 680, fol. 186r, 195v-196v.

144. MNL Budapest, OL DL 25312 (5 Sep 1523), "Nos igitur attentis premissis vestris in hac parte supplicationibus inclinati vobis, ut adhibitis vobiscum fratribus dicti ordinis seu aliis, qui vobis videbuntur, ossa huiusmodi in ecclesiam monasterii vestri predicti in loco decenti transferre possitis auctoritate apostolica, qua etiam per litteras sanctissimi domini nostri papę nobis concessa fungimur in hac parte tenore presentium concedimus et indulgemus".

145. Meyer, "The Curia: The Apostolic Chancery", p. 253; Frenz, *Die Kanzlei*, pp. 97-100, 193-198.

146. ASV, Reg. Vat. 680, fol. 41r-42r, "Nos volentes illa tibi concedere, per que te aliis valeas reddere gratiosum circumspectioni tue hac vice postquam limites legationis tue intraveris concedende auctoritate apostolica predictum tabellionatus officium quinquaginta personis infra limites huiusmodi constitutis, quas ad id elegeris, eciam si earum alique cum unica et virgine

and lesser orders, including protonotaries, sub-deacons, acolytes or chaplains,[147] and when given such a faculty, they could even grant doctoral degrees.[148]

The example of Cardinal Marco Barbo illustrates even further the consequences of various faculties, which could be labelled as "political". That is, faculties could have a clear connection to political negotiations of the legate and the political situation of the region. The legate, in this case, was endowed with special faculties to excommunicate supporters of King Casimir of Poland and various heretics and bless favourites of King Matthias Corvinus; to absolve the Grand master of the Teutonic Knights as well as the knights themselves from an oath of fealty to the King of Poland (as mentioned above); to deprive the former supporters of King George of Poděbrady of all previously granted indults and of all feudal property; to distribute according to his will all ecclesiastical possessions in the Kingdom of Bohemia; to confirm a peace, if it was concluded between the Kings of Poland and Hungary and between the King of Poland and the Teutonic Knights; and even to divide the Kingdom of Bohemia, if needed because of peace.[149] The political consequences will not be treated here, suffice it to say that legates were clearly endowed with many spiritual powers that did not merely concentrate on the well-being of the lay population of the province, but gave more power to their political and diplomatic deeds.

A number of additional faculties can be found in the Vatican registers which limited or enhanced the scope of the powers of legates. Conceding such faculties was wholly in the power of the Pope, who could thus boost the position of the

coniugate, vel in sacris ordinibus constituti fuerint, si eas ad illud post diligentem informationem examinationis idoneas esse repereris iuramento, prius ab earum singulis iuxta formam presentibus annotatam recepto plenam et liberam tenore presentium concedimus facultatem. Forma autem iuramenti, quod quelibet earumdem personarum prestabit, est talis: Ego diocesis ab hac hora inantea fidelis ero beato Petro et sancte Romane ecclesie ac domino meo domino Sixto pape quarto et successoribus suis canonice intrantibus. Non ero in consilio, auxilio, consensu, vel facto, ut vitam perdant aut membrum, vel capiantur mala captione. Consilium, quod michi per se vel literas aut nuncium manifestabunt ad eorum dampnum scienter nemini pandam. Si vero ad meam noticiam aliquid devenire contingat, quod in periculum Romani pontificis aut ecclesie Romane vergeret seu grave damnum illud proposse impediam, et si hoc impedire non possem, procurabo bona fide id ad notitiam domini pape perferri. Papatum Romanum et regalia sancti Petri ac iura ipsius ecclesie specialiter, si qua eadem ecclesia in civitate vel terra, de qua sum oriundus, habeat adiutor eis ero ad defendendum et retinendum seu recuperandum contra omnes homines. Tabellionatus officium fideliter exercebo. Contractus, in quibus exigitur, consensus partium fideliter conficiam nil addendo vel minuendo sine voluntate partium, quod substantiam contractus immutet. Si vero in conficiendo aliquod instrumentum unius solius partis, sit requirenda voluntas, hoc ipsum faciam, ut scilicet nil addam vel minuam, quod inmutet facti substanciam contra voluntatem ipsius. Instrumentum non conficiam de aliquo contractu, in quo sciam intervenire seu intercedere vim vel fraudem. Contractum in prothocollum redignam, et postquam in prothocollum redegero, maliciose non diferam contra voluntatem illorum seu illius, quorum seu cuius est contractus, super eos conficere publicum instrumentum salvo meo iusto et consueto salario. Sic me deus adiuvet et hoc sancta Dei euuangelia". Cf. Tangl, ed., *Die päpstlichen Kanzleiordnungen*, p. 50.

147. ASV, Reg. Vat. 680, fol. 153v-154r.

148. ASV, Reg. Vat. 680, fol. 254rv.

149. ASV, Reg. Vat. 680, fol. 65r-73v, 77v-80v; some of the documents published in Theiner, ed., *Vetera monumenta Hungariae*, vol. 2, pp. 431-440, nos. 613-615, 621, 624.

legate in terms of his political negotiations within the assigned region and – even more importantly – in terms of the local church and local dioceses, where the legate could completely overturn the ecclesiastical structures. The legate could not only interfere with the judicial powers of the local episcopate, but could bring graces that could be reached otherwise only in Rome.

Once the legate obtained his faculties, his powers and authority were not limited in any way. The activities of the legates were still monitored, however, by the papacy or by other papal representatives. Papal nuncio *cum potestate legati de latere* Bartolomeo Maraschi, for example, was charged with the task of observing the activities of a simple nuncio Bartolomeo da Camerino. Strange and even "sinister" information about the latter reached Rome and thus Maraschi had to find out the truth, so as to allow the Pope to decide whether the faculties given to Camerino should be abolished or not.[150] Much more was done in the case of nuncio *cum potestate legati de latere* Alexander Numai, whose story was mentioned earlier. He was deprived of his authority and his faculties. Supposedly, he had even used faculties that were not given to him, as the Pope was informed by "Germans and Italians". His position seemed quite problematic, but with the support of the Emperor, he was allowed by the curia to remain at the imperial court as a private agent and later all his powers were given back to him. These events clearly reveal that faculties and the powers entrusted to legates or nuncios could still be subject to a certain control from the side of the Papal Curia and in the case of certain kinds of misuse of these faculties, legates or nuncios were consequently punished.

Legates (and nuncios with the power of a legate *de latere*) and their faculties were naturally welcome in all parts of Europe. The local population did not need to set out on a long journey to Rome to acquire certain spiritual benefits and graces to remove their sins and worldly punishments or to legally get around the requirements of canon law. Papal nuncio Angelo Pecchinoli asked, for example, Pope Innocent VIII to send him extra faculties for setting up portable altars and awarding indulgences. Hungarian lords, especially in regions close to the Ottoman Turks, did not understand that their faculties gave them powers to award such benefits only to a limited number of people. They would have a need of more.[151] This idea was best expressed by Sigismund, King of Poland, in his petition (that was mentioned in the beginning of this sub-chapter) to Pope Leo X, in which he asked the Pope to extend the faculties of nuncio Zacharia Ferreri to Poland, originally valid only for Lithuania and Muscovy. King Sigismund wrote that the nuncio could not use these faculties in any case, as the population of those lands was predominantly of the Greek rite and would not need them. "It will be a thing unusually pleasing to me and useful to my subjects, if what they now ask from Rome or Hungary [i.e. from other legates], they could have at home".[152] The

150. ASV, Arm. XXXIX 16, fol. 49r (11 Oct 1483), "... de ipso Bartolomeo nonnulle sinistre informationes date sunt et nescimus, si ille vel ex veritate re vel ex conlatione aliorum proficiscuntur. Itaque iudicio et examini tuo placuit relinquere verum facultates ipse dande aut denegande sint..."; Arm. XXXIX 16A, fol. 2v (2 Jan 1484).

151. BMV, Lat. X 175 (=3622), fol. 145r.

152. Wojtyska, ed., *Acta*, vol. 2, pp. 48-49, no. 18 (post 14 Mar 1520).

presence in a kingdom of a legate or nuncio with extensive faculties definitely made the journey to salvation much easier for its inhabitants.

As mentioned earlier, faculties could be utilised for political ends. Their original purpose seems to have been entirely different, however, as they mirrored the spiritual authority of the Pope and should have helped with the administration of the province as well as enable individuals to be granted special graces reserved to the Pope only. This can also be confirmed with the above-mentioned 1518 case of four legates (and two collegates), who were sent from Rome expressly without faculties, *sine facultatibus*. This means they had their powers as legates *de latere*, but no special mandates that would enhance their authority, or at least that was the original intention on the part of the Curia. The communication with legates and the respective rulers has been preserved in one of the registers in the Vatican archives. Most of the letters relate to political matters, questions of accepting the legates, problems of preparing the crusade and the like, as the legates were mostly sent for facilitating the crusade.[153] A letter was addressed to Cardinal Tommaso De Vio, however, which gave him the faculty to proceed against preachers who criticised the indulgences in Germany.[154] The Pope had to use the legate who was in place to solve pressing problems within the Church: the letter mentioned the indulgences and their critics, but no word was dedicated to the fact that Cardinal Tommaso had been dispatched with no faculties. It seems that once the legate was in his province, the Pope communicated with him as with other legates and did not follow up the original decision of sending legates without faculties too strictly.

The structure of the Papal Curia became more complex in the later Middle Ages and included several tribunals and offices. At the head was the Pope, to whom the plenitude of power, *plenitudo potestatis*, belonged, which he delegated to these offices. The structure itself was designed for the stationary Curia of Rome or other residences of the Pope, and was complemented in a somewhat mobile fashion by other offices. Papal legates and delegated judges were part of the delegation of the papal plenitude of power and have to be treated together with the rest of the Curia. The office of legates *de latere* itself had powers which were further augmented with faculties for specific cases. These still, however, represented an extended arm of papal power over western Christendom.[155]

2.3. *Geographical and temporal limits of the legation*

There is in general a crucial question concerning the substance of the scope, validity and limitations of such authority for representation and delegation of

153. ASV, Arm. XLIV 5, passim; cf. regests in Nanni, ed., *Epistolae*, vol. 1.

154. ASV, Arm. XLIV 5, fol. 268r-269v (9 Nov 1518), "… Tibi nihilominus contra presumentes et inobedientes procedendi illosque debitis pęnis, quibus tibi videbitur, puniendi plenam et liberam etiam per presentes concedimus facultatem".

155. Recently studied with the rest of the Curia in Sisson and Larson, eds., *A Companion* by Müller, "The Omnipresent Pope".

powers. This general statement is, obviously, equally valid for the legatine system of representation, as the apostolic authority was transferred to the individual prelates who represented the Pope himself. The Pope transmitted the plenitude of power, *plenitudo potestatis*, to legates but it also had its limitations in geographical and temporal terms. This means that the authority had to be positively defined in terms of geographical scope.

The geographical restrictions of the legation created a legatine province that always had to be defined before the legate set out from the Curia. Legatine provinces were never stable and may have changed with every new legation. Moreover, they did not have to copy the division of the dioceses and provinces of the standard church administration. It is crucial, as Robert C. Figueira has remarked, to realize that the organisation of the Church is based on the territorial model through the diocesan administration. Within the framework of this administration, the metropolitan provinces are the archdioceses, within the borders of which the archbishop exercised his jurisdiction. The legatine provinces are, however, part of a different system, or rather they do not need to be standardised or coincide with the standard administration on the diocesan level. Historians need to always be aware of this fact when metropolitan or legatine provinces are discussed. The legatine province denotes "that area assigned to a legate and within which he could employ all of the powers pertaining to him by virtue of his office".[156]

The legatine province constituted a crucial point in the definition of the legation, as the canon law of the twelfth and thirteenth centuries already indicates. Figueira has analysed the definitions of the legatine provinces in the *Liber extra* and in the glosses of the decretalists. The criteria varied: the definition of the province may have followed political divisions or ecclesiastical or simply geographical or even a combination of all of these. Various terms can be found in canon law that reflect these criteria; they may be clearly defined political units (e.g. the Kingdom of Sicily), less clearly defined geographical terms (e.g. German parts), areas around metropolitan churches (e.g. parts surrounding Toulouse), or groupings of metropolitan provinces.[157] This overview holds true not only for the sources of canon law, but also for the actual definitions of the legatine provinces found in the titulatures of the individual legates, where the destinations are necessarily described. Within vaguely defined European regions, the actual provinces may vary substantially. An example of this might be the multiple creations, when the whole of Europe was supposed to be divided into parts that were administered by individual legates. The popes created a number of legates which were dispatched from Rome simultaneously in the years 1471, 1500 and 1518, usually with commissions to facilitate a crusade. If one also takes into account the creations of 1455, which were almost simultaneous, the overview looks as in Table 1:

156. Figueira, "The Medieval Papal Legate", pp. 74-76, quote on 76.
157. *Ibid.*, 76.

Table 1. Overview of the legantine provinces at multiple creations.

1455 Calixt III	1471 Sixtus IV	1500 Alexander VI	1518 Leo X
Alain de Coëtivy *France*	Bessarion *France, Burgundy, England*	Juan Vera *France, Spain, Portugal, England*	Bernardo Dovizi da Bibbiena *France*
Nicholas of Cusa *England, Germany*	Roderigo Borja *Spain*	Raymund Peraudi *Germany*	Lorenzo Campeggi (& Thomas Wolsey) *England*
Juan Carvajal *Germany, Hungary, Poland*	Angelo Capranica *Italy*	Pietro Isvalies *Hungary, Bohemia, Poland, Russia &c.*	Egidio di Viterbo *Spain*
Dionysius Szécsi *Hungary*	Marco Barbo *Germany, Hungary, Bohemia, Poland, Denmark, Norway, Sweden*		Tommaso De Vio (& Matheus Lang) *Germany*
Lodovico Trevisan *fleet*	Oliviero Carafa *Naples, fleet*		[Tamás Bakóc] *Hungary, Poland*

In this case, the provinces are designed according to kingdoms or political units in general, and form different groupings on the basis of geographical convenience. Different popes had different interests and placed an emphasis on different regions. France, for example, twice had a legate who was only sent to the kingdom, in other instances, however, the kingdom of France was only part of a a much larger legatine province.

In order to analyse more closely the definitions of legatine provinces, the example of Central Europe may be utilised, as the situation varies the most in this region. The previous table indicates that Central Europe was treated by papal diplomacy as a region, usually as central or east-Central Europe, i.e. anything east of Germany or sometimes including Germany. In the crusading designs of the later Middle Ages, it played a crucial role.[158] Central Europe, as defined here was never clearly delineated, however, and thus all the legates and nuncios who received their provinces in the region never copied previous legatine provinces. Also, the individual countries, here Germany, Hungary, Bohemia and Poland, to follow the example of France, were sometimes taken into account as the destination of a single legate, but most often there were combinations that constantly changed.

The narrowest possible delimitation mentioned one single kingdom or other country. Dionysius Szécsi, as Archbishop of Esztergom, for example, held the title of *legatus natus* for the Kingdom of Hungary. Since the title was mostly empty in the fifteenth century, the archbishop was also created legate *de latere* with the powers limited to the kingdom itself.[159] The country that most often stood alone in

158. In detail see Kalous, "Středovýchodní Evropa"; idem, "Papal Legates and Crusading Activity".

159. E.g. MNL Budapest, OL DL 15888 (31 Oct 1463), "apostolice sedis legatus natus ac in regno Hungarie eiusdem sedis legatus de latere"; similarly, he was called *bone memorie*

the legatine provinces was naturally Germany (*Germania*, *Alemania*), as frequently the legates were sent to the Emperor, to the imperial diets or negotiations with the princes of the Empire. Cardinal Francesco Todeschini Piccolomini was a legate *de latere* in Germany in 1471 and his task mostly involved negotiations in the imperial diet in Regensburg. His mandates narrowed his powers to the German lands, but the terms *Germania* or *Alemania* were more thoroughly defined and described, as, for example, in the faculties Francesco acquired from Pope Paul II.[160] There are, in contrast, extremes when one single legation would encompass half of Europe, as in the case of Cardinal Marco Barbo, whose legatine province first included the German lands and Kingdoms of Hungary, Poland and Bohemia, only to be later extended to the Scandinavian Kingdoms of Denmark, Norway and Sweden.[161] Different sources presented the province differently: it is most precisely defined in the faculties. The consistorial diary, only mentioned, however, the most important ones with the addition "and others".[162] Similarly, the legatine province of nuncio Bartolomeo Maraschi (*nuncius cum potestate legati de latere*) was, in addition to Central Europe, extended to the Kingdom of Denmark.[163] The Pope also assigned a large province to Cardinal Pietro Isvalies, who was sent to Central Europe again, but unlike Cardinal Marco Barbo, his extension was not directed towards the north but rather to the east.[164] More than twenty years later, Cardinal Tommaso De Vio

by Pope Paul II in 1467, Lukcsics, ed., *Monumenta*, vol. 3, p. 188 (4 Jul 1467), "... ac in regno Ungarie eiusdem sedis de latere et natus legatus fuit".

160. BAV, Vat. lat. 10637, fol. 588r-611v (in all faculties the same titulature), "in Alamanie et totius Germanię ac universis et singulis provinciis civitatibus terris et locis eiusdem Germanię sacroque Romano imperio subiectis apostolicę sedis legato".

161. ASV, Reg. Vat. 680, fol. 34r (21 Jan 1472) (Theiner, ed., *Vetera monumenta Hungariae*, vol. 2, p. 441, no. 626), "Marco tt. sancti Marci presbitero cardinali in Alamania ac totius Germanie necnon universis et singulis provinciis, civitatibus, terris et locis eiusdem Germanie sacro Romano imperio subiectis ac Hungarie et Polonie regnis apostolice sedis legato salutem et apostolicam benedictionem. Cum nos pridem pro nonnullis arduis Christiane religionis negotiis ad Germaniam ac Hungarie Polonie et Boemie regna legatum de latere duxerimus destinandum ..."; fol. 35v (2 Apr 1472; Theiner, ed., *Vetera monumenta Hungariae*, vol. 2, pp. 435-6, no. 620), "Nos attendentes, quod dilecti filii prelati, principes, barones, milites, nobiles et comunitates Datie, Novergie et Svetie regnorum ad premissa peragenda nec non felicem et prosperum statum deducenda quin plurimum utiles esse potuerunt legationem tuam huiusmodi ad omnia regna predicta illarumque provincias civitates terras et loca extendimus...".

162. ASV, Arm. XXXI 52, fol. 77r (22 Dec 1471) (Eubel, *Hierarchia catholica*, vol. 2, p. 37), "[legatus de latere] apud imperatorem et regem Ungarie et alios".

163. ASV, Reg. Vat. 549, fol. 75r (7 Jun 1483), "ad Alamaniam ac universa et singula provintias civitates terras et loca Germanie sacro Romano imperio et illius electoribus ac subditis subiecta necnon Ungarie Polonie Boemie et Datie regna apostolice sedis cum plena potestate legati de latere nuntio et oratori...".

164. BAV, Vat. lat. 3922, fol. 305v (1501), *littere confessionales* printed in Olomouc (with other copies in archives and libraries in e.g. Budapest, Kraków, Olomouc and Brno), "ad Hungarie Bohemie et Polonie regna necnon Prussiam Russiam Livoniam Littuaniam Valachiam Slesiam Lusatiam Moraviam Transilvaniam Dalmatiam Sclavoniam Croatiam Corbaviam et Moscoviam omnesque et singulas regnorum et provinciarum predictarum civitates terras atque loca illis subiecta et alia eis adiacentia apostolice sedis de latere legatus"; the same titulature in a charter in matrimonial matters, SOkA Olomouc, fond AMO, Sbírka listin, inv. no. 385 (30 Apr 1501).

used almost the same description for his legatine province (in some charters with the Kingdom of Poland, which was absent from the longer titulature) with Germany, strangely enough, added only at the end.[165]

The last example reveals several important issues. First of all, the description of the legatine province is not always the same even in the charters that were published by the legate. The reason might be that when the charter or letter was relevant for only a part or a single kingdom within the legatine province, the chancery of the legate would not believe it necessary to list all the countries. It might also be possible that some of the faculties and powers were limited to certain parts of the huge province. The faculties, i.e. documents published by the Papal Chancery, of Angelo Pecchinoli, who was sent to Central Europe as a nuncio *cum potestate legati de latere*, had different definitions of the province in the Vatican registers (the question might be, whether the originals kept the entire province for all the faculties, but that does not seem to be the case, as the registers would usually copy the whole titulature).[166]

The second issue constitutes a further problem for the exact demarcation of the legatine province. The lists of countries and lands would often include phrases that further enhanced the powers geographically, but without any strict geographical delineation. In the case of Angelo Pecchinoli the phrase reads "and to other to them [Germany, Hungary, Poland, Bohemia] adjacent parts and kingdoms". This expression would have meant that the nuncio would be able to wield his powers in all the regions around the above-mentioned kingdoms, which – to go to the extreme – would include enormously large parts of Europe. There are, however, no traces of the legate using his powers in such a way and in all probability the legates and nuncios did not use their faculties in this manner. The case of Cardinal Tommaso De Vio, mentioned two paragraphs above, reveals another modification of the extensions of the legatine province stating that the powers stretch to "other whatsoever places where we would happen to divert". This would mean an even larger province: basically, all the places of Latin Christendom where the legitimacy

165. Prímási és főkáptalani levéltár Esztergom, sign. Eccl. Vetus., 81 sz. (24 Apr 1524), "ad Hungarie Bohemie et Dacie regna necnon Prussiam Russiam Livoniam Lithuaniam Valachiam Slesiam Lusatiam Moraviam Transsilvaniam Sclavoniam Croatiam Dalmatiam et Moscoviam omnesque et singulas illarum et regnorum predictorum provincias civitates terras atque loca illis subiecta et alia eis adiacentia necnon universam Germaniam et ad alia loca ad que nos declinare contigerit apostolice sedis legatus de latere"; MNL Budapest, OL DL 23922 (13 Apr 1524), "ad Hungarie Bohemie et Polonie regna necnon universam Germaniam ac alia quecumque loca ad que nos declinare contigerit sedis apostolice legatus de latere"; or even shorter in MNL Budapest, OL DL 25312 (5 Sep 1523), "ad Hungarię Bohemię et Polonię regna sedis apostolicę legatus de latere".

166. ASV, Reg. Vat. 734, fol. 235r (all 1 Sep 1488), "ad regnum Ungarie cum plena potestate legati de latere nostro et apostolice sedis nuntio oratori…"; fol. 229v, "ad nonnulas Ungarie et Boemie partes nostro necnon sedis apostolice oratori et nuntio cum potestate legati de latere…"; fol. 239v, "ad nonnullas Germanie Ungarie Polonie et Bohemie ac alias illis adiacentes partes atque regna nostro necnon sancte sedis apostolice nuntio et oratori cum potestate legati de latere"; the longer definition also in the general recommendation letter, fol. 231rv.

of the Pope was acknowledged, if the legate wanted to travel. This alteration is not attested to in contemporary sources as being utilised by the legates and is not mentioned outside the titulatures or used as a basis for legitimising the power of a legate outside the primarily assigned province. Cardinal Ausias Despuig (De Podio), on legation in Germany in 1479, had a special faculty, which enabled him to use all his faculties that were linked to his province after he reached twenty-five miles beyond the limits of the City of Rome. This was a modification of the extensions of Angelo Pecchinoli and Tommaso De Vio, but with a strict limitation in terms of where he could start wandering to whatever places he wanted. When he returned he could use his faculties up to this limit once again.[167] Cardinal Giovanni d'Aragona had a similar faculty, with which Pope Sixtus IV allowed him to use all his faculties in lands adjacent to his province, in places he would pass through and for people who would come from whatever place.[168] Moreover, the legate received an almost identical faculty as Cardinal Ausias that he could start his legation twenty miles outside Rome, where all his faculties became effective.[169] The actual usage of the faculties outside the legate's province is not known once

167. ASV, Reg. Vat. 680, fol. 153r (7 May 1479), "... Nos igitur cupientes, ut eo plenius universis ad te confluentibus in eorum oportunitatibus valeas subvenire tibi, ut extra limites tue legacionis huiusmodi per quascunque provincias et dominia quecunque ac illis adiacencia oppida, civitates, terras et loca, ad quas et que te declinare contigerit per tuum a Romana curia gressum et reditum ad urbem demptis viginti quinque miliaribus a dicta urbe distantibus, quo ad personas in illis comprehensas legacionis de latere fungaris officio et premissis valeas tibi concessis facultatibus, uti quamdiu te ibidem contigerit permanere ac si dominiorum et provinciarum eorundem legatus cum predictis facultatibus deputatus fores, auctoritate apostolica tenore presencium concedimus facultatem".

168. ASV, Reg. Vat. 680, fol. 185v (1 Jun 1479), "... apostolica auctoritate concedimus, quod postquam de curia predicta exiveris etiam antequam dicta regna civitates terras et loca circumiacencia et alias partes huiusmodi ingrediaris in omnibus et singulis tibi tam prefate legacionis, quam per quavis alias literas nostras concessas facultatibus in commissis negociis ... tibi perpetuata potestas et iurisdictio attributa in eo vigore eaque firmitate possis in premissis omnibus et singulis etiam cum personis undecumque venientibus per predictis procedere ac si infra regna et terras ac loca existeres antedicta et similiter in eisdem regnis civitatibus et locis cum quibuscumque personis undecumque venientibus, ut prefertur, decernentes omnes et singulas tibi per nos concessas facultates et legacionis auctoritatem non solum ad expressa regna provincias civitates et terras, sed ad omnia loca circumvicina et per que te transire seu in quibus moram facere contigerit se extendere et extendi debere".

169. ASV, Reg. Vat. 680, fol. 201rv (1 Jun 1479), "... apostolica auctoritate concedimus, quod postquam de curia predicta per viginti miliaria exiveris etiam antequam dicta regna civitates terras et loca circumvicina et alias partes huiusmodi ingrediaris in omnibus et singulis tibi tam prefate legacionis, quam per quasvis alias litteras nostras concessas facultatibus in commissis negociis sit tibi perpetuata potestas et iurisdictio attributa in eo vigore, eaque firmitate possis in premissis omnibus et singulis eciam cum personis undecumque venientibus in predictis aut quibuscumque et quomodocumque petentibus pro se vel aliis procedere, ac si infra regna et terras ac loca existeres antedicta et similiter in eisdem regnis civitatibus et locis cum quibuscumque personis undecumque venientibus, ut prefertur, decernemus omnes et singulas tibi per nos concessas facultates et legacionis auctoritatem non solum ad expressa regna provincias civitates et terras, sed eciam ad omnia loca circumvicina et per que te transire seu in quibus moram facere contigerit eundo et redeundo se extendere et extendi debere".

again, but these modifications greatly enhanced the powers of the legates and enabled them to use the faculties wherever they went, possibly even in their own dioceses, which would mean they could benefit from the legations at home.

This is not entirely impossible, as the authority of the legates could have been officially extended to their home dioceses. The case of Cardinal Marco Barbo illustrates this. The legate's province was not extended only as far as the Scandinavian kingdoms, but as the Patriarch of Aquileia he received further faculties which enabled him to utilise the powers of legate *de latere* and all his faculties in his own diocese. The legatine province was thus further enlarged with one adjacent metropolitan province.[170] The cathedral of Aquileia was even provided with indulgences for all who would visit the church on Easter Thursday and Sunday.[171] The legatine province could have been extended to places the legate did not go to or even did not have a chance to go to. The provinces which included the Kingdom of Hungary were sometimes extended to the originally Christian areas which were now ruled by the Ottoman Turks (as in the case of Cardinal Juan Carvajal during his second legation or nuncio Girolamo Lando),[172] or close to the areas occupied by the Ottomans.[173]

The legatine province could be defined not only in geographical terms, but by the the limits of the worldly rule of a single ruler, in late medieval Central Europe this being, for example, the King of Hungary and Bohemia Matthias Corvinus in the case of the legates Gabriele Rangoni[174] or Giovanni d'Aragona.[175] The extent of the

170. ASV, Reg. Vat. 680, fol. 61v-62r (18 Feb 1472), "Nos volentes te, qui grato animo ac cum magnis cordis affectibus iniunctum onus suscepisti, speciali honore ac favoris gratia attollere circumspectioni tue, ut tam in ecclesia Aquilegiensi cum ex concessione et dispensatione sedis apostolice preesse dignosceris, quam per totam civitatem et diocesim Aquilegiensem huiusmodi videlicet eundo, stando et reddendo, ut prefertur tam officio legati de latere, quam omnibus et singulis facultatibus et indultis tibi sub quavis verborum forma occasione legationis huiusmodi concessis et forsitam concedendis uti et fungi libere et licite valeas in omnibus et per omnia, ac si legatio et facultates predicte ad ecclesiam civitatem Aquilegiensem diocesim huiusmodi se extenderent tuque tunc infra nationem Alamanie civitates et loca predicta constitutus fores, auctoritate apostolica tenore presentium plenam et liberam facultatem elargimus et etiam potestatem".

171. ASV, Reg. Vat. 680, fol. 86rv (29 Aug 1472).

172. For Juan Carvajal, e.g. MNL Budapest, OL DL 14492 (29 May 1456), "per Germaniam Hungariam regna et terras Turchis subiectas et illis finitimas apostolice sedis de latere legatus specialiter deputatus"; for Girolamo Lando, e.g. MNL Budapest, OL DL 16177 (12 Mar 1465), "sanctissimi in Christo patris et domini nostri domini Pauli divina providencia pape secundi dicteque [apostolice] sedis in regno Hungarie ac membris eius inque locis et terris Turchis subiectis cum potestate legati de latere legatus".

173. ASV, Arm. XXXIX 7, fol. 113v (28 Jul 1457; Theiner, ed., *Vetera monumenta Hungariae*, vol. 2, p. 298, no. 467), "per loca omnia regnorum Hungarie et Bosne ac Servie et in quibuscumque aliis terris et locis christianorum Turchis vicinorum ...".

174. E.g. MNL Budapest, OL DL 17835 (18 Jul 1476), "apostolice sedis cum plenitudine potestatis legati de latere in regnis Hungarie et Bohemie ac omnibus terris in locis temporali dominio serenissimi principis domini Mathie regis Hungarie Bohemie etc. subiectis legatus etc."; also, DL 18073 (24 Jul 1478), DL 18295 (10 Dec 1479).

175. E.g. MNL Budapest, OL DL 18975 (18 Jun 1484), "ad regnum Hungarie et ad omnes alias et singulas provintias, civitates, terras et loca serenissimo principi et domino Mathie Hungarie Bohemieque etc. regi subiecta apostolice sedis legatus"; also, DL 18972 (11

legatine province thus could have been unstable, just as the worldly government of a ruler continually changed based on the successes or losses of his external policy. The government of Matthias Corvinus extended to the Kingdom of Hungary and as of 1469 to the Kingdom of Bohemia (elected by the Catholic estates) and Austria during the 1480s (as Duke of Austria as of 1487).[176] Did the extent of the legation also change and grow? This is highly probable, although no discussion on this topic or any source that would elucidate the situation is known to me.

Legates visited individual provinces according to the needs of the papacy. Permanent representatives were still very rare in the fifteenth and early sixteenth centuries (certain instances which were mentioned previously in chapter one may be considered more or less permanent) and thus the legates were sent with individual tasks to individual provinces. Some exceptions may be the above-mentioned multiple creations, when most of Latin Europe was to be addressed by papal legates with the task of organising a crusade. These cases as well as all the above-mentioned examples clearly indicate that the legatine provinces were never stable and could change a great deal, while in contrast certain areas of the western, eastern and central parts of Western Christendom were usually combined.

The province was made for the legate and, one might argue, the province made the legate. Although this statement might seem somewhat problematic, it holds as valid, as in general, the presence or absence in his province defined the powers of the legate. They varied in the periods before the legate entered his province, after he entered and was present in his province, and after he left with no intention of coming back. Canon law strictly defined these situations and one may find various reasonings in the *Liber extra* and the works of decretalists as Robert C. Figueira has shown in his study, where he organised and commented on their ideas and opinions. The commentaries were based on canon and Roman law that defined the office and jurisdiction in general, as the limitations of the legatine powers in relation to the province related mostly to jurisdiction and the legates' judicial authority.[177]

According to the papal ceremonial, which will be dealt with later, the legate assumed some of his authority immediately after he left the territory of Rome (or in general the diocese where the Pope resided): he could assume the papal garment (red mantle and biretta), he could bless the people and have a cross carried in front of him. Apart from these, after leaving Rome the legate, had (in the terminology of Roman law) *iurisdictio voluntaria*, which in practice meant that he could preach, or absolve "a certain type of excommunicate" (some decretalists would claim it was the excommunicated for violence against the clergy; Guillaume Durand registered the powers of the legate to absolve those excommunicated *ipso facto*, i.e. with the illegal act itself). The legate, moreover, had the right to exercise this authority over all Christendom and not only among the inhabitants of his particular province.[178]

Jun 1484); elsewhere he is named as "sancte sedis apostolice legatus ad regnum Vngarie et partes eiusdem dependentes a latere electus confirmatus et missus", Fuchs, ed., *Urkunden und Regesten*, p. 215, no. 1994 (23 Nov 1483).

176. Kubinyi, *Matthias Rex*, passim; Kalous, *Matyáš Korvín*, passim.

177. Figueira, "The Medieval Papal Legate", with the list of main points on pp. 101-103.

178. *Ibid.*, pp. 78-80, 101-102.

Additional types of jurisdictions could only be started after the legate entered his province. Entering the province did not mean merely arriving or coming to the province itself. The legate had to be ceremonially accepted by the clergy and received by the local bishop and the landlord. He assumed all the powers linked to his legation in general as well as specifically with his mandates. The ceremonial and the authority will be addressed later. The entry was, however, a legal act that changed the authority of the legate and had to be publicly proclaimed, so that it was known and acknowledged by all. According to Guillaume Durand, the legate should first send a notification of his coming, just like Christ had a messenger in St John the Baptist, and then humbly enter the province on a donkey as Christ entered Jerusalem.[179]

The discussion of canonists was also related to the question of travelling and leaving the province. If the legate publicly entered the province and assumed his jurisdiction and authority, in what way did the authority change when he was not present in the province? What was the authority of the legate after he left the province for good with no intention of coming back? These are questions that the canonists tried to solve in relation to the decretals of *Liber extra* within the chapter on the legate *Novit ille* (X 1.30.7) and *Excommunicatis* (X 1.30.9).[180] The discussion "ranged through legatine activities such as pre-arrival and post-departure jurisdiction, interdict, subdelegation of cases, conferral of benefices, excommunication and absolution;" the legatine provincial jurisdiction was commented on as well as minute details concerning the validity of legatine decisions after the legation ended.[181] Guillaume Durand summarised all the material of earlier decretalists in his *Speculum iuris.* When the legate left the province he still held the jurisdiction, but could not exercise it; if he came back shortly after, he could regain the exercise, but if he had no intention of returning he lost the jurisdiction. The jurisdiction and authority of the legate belonged to the entire legatine province, which meant that he could freely move between the metropolitan provinces of his legatine province and retain jurisdiction in all of them. Durand, as other decretalists, went into such details as discussing the legitimacy, authority and jurisdiction of the legate *de latere*, if he intended to leave aboard a ship, but was blown back to the port by adverse winds. He could retain his jurisdiction, if it happened quickly after the intended departure, or if those who exercised jurisdiction in the province (a lesser legate is discussed) after his departure willingly conceded it to him.[182] All the above-mentioned matters were also treated by the later canonists without all that many changes. Pietro Andrea Gambaro, Jean Bruneau and Gonzalo García de Villadiego discussed these matters in detail, but mostly followed earlier canonists including Guillaume Durand.[183]

179. *Ibid.*, p. 99.
180. *Ibid.*, pp. 80-95.
181. *Ibid.*, pp. 95-96.
182. *Ibid.*, pp. 98-101.
183. *Tractatus universi iuris*, vol. 13/2, fol. 151v-154r, 230v-258r (passim, conclusiones IX, X, XI, XVI, XXV, XXVI), 258r-282v (passim).

This debate necessarily leads to the question of ending a legation. How could a legation come to an end? A legation in general entailed various stages: the legate was created in Rome in a consistory, started his legation at the gates of the City and took full possession of his legatine province only after he ceremonially and publicly entered. One had to proceed in a similar fashion when the legation ended. From the point of view of the province, the legation was finished after the legate left with no intention of returning and from the point of view of the legate, ended upon returning back to Rome and being received by the College of Cardinals and by the Pope, when the legate gave a report of his deeds.

The legation ended for the province when the legate left, even though the subdelegated cases could still be judged with the original authority of the legate. Leaving the province was final, unless in special cases (like leaving the province aboard a ship and being blown back) or in cases where special faculties and indults changed the situation. These can be shown in practice. As has been discussed there were indults that allowed the legates to utilise their faculties and other powers outside their legatine provinces. Cardinal Giovanni d'Aragona, in addition, received a faculty during his first legation to Hungary, Bohemia and Poland in 1479-1480 to leave and re-enter his province without losing his authority.[184] This power to leave and re-enter the province could even be given to a simple nuncio, as in the case of Francesco Petrucci, a nuncio to France in 1478, whose commission was extended to Germany, in particular the Swiss Confederation in 1479.[185]

Since the legate was sent to his province from Rome and eventually returned back to Rome, there was usually no need to use any temporal limitations. The mission typically lasted during the legate's stay in his province and ended with his departure or in some other manner that would have to be defined in the bull of legation or other faculties that could modify the normal procedure. Occasionally, the legation could be restricted to a certain period of time as the canonists were also defined. Canonists would present various manners of ending the legation. According to Bernard of Pavia, they were as follows: 1. lapse of the date, if the legation was granted for a certain period of time; 2. recalling of the legate; 3. death of one or the other, i.e. the legate or the Pope, regardless of whether the legation had begun or not.[186] Guillaume Durand listed four possible ways of ending the legation: 1. lapse of the time the legation was granted to; 2. recalling, i.e. the legate was recalled or left his province because of some other reason and

184. ASV, Reg. Vat. 680, fol. 185r (1 Jun 1479), "... Nos attendentes, quod forsan pro expeditione negociorum eorundem vel alias nonnunquam te continget limites tuę legacionis huiusmodi, postquam illos intraveris, exire et propterea ipsa tua legatio finiri videatur, et premisse providere volentes, volumus et tibi auctoritate apostolica tenore presencium concedimus pariter et decernimus, quod liceat tibi limites dictę legationis postquam illos intraveris, ut prefertur, quotiens tibi placuerit exire. Et nihilominus possis illos reintrare et officium legacionis huiusmodi cum omnibus et singulis commissionibus et facultatibus generalibus et specialibus per nos tibi quomodolibet concessis et concedendis in illis partibus exercere".

185. ASV, Reg. Vat. 679, fol. 173r.

186. *Bernardi Papiensis Summa*, p. 18, "Durat quamdiu placet mittenti; finitur vel elapso termino, si est ad terminum data legatio, vel revocatione secuta, vel alterutrius morte interveniente, sive coepta fuerit legatio sive nondum coepta".

did not return (a detailed discussion of the conditions of regaining jurisdiction follows); 3. fulfilling the task the legate was assigned by the Papal Curia; 4. death of the legate or the one who sent him, unless the legate had begun to exercise the jurisdiction in lawsuits.[187] Typically for canon law, opinions in these matters varied. The death of the Pope did not have to bring about the end of the legation: one of the decretals of Pope Clement IV, which entered *Liber sextus* as chapter two of the title *De officio legati*, stated clearly that the legate had ordinary jurisdiction in his province and thus his legation could not end with the death of the Pope.[188] Gonzalo García de Villadiego dedicated a good part of his treatise to the end of a legation, but again recounted what appeared in the earlier commentaries on canon law. He added that *sede vacante* the cardinals could not revoke a legate and concluded with stating that a legate did not have a successor, which clearly confirms that even though the legation might be regarded as an office, a special nomination was needed for each and every legate.[189]

Ending the legation in practice to some extent followed the claims of canon law. Even though temporal limitations to the legations were rare, they can be found among the legates of the fifteenth and early sixteenth centuries. Cardinal and Archbishop of Esztergom Tamás Bakóc was sent, for example, to Hungary, Bohemia and Poland in 1513 and had his legation officially prolonged in 1518 by one more year after the original deadline (which, however, was not specified).[190] Generally, which is not surprising, legates ended their legations by leaving the province, following the basic

187. Durantis, *Speculum iudiciale*, p. 56, rubr. *De legato*, §8, "Finitur autem legati iurisdictio quatuor modis principaliter. Primo tempore, quando videlicet ad tempus datus est. ... Secundo revocatione, ex quo videlicet revocatus, vel alio modo provinciam egreditur non reversus. ... et tunc finitur legatio quoad se, sed non iurisdictio in causis coeptis per alios, quibus eas delegavit: et intellige causas coeptas esse per solum citationis edictum ... Causas autem incho[a]tas per se, vel per auditores curiae suae perficere nequit, postquam revocatus vel egressus est: cum desinat esse legatus, et factus sit privatus. ... quod etiam egressus retinet iurisdictionem, licet eam exercere non possit. ... sed si egreditur: ut statim revertatur, iurisdictio intermittitur, non finitur. Et secundum hoc intellige. ... Nec enim videtur egressus, qui statim reversurus est. ... Superflua ergo videtur indulgentia, quam quidam legati obtinent: ut si contigerit eos propter aliquam causam exire provinciam suam, reversi ad illam possint hoc non obstante legationis officium exercere. ... Sed si vocatus a principe exierit, non debet absque speciali mandato redire. Quid ergo si legatus revocatus forte, vel ob aliam causam, provinciam egreditur animo non redeundi: sed audita morte papę potius vult in loco pascuae manere, quam ad sedem apostolicam redire: nunquid poterit ad provinciam redire et ibi legationis officium reassumere? Responsio patet ex praemissis, quod non: nam egrediendo illam animo non redeundi, privatus est dignitate et exercitio iurisdicionis. ... Tertio, ex quo aliquod negotium retulit ad apostolicam sedem, quoad illud negotium eius iurisdictio est finita ... Quarto, morte ipsius legati, vel illius, qui eum misit: et hoc quando personalis est legatio, secundum dominum meum extra de pręsumpta mandata. non tamen, quoad causas coeptas ... quia quoad illas remanet legatio, non obstante morte mittentis. si autem ratione dignitatis competit legatio, tunc morte alterius non expirat".

188. VI 1.15.2 (Friedberg, ed., *Corpus*, pt. 2, col. 984).

189. *Tractatus universi iuris*, vol. 13/2, fol. 278rv.

190. ASV, Arch. Concist., Acta Vicecanc. 2, fol. 80v (14 Jun 1518), "Prorogavit legationem in regno Ungarię reverendissimo domino Tho[mae]. tt. sancti Martini in Montibus presbitero cardinali Strigoniensi ad annum post finitum tempus, pro ut erat ante".

disposition of canon law. Recalling a legate was not so common; usually the legates fulfilled their tasks and returned. Cardinal Marco Barbo was called back several times in letters from Cardinal Giacomo Ammannati Piccolomini, but these were in no way binding as Cardinal Ammannati did not possess any official authority to call the legate back.[191] A case of a legate, who was recalled by the Pope, was Cardinal Raymund Peraudi. The Pope himself called him back through the nuncio Mariano Bartolini, who was sent to the King of the Romans in 1504. His instructions stated that he should strongly encourage the legate to return to Rome. Raymund Peraudi was a legate in 1500-1504 during the pontificate of three different popes, so not even the rule that the legate should go back applied.[192] When he did not want to obey, Peraudi was even approached as an ordinary cardinal and not a legate.[193] Interestingly enough, some thirteen years earlier, Peraudi wrote to Pope Innocent VIII in 1491 that he would come when called back "so that it is not spoken about me as about the late bishop of Forlì [Alexander Numai], who, when he was often called back by the late Sixtus, refused to come as it pleased to the Emperor".[194]

A legate (or a nuncio *cum potestate legati de latere*) could be recalled by a single brief. The case of the papal nuncio Bartolomeo Maraschi from January 1485 reveals, however, that although his legation began with the previous pontiff, he was called back by Pope Innocent VIII.[195] As mentioned above, recalling the nuncio was not final and his legation was probably prolonged as were the concessions of the nuncio in November 1485 by the Pope.[196]

As stipulated by canon law as well as common sense, the legation ended with the death of the legate, if it occured during the legation itself. The papal nuncio Alexander Numai of Forlì died in August 1483 while on mission in Austria. He was actually a resident envoy at the imperial court and had stayed there for a prolonged period of time. As he did not travel around with a retinue, which would typically be the case of legates who were sent from Rome to complete a task and govern the province, the Pope sent another nuncio to bring his belongings back to Rome. Two years after his death, the papal nuncio Benedetto Mansella was dispatched from Rome with the task of bringing back money and other things.[197] It might be a coincidence, or maybe the reason behind Benedetto's mission, when

191. Ammannati Piccolomini, *Lettere*, vol. 3, pp. 1577 (28 Jul 1472), 1805-1806 (14 Mar 1474).

192. ASV, Misc., Arm. II. 30, fol. 176v (22 Feb 1504), "Si vero dilectum filium nostrum Raymundum tituli sancti Vitalis presbiterum cardinalem Gurgensem in curia regis Romanorum nactus fueris, aut in aliquo loco in Germania, ubi aliquid rebus nostris possit prodesse, hortaberis nomine nostro, ut pro sui cardinalatus officio proque sua laudabili consuetudine causae sanctae Romanae ecclesiae tam insigni iniuria a Venetis, ut supra demonstravimus, ut ipse suis affectae ubicunque opus erit faveat; et tam apud ipsum Romanorum regem, quam apud alios, faveat; et ad suscipiendam eius protectionem inducat. Hortaberis etiam, ut ad nos redire festinet, qui magno desiderio tenemur eum videndi atque amplectendi".

193. BAV, Vat. lat. 4739, fol. 27r-28v. See also the § 3.1. in the following chapter.

194. BMV, sign. Lat. X 178 (=3625), fol. 173v.

195. ASV, Arm. XXXIX 18, fol. 91r (3 Jan 1485).

196. ASV, Arm. XXXIX 19, fol. 18rv (29 Sep 1485).

197. ASV, Arm. XXXIX 18, fol. 228rv (5 Aug 1485) (Theiner, ed., *Vetera monumenta Hungariae*, vol. 2, p. 505, no. 694, 695).

in the spring of that year the Emperor allowed the Viennese burghers to use the silver of the nuncio's legacy (only the tableware, not jewels) for minting coins to pay the garrison that protected the city.[198] A similar situation arose with the death of Cardinal Raymund Peraudi. Although he died in Rome, some money was left behind in Germany that belonged to the Papal Chamber. The Papal collector Günther von Bünau was commissioned to bring the money back to Rome and allowed to use the accounts of the legate.[199] Thus, even if the legate did not die in his province, but right after his return to Rome, his passing away might have resulted in certain troubles in finalising the legation.

What was not discussed by the canonists was the rare situation, when the legate himself wanted to end his legation. There was no official legal procedure, so the legate naturally merely asked the Pope for permission to leave the province prior to having completed his task. This was not a purely hypothetical matter. For example, Cardinal Bessarion, whose legation to Germany (namely to the imperial court in Vienna) in 1460 dealt mostly with political matters, requested such permission from Pope Pius II. Problems in politics and diplomacy, an inability to negotiate with the Electors of the Empire and the fact that his undiplomatic behaviour provoked such an open protest in the imperial diet led him to his request. Pius II, however, after discussing the matter with the cardinals did not grant the permission and Cardinal Bessarion had to stay in Vienna for almost one more year.[200] Cardinal Bernardino Lopez de Carvajal, legate *de latere* to the King of the Romans/elected Emperor, requested permission to return to Rome, which was granted by Pope Julius II, even if the Pope expressly mentioned that the legate's task – peace among Christian princes and using their forces against the Ottoman Turks – was supposed to be completed. "But as there was no lack of effort on your and on our side and because of the truce, we permit you to come back to us," the Pope concluded in his brief.[201] Thus, even if the task was not completed, the decision concerning the legation was in the hands of the Pope and the Papal Curia.

198. Opll and Perger, eds., *Kaiser Friedrich III*, p. 84, no. 215 (26 Mar 1485).

199. ASV, Arm. XXXIX 22, fol. 509rv (23 May 1506), 542v-543v (4 Aug 1506).

200. Mohler, *Kardinal Bessarion*, vol. 1, pp. 302-303; Enepekides, "Die Wiener Legation", pp. 76-80; Smołucha, *Polityka kurii rzymskiej*, pp. 212-215.

201. ASV, Arm. XXXIX 28, fol. 403v (5 Jul 1508), "Cardinali sancte Crucis. Venerabilis frater salutem et apostolicam benedictionem. Ex litteris circumspectionis tue tuorumque relatione cognovimus desiderium tuum ad nos redeundi. Vellemus ea perficere potuisses, quorum causa missus fueras, ut reconsiliatis videlicet principibus christianis inter se dissidentibus, bellum in perfidos Turchos christianam rem publicam labefactantes converteretur, sed quoniam nec nostrum, nec tuum studium defuit et iam arma utrinque per inducias deposita sunt, contentamur, ut ad nos redeas. Cum bona tamen venia et licencia carissimi in Christo filii nostri Maximiliani Romanorum imperatorem semper augusti, quem in visceribus gerimus caritatis. Datum Rome die v Julii 1508 anno quinto".

3. *Modus operandi*

The theory of papal power and authority in his province and outside and the definition of the extent of the province as well as special mandates for the legation constituted essential prerequisites before a legate could set out for his legation. What did the practice of the legatine missions look like? What regulations, if any, did it follow? What standards had to be observed? How did the legates reach their provinces and when in place how did they constitute their power? These questions and many more might arise after treating the theoretical part of their office. They can only be answered with the help of normative sources as well as actual sources for individual legates and legations. Apart from the regulations on canon law, the standardized behaviour of legates was defined in handbooks or recommendations to legates as well as in practice transmitted by tradition. Instructions for individual legates might have helped as well; they were copied for other legates and shared as they might teach them to behave in the proper way for a legate as representative of the Pope who needed to respect certain rules and regulations. The practice of legation, however, is best attested to by ad hoc sources created by the legates themselves in the form of charters or letters, or by external observers, even chronicles or correspondence, private or political.

3.1. *Ceremonial*

Although papal ceremonial was basically formalized during the High Middle Ages, new trends and tendencies also appeared in the fifteenth century, specifically at the turn of the century and with the activity of papal masters of ceremonies of that period. It belonged to the sphere of ritual and liturgy, even if it regulated the extra-liturgical operation of the papal court.[1] The ceremonial contained not only principles for the actions of the Pope, but also a code of conduct for cardinals, standardized rituals for all crucial events such as their creation, acceptance to the Sacred College, accepting the red hat, etc. Since legates *de latere* could only be selected from among the cardinals, and since they were personal representatives and embodiment of the Pope, it was essential

1. Schimmelpfennig, *Die Zeremonienbücher*, pp. 132-138.

that the papal ceremonial also regulated their behaviour – as representatives of the Pope and as cardinals. Certain parts and chapters of the papal ceremonial are thus directly dedicated to cardinals and papal legates.[2]

The basic sources for the legatine ceremonial are books of papal ceremonial as well as liturgical books in general. These focus on the role and position of the Pope and cardinals during a Holy Mass as well as during other liturgical rituals, while ceremonial books deal with all the ritualistic and formal organisation of the papal court, especially concerning all events in the presence of the Pope himself. The ceremonial books take their origin from *Ordo Romanus* from the thirteenth century. For the later Middle Ages, but heavily based on the thirteenth-century sources, a series of texts entitled *Ordo Romanus XIV* (attributed most often to Cardinal Giacomo Stefaneschi)[3] is of crucial significance. There are prescriptive texts and ceremonial diaries from the second half of the fifteenth and early sixteenth centuries written by the papal masters of ceremonies (*magistri ceremoniarum*) Agostino Patrizi Piccolomini, Johannes Burckard and Paride Grassi.[4] As sources for the ceremonial one may find records of consistory diaries or similar notes from the consistory or the Curia in general such as *Acta vicecancellarii*, which are all held in the Vatican archives.[5] The behaviour of papal legates was consequently also governed by the general guidelines of diplomatic operations in the Middle Ages and the Renaissance, which were described in detail by diplomatic manuals for ambassadors of the period, substantially ritualised and had written as well as unwritten rules.[6]

The journey of a legate had the form of a ritual right from the start, when the legate was nominated, created (Latin uses the word *creare* as in the case of creating cardinals) till the end when the legate returned to Rome or to the Pope in general. He was accepted back at the Curia with the formal *aperitio oris*, the opening of the mouth, when he reported on the details of his mission in the consistory and began to participate in the revenues of the Sacred College. The entire legation had a clear framework that was given by the legate's authority and his province as well as by the ceremonies in Rome on both ends. Between these Roman ceremonies, the legate had to behave according to clear rules in his province and in a manner which was expected for a first-class representative and embodiment of the Pope.

2. On the ceremonial of legates Wasner, "Fifteenth-Century Texts"; Maleczek, "Die päpstlichen Legaten", pp. 68-82.

3. Schimmelpfennig, *Die Zeremonienbücher*; Dykmans, ed., *Le cérémonial papal*, vol. 2, pp. 133-138.

4. Dykmans, ed., *L'oeuvre de Patrizi Piccolomini*; for the overview of manuscripts see Salmon, *Les manuscrits*, vol. 3; for Grassi, most importantly Dykmans, "Paris de Grassi".

5. Eubel, *Hierarchia catholica*, vol. 2; Eubel and Schmitz-Kallenberg, *Hierarchia catholica*, vol. 3; ASV, Arm. XXXI 52; ASV, Arch. Concist, Acta Vicecanc. 1-3.

6. Mattingly, *Renaissance Diplomacy*; Queller, *The Office*; Schwinges and Wriedt, eds., *Gesandtschafts- und Botenwesen*; Zey and Märtl, eds., *Aus der Frühzeit*; Lazzarini, *Communication and Conflict*; Andretta, Péquignot and Waquet, eds., *De l'ambassadeur.* Cf. treatises in Hrabar, ed., *De legatis*; Barbaro, *De officio legati.* On rituals connected to international diplomacy and international relations in the later Middle Ages see Trexler, *Public Life*, pp. 279-330.

3.1.1. *Rome*

Rituals and ceremonies in late-medieval and Renaissance Rome developed over the period in question into a complex system. They were designed by the aforementioned papal masters of ceremonies, namely Agostino Patrizi Piccolomini, Johannes Burckard and Paride Grassi. Their handbooks defined the papal liturgy of the Roman ceremonies and their diaries described them in detail with the intention of replication, modelling or at least reference for later use. Ceremonial and related rituals should express the papal claims for the renewed secular (in Italy) and ecclesiastical (in the whole of Christendom) government. A great procession took place at the papal coronation, which itself was a large-scale pageant. After the coronation, the Pope took over the rule over Rome and progressed from St Peter's basilica to the basilica of St John in the Lateran, the Roman cathedral. The *possesso*, as the procession came to be known in 1471, was modelled after the Roman triumphs and even matrimonial festivities as the Pope celebrated his marriage with the Roman church. Another presentation of spiritual power consisted of the traditional papal benediction regularly spoken from the loggia of St Peter's basilica. Additional processions took place in Rome, important ones being especially the feasts of Corpus Christi and the Assumption of the Virgin Mary (from St Laurence to the basilica of Santa Maria Maggiore).[7] The ceremonies of cardinals in general and legates *de latere* in particular fit into the frame of such Roman festivities.

The very beginning of the legation, the naming and preparation for the journey, was also accompanied by rituals and ceremonies in Rome or in general the place where the Pope resided. The papal ceremonial of Agostino Patrizi Piccolomini provided instructions on how things should be done. In a secret meeting of the consistory, the Pope would first announce the general problems and reasons for sending a legate or legates and had the cardinals vote as to whether there was a need to dispatch legates. When they agreed, he suggested persons, cardinals, whom he wished to take that office and the tasks. These then left the consistory and the meeting continued without their personal presence. When everything was decided, they were called back in. The pontifex then praised the character of the one designated as legate, specified the individual legatine province and officially entrusted him with the office of the legation. The cardinal himself raised, expressed his thanks for the trust they all had in him, but asked the rest of the cardinals to choose a more worthy candidate. The Pope, however, was supposed to insist and the new legate accepted the assignment and expressed his thanks by kneeling down, kissing the Pope's foot and hand and being given in return a kiss on the mouth from the Pope as well as from the other cardinals. When the consistory ended, the legate was supposed

7. On the complex of Roman ceremonies, see Savettieri, "Lo spettacolo"; on *possesso* Fosi, "Court and City". See also, Stinger, *The Renaissance*; and on the context of the Renaissance City Paschini, *Roma nel Rinascimento.* On papal ceremonial books Schimmelpfennig, *Die Zeremonienbücher*; and for the later period Bölling, *Das Papstzeremoniell*, on the changes of the period esp. pp. 79-112. On legatine ceremonial of the late sixteenth century see Fosi, "'Parcere subiectis'"; and the *Tractatus de legato* of the master of ceremonies Paolo Alaleone in BAV, Vat. lat. 12285, fol. 4r-12r.

to be accompanied by the rest of the Sacred College to his home. The newly created legate rode on horseback between two cardinal deacons, who were also on horseback, at the end of the entire procession. Outside his home, he again expressed his thanks to all the cardinals, took leave from them cardinal by cardinal and began to prepare himself for his journey. During the period between his creation and his leaving Rome, the cardinal legate would visit other cardinals on an individual basis. The procedure was the same as in the case of newly created cardinals, who were to be accompanied to their homes and then expected to pay visits to other cardinals.[8] The text of *Ordo Romanus XIV* planned a meal of the legate with the Pope right after his creation; otherwise, the procedure did not contradict Patrizi Piccolomini.

Many examples of ceremonial events could be found in the consistorial diary of this period and describe the practical side of it. After the creation of legates, they were accompanied by the rest of the Sacred College to their homes. The same can be read in the diaries of Johannes Burckard and Paride Grassi. Paride Grassi used a special occasion to speak about the creation of legates. Pope Leo X created four legates to various parts of Europe on 3 March 1518. In his *Diarium*, the papal master of ceremonies described a longer discussion about the number of legates and why there was no legate sent to Hungary.[9] What is of importance here, however, is his description of the procedure by which they were created. As Grassi stated, many people argued that the legates should have been accompanied to their homes by the remaining cardinals in the order of the significance of their destination – first to the Emperor, followed by the one to the King of France, the King of Spain and finally to the King of England. It was instead performed in the traditional way of convenience concerning the journey through the streets of Rome, including the first visit to a cardinal who stayed in the palace.[10] The preparations for the legation meant not only visits to the houses of other cardinals, but also real and practical preparations for the journey and the travels, organisation of the retinue, securing the running of the household, etc. The time that elapsed between the creation and actual departure might vary and could take anything from between a few days to a few months. In 1472, for example, Cardinal Marco Barbo left two months after his creation; Cardinal Giovanni d'Aragona left nine days after his creation in 1483, but more than four months after in 1479 upon another occasion; and it took Cardinal Juan Carvajal in 1447 and Roderigo Borja

8. Dykmans, ed., *L'oeuvre de Patrizi Piccolomini*, vol. 1, pp. 156-158.

9. Cf. Kalous, "Papal Legates and Crusading Activity", pp. 83-84.

10. Grassi, *Diarium*, p. 404, "… et ducti sunt a collegio, ut moris est. Nam primo in palatio ad cameras suas ductus est cardinalis sanctae Mariae in Porticu, … istos legatos esse debere in ordine legationum, et non in ordine episcoporum cardinalium, scilicet ut primo et primus esset, qui iret ad imperatorem, secundus, qui iret ad regem Francie, tertius, qui iret ad regem Hispanie, ultimus, qui iret ad regem Anglie, habita ratione legationum, ad quas proficiscebantur, et non habita ordinis ipsorum ratione. Tamen ego non volui nisi respicere ad ordinem, quo ipsi cardinales sedent, et sic fuit bene factum. Ducti autem fuere ad aedes juxta commoditatem ipsarum aedium. Primo enim Sanctae Mariae in Porticu in Palatio, deinde Faranesius, tum Campeggius, ultimo Aegidius; alia ut alias".

in 1472 almost six months to leave after they were created legates to Germany, Bohemia and Hungary and Spain and Portugal respectively.

Additional ceremonies and rituals took place in the city on the day of the legate's departure. The legate took leave from the Pope in another secret consistory. In his ceremonial, Agostino Patrizi Piccolomini described the ideal departure of a legate. After the secret consistory, the legate was led by all the cardinals beyond the gates of the city, where he would thank them all and they would return to their homes. The significance of the gates consisted of the fact that the legate could make use of his general legatine powers upon leaving the "territory of the city where the Pope resided". He could grant blessings, he could wear the papal colours and carry a cross in front of his procession. These were the consequences of the legation itself; the cardinal legate, moreover, ceased to participate in the benefits and income of the College of Cardinals.[11] In *Ordo Romanus XIV*, the cardinals waited for the legate outside the city and took their leave of him.[12] As the ceremonies could take more time at the Curia and the procession itself also lasted longer, it was not untypical for the legates to take leave of the cardinals at the gate, but remain overnight at Santa Maria del Popolo, as attested, for example, in the cases of Cardinals Marco Barbo, Giovanni d'Aragona and Bernardin Carvajal. Bernardin's departure and the entire legation were described in detail by Johannes Burckard: Bernardin himself had dinner at the monastery of the church of Santa Maria del Popolo and slept in the hospital of St James, situated between the present-day streets Via del Corso and Via di Ripetta, i.e. still in Rome itself.[13] The legates who travelled to the north, i.e. most of the legates dispatched to the rest of Europe, left Rome at the Porta del Popolo, which became ceremonially the most significant gate into the City, and thus one of the few which were refurbished in the Early-Modern period. The road leading towards the gate from the direction of the papal palace was also constructed at the start of the sixteenth century into a modern, straight street fit for ceremonial traffic: Via di Ripetta was reconstructed by Pope Leo X during his pontificate and renamed Via Leonina.[14]

To employ the same example, Paride Grassi wrote about the departure of the legates in 1518. Cardinal Alessandro Farnese was sent to the Emperor and although his legation did not take place, as he later became ill, he left Rome in

11. Dykmans, ed., *L'oeuvre de Patrizi Piccolomini*, vol. 1, pp. 157-158, "Adveniente die profectionis, fit secretum consistorium, et in fine exiens a <latere> pontificis deducitur ab omnibus cardinalibus, ordine predicto, usque extra portam civitatis. Et ibi postquam egit gratias et osculatus est omnes cardinales, proficiscitur in pace. Alii autem revertuntur ad domos suas. Cardinalis legatus, postquam exivit territorium civitatis ubi pontifex residet, incipit benedicere, capit mantum rubeum et prefertur ante eum crux. Et dum est in legatione non participat de emolumentis camere apostolice sive annatarum".

12. Dykmans, ed., *Le cérémonial papal*, vol. 2, p. 498, "Sed in die recessus ipsius, omnes cardinales debet extra villam ipsum in convenienti campo expectare, et ibi recipere commeatum ab eo, facto primitus osculo, depositis capello et birreto per eosdem".

13. Eubel, *Hierarchia catholica*, vol. 2, p. 42, no. 411 (Giovanni d'Aragona); Celani, ed., *Johannis Burckardi Liber*, vol. 1, p. 615, the whole legation on pp. 615-658.

14. Gualandi, "'Roma resurgens'", pp. 143-144.

a ceremonial way accompanied by the entire College of Cardinals.[15] The three other legates left together. They were accompanied, as was the usual fashion, by the College, but only to the bend of the street *de populo*, which was even called *diversorium solitum.* This means they were not accompanied to the gates, which might be considered an innovation.[16] Similarly, Cardinal Farnese's replacement, Cardinal Tommaso De Vio left the palace towards Porta del Popolo, but was only accompanied to the same place.[17]

The place located at the middle of the journey between the papal palace and the gate that led to the north of Rome, *Porta del Popolo*, was becoming popular in the early sixteenth century for a number of reasons. There could have been legal and traditional reasons involved, but also reasons of convenience in terms of the space and suitability of the street. This was first mentioned in the awkward case of a legate who was supposed to go to Perugia. He was, however, not a full legate *de latere* with all the relevant powers, because he represented the Pope in the lands of the Church. Paride Grassi attempted to demonstrate in a discussion with the legate, as well as with Pope Julius II, that the legate could not leave the city in the ceremonial way of the legates *de latere* proper, who represented the Pope outside Italy. Cardinal Antonio Ferrero was created a legate *de latere* for Perugia in January 1506, and was to leave Rome on 27 April 1506. Grassi reported a heated discussion, in which the reader learns that the legate had already spread the word that he was going to leave the City in the most ceremonious way. He provided examples from the history of legates to Perugia who were accompanied by the College of Cardinals, which was rejected by Grassi, who stated that it was on other occasions, when the cardinals, once legates to Perugia, were sent to some other destination. They agreed on a compromise, which would entail that the cardinals would accompany the legate up to the Church of St Ivo dei Bretoni, which is roughly in the middle between the palace and the gate.[18] It is true that Paride Grassi was right when he rejected the argument that legates to Perugia were accompanied by the College. However, there was a case – which was not part of the argumentation – when a legate to Perugia was accompanied by the cardinals. Cardinals Latino Orsini and Richard Olivier de Longueil were named legates to the Marches and to Perugia respectively in 1464. They were accompanied by the College of Cardinals from the Curia, which then resided at St Mark's, to the *Porta del Popolo.*[19] Such a compromise for legal reasons

15. Grassi, *Diarium*, p. 405, "… ductus a collegio ad portam, quae est ante Turrionem plateae sancti Petri, ubi extra eam cardinalis legatus osculatus est omnes et singulos cardinales, et sic vale dicto abiit versus Crucem Montis Marii. Alia ut alias".

16. *Ibid.*, p. 408, "In fine consistorii hi tres legati, genu flexi fuerunt cum lectione solita per papam licentiati, et a collegio ducti ad diversorium solitum circa angulum viae de populo et abierunt in nomine domini".

17. *Ibid.*, p. 411, "… denique ductus a Sacro Senatu, non per eam viam, qua fuerat cardinalis de Farnesio, id est, per portam guardiae palatii, sed usque ad aedes archiepiscopi Nicosiensis versus ad populum: nam cum usque ad eum locum etiam tres ducti simul fuissent, placuit papae et legato, ut similiter senatus eo accederet, prout fuit".

18. BAV, Vat. lat. 4739, fol. 203v-205v (ed. Kalous, "Through the Gates", pp. 42-44).

19. ASV, Arm. XXXI 52, fol. 67r (not registered by Eubel, *Hierarchia catholica*, vol. 2, p. 34), "Die Veneris XVI mensis Novembris anno a Nativitatis domini MCCCCLXIII pontificatus

might even change the structure of the departure of other legates. Grassi documented several other departures of legates who were on their way to the King of France (Gabriele de' Gabrielli) and to the Emperor (Bernardino Lopéz de Carvajal), and were only accompanied to the middle of the usual journey. This was convenient for the former, because he left Rome the following day in a boat on the river, whereas in the latter case, Grassi mentioned a heatwave, due to which they stopped earlier.[20]

When a legate returned to Rome, the situation would be comparable to his departure. He had to be accompanied by the College of Cardinals from the gates to the papal palace, from where – after being accepted in public consistory by the Pope – he would be accompanied by the cardinals to his home. *Ordo Romanus XV* defined the return of the cardinal, who should be associated by the College of Cardinals, but only if he returned from an official legation (as a legate or nuncio). If a cardinal returned due to having been away from the Curia privately, he was not supposed to have any such ceremonial entry (only perhaps when greeted by friends, etc.).[21] It is defined here in a negative manner that the legate should be accompanied by the College of Cardinals from the gates of the city. Patrizi defined the return of a legate the same as the entry of a new cardinal (who was created cardinal while outside Rome). The legate was to be met at the gate of the city and accompanied to the papal palace. It was understood that he was to be met by the other cardinals, as Patrizi refers back to the discussion of the entry of a new cardinal without a hat. They accompanied him on horseback as usual.[22] Patrizi could also draw here on the

domini Pauli anno primo reverendissimus dominus Latinus cardinalis de Ursinis in Marchia et dominus Ricardus cardinalis Constanciensis in Perusium legatos de latere a domo seu palatii sancti Marchi, ubi tunc prefatus dominus noster Paulus residentiam faciebat, post finitum consistorium discesserunt associati, ut moris est, ab aliis dominis cardinalibus usque ad portam sancte Marie de populo".

20. BAV, Vat. lat. 12273, fol. 112rv, "... Omnes cardinales intra urbe fuerunt praesentis et associarunt legatum, usque ad media via de Populo apud domo domini comitis olim de Mirandula, ut supra anno praeterito pro cardinali s. Vitalis legato Perosino factum fuit in omnibus et per omnia, nisi quod hic omnes cardinales osculatus est et in facie ille non et post omnium discessum, legatus ad domum suam per viam porticulam ante domum sericostum olim vicecancellarii reversus est, et in mane sequenti galeas porrexerit apud voltam s. Pauli in flumine existentes quisque praelatus secum duos in navium duxit, alii omnes per terram"; fol. 117v-118r, "... et ipse denique legatus fuit associatus a collegio per viam versus sanctae Mariae de Populo usque ad portam propter calores, sed usque ad domum olim comitis Antonii de Mirandula, id est in via revolutione longe sint, et ultra illam sub umbra unde abiis cum suis ad monasterium praedictum et ibi fecit prandium et in aurora sequenti arripuit iter etc.".

21. Dykmans, *Le cérémonial papal*, vol. 4, pp. 234-235, "Nota quod si cardinalis veniat, quod si fuit extra curiam per aliquod tempus pro negotiis suis, vel ratione solatii, non tamen nuntii vel legati, quando redit et intrat civitatem, ubi Romana curia residet, cardinales alii non debent ei ire obviam, sed mittunt eorum familiares ad associandum illum. Item si aliqui cardinales amore vel ex nobilitate aut consanguinitate occurrant ei obviam, si sit unus qui intrat, et alii qui ei obviant plures sint in pari numero, ille qui noviter venit solus debet precedere, et alii post eum bini et bini, deinde patriarche, deinde protonotarii et alii iuxta ordinem suum".

22. Dykmans, ed., *L'oeuvre de Patrizi Piccolomini*, vol. 1, p. 163, "Si autem novus cardinalis iam habuit capellum, sive est legatus apostolicus aliquis ille qui venit, recipitur apud portam, deducitur ad palatium, et deinde ad consistorium ad pedes pape, ut de novo cardinali sine capello diximus".

practice of the fourteenth century, as documented by *Ordo Romanus XIV*, which even prescribed that the cardinals should await the legate outside the city.[23] As in the case of departures, the consistorial diary and the diaries of Johannes Burckard and Paride Grassi contained numerous examples of legates returning to Rome. In October 1504, for example, Cardinal Raymund Peraudi returned from a legation to the King of the Romans. His return proves the practice that was mentioned above in *Ordo Romanus XV*, namely that the ceremonial entry belonged only to the legates and not to simple cardinals. The discussion concerned whether or not he should be accompanied by the cardinals when he had not shown respect for the summons of the Pope and did not behave like a proper legate. It was finally decided that he would receive the ceremonial entry.[24]

The borders of the city were crucial for legates. When they left, they became the direct representatives of the popes and upon their return, they once again began to be part of the College of Cardinals and participated in the benefits of the Sacred College. Burckard's and Grassi's examples may even illustrate what the role of the ceremonial was, and what was crucial in terms of departure or acceptance of the cardinal back to the position in Rome. Cardinal Pietro Isvalies ceremoniously left the papal palace after the secret consistory on 16 November 1500 and was accompanied by all the cardinals outside the gate San Pellegrino (*porta Viridaria*). He actually had lunch outside Rome, but secretly came back and stayed in his house for three more days. Late in the evening on 19 November he went to the papal palace with six or seven people and left after meeting with the Pope. One could conjecture that he had to remain in Rome for some additional time, as his instructions were only dated to 18 November and he could have been given them during his last visit to the Pontiff.[25] Eighteen years later, on 18 November 1518, another papal legate, Cardinal Lorenzo Campeggi, returned to Rome from his legation to England. He had to remain secretly in his home for three days before he was accepted by the College of Cardinals and led to the papal palace. To be ceremonially accepted by the Pope he had to return back to the gate in order to be met by the cardinals and accompanied to the palace. Thereafter he could visit others and begin to be a valid member of the College again.[26] This can

23. Dykmans, ed., *Le cérémonial papal*, vol. 2, pp. 498-499.

24. BAV, Vat. lat. 4739, fol. 27r-28v, "Reverendissimus dominus cardinalis Curcen. a sancte memorie Alexandro legatus ad partes Alemanie destinatus habuit in eius ad urbem regressu consistorium publicum. Licet ut dictum fuit aliqui obstiterint, ne acceptaretur in publico consistorio allegantes, primo papam, qui eum destinavit mortuum esse; secundo quod idem papa iamdiu ipsum revocaverat a legatione; tertio quod idem cardinalis sic revocatus iam amplius non se gerebat in partibus illis ut legatum, sed ut simplicem cardinalem. Et quod in veniendo usque ad urbem non ut legatus sugerens legationis munere veniebat, sed ut simplicis cardinalis. Tamen sanctissimus dominus noster Julius II. audiens in arbitrio sue sanctitatis esse eum acceptare ut legatum et non acceptare duxit ex eo, quia ipsum diligebat ut legatum acceptare. Itaque die dominico, que fuit XX mensis Octobris anno 1504".

25. Celani, ed., *Johannis Burckardi Liber*, vol. 2, p. 248.

26. Grassi, *Diarium*, p. 433, "... cardinalis de Campeggio ex sua anglicana legatione reversus, pridie aut nudius tertius, quo tempore in domibus suis secrete latuit, hodie summo mane ad sanctam Mariam de Populo, ut fieri per omnia solitum est, et ibi a collegio sacro

also be demonstrated with the example of another legate who was created together with Cardinal Campeggi. Cardinal Bernardo Dovizi da Bibbiena, who returned from the legation to the King of France before Christmas 1519, was severely reproached by Grassi for being seen and visited in the City before his official entry. He should have either stayed in secret or left the City. The consistory could only take place on 9 January of the following year, which meant his entry had to be postponed for more than two weeks.[27]

The legation ended in several stages. It first came to an end in the province once the legate left its territory. According to the *Ordo Romanus XIV*, the legate needed special permission to be able to enter Rome, however, such a practice is not attested to in the sources of the fifteenth century, although this permission definitely did not have to be in the form of a formal charter.[28] As is apparent from the previous paragraph, merely entering Rome did not end the legation itself. The cardinal legate had to be received by the Pope in the public consistory, and consequently shortly after that in a secret consistory, where the legate officially spoke about the results of the legation. The *aperitio oris*, the opening of the mouth, meant not only a report on the legation, but also the full acceptance of the cardinal into the Sacred College once again. Such an account was given in the consistory on 15 November 1474 by Cardinal Marco Barbo, after he had returned from his legation to Germany and Central and Northern Europe on 26 October.[29]

The departure and the return of a legate also had other consequences. These days belonged to times of a special mode of the Papal Curia. Like on other important feast days and celebrations, the arrival of kings or royal sons or brothers, the first arrival of a cardinal and the coronation of the Pope there was no papal audience, i.e. the central Roman tribunal, *Rota Romana*, could not hold a session. These kinds of days are listed in a contemporary inventory written by Gaspare Biondo,[30] but also attested to by the practice of the most famous medieval papal tribunal.[31] Paride Grassi, papal master of ceremonies,

receptus est, et visitatus, ac inde cum solitis ceremoniis conductus ad publicum consistorium, in quod papa venit …, ipse legatus ingressus est, et admissus a papa cum hilari facie et in fine familia legati osculata est pedem pape. Finito consistorio, collegium duxit legatum ad edes suas, ut moris est… Deinde ipse legatus visitavit papam una die et alia visitavit cardinales, incipiens a decano collegii et inde per suam commoditatem illa die et alia et postea palatinos".

27. *Ibid.*, p. 441, "… fuit consistorium publicum pro admissione reverendissimi domini cardinalis sancte Marie in Porticu, ex sua gallica legatione reversi et licet ante festa natalia fuerit in urbe, tum quia consistorium fieri non potuit, usque modo dilatum fuit. Et ipse fuit a pricipio palam et publice visus et visitatus, quod cum esset male factum, reprehendi eum et monui, ut secretius maneret, aut ex urbe recederet. Et sic fuit. Cardinales eum hodie [9 January 1520] ex monasterio de Populo confluxerunt ad palatium, ut moris est".

28. BAV, Vat. lat. 12348, fol. 105r, "Item sciendum est, quod cardinalis legatus vel nuncius non consuevit redire ad curiam Romanam, nisi prehabita super hec licencia speciali domini pape".

29. Ammannati Piccolomini, *Lettere*, vol. 3, pp. 1890-1891, no. 767.

30. Cherubini, "L'intensa attività", pp. 144-145, no. IV.32, "Die qua aliquis de dominis cardinalibus legatus vel nuntius pape de curia recedit. Die qua revertitur de legatione et intrat dictam curiam".

31. Salonen, *Papal Justice*, pp. 69-70.

who organised a number of departures of legates even remarked on 17 May 1507 that due to the departure of Cardinal Antonio Gentile Pallavicini to France he told the auditors in the morning to stop their work.[32] Seventeen years later, in 1524, unlike the habit, the auditors of the Rota held a normal session, even though Cardinal Lorenzo Campeggi ceremonially rode from the palace as a legate to Germany and Hungary, because they were not told in advance.[33] Such events were, then, not only crucial for the legate himself as he began and ended his legation with such significant and complex ceremonies, but also for the Papal Curia, which had a special routine as well as the City of Rome, which experienced yet another festivity. For the countries of destination, however, the legation only began after the legate entered the province.

3.1.2. *Outside Rome*

All that came about between the two dates of departure from and return to Rome constituted the legation itself. This was also subject to regulation of the papal masters of ceremonies, because even if the legation began with intricate rituals and ceremonies in Rome, the legate only assumed the legatine authority after leaving the City and even more so after entering his legatine province. Only then could he assume the powers entrusted to him in special mandates.

The role of the legate changed after the departure: as he left the gates of the City, he began to impersonalise the Pope. Even prior to reaching his province, he could use the symbols of papal power after leaving Rome, which means, he could have a legate's cross carried in front of him and could bless people. Moreover, apart from these papal insignia, legates were entitled to wear the papal dress, the red papal mantle and the red biretta. The colour red traditionally belonged to the Pope and the papal garment. By this time, however, it was being used for cardinals in general, in all probability since the reign of Pope Boniface VIII although the exact date cannot be ascertained.[34] As already noted by Franz Wasner, Agostino Patrizi Piccolomini was so concerned about the proper dress and formal decorum of legates that he continually tried to prohibit other cardinals from wearing red. Such a dignity, he argued, belonged only to the legates *de latere*, who travelled outside Italy, as Patrizi specified both in notes on legatine ceremonial and writings

32. BAV, Vat. lat. 12273, "Die Lunae 17 Maii [1507] fuit concistorium publicum pro recessu reverendissimi domini cardinalis s. Praxedis legati ad regem Franciae, pro qua re summo beni petii a papa an vellet, quod intimarem auditoribus rotae ut ab audientia cessarent, quod sic itaque ego auditoribus iam collectis in rota intimavi hoc ut cessarent ab audientia et similiter feci fieri per unum cubicularium clericis camere, qui etiam similiter cessarunt a camera, ut moris est".

33. BAV, Chig. L I 22, fol. 116rv, "Die Lunae prima Februarii 1524 fuit consistorium et reverendissimus dominus Laurentius Campegius legatus in Alemaniam recessit licentiatus a papa cum coeremoniis et benedictionibus solitis et associatus a collegio cardinalium usque ad domum Nicosiae apud sanctam Mariam de Populo me interveniente etc. et papa voluit, quod auditores sederent tenerent termino et expedirent causas disponendo contra stylum et fingendo, quod eis non fuisset intimatum de recesso legati".

34. Wasner, "Fifteenth-Century Texts", p. 315.

on papal ceremonial in general.[35] Papal insignia were crucial for the representation of the head of the Church as well as the presentation of the legatine authority. The splendour of the papal legates is actually attested to in sources much earlier. The Bohemian chronicler, Cosmas of Prague, for example, wrote about legate Rudolf (correctly Gregorius), who "used such authority and power as if the Pope himself was present"[36] – the first official promulgation of such a practice came with Pope Innocent III in 1215 and was incorporated into *Liber extra.* This decretal focused on the patriarchs, who were not allowed to have a cross carried in front of them in Rome or in the presence of a legate.[37] Their authority was subordinated to that of the Pope and thus also to legates. Guillaume Durand states that the legates and nuncios of the Apostolic See should be honoured as representatives of the Pope.[38] Although he mentioned legates and nuncios together, what he probably had in mind was the case – typical in the fourteenth century – when cardinals functioned as nuncios as well. The ceremonial of nuncios has not been sufficiently described as sources are to a large extent lacking. Clearly, however, nuncios who were not cardinals could not assume such a high position and dignity as cardinal legates, as they did not impersonalise the Pope.[39]

The above-mentioned texts of papal masters of ceremonies could be utilised to a great extent in order to analyse ceremonial and ritual behaviour in Rome. When leaving Rome, however, there is a lack of such clear descriptive and normative sources that would provide direct guidelines. Certain notes on legatine ceremonial could become part of general papal ceremonial, could have been given to individual legates or created for their use by the masters of ceremonies. Such prescriptive sources consequently have to be cross-checked with local narrative sources or descriptions by the legates themselves or members of their retinues.

In principle, legates were to be honoured throughout the entire journey and most importantly, when they entered their legatine province. Coming to the main city of the province did not only entail the arrival of a papal representative, but

35. *Ibid.*, pp. 330-331; see, Dykmans, ed., *L'oeuvre de Patrizi Piccolomini*, vol. 2, pp. 502-503, "Reverendissimi domini cardinales, cuiuscumque sint ordinis, utuntur semper in capella et in publico cappa ampla supra rochetum, coloris violacei, plus vel minus clari, aut obscuri indici sive aerei, et aliquando rubei, sed rarius. Nam rubeus color proprie ad papam pertinet et ad legatos qui mittuntur de latere extra Italiam vel ad aliquod magnum negotium, nam in istis casibus pontifex solebat donare legato mantum rubeum cum caputio, et in illo habitu dabat audientiam legatus in sua provincia"; about cardinals' dress most recently, Richardson, *Reclaiming Rome*, pp. 122-140; Märtl, "Zwischen Habitus und Repräsentation", with discussion on legates.

36. Bretholz, ed., *Die Chronik*, p. 125, "Quo cum pervenisset missus apostolici, invenit ducem Wratizlaum in urbe Praga, cui offerens apostolicam benedictionem et universalis patris adoptivam filiationem tanta auctoritate usus est et potestate, ac si idem summus pontifex ipse presens fuisset". Discussing the problematic name, Schumann, *Die päpstlichen Legaten*, pp. 17-22.

37. X 5.33.23; cf. Wasner, "Fifteenth-Century Texts", pp. 300-302.

38. Durantis, *Speculum iudiciale*, p. 30 (rubr. *De legato*, §1, 3), "Honorandus autem est legatus, et nuncius Apostolicae sedis, ac benigne tractandus, tanquam domini Papae uicem gerens ...".

39. Wasner, "Fifteenth-Century Texts", p. 304; Kyer, *The Papal Legate*, pp. 160-167.

also had a constitutive character. The legate entered and took possession of his province, literally taking over the authority of local bishops. Thus, the entry to the city (and thus to a province) represented the basis for the legatine authority. According to the notes of Cardinal Juan Carvajal, the legate was supposed to be honorifically received in a procession, kiss the cross which was offered to him before entering the city (some texts prefer that the legate dismount from his horse first), and be accompanied to the main church of the city (or a cathedral). Apart from blessing the people, the legate announced the indulgences he could grant. This was the basis of the ceremonial generally also shared among other authors of legatine ritual guidelines. Johannes Burckard even added that the legate could enter the city under a canopy, a baldachin, if it was available.[40]

The legatine entry to a city could resemble in some sense that of a king, who first entered the capital of a land or province.[41] Such entries were not untypical and most of the population of the city could make the comparison themselves, rather than comparing them to entries of bishops, which did not occur that often outside Italy.[42] To secure proper reception by the city and its inhabitants, including the secular and ecclesiastical powers, the legate should announce his arrival and let the city know in advance.[43] Entering the capital city of a province meant taking over the province and thus it was seen as a crucial act: even the cardinal's hat, which cardinals received in a public consistory, was to be used at this occasion, as Paride Grassi remarked in his treatise on the creation of new cardinals.[44] It is clear, however, that for a city the entry of a legate could constitute one of the greatest festivities in many years as can be seen with several examples.

Cardinal Juan Carvajal entered the city of Prague, capital of Hussite Bohemia, in 1448. After success in Vienna, Carvajal wanted to overcome the Utraquists of Bohemia and bring them to an observance of the Roman See. Even if such a situation heralded a possible conflict, the legate received a spectacular greeting according to all possible rules, as they welcomed him in a procession outside the city and brought him back to Prague under a canopy. A contemporary song even asserted that "the lords came to meet him with banners and received him under a canopy in great glory singing *Te Deum laudamus* and thanking God for sending us such a man." According to the same song, however, the baldachin was destroyed even before entering the city by a huge storm, a divine punishment for such great haughtiness, thus symbolising the outcome of the legation, as – in the words of the song – the legate rather than praising the truth began to disparage it.[45] Another report, one from the retinue of

40. Wasner, "Fifteenth-Century Texts", pp. 311, 324, 328, 330-331, 340, 344-345, 357.

41. Kipling, *Enter the King*.

42. Maciejewski, *Adventus Episcopi*; Miller, "The Florentine Bishop's Ritual Entry".

43. Wasner, "Fifteenth-Century Texts", p. 311, 331.

44. BAV, Vat. lat. 4739, fol. 148v, "... Idem capellum similiter cum suis flochis magnis portabunt intra tempus visitationis antiquorum cardinalium, sed illud postea debent servare per legationibus si quando ad illas mittentur in die ingressus civitatis principalis de suo legatione".

45. *Výbor z české literatury*, vol. 2, p. 97, "A podlé své neupřiemosti ihned nebyl bez pomsty; z božieho dopuštěnie stalo se jest povětřie, dobře hrozná búře, dřieve než do Prahy

the legate himself, merely states that he was "solemnly received" and no further details appear. Such a short note means the ritual respected traditional ways of receiving the legate into a city.[46] A description of a Prague historiographer, however, provides additional details:

> In the same year around the Ascension [2 May 1448] a legate came to Prague, cardinal *Sancti Angeli*, called Paul [*recte* John, Juan] from Rome [with the intention] of improving the state of the Kingdom of Bohemia and bringing it to proper order. And when the legate came towards Prague, they all went forth to meet him with such a solemn procession, as if accepting a new king. For in that procession pupils came from all of Prague, small and big, canons, all the doctors, masters, bachelors and students, priests, monks and all crafts from all the Prague towns under their banners left Prague; and went as far as Krč.[47] And the city councillors of the Old Town (*Staré Město*) went first under the canopy, followed by the New Town (*Nové Město*) councillors and those of the Lesser Town (*Malá Strana*) with silver sticks, as is their ancient tradition. And thus, they received him under the canopy and took him to Prague, singing: *Advenisti desiderabilis, o pater amabilis, quem expectabamus in tribulacionibus nostris, advenisti cum donis celestibus, ut benediceres omnibus bone voluntatis hominibus*, that is 'You have come to visit, our beloved father, for whom we have been waiting in our distress, you have come with celestial presents to bless all the people of good will.' And when he went through the New to the Old Town, they rang the bells in all the churches and monasteries and they took him up to the Church of the Virgin Mary before Týn and then to the inn at the Elephants.[48]

Another manuscript of the chronicle adds, that "no one heard for a long time that any mortal man would be shown such an honour as in the case of this legate".[49] In Utraquist Prague (prior to its capture by the Utraquist George of Poděbrady later that same year), the first contact with the legate was made in a very ceremonial way following the traditional rules and guidelines, although no mention is made of kissing the cross by the legate before he entered the city, indulgences or the solemn mass.[50]

vjeli, až se korúhve ztrhaly, nebesa se zrušila, a to boží pomsta byla té veliké pýchy". In Czech the word "nebesa" is used for a baldachin and it also means "skies" or "heavens", thus placing greater emphasis on the heavenly punishment. A baldachin was used by Cardinal Bernardin Carvajal when legate, cf. Celani, ed., *Johannis Burckardi Liber*, vol. 1, p. 616, 638.

46. Gómez Canedo, *Don Juan*, p. 303, "Primo dominus legatus uenit Pragam in vigilia Ascensionis Domini hora XVIII uel quasi et ibi honorifice susceptus anno domini 1448".

47. A village roughly four kilometres outside the city gates.

48. Šimek, ed., *Staré letopisy*, pp. 104-105. A welcome speech for the legate, a *beneventatio*, is also attached: "Egreditur, o pater reverendissime et domine amantissime, obviam paternitati tue tota Pragensis inclita civitas. Egrediuntur et alma doctorum, magistrorum, baccalaureorum et studentium ancilla paternitatis tue universitas. Egrediuntur et principes civitatum, magister civium et consules cum populo gaudentes, o pater, de felici adventu tuo dicentes: Advenisti desiderabilis, o pater amabilis, quem expectabamus in tribulacionibus nostris. Advenisti cum donis celestibus, ut benediceres omnibus bone voluntatis hominibus. Ingredere, o pater, civitatem nostram cum donis celestibus, age pacem populo desiderabilem, age sanctam unitatem, age salutem, concordiam salutarem, ut hec inclita civitas per te, pater, donis repleta celestibus decantare possit illum angelicum cantum vere salutarem: Et in terra pax et salus bone voluntatis hominibus. Quod prestare dignetur, o pater, altissimus in secula seculorum benedictus".

49. Palacký, ed., *Staří letopisové*, p. 138.

50. Cf. on these topics Wasner, "Fifteenth-Century Texts", pp. 324, 352-354.

The second largest city of the Bohemian Lands, Wrocław, the unofficial capital of Silesia, was a Catholic city unaffected by Utraquism. Descriptions of the solemn acceptance of legates and even nuncios can also be found here. In the autumn of 1459, Girolamo Lando and Francesco da Toledo came to the city, which welcomed them in a procession with holy relics, "as befits the arrival of apostolic legates". The city scribe and chronicler, Peter Eschenloer, narrated lengthily about the solemn reception of the "legate" Girolamo Lando, whom the curia officially named *nuntius et orator cum potestate legati de latere.* Although the papal representative was not a cardinal, his arrival nevertheless aroused the greatest interest in Wrocław. The chronicler even competed with Prague mentioning that the "legate" was not greeted with such splendour. He speaks of the "legate" that came on a mule and was received by the prelates and most important burghers, and who let himself be kissed by them. Even at the first meeting, according to Eschenloer, he began a conversation asking about the burghers' names and commenting on the military power of the city. He was impressed by the number of people who greeted him outside the city and were arranged according to their ranks and affinities totalling some four thousand men, Eschenloer states. After entering the city, the streets as well as the houses and their roofs were filled with people of both sexes who wanted to see the legate. Girolamo then addressed the city in a lengthy sermon in the cathedral, in which he emphasised the need for peace and the Turkish threat and most importantly urged the city to seek reconciliation with the king. The response from the city came only after a heated discussion, as the burghers were not united in their ideas on making peace with the king. Eschenloer observed that some agreed and "many cursed the coming [of the legate], which they blessed the day before".[51] The city scribe entered in his *Historia* several speeches and letters related to the problematic revolt against the king. There is no discussion, however, as to whether the entry of the nuncio provided the burghers with an occasion for self-presentation and simultaneously the city had the need to honour the representative of the Pope, who, they thought, would support them against the 'heretical' king.[52]

Although Lando was not a cardinal and thus not a legate *de latere*, he followed some unofficial habits of the legatine entry to a city. To model the entry on the arrival of Christ to Jerusalem, the legates often rode a mule when entering the city. Girolamo Lando did, according to Eschenloer, the same. Moreover, to show that the mule was to be used only for the entry, he left the beast behind in Wrocław and later wrote back to the city council about it. Writing from the Papal Curia, which at that time (July 1460) resided in Siena, he said he would be happy if the burghers could return it to him through Fantino della Valle, the

51. Eschenloer, *Historia*, pp. 63-70, quote on p. 70, "… mirati omnes de legatorum persuasione, diversas in partes oracio voluta fuit, alii sic, ceteri taliter qualiter de ipsis senciebant, fit murmur in populo, multi maledicunt adventum, quem pridie benedixerant"; cf. German version, idem, *Geschichte*, pp. 292-300.

52. Idem, *Historia*, pp. 63-99; idem, *Geschichte*, pp. 292-350. Cf. also Drabina, "Działalność dyplomatyczna Hieronima Lando".

king's procurator at the Curia, who was going to go to Bohemia and bring it back when returning to the Curia.[53] When the nuncio arrived at the city for the second time after two years, in mid-November 1462, he was ceremoniously greeted once again and even met by the *wagenpurk* (*Wagenburg*, military carriages typical for Bohemian warfare in the fifteenth century) and a number of riders at a distance outside the city *in Parchwicz*, present-day Prochowice, some fifty kilometres north-west of Wrocław. The city scribe, however, did not mention whether Girolamo came on his mule again.[54]

Cardinal Marco Barbo left Rome in 1472 for his legation in Central Europe and his arrival to Wrocław is also well documented. He began his mission, however, at the Imperial court and then the court of the King of Hungary. His journey next brought him to Kraków and the court of Casimir, King of Poland, as the legate himself and the Polish chronicler Jan Długosz have informed us. According to Długosz, the King and his entourage met and welcomed the legate in Wieliczka, more than ten kilometres outside the royal city of Kraków. Together with the King came his sons, who addressed the legate with individual Latin speeches, as was apparently the tradition in Poland (similarly, the papal nuncio Alexander Numai was also addressed by them two years earlier when visiting Kraków). After being received, Marco Barbo was accompanied to the city, where he visited all the churches of Kraków in a procession, took part in a splendid banquet the following day and a day later had an official audience with the King.[55] The cardinal himself wrote in a travel report only very laconically "after my arrival in Kraków and the solemn mass I was heard by the most serene lord King of Poland".[56] Like Juan Carvajal, he had no need to describe all the festivities and ceremonies.

Peter Eschenloer recorded Barbo's arrival to Wrocław, where he went after his visit to the King of Poland. Reportedly, the Poles were all that friendly to the legate and even, Eschenloer writes, dispatched a band of "bad people" to capture or kill him. The scribe undoubtedly exaggerated in order to emphasise the merits of the Wrocław burghers who sent one hundred and fifty riders to meet the legate in Namysłów fifty kilometres east of Wrocław (fifty kilometres seems to be the typical distance the Wrocław horsemen were willing or obliged to go to greet the legate). The legate himself came to Wrocław with eighty people on 21 November 1472, "with great joy, singing and processions"; and supposedly "no one saw such a great prelate in Wrocław before". The legate then stayed in the palace of

53. Markgraf, ed., *Politische Correspondenz*, vol. 1, pp. 45-46, no. 42.

54. Eschenloer, *Historia*, pp. 102-103; idem, *Geschichte*, pp. 388-389; cf. also his trip to Poland, *Joannis Dlugossii Annales*, 1462-1480, p. 50, "Tardius itaque venientem Casimirus rex avidius excepit, cui Pyotrcoviam feria sexta in crastino sancte Catherine ingredienti ab omnibus prelatis et baronibus Polonie obviam itum est".

55. *Joannis Dlugossii Annales*, 1462-1480, pp. 291-292; Eschenloer, *Geschichte*, p. 900, only states, "Gar czirlich empfingen jn die Polen, adir wenig folgeten sie seiner lere"; for the Latin welcome speech of *scholasticus* of Kraków and Prince Casimir for Marco Barbo as well as those for Alexander Numai, see Szujski, ed., *Codex epistolaris*, vol. 2, pp. 338-339, 341-343. For the legation, cf. Kalous, "Papežský legát Marco Barbo"; Drabina, "Misja dyplomatyczna".

56. BAV, Vat. lat. 5641, fol. 201r.

the Wrocław bishop Rudolf of Rüdesheim, also a papal legate, though of lower rank. When in Wrocław, the cardinal visited all the city churches on foot and was hailed by the city scribe as "a very earnest and humble lord, full of wisdom and justice".[57] Even if all this information might be gathered from the writings of the city scribe, the legate did not make any mention of the welcome in his report, only matter-of-factly stating that "after I entered Wrocław on Saturday before the feast of St Clement, my auditor came back…".[58] Neither the legate nor the city scribe expressly mentioned the indulgences that could have been granted according to the ceremonial instructions or even the faculties of the legate himself.[59] It should be once again made clear that the solemn entry was a matter of the moment and had a constitutive character, but did not need to be mentioned or presented when reporting on serious matters of papal business.

A year earlier, in 1471, a great personality was seen in Regensburg, when Cardinal Francesco Todeschini Piccolomini took part in the *Reichstag*.[60] This was the master of ceremonies and his secretary Agostino Patrizi who recorded the travels and the entire legation. The report makes it clear the legate made a ceremonial trip through Italy, visiting Siena, the place of his origin, and other towns. Beyond the Alps, he first visited Duke Sigismund in Innsbruck, who welcomed the legate with great joy, honour and reverence and came to meet him "to the roots of the mountains" to accompany him to the main church of the town. The legate intended to go straight to Regensburg for the diet, but was asked on the way to stop in Landshut, as the Duke of Bavaria Louis was ill. A delegation with the son of Louis and Martin Mair, a learned lawyer and diplomat, who greeted Francesco with a speech in the name of the Duke, met the legate outside the city and with a great pomp brought him to the gates. Finally, entering Regensburg, Cardinal Francesco met forty armed riders in Langquaid some twenty-five kilometres south of the imperial city of Regensburg. They accompanied the legate and his retinue to the city with great pomp, but the Emperor had not arrived yet and the legate could not use his Latin speech written for him still in Rome by Antonio Lolli. Those present in the city were able, however, to give the legate a welcome worthy of a cardinal and representative of the Pope.[61]

In 1518, Cardinal Lorenzo Campeggi was created one of the legates for the organisation of the crusade, which brought him to England. The bishop of Worcester wrote to Cardinal Wolsey (who was created a collegate to Campeggi) from Rome about the plans:

> Campeggio is to be received with accustomed pomp, at London or elsewhere, if the King so decree. Within two or three days after, he is to visit the King, and pronounce a general oration; and a day or two after, present the apostolic letters to Wolsey, by which

57. Eschenloer, *Geschichte*, p. 903.

58. BAV, Vat. lat. 5641, fol. 208v.

59. ASV, Reg. Vat. 680, fol. 54v. Cf. Wasner, "Fifteenth-Century Texts", pp. 315, 335, 346.

60. Strnad, "Francesco Todeschini-Piccolomini", pp. 207-249.

61. *Deutsche Reichstagsakten*, vol. 8, pt. 2, p. 467; Strnad, "Francesco Todeschini-Piccolomini", pp. 236-238.

he is joined with Campeggio in the legation. Thenceforth they are to act in common; nor is Campeggio to do or [say anything] without Wolsey, who shall be mentioned first in the commission, as the senior Cardinal. On the same or the following day they are to present the letters to the King with due pomp. One cross is to be carried before them viz., Wolsey's, as he is first named in the letters; and so it was established in the consistory, "prae omnibus aliis legatis".[62]

Campeggi's coming to England was even more complicated as he shared his legatine position with Cardinal Wolsey, present in England. Thus, he began to organise his arrival to their common province while on his journey sending a letter to Wolsey from Lapalisse in Central France between Lyons and Bourges.[63]

It would be possible to provide many more examples along these lines, with the last one also from a later period serving to illustrate that although the system of papal diplomacy changed, in the 1520s and 1530s, the dignity of a cardinal legate remained unchallenged. It concerns Cardinal Lorenzo Campeggi again, who left Vienna, where he primarily resided during his legation in Central Europe, and visited the court of Louis II, King of Hungary, in Buda in December 1524. The King rode "one Italian mile" outside his city to greet the special guest, who was traditionally addressed in a welcome speech (this time by the archbishop of Esztergom). Since the report comes from a letter of Campeggi sent back to Rome, no details can be ascertained. After the welcome, Cardinal Lorenzo found his accommodation in the city and two days later had breakfast with the royal couple and then spoke in the royal council about his legation and the great significance of the Kingdom of Hungary for papal policy.[64]

A legate's entry to a city represented a great event not only for the general population of the city, but most crucially for the local church. Local bishops naturally took part in welcoming and receiving the coming legate and were supposed to play a key role as shown by the Pontifical, a book of sacraments and sacramentals, administered by a bishop and other ceremonies. These books that defined a bishop's role in rituals and ceremonies were also written by authors who wrote other ceremonial handbooks. Thus, already the Roman Pontifical of Guillaume Durand contains an entire section on receiving a legate (*Ordo ad*

62. Brewer, ed., *Letters and Papers*, vol. 2, pp. 1294-1246, no. 4179 (20 May 1518)

63. *Ibid.*, p. 1300, no. 4194 (28 May 1518).

64. Fraknói, ed., *Relationes oratorum*, pp. 101-108, no. 32 (29 Dec 1524), "... El Re con la corte soa mi venne incontro un miglio Italiano et piu, et Strigoneinse nel primo affronto fece le parole et accommodatamente. Dipoi alli XXI in pleno consilio dissi alcune poche parole, come Vostra Signoria vedera per al inclusa copia overo aligata, et dal detto Strigoniense mi fu risposto convenientemente, et quella mattina medesima fui in pranzo con el Re et Regina"; on pp. 106-108, Lorenzo's speech in the royal council (21 Dec 1524), "... cum sub illius profectionis meae ex urbe tempus Sanctissimus Dominus Noster et Sacrum Collegium cognosceret Reverendissimum in Christo patrem Dominum Cardinalem Santi Sixti [Tommaso De Vio], tunc apud Maiestatem Vestram et in Nobilissimo hoc regno Legatum Apostolicum, Romam honestis quibusdam de causis redditurum esse; ne Apostolicae Sedis officiis et authoritate Regnum hoc, his praesertim temporibus difficillimis, destitui videretur, praedictae Legationi Germanicae Hungarica quoque, Boemica et Polonica, adiacentiumque locorum et Regnorum mihi, tanto oneri certe impari, adiuncta fuit ...".

recipiendum processionaliter prelatum vel legatum).[65] Similarly, the papal masters of ceremonies Agostino Patrizi Piccolomini and Johannes Burckard compiled a modernised version of the Roman Pontifical that was printed in Rome in 1485. They also include such a chapter, but (as is the rule in other parts as well) their description tends to be much more detailed.[66] Such texts, then, also appeared among the notes of legatine and papal ceremonial.[67] The local bishop ceded his legal status to the newly coming legate and thus the entry of a legate could have resembled the arrival of a newly elected bishop,[68] although naturally, this was only temporary. According to the Pontifical, when the legate came to the vicinity of an episcopal city, the local clergy led by a bishop left in procession the cathedral and marched outside the gates of the city. They carried a cross (or holy relics, Durand adds) in front of the local bishop, who bears his *pontificalia*, including the mitre and the staff. When they met the legate, he was supposed to kneel before the cross (or the relics) on a prepared carpet and kiss them. Then, singing an antiphon according to the status and number of legates, the procession would bring the legate in to the city. Patrizi and Burckard also planned a welcome by the city magistrate at the gates of the city, who should accept the legate under a baldachin. At the door of the cathedral, the legate was given an aspergillum and sprinkled himself and then all the people standing by with holy water. He then placed blessed frankincense into a thurible and was censed by the local bishop. According to the older version of the Pontifical and *Ordo Romanus XIV*, a gospel book was offered to the legate for kissing before entering the church. The legate consequently prostrated before the high altar while the local bishop recited certain prayers and after an antiphon to the patron of the church the legate stood up at the main altar, prayed, blessed people and offered indulgences. When finished, he was accompanied to his place of accommodation. Cardinal Francesco Todeschini Piccolomini described the ideal entry in a very similar way in 1484 in a text that was perhaps drafted by Agostino Patrizi Piccolomini, thus having the same sources as the pontifical of 1485.[69] From the point of view of the legate, it only adds that when approaching the city the cardinal-legate should dress in his cardinal's mantle.

Such instructions were given not only to bishops, but also to priests in general. *Liber sacerdotalis* of Alberto da Castello,[70] printed in 1523 provided guidelines for receiving legates or high-ranking prelates. They should be met at the gates of the city and specific antiphons should be sung for them. The ceremony copies that of the bishops: the legate is offered a cross to kiss and with singing the antiphons and under a baldachin the legate is taken to the principal church of the city. At the entrance to the church, the legate is offered an aspergillum and sprinkles himself

65. Andrieu, ed., *Le pontifical romain*, vol. 3, pp. 627-629.

66. Patrizi Piccolomini and Burckard, *Pontificalis liber*, fol. [260r-261v].

67. BAV, Vat. lat. 12348, fol. 134v-135r (ed. Wasner, "Fifteenth-Century Texts", pp. 352-354).

68. Maciejewski, *Adventus Episcopi*; Miller, "The Florentine Bishop's Ritual Entry".

69. Wasner, "Fifteenth-Century Texts", pp. 328-329.

70. On the book see Righi, *Il "sacerdotale"*; Vogel, *Introduction*, p. 222; and Kalous, "Late Medieval Nuptial Rites", p. 59.

and others with holy water, with frankincense being used in the same way as in the Pontifical. After some prayers with the legate sitting in a faldstool at the main altar, he announces the indulgences, blesses the people and finally is accompanied by the priest to his lodging house.[71]

The guidelines of the Pontifical and the *Liber sacerdotalis* constituted the local knowledge about the ceremonial of a coming legate. Moreover, the above-mentioned examples seem to corroborate this knowledge. What was, however, crucial from the point of view of the local church was that the legate accepted certain powers of the bishop, especially jurisdictional ones, and thus it was crucial to present this power and have it confirmed and legitimised at the local cathedral.

The general ideas on diplomacy and diplomatic traffic must also be taken into account here. They also specified the procedure for welcoming representatives of significant political personalities. For such greetings, Bernard du Rosier, for example, advised the sending of people who would match the coming ambassadors in status.[72] When a king, then, greeted the legate himself, it is clear that from this point of view that he regarded the visit of a legate as crucial and important, as seen in previous examples. When Cardinal Giovanni d'Aragona, for example, was on his way to Hungary, Jan Filipec, bishop of Várad (Oradea) went to meet him on his way. They met close to Passau, a long distance before the borders of Hungary: in this way the King, whose envoy accompanied the legate for the rest of the trip, showed respect to and honoured the arriving cardinal and his brother-in-law. The bishop was supposed to make the journey more pleasant and even lead the way, as he was familiar with the region.[73] These general rules that respect the status of the persons in question apply for the legatine ceremonial as for meeting visitors in their residences. Cardinal Juan Carvajal, for example, wrote that he met the Emperor outside the gate of his residence, the kings below the stairs and other princes only in the middle of the staircase.[74] The procedure in such situations respects the general guidelines of diplomatic relations.

An even more specific situation came about when a legate met a king or any other secular ruler. Among the notes on legatine ceremonial, certain hints on the relation to secular power may be found.[75] Meetings of the highest representatives of secular and ecclesiastical powers always caused problems of protocol. Unsurprisingly then, descriptions of and guidelines for such meetings form a significant part of the legatine ceremonial instructions. Agostino Patrizi Piccolomini wrote that "when a legate comes to a kingdom or province and approaches a town or castle, where the

71. Castellano, *Liber sacerdotalis*, fol. 310v-313r.

72. Hrabar, ed., *De legatis*, p. 11 (Bernard du Rosier, *Ambaxiator Brevilogus*, cap. XI).

73. Fraknói, ed., *Mátyás király levelei*, vol. 1, pp. 455-456, no. 308, King Matthias wrote to Giovanni d'Aragona, "... expedivimus reverendum patrem dominum Ioannem episcopum Waradiensem, quem jussimus ire crastino in occursum reverendissime paternitatis vestre usque Pathaviam. Is accepit a nobis in mandatis, ut se paternitati vestre associet, et via commodiori conducat. Qui bene diriget iter paternitatis vestre et viam illi aptiorem melioremque ostendet, tamquam is qui optime novit locorum situs".

74. Wasner, "Fifteenth-Century Texts", p. 313, 325.

75. *Ibid.*, pp. 311-314.

king of that kingdom resides, the king must come out of the walls of the town or castle to meet him." It is then obvious to Patrizi that a legate should stand on the right hand side of the king, because the legate is superior to the king. He might allow the king to be on his right, but only once, so that it would not seem that he was subordinate to the king.[76] When comparing the ideal with reality in the case of Marco Barbo, we only know that Casimir, King of Poland, met the cardinal well outside the city of Kraków and that in turn the cardinal invited the king to his own residence, but again it was described by Marco Barbo very laconically. He reported that "the most serene King of Poland came to me with notable prelates, barons and counsellors, whom (the king) I have received with appropriate respect."[77]

Meeting secular sovereigns constituted one major part of a legate's job. These meetings cannot be listed here, of course, but certain examples illustrate the point. In 1489, for example, peace negotiations between King Matthias of Hungary and the King of the Romans Maximilian took place in Linz in Austria. When entering the church, it was the King who was in the middle between the Hungarian ambassador Jan Filipec, bishop of Várad, on his left, and *der Legat* on his right. It is clear that the most significant place was reserved for the King of the Romans; the "legate" was a nuncio with the power of a legate *de latere* Raymund Peraudi, later one of the most crucial representatives of the Pope in Germany.[78] Since Raymund Peraudi's position was only an orator, nuncio and commissary, he could not bless people and did not wear the papal/cardinalitial dress. Nuncio did not impersonalise the pope and thus he did not have to acquire a position of highest importance as the legate *de latere*, a cardinal, required. However, the ceremonial of such nuncios has not been as yet treated in such detail as the ceremonial of legates, primarily due to the available sources.

A revealing instance of an encounter of a papal legate *de latere* and a king comes from Hungary. In 1523, Cardinal Tommaso De Vio operated in the region and met Louis and Mary, King and Queen of Hungary and Bohemia in Bratislava (Pressburg, Pozsony). A general meeting was held in Wiener Neustadt concerning a possible crusade against the Ottoman Turks in the presence of the Archduke of Austria, the King of Hungary and Bohemia and a representative of the King of Poland, his envoy and counsellor Krzysztof Szydłowiecki. He reported on the events in Wiener Neustadt and later in Bratislava, where the court of King Louis and Queen Mary moved. Szydłowiecki, for example, described a situation in the main parish church of St Martin in Bratislava during the Feast of All Saints. Both the royal couple and the papal legate took part in the celebrations and the legate wished to be given the gospel before the King and Queen. The Hungarian lords, who guarded the rights of the kingdom, however, viewed this, as an infringement of the sovereignty of the King and the gospel was finally not given to anyone. Also the sides in the church were clearly divided between the secular and spiritual

76. *Ibid.*, pp. 331-332.

77. BAV, Vat. lat. 5641, fol. 205r.

78. Nehring, "Quellen", p. 252, "Der Legat uff der rechten seyten und der Bischove von Waradein uff der lyncken seyten des Römischen Konigs ..."; cf. Nehring, *Matthias Corvinus*, p. 190.

powers: the King and the Queen, the Polish ambassador and other lords were standing on one side, while the other side was occupied by the legate and the bishops. After the mass ended, the legate bestowed a blessing on the people.[79] According to the ceremonial notes, legates were supposed to visit churches at major feasts and bless the people;[80] and this was done by Cardinal Tommaso. He pronounced a blessing also upon other occasions, for example, at the feast of St Martin, the patron saint of the parish church.[81] When the new Pope, Clement VII, was elected and the news reached Bratislava, the legate celebrated a Holy Mass himself in front of the royal couple and other lords in the parish church of St Martin. After the blessing, a solemn *Te Deum laudamus* and firing of cannons, the papal legate participated in a festive dinner with King Louis, Queen Mary, the Polish ambassadors and the Archduke of Austria.[82] Although a description of meeting a king in a church cannot be found among the ceremonial instructions for legates, it might be inferred that cardinal legates must have represented a certain dignity and specific powers that even distinguished them from the secular rulers.

Such a standard might be inferred from a negative comment by Paride Grassi, when he mentioned Cardinal Tamás Bakóc in Hungary. Bakóc was of humble origin and only rose to power through serving King Matthias Corvinus and by means of ecclesiastical and chancery positions in Hungary. As bishop of Győr he worked as royal secretary, later became bishop of Eger, High Chancellor under King Wladislas and finally archbishop of Esztergom, the primate of Hungary. In 1500 he was created a cardinal and in 1513 a strong, but losing candidate for the throne of St Peter. Sent to Hungary as papal legate *de latere* by the successful Leo X a few months after the election, he remained there until his death in 1521. Under King Louis, in 1518, Paride Grassi still called him *creatura regis*, as

> … the cardinal of Esztergom is not a useful legate, because he is of the same nation and basically a creation (*creatura*) of the king of Hungary. He does not behave as a legate, but rather as the king's chaplain, because when he should be, as a papal legate, superior to the king, not only is he not above the king, he is below him, and in all matters behaves like a subordinate and his minister, because when the king washes hands, he passes him the towel and during mass he administers peace and the book, which he should not do. And therefore, in these and other things, the legate lowers the honour of the Holy See, because the legate should be above any king.[83]

79. Zombori, ed., *Krzysztof Szydłowiecki*, p. 160, "Die dominico in festo omnium sanctorum serenissimus rex et regina fuerunt in ecclesia parochiali, in qua fuit et legatus apostolicus et quia voluit legatus, uti ei prius offeratur evangelium et alia et domini Hungari noluerunt omnino admittere volentes, ut omnia cerimonialia prius afferrantur regi et regine et ob eam causam neque regi et regine neque legato oblatum est evangelium nec alia cerimonialia etc. In ea parte, ubi serenissimi rex et regina steterunt, primum locum tenuit in stallo dominus orator regis Polonie, deinde illustrissimus dux Carolus, Georgius marchio post hoc voyewoda Transilvanie tandem marchio Vilhelmus et sic alii domini. In alia parte legatus ex opposito regis et in illa parte domini Hungarie episcopi steterunt. Post missam legatus dedit benedictionem".

80. Wasner, "Fifteenth-Century Texts", pp. 314, 322.

81. Zombori, ed., *Krzysztof Szydłowiecki*, p. 168.

82. *Ibid.*, p. 190.

83. Grassi, *Diarium*, pp. 402-4.

Here, Paride Grassi, defined what should not have been done and thus what was expected from the legate in relation to the highest secular power.

The meetings of legates and kings, however, did not have to involve a conflict between the two or a conflict with the ideal. As legates were present in royal courts, they also took part in the court ceremonies. Cardinal Pietro Isvalies, for example, participated in a solemn Eucharistic procession in 1501 in Buda, the capital of Hungary, and paid for a wine fountain for the celebration. A more significant occasion was, however, the royal wedding of King Wladislas and the French princess Anne of Foix and Candale, which took place in 1502. Paride Grassi preserved in his *Diary* a liturgical *ordo* for this wedding that was used by Cardinal Pietro in Székesfehérvár, the royal coronation city.[84] Gabriele Rangoni in the double role of a papal nuncio and bishop of Eger took part in the royal wedding of 1476 of the King of Hungary Matthias Corvinus and his Queen Beatrice d'Aragona. Possibly out of courtesy to the new Italian queen, it was Rangoni who welcomed her with an Italian speech when she first met the king, served the first mass that was visited by the queen and her Italian retinue in Székesfehérvár, where the queen was crowned, and most crucially it was Rangoni again who performed the wedding ceremony itself in Buda.[85]

The movements and travels of the legate around his legatine province had clear rules and recommendations so that the dignity of the highest representative of the head of Christendom was preserved. It even had to be respected by the secular rulers in their own territories, which could have been a cause of troubles or various adjustments that stemmed from the current situation. The Emperor and the kings were the only match to the legate wherein his position in festivities and ceremonials could have been contested.[86] The legate, however, acted mainly as an ecclesiastical personality of the highest position, surpassing all the other prelates of the region. He, thus, had to behave with a certain dignity and represent his office with participation in church festivities and rituals as well as with appropriate modesty, as avoiding pomp was also recommended.[87] The pomp and solemnity of papal legates travelling around their province was, however, still great with them behaving as if the pope himself was present, not only in the High Middle Ages but also in the later period.

3.2. *On the road*

A legation naturally meant being on the road. Legates had to find their way to their province and then rarely remained tied to one place within the large territory assigned to them, even though they also had their "residences". The travelling of the legates was in no way special and the legates did not differ all that much from other travellers of the day. Their standing undoubtedly attracted attention, but in

84. Kalous, "Late Medieval Nuptial Rites".
85. Contemporary reports summarised in idem, "Tři týdny slávy", pp. 194-203.
86. Cf. Wasner, "Fifteenth-Century Texts", pp. 313, 338.
87. Cf. *ibid.*, p. 322.

the same way as members of royal families, kings and queens, or bishops and other prelates travelling around Europe. Just like these travellers of the highest social standing, they had a larger retinue of followers, which could have special rules and instructions with individuals even receiving particular tasks within the office of the legation.

3.2.1. *Travelling*

Concerning the travelling itself, no general recommendations or rules existed, which would limit or define the mode of travel. Legates encountered the same dangers on their travels as others, including risks of disease, but also threats of robbers or the military power of secular landlords. Not even the status of a papal legate could protect them from all the perils on their travels. As is apparent from the previous section, the legate would wear a distinctive dress and was supposed to enter larger cities in a special way, but these were all the restrictions.

Although there were no general rules, certain specific recommendations for the trip or descriptions that could have been used later as guidebooks could be found. First, the instructions that the legate received before his departure would tell him whom to visit first and how to proceed in the province. As for the travels to the province itself, unofficial instructions for a legate in the early 1470s, probably for Cardinal Marco Barbo (the instructions could even have been written for or maybe by Cardinal Francesco Todeschini Piccolomini, as they appear in a manuscript connected to his activities), provide a description of two possible journeys from Italy to Germany. One of them was easier, but frequently attacked by the Turks, the other more difficult and longer, but safer in terms of the Ottomans. The first one led "from Udine to Venzone and then to Malborghetto and Villach, then eventually through Carinthia, Carniola and Styria, provinces of the house of Austria to Wiener Neustadt". The other way led "from Venzone to the left" through Brenner Pass to Innsbruck "and then either on the ground or on the River Inn to the Danube".[88] Cardinal Francesco Todeschini Piccolomini travelled in 1471 by the western way over the Brenner Pass to Innsbruck, which for him was even more convenient as his goal was not Vienna or Wiener Neustadt, but Regensburg and the *Reichstag* there. He travelled from Rome (18 March) through Pienza, Siena, Florence, Bologna, Mantua to Verona (5 April). On 7 April, he journeyed via Volargne and began to climb up towards the mountains through Borghetto, Rovereto to Trento. After a three day rest there, the company left Italy crossing the River Avisio outside the town. They spent Easter in Bolzano and then through Bressanone (Brixen) went towards the Brenner Pass and Innsbruck (18 April) on the other side.[89] The travels then had to be planned in advance in relation to the feasts of the period. Francesco had to remain in a decent place to celebrate Easter properly.

In addition, official instructions might provide directions for the travels. Cardinal Pietro Isvalies, who left Rome for his legation on 19 November 1500,

88. Roma, Biblioteca Angelica, ms. 1077, fol. 21v.
89. Strnad, "Francesco Todeschini-Piccolomini", pp. 230-233.

was advised by his instructions to cross the Italian peninsula to Ancona and from there sail on ship to Senj, from where he would reach Hungary and Buda easily through Zagreb, avoiding the difficult route over the mountains.[90] A similar route was taken thirteen years later by Cardinal Tamás Bakóc who travelled back to Hungary as a legate *de latere*.[91] Travelling to the province might entail many dangers and a voyage on the sea could have represented an extra danger. Cardinal Tamás, who travelled in November, sailed with his retinue with two galleys and one cargo ship. He reached Senj safely after a storm, but the two other ships were blown off course and only re-joined him later.[92] Roderigo Borja, who spent a year as a papal legate *de latere* in Spain and travelled back to Rome on ships in October 1473, had even less luck. When returning to Rome, his ships were caught in a storm, in which the two ships collided. One of them sank with all the people aboard (180 people according to Platina, 75 according to Ammannati Piccolomini), the other, which carried the cardinal, managed with a destroyed stern to reach the port of Livorno.[93]

Additional dangers which frequently appeared included the previously mentioned Turkish raids, but also winter and diseases. Papal nuncio Angelo Pecchinoli wrote the first report from his mission to Central Europe on 31 January 1489, almost five months after leaving Rome. He even commented on the severe winter, which did not allow him to write and most importantly to send an envoy with the report earlier.[94] Similarly, papal nuncio Bartolomeo Maraschi, when asked in October 1483 to provide someone from his retinue to accompany a Turkish ambassador to Rome, could supply someone, but not from the original company, as one died on the way and others stayed behind in various places because of diseases.[95] Apart from natural conditions, humans could change the luck of legates. Like other travellers they were exposed to the dangers of the road including robbers. Tamás Bakóc, as reported by Marino Sanudo in Venice, was waylaid by robbers after his problematic voyage on the sea. Allegedly, he lost in the robbery a hardly credible amount of 200,000 ducats.[96] Long-distance travelling represented the same trouble for legates as for other travellers.

Even though, as mentioned earlier, the legates had more or less stable residences when present at royal courts (and published letters, as Angelo

90. Theiner, ed., *Vetera monumenta Poloniae*, vol. 2, pp. 269-276, no. 297 (dated 18 Nov 1500), here p. 269.

91. Fraknói, *Erdődi Bakócz*, pp. 138-142.

92. *Ibid*., pp. 141-142.

93. Tommasini, ed., *Diario della Città di Roma di Stefano Infessura*, p. 78; Ammannati Piccolomini, *Lettere*, vol. 3, p. 1752; Gaida, ed., *Platynae historici Liber*, pp. 411-412.

94. BMV, Lat. X 175 (=3622), fol. 127r, "Quod ad sanctitatem vestram, postquam illi de primo ingressu meo Viennam significavi, non scripserim, in causa est, quod solito asperior hiems, que ingruit, volentes ad Italiam proficisci deterret. Tam et si tutum non putaverim passim omnibus litteras credere, quomodo fit, ut nuntium hunc familiarem meum ad rem hanc delegerim, ut minus timeam, litteras et que scribo videri posse".

95. ASV, Misc., Arm. II 56, fol. 348rv, "… Respondi me hominem daturum, non tamen ex antiquis meis, cum aliquis esset mortuus in itinere, alii infirmi variis locis relicti".

96. Sanudo, *I Diarii*, vol. 17, col. 424.

Pecchinoli in Vienna *in domibus nostre residencie*, or in Buda *in domo solite nostre residencie*)[97] they were definitely not stationary. They travelled around their province in order to be able to complete their tasks. Such travels could within a few short months encompass vast territories of their legatine provinces. The example of Nicholas of Cusa demonstrates this kind of activity. He was almost continuously on the road, staying in certain places for more than a week and only occasionally remaining in a city for more than two weeks: in Bamberg (over Easter 1451), Trier, Mainz and Cologne, where he spent Christmas 1451.[98] As Erich Meuthen has shown, out of the 456 days of Cusa's legation, 277 could be directly linked with sources and specific places; the legate changed places over ninety times during this period. Such data can also show that the normal travel speed was about 30-40 kilometres per day, as was usual at the time.[99] Nicholas of Cusa travelled around Germany, which was his legatine province together with Bohemia, which he never entered. An even larger province must have been attended to by Marco Barbo, whose province entailed Germany, Hungary, Poland, Bohemia and then even the Scandinavian kingdoms. He travelled first to the court of the Emperor in Wiener Neustadt, then through Vienna went to the court of King Matthias Corvinus in Buda, from where he travelled to the court of King Casimir in Kraków. After a longer stay in Silesia (Wrocław, Nysa), he returned to Vienna, Hungary and from there to Opava in Autumn 1473. After negotiations there, he reached Vienna again and thereafter stayed in the German lands (Augsburg, Mainz, Nuremberg, Basel) before he left his province for Rome.[100] Whereas Cardinal Nicholas of Cusa was commissioned to reform the church of Germany, Cardinal Marco Barbo carried out mostly political negotiations with local rulers and organised political conventions. Thus, the first travelled all around the province and was attested to in a number of places, while the latter stayed at royal courts or larger cities where he organised political talks. The above-mentioned Angelo Pecchinoli actually only followed one royal court, which had two main residences, Buda and Vienna. Although he primarily stayed at the court, from a letter of the run-away Bishop Agostino Luciani (an Italian bishop in Prague, Bohemia, who cooperated with the Utraquists) we learn that he might have travelled to Poland (or at least such a rumour was reported).[101]

When travelling around the province, the legates, usually Italians, naturally teamed up with other Italians. The example of Cardinal Pietro Isvalies indicates that when he travelled within Hungary, he was accompanied by the then

97. Munich, Bayerisches Hauptstaatsarchiv, fond Kloster Niederaltaich Urkunden (790-1801) (www.monasterium.net), no. 1042 (31 Dec 1488, Vienna); MNL Budapest, OL DL 56234 (26 Oct 1489, Buda).

98. Meuthen, "Das Itinerar"; idem, ed., *Acta Cusana*, vol. 1/3a, no. 964 (inserted itinerary table).

99. Idem, "Das Itinerar," p. 475.

100. Kalous, *Plenitudo potestatis*, pp. 245-247; see also Drabina, "Misja dyplomatyczna"; Untergehrer, *Die päpstlichen nuntii und legati*, pp. 378-380.

101. BMV, Lat. X 175 (=3622), fol. 145v.

ambassador of Venice in the kingdom. They arrived together in Esztergom in April 1502 and then left by a boat on the river in the direction of Visegrád, the fancy royal castle and palace, as Domenico Runcio, the chaplain of Queen Beatrice, reported.[102] Even in the province itself, the legates could encounter danger on the way. Sometimes, however, the reasons could not be ascribed to everyday dangers on the road, but were rather related to their status and political negotiations. Peter Eschenloer even mentioned that the King of Poland did not hesitate to threaten the legate Marco Barbo, who travelled from Kraków, the royal residence, to Wrocław in Silesia. Although Eschenloer himself could have enlarged the danger for the rhetorical purposes of his chronicle, the burghers of Wrocław, he says, sent some hundred and fifty equestrians to protect the legate on his way.[103] A predecessor of Marco Barbo was also followed by horsemen, who, however, did not protect the legate, but wanted to ensure that he returned what they asked for. Cardinal Juan Carvajal, after visiting Prague, carried away the originals of the Basel Compacts, treaties between the Council of Basel and the Bohemian Utraquists. He was stopped by the burghers who requested the charters and when he refused to do it immediately, they sent 400 horsemen to Benešov, the next town on the way, where he promised to give everything back.[104] The legate was even bullied in the city of Prague, so this incident was instead linked to the political negotiations rather than the dangers of the road.

This chapter began with certain unofficial instructions that explained not only the road itself, but also the political and societal situation in the destinations. Since cardinals could stem from distinguished (even royal) families, they would have been advised not only by the curia or previous legates, but also by the general ways of courtly literature. Although various moral writings were a popular genre of the period, only one such book is known to me which would instruct a legate as to what to do on the road. Diomede Carafa, a humanist author in the service of the King of Naples, wrote among other pieces the *Memoriale al Cardinal d'Aragona*, where he, according to Tommaso Persico, advised the cardinal how to behave on the road in a similar way, as he did for his sister Beatrice d'Aragona, who travelled to Hungary as well (as a new spouse of the King of Hungary). Only two pages of the text survived, unfortunately, so no details can be given, except for the emphasis on *humanitas* in the cardinal's behaviour.[105]

Legates, by definition travellers, encountered the same problems as other people on the road. They suffered from winter and diseases, and sometimes, not even their status could protect them from robbers and highwaymen. Although they carried the highest possible authority, they could be assaulted either by common robbers, who sought out wealth, or because of their activities by those, who wanted to stop them.

102. AS Modena, Ambasciatori b.3/32,1 (www.vestigia.hu).

103. Eschenloer, *Geschichte*, p. 903.

104. Urbánek, *České dějiny*, vol. 3/2, pp. 235-259.

105. Persico, *Diomede Carafa*, p. 217-218; Petrucci, "Carafa, Diomede," in *DBI*, vol. 19, 1976, pp. 524-530; Bentley, *Politics and Culture*, pp. 141-147; Vecce, "I memoriali ungheresi", pp. 482-484, text edited on pp. 486-487.

3.2.2. *The retinue*

The retinues of legates have been mentioned several times. Naturally, cardinals or other prelates never travelled alone, but were accompanied by a larger or smaller number of people, who secured communication with the papal centre, worked in the legatine chancery, served the cardinal, etc. The legates chose their companions before their journey began, thus most of them accompanied the legate from Rome, even though locals could have joined the circle when the legate arrived in his province.

The number of people in the entourage did not have a precise count in the later Middle Ages, but was limited by canon law, especially due to reasons of financing the legation. A canon of the Third Lateran Council required that the legate did not travel with more than twenty-five people.[106] The Fourth Lateran Council also required that legates and nuncios limit the number of their followers.[107] These limitations were not really followed, however, in the later period. As the system of financing the legations changed in the late medieval period, the limitations lost their importance, and the train of the legate *de latere* could entail several hundred people.[108] Wolfgang Untergehrer counted the numbers of individual retinues of simple nuncios and nuncios with the power of legate *de latere* for the period of 1447-1484: for the first category it was between 4 and 24 people, for the latter between 18 and 50 people.[109] The legates usually employed members of their household or curial acquaintances who had some experience of cooperation with them and experience with the required tasks.

Cardinal Marco Barbo's retinue may serve to illustrate such a situation. His retinue consisted of curial prelates and his *familiares*, who had appeared in his presence before. Many of these later became active in papal service on their own either at the Curia, or as papal envoys. The Dominican Leonardo Mansueti da Perugia held the office of *magister sacri palacii* at the time of Barbo's legation, but served as a papal nuncio to Perugia in 1440. He accompanied Marco Barbo and served as a messenger between the legate, the Pope and the King of Hungary, as various sources indicate.[110] Leonello Chieregato, bishop of Rab (It. Arbe) in Dalmatia, accompanied the cardinal, but returned to Rome earlier and sent

106. The Third Lateran Council, canon 4 (Larson and Pennington, eds., *Concilium Lateranense III*, pp. 129-131); X 3.39.6 (Friedberg, ed., *Corpus*, pt. 2, col. 623).

107. The Fourth Lateran Council, canon 33 (García y García and Melloni, eds. *Concilium Lateranense IV*, pp. 183); X 3.39.23 (Friedberg, ed., *Corpus*, pt. 2, col. 632).

108. Maleczek, "Die päpstlichen Legaten", pp. 54-55.

109. Untergehrer, *Die päpstlichen nuncii und legati*, pp. 143-145.

110. BAV, Vat. lat. 5641, fol. 207v, "Dominum vero magistrum sacri palatii ibi [in Nowy Sącz] inveni [17 Sep 1472], quem in crastinum transmisi ad dominum regem Ungarie bene instructum de omnibus, que in Nova Civitate cum domino rege Polonie tractata fuerunt", cf. also fol. 206r, 208r; ASV, Reg. Vat. 680, fol. 35r (dated between 25 Aug 1472 and the end of the year) (Theiner, ed., *Vetera monumenta Hungariae*, vol. 2, p. 440, no. 625), "Veniens a circumspectione tua ad nos dilectus filius Leonardus de Perusio, sacri nostri palatii magister..."; *magistri sacri palatii* were often charged with papal missions; see also Taurisano, *Hierarchia*, p. 9; Mortier, *Histoire*, vol. 4, pp. 488-541.

letters to the legate while he was still on his legation.[111] During his presence in the legate's retinue, Chieregato worked as his commissary in jurisdictional cases and like Mansueti helped the cardinal in the Polish-Hungarian negotiations; he later became a nuncio in the service of Popes Innocent VIII and Alexander VI, especially in France and Germany.[112] Like these two members of the retinue, Bartolomeo Massa, the legate's auditor, took part in the Polish-Hungarian peace talks. Massa was also known to Marco Barbo previously, as they collaborated when Marco Barbo bore the function of *camerlengo.*[113] Giovanni Gigli, who also later had a career in papal diplomacy as a collector in England in the 1470s and 1480s, was another auditor of the legate.[114] Giovanni Lorenzi appeared as the legate's secretary during the legation and continued to fulfil this function later after his arrival back in Rome.[115] And other, less well-known, members of Marco's household took part in the trip as members of the train, namely Giovanni de Pelegrina, Francesco de Baufremes, Tommaso da Polcenigo[116] or Konrad Altheimer, who are mentioned as members of the household in the legation.[117] Others only appear on the charters or letters themselves, namely Cesar de Pagnanis (known to be the familiaris of Marco Barbo as early as 1482),[118] Jacobus de Perusia, Johannes Lapicide, M. de Aleprandis, C. de Amelia or A. de Sancto Vito. The last name mentioned reveals even more details. Andreotto de Santovito appeared to be ordained to four minor orders and to subdiaconate in *Camera Apostolica* as *familiaris* to Marco Barbo in December 1466 in the first case and in June 1471 in the other.[119] Moreover, Angelo Fasolo, bishop of Feltre, whom Marco took along, was made the legate's vicar in the Patriarchate of Aquileia and Marco corresponded with him.[120]

Legates usually also took certain locals into their service, who could be very useful, as they knew the local situation, spoke the local language and could even have some previous experience. The example of a certain John the Hungarian

111. Paschini, *Leonello Chieregato*, pp. 20-37.

112. BAV, Vat. lat. 5641, fol. 207v, 215v (as an auditor), see also Foa, "Chiericati"; Paschini, *Leonello Chieregato*.

113. Fraknói, ed., *Mátyás király levelei*, vol. 1, p. 297, no. 211 (12 Mar 1474); cf. Baczkowski, *Walka Jagiellonów*, p. 91; Drabina, "Legaci apostolscy", p. 268. For the previous cooperation, Cherubini, "L'intensa attività", pp. 109-112, no. III.14.

114. NA Prague, ŘF, inv. no. 52 (18 Jun 1473) (www.monasterium.net; 17 Mar 2017); Lukcsics, ed., *Monumenta*, vol. 4, p. 452; similarly, Stiftsarchiv Klosterneuburg, St. Dorothea, CanReg, 1473 XII 11 (www.monasterium.net; 17 Mar 2017). Cf. Weiss, "Lineamenti", who, however, does not know about the trip with Marco Barbo; Davies, "Bishop John Morton", pp. 21-25; he also remained in contact with Marco Barbo later, cf. Paschini, ed., *Il carteggio*, pp. 34, 146.

115. E.g. MNL Budapest, OL DL 17479 (12 Aug 1473); NA Prague, ŘF, inv. no. 52; Paschini, ed., *Il carteggio*, p. 13.

116. He also appeared in a letter in MNL Budapest, OL DL 17506 (13 Nov 1473).

117. Vale, *Itinerario*, p. 20.

118. Battioni, ed., *Camera Apostolica*, vol. 2, pp. 400-401, no. 473 (9 Jul 1482).

119. Cf. Salonen and Hanska, *Entering*, p. 241; I would like to thank Jussi Hanska for further personal clarifications.

120. BAV, Vat. lat. 5641, fol. 149rv; Cherubini, "Fasolo"; Vale, *Itinerario*, pp. 20, 47-55.

(*Johannes Hungarus*) is telling, as the above-mentioned papal nuncio Bartolomeo Maraschi employed him as someone, who had already served another nuncio Alexander Numai. He was even sent to Rome with a Turkish ambassador, as Maraschi's own servants were either ill or dead.[121] Cardinal Tommaso De Vio brought the Hungarian Tamás Nádasdy along with him from Rome for his legation in Hungary, where he served as a translator. After the legation ended, Tamás became a secretary in the chancery of the King of Hungary.[122] Angelo Pecchinoli, papal nuncio who remained in the region for two years, employed several notaries including Johannes Ginorus of, in all probability, Italian origin and Jacobus de Bodogazonfalva, i.e. Boldogasszonyfalva (many places were known with such a name, the village of the Virgin), who was surely of local origin. Jacobus, moreover, had served the papal legate Ladislaus (László) Geréb, bishop of Transylvania, who himself for obvious reasons, had a number of companions of local origin. Through this position, it seems, they could have entered the network of the legatine service and then even been employed by the newly arriving Italians. Similarly Giovanni d'Aragona, who entered the local structures as the Archbishop of Esztergom, utilised the possibilities of employing locals.[123]

As the legate represented the papacy in its legal and jurisdictional authority and also took over the local jurisdiction, he needed to publish letters and charters. The jurisdictional rulings of papal tribunals had to be confirmed by papal letters, so also the legatine decisions had to be announced in the same way. The legate then had a chancery at his disposal, which drafted and published the letters. How did the chancery work? Who were the personnel? There are only limited number of documents, however, which clarify the activities and system of the legatine chanceries. These included instructions concerning the work of the chancery as well as actual evidence of its activity. The direct representation of the Pope entitled the legate to publish the charters in the same way as in the case of the Papal Chancery.[124] It was one of the legates, Cardinal Juan Carvajal, who described in detail how the chancery should be led. According to his notes, the chancery should be formed by ten or eleven people: the head of the chancery was a bishop (in this particular case the bishop of Assisi), who had a secretary and an auditor at his disposal. These accepted the supplications and checked whether they correspond to the legatine faculties, then signed the letters, etc. The bishop assigned the work to seven or eight scribes, the secretary prepared a concept and the auditor checked it. The letter had to be sealed by the legate's

121. ASV, Misc., Arm. II 56, fol. 348v, "… darem tamen virum bonum et aptum Joannem quendam Hungarum, qui episcopo Forliviensi servivit, quique aliquando ad pedes sanctitatis vestre accessit".

122. Bónis, *A jogtudó értelmiség*, p. 325; Kubinyi, *Főpapok*, p. 119; idem, "The Hungarian State", p. 85.

123. A number of letters appear with their signatures, for some references see Bónis, *Szentszéki regeszták*, pp. 440-486.

124. See, Schmitz-Kallenberg, ed., *Practica Cancellariae*, pp. XVII-XIX; Göller, "Aus der Kanzlei", pp. 319-324; Wasner, "Fifteenth-Century Texts", pp. 316-322; Maleczek, "Die päpstlichen Legaten", pp. 56-62; see also Frenz, *Die Kanzlei*; idem, *Papsturkunden*.

seal which was held by *magister domus*, and inscribed in the registers. This would have cost a maximum of "thirty-four Czech Groschen, i.e. one ducat".[125]

This sum of one florin for a charter is confirmed by another exceptional source, namely an ordo for a legation that was written about 1482/3 by Antonio Romagnano for Cardinal Domenico della Rovere, who went for his legation in 1483 to Savoy. The author recalled the legation of Francesco Todeschini Piccolomini some twelve years earlier, where he served as an auditor to the legate. Apart from the price for the charter, he mentioned that the legate was supposed to name clerks for his legation, namely two abbreviators, two auditors, two registrators of supplications and bulls, one *datarius*, as many scribes of bulls as he needed, one notary, who signed the bulls, one treasurer of the chancery, one secretary and one master of ceremonies, who assisted with public acts. This means that the chancery would have had eleven clerks plus scribes; *camerarii* are mentioned, who do not appear in the initial list of nominations, are also mentioned. Moreover, Antonio did not name any head of the chancery, where Juan Carvajal's overview requires a bishop. All in all, however, he provided a good overview for the new legate for the running of a legate's chancery.[126]

The nephew of Cardinal Juan Carvajal Bernardin, who also reached cardinalate, represented the Pope as papal legate *de latere* at the King of the Romans in 1496-1497 and 1507-1509. Bernardino Lopez de Carvajal's chancery was very well described by Johannes Burckard, who served as registrator of the chancery during Bernardino's first legation. He incorporated the report of the legation into his Roman diary.[127] It is striking, that after some fifty years, the chancery of the legate employed fifty-one people. The composition of the chancery included "seven referendarii, one datarius, thirteen abbreviators, fourteen scribes, one master of the registers (Burckard), seven registrators for the register of supplications and eight registrators for the register of bulls." The taxes for publishing a bull, however, rose only by fifty percent, i.e. a ducat and a half. This was more than half a century earlier, but still much less than the ten ducats which were a usual payment at the Papal Chancery.[128]

Such descriptions are unfortunately not common and thus the chancery notes on individual charters or certain indirect sources have to be used. They would not show the total extent of the chancery, but rather the names of the clerks. In the case of the papal nuncio Lorenzo Roverella, for example, Geraldus de Bolzanis de Regio is named as *cancellarius legati*,[129] and Angelo Cialfi, as *registrator* of the nuncio, even with a short intermission in this function as

125. Wasner, "Fifteenth-Century Texts", pp. 318-319, 325-326. See also the costs recorded in the chancery notes on the charters themselves. In the case of Juan Carvajal, e.g. 21 grossen for the seal and 35 solidi for the scribe, MNL Budapest, OL DL 15168 (31 May 1457); or Marco Barbo, 16 grossen for the scribe, seal and registration, MNL Budapest, OL DL 17479 (12 Aug 1473).

126. Dendorfer, "Ein kurialer Ordo", pp. 77-92, text edited on pp. 90-92.

127. Wasner, "Fifteenth-Century Texts", pp. 319-322, 348; Celani, ed., *Johannis Burckardi Liber*, vol. 1, pp. 653-654.

128. Wasner, "Fifteenth-Century Texts", p. 318.

129. AS Roma. Camerale I, Depositeria della crociata, vol. 1235, fol. 184v.

Cialfi worked as papal collector in Germany (1470-1472) commissioned by the nuncio; the charters were also signed by Henricus Labenter.[130] The chancery notes of the letters of Cardinal Marco Barbo, whose retinue was mentioned earlier, reveal that the chancery itself was well organised and possibly quite large. The clerks were not continuously in the presence of the legate, as they were also dispatched as envoys and messengers of the legate himself. The prelates who accompanied the cardinal, and later even became significant on their own, also made up his chancery. The chancery members could also serve more than one legate, as they formed certain skills during their service that could have been useful for others. Cardinal Tommaso De Vio had at his disposal Giovanni Battista Flavio as a secretary and the charters mention other names: B. Communellus, N. Faber as taxators and Johannes Dissoncourt as scribe in 1523-1524.[131] The last person, however, had served Cardinal Tamás Bakóc earlier and appeared signing his letters in 1515.[132] It would be possible to list many names that appear on the charters. What is, however, crucial here is that there appear to be certain personnel that might have migrated from one legate to another after the mission of the first ended or after he died in the province.

As is clear from the above-mentioned cases, a number of clerks of the chancery and other prelates accompanied the legate and they could take part in the negotiations. They also took on other roles in the retinue, namely representing the legate in his judicial authority. Such authority could have been assumed by the auditors, commissaries, and subdelegates and given to them by a delegation by the legate.[133] The auditor presided over the legate's tribunal, which copied in its functions the curial tribunals. Usually, auditors were prelates educated in law who followed the legate in his train, but who often stayed in a certain place, where the tribunal had its sessions and where not only the appeals, but also cases in the first instance were heard. This stemmed from the fact that the legate assumed the jurisdictional authority of the ordinary judge, namely the local bishop, as mentioned earlier. Gabriele Rangoni had at his disposal, for example, two clerks, Angelus de Gizalphis and Clemens de Turun, who appeared in sources as *auditores causarum curie legationis nostre*,[134] and functioned in the same way as the *auditores (generales) causarum sacri palatii*, who worked at papal

130. See NA Prague, fond Řád Františkáni, Listiny (Charters), inv. no. 41 (27 Aug 1468, Olomouc).

131. MNL Budapest, OL DL 25312 (5 Sep 1523), Dl 23922 (13 Apr 1524); Prímási és főkáptalani levéltár Esztergom, Eccl. Vetus., 81 sz. (24 Apr 1524).

132. NA Prague, fond I-ŘKř, no. 538 (www.monasterium.net; 17 Mar 2017).

133. E.g. Bónis, *Szentszéki regeszták*, passim; e.g. Augustinus de Monellis, *utriusque iuris doctor, reverendissimi in Christo patris et domini domini Gabrielis Dei gratia episcopi ecclesie Agriensis, apostolice sedis etc. legati causarum auditor generalis*, and in some cases *subdelegatus* of Gabriele Rangoni, see Lukcsics, ed., *Monumenta*, vol. 4, pp. 467-80; Georgius de Priolis, *iudex commissarius legati* or *auditor generalis* of Giovanni d'Aragona; Philippus de Segardis Senensis as *auditor generalis* of Pietro Isvalies; Mariano Bartolini, *auditor generalis* of the same; Johannes Lopecz, *commissarius supremus causarumque auditor generalis* of Angelo Pecchinoli active in Buda, MOL Budapest, OL DL 90200 (31 Mar 1489).

134. Lukcsics, ed., *Monumenta*, vol. 3, p. 264.

tribunals (*audientia causarum*, later known as *rota romana*).[135] These auditors differed from the chancery auditors in the same way as at the Papal Curia itself.[136] Auditors, then, constituted crucial members of a legate's retinue.

Legates could entrust commissaries with treating specific individual cases, unlike auditors, who assumed a general authority. A commissary then accepted part of the legate's authority, including the judicial one, even if it concerned the *forum internum*, matters of conscience and penitence.[137] Papal nuncio Lorenzo Roverella, for example, named commissaries who could publish indulgences and letters of confession (*litterae confessionales*), which enabled the addressee to elect an adequate confessor and receive absolution even in cases reserved to the Apostolic See, distributed for the financial support to the crusade against the Turks. Several persons appeared as such commissaries in 1470, for example even the local priests and significant personalities, such as Gabriel (Gábor) Matucsinai, royal vice-chancellor and parish priest of Buda, or Ladislaus (László), an abbot of the Benedictine monastery at Báta, a major pilgrimage site close to the Danube.[138]

The last category mentioned above, subdelegates, did not appear in the fifteenth-century sources all that often. Subdelegation was defined in canon law as a further, third level of papal judicial authority, as in this case, the judge's power was derived from the legate's or delegated judge's authority.[139] As an example, Baldassare Turini may be mentioned, as he represented Girolamo Lando. Baldassare remained behind in the city of Wrocław as a *subdelegatus* of Lando in 1464-1466.[140] Gabriele Rangoni also had a *subdelegatus* in the person of Augustine de Monellis, who otherwise performed the function of an auditor.[141] And the last example that can be mentioned here, comes from the early sixteenth century, when Cardinal Tamás Bakóc created *vicelegatum* for the crusade he was supposed to organise as legate *de latere* in Hungary.[142]

The image presented indicates a large company which would travel with the legate fulfilling partially obligations commissioned to the legate himself. These people originated in the Papal Curia or in the household of the cardinal, who had become a legate. Apart from these, there seems to have been general personnel, people who entered the services of legates in the province, either locals or foreigners who stayed in the region. They made up a group with a certain expertise whose members were certainly welcomed by the incoming legates. Not

135. Cf. Salonen, *Papal Justice*; eadem, "The Curia: The Sacra Romana Rota".

136. Frenz, *Papsturkunden*, p. 117.

137. Cf. Goering, "The Internal Forum", pp. 379-428. *Forum internum* is a post-Tridentine term for matters of conscience and penitence; corresponding terms in the Middle Ages are *forum poenitentiae*, *poenitentiale*, and *forum conscientiae* (p. 379).

138. MNL Budapest, OL DL 17005 (17 May 1470); DL 88508 (25 Jul 1470).

139. See, Figueira, "Subdelegation".

140. Palacky, ed., *Urkundliche Beiträge zur Geschichte Böhmens*, pp. 324-325, no. 314 (22 Jan 1464); Eschenloer, *Geschichte*, pp. 432-434.

141. Lukcsics, ed., *Monumenta*, vol. 4, pp. 467-480.

142. Fekete Nagy, Kenéz, Solymosi and Érszegi, eds., *Monumenta rusticorum*, pp. 65-66, no. 22.

surprisingly, taking into account the above-mentioned, many legates or nuncios kept reappearing in the region or in the service of the Pope as papal diplomats. These also created a group of experts who by gaining experience in the legations (either as servants to legates, or as legates themselves) became invaluable specialists in the diplomatic practice and in the regions they visited. Tilmann Schlecht, for example, who served Cardinal Juan Carvajal on his second legation to Central Europe as a notary, was sent to the region in late 1471 with the task of concluding peace between the warring kings.[143] His case, like others from the retinue of Marco Barbo, displays the situation quite illustratively. Even though a group of professionals was not yet created, they can nevertheless be regarded as a semi-professional group of prelates and clerks who dealt with papal representation in general and politics in the individual regions.

3.3. *Financing a legation*

Apart from the letters confirming their authority, all the companions and clothing, the legates needed money. The problem of financing the legation had to be clearly solved, so that the cardinal could travel with a relatively large retinue and with everything needed to represent the pope properly with all the appropriate dignity. Who was supposed to pay, however, the expenses of the legation? Where would the money come from? How much money would be needed? Such questions naturally appear when studying the representation of papal power in the countries outside Rome and Italy. As the system of papal legation changed throughout the centuries of the Middle Ages, the organisation of the financing also reflected these changes as well as changes within society, the political claims of the papacy as well as the needs of the Church. These changes also naturally included adjustments in financing.[144]

3.3.1. *Procuration*

A complicated argumentation with a simple result was used in order to secure financial support for the legates. One of the duties of a bishop or archbishop was to visit his diocese or province for reasons of teaching and inspection. In the same manner that a landlord and his representatives were entitled to receive food and lodging from the Church and the nobility, the bishop was entitled to acquire the same from the Church institutions within the area of his authority, that is the *procuratio canonica.* The pope consequently asked the bishops and archbishops to do the same for his legates. And finally, the papal legates, as direct representatives of the Pope, who was the ordinary judge of all and thus authorised to collect *procuratio canonica*, were also entitled to benefit from the

143. MNL Budapest, OL DL 14492 (29 May 1456); an early report of Schlecht in Kronthal and Wendt, eds., *Politische Correspondenz*, vol. 1, pp. 78-79, no. 109 (29 Nov 1471).
144. Maleczek, "Die päpstlichen Legaten", pp. 46-54. This section is an updated version of Kalous, "Financing a Legation".

same privilege in the individual dioceses, parts of their legatine provinces, as it was included in the decretal law of *Liber extra* (X 2.26.11; X 3.39.17).[145]

When dispatching legates, the Pope needed the support of the local church, namely the archbishops. The Patriarch of Aquileia swore to Pope Gregory VII as early as 1079 that he would support the "Roman legate" with all his necessities.[146] By the end of the twelfth century, this was one of the essential parts of the oath of the archbishop when accepting the *pallium*, as Hubert Walter, Archbishop of Canterbury, did in 1193 to Celestine III.[147] Later, such an oath would also be taken by bishops and abbots, who promised not only to help, but also to secure safe conduct and not to permit any injustice to the "legates or nuncios".[148] The province and the individual lands were to feed the legate during his travels for the entire period of his stay.

The procurations were secured by the popes for the legates as their first stable and systematised income and were used as such up until the later Middle Ages. It is clear that the procurations were mostly typical before the fifteenth century.[149] They may have secured quite a substantial income for the legate, as the case of Gentile da Montefiore, a legate in Hungary (1307-1311) shows.[150] Cases from the Kingdom of Bohemia of the second half of the thirteenth to the late fourteenth centuries also indicate that the financial burden of the support for the legate put great pressure on the province.[151] The payments by the province to the legate were often subject to criticism, even if the level of support for the individuals was limited by the Third and the Fourth Lateran Councils, as mentioned in the previous section. Pope Benedict XII further limited the support that could be drawn from the procurations and called for moderation (Extrav. comm. 3.10.un).[152] The procurations, as stated above, began to disappear along with support for the legates in their provinces, during the later part of the fourteenth century, connected to the troubled times of the schism. Although Gonzalo García de Villadiego asserted that legates could claim procurations on the basis of previous canonical tradition, he stated quite clearly that "at present, so that the subjects are relieved from the procurations of the legates, the Apostolic Chamber is accustomed to establishing a salary".[153]

145. Friedberg, ed., *Corpus*, pt. 2, cols. 385, 627-628; Ruess, *Die rechtliche Stellung*, pp. 187-188; Figueira, *The Canon Law*, pp. 332-348, 409-415; Robinson, *The Papacy*, pp. 162, 266-267.

146. "Legatum Romanum eundo et redeundo honorifice tractabo et in necessitatibus suis adiuvabo", cited in idem, "The institutions", p. 406.

147. Tangl, *Die päpstlichen Kanzleiordnungen*, pp. 50-51, no. 18; Robinson, "The institutions", p. 406.

148. Tangl, *Die päpstlichen Kanzleiordnungen*, pp. 51-52, no. 19.

149. Maleczek, "Die päpstlichen Legaten", pp. 46-49; Ruess, *Die rechtliche Stellung*, pp. 187-204.

150. Maleczek, "Die päpstlichen Legaten", p. 46; Pór, ed., *Acta legationis*, pp. 416-472.

151. Krofta, "Kurie a církevní správa" (1908), pp. 425-434; Szczur, *Skarbovość*, pp. 231-233.

152. Friedberg, ed., *Corpus*, pt. 2, cols. 1280-1284.

153. *Tractatus universi iuris*, vol. 13/2, fol. 270r.

3.3.2. *Central payments*

As early as the fourteenth century, in connection with the Avignon papacy and most significantly the Great Schism, the system would have had to be adjusted to the new financial situation of the Church and with the papacy itself. New payments from the centre were offered to the legates as part of their legatine duties. In the beginning of the fourteenth century, during the pontificate of Pope John XXII, instances can be found of special financial support for the nuncios by the papacy, while later the central payments of the legates or nuncios can be substantiated with documentary evidence.[154] The fourteenth century can be understood, however, as a transitional phase in the legatine system and in terms of the system of their financing. Cardinal legates were members of the cardinals' college and thus able to participate in the income of the college. It is, however, in the beginning of the fourteenth century that this income began to be reserved exclusively for those cardinals who stayed at the Curia. This practice is confirmed by the constitution of Clement V of 1312, which expressly states that all the cardinals are entitled to participate in the income of the college (that is the cardinals' share in the common and the petty services, *servicia communia* and *servicia minuta*) excluding those who at the time held legatine office.[155]

The income from the legatine province was thus even more crucial to sustaining the legate. The constitution of 1312 was circumvented for various reasons, however, fairly soon after. There was a growing number of cardinals sent from the Curia as nuncios in the fourteenth century, who participated in the income of the college, but had no right to the resources of the local church.[156] Even if the general rule that the legates do not have a share of the college's income was valid throughout the fourteenth and fifteenth centuries,[157] there was another way around this restriction. Especially, after the end of the schism and final victory of the popes over the conciliarists, it became a frequent practice to issue exemptions for the cardinals. These were simple papal concessions involving the right to participate in the revenues of the College of Cardinals, a special exemption from the rule, which could take various

154. Baumgarten, *Untersuchungen*, p. 4, no. 8, p. 6, no. 10.

155. *Ibid.*, pp. 1-2, no. 3, "De fratrum nostrorum consilio, hac in perpetuum valitura constitutione sanccimus, ut Sancte Romane Ecclesie cardinales presentes pariter et futuri, qui sunt vel deinceps erunt, de nostra vel successorum nostrorum Romanorum pontificum licentia speciali absentes a loco, in quo Romanus pontifex cum sua curia duxerit residendum, illis tamen, qui legationis funguntur adpresens vel imposterum fungentur officio dumtaxat exceptis, ad omnes fructus, redditus et proventus ac obventiones inter cardinales dividi consuetos, undecumque et ex quacumque causa proveniant, quocumque nomine censeantur et in quibuscumque consistant, velud presentes admicti per omnia debeant, et quo ad plenum in illis participium, habeantur pro presentibus, consuetudine quacumque contraria non obstante. Per hanc autem constitutionem omnem aliam super hoc editam revocatam esse decernimus et prorsus viribus vacuatam".

156. Kyer, *The Papal Legate*, pp. 28-31; idem, "*Legatus* and *nuncius*", pp. 475-477; Lützelschwab, *Flectat cardinales*, passim.

157. Dykmans, ed., *Le cérémonial papal*, vol. 2, p. 500; Dykmans, ed., *L'oeuvre de Patrizi Piccolomini*, vol. 1, p. 158.

forms. For example, Cardinal Jean Le Jeune was a legate to Milan in 1447 and participated in the income of the Sacred College and in the same year Cardinal Juan Carvajal left as legate *de latere* to Germany and took a share in the income of the College for six months. Cardinal Nicholas of Cusa served as a legate to Germany in 1451 and participated in the income for the entire year.[158] Cardinals Marco Barbo in 1472-1474, Giovanni d'Aragona and Ausias Despuig in 1479, for example, were conceded the right to participate in the revenues for the whole duration of their legation.[159] The situation was, however, not always so clear. It was explicitly stated in the consistorial diary in October 1451 that the five cardinals who were not present at the curia should not participate in the income. One of them was Cardinal Guillaume d'Estouteville who was created legate *de latere* to France in August. It was later, however, agreed by the cardinals representing the College, that Cardinal Guillaume should participate in the revenues for one year after his departure on 16 September 1451, but he did not have any share in the income of the cardinals' chamber from the churches of Salzburg, Canterbury, York, Lichfield and Carlisle. He was instead entitled to receive 1,000 gold florins of the Chamber, which were assigned to him from the income of the church of Poitiers. No further participation was allowed; the cardinal only began to participate in the revenues again after his return in January 1453.[160] The situation was even more complicated when the cardinals were absent without a legatine commission. In any case, many legates were able to obtain some extra income from the College of Cardinals, even when absent from Rome.

At the same time, further income may have been secured from the original benefices of the legate, who might also be awarded a faculty to extract money from his benefice, where he was not present, because of his stay in the legatine province.[161] A special situation in terms of benefices came about in Hungary, were the King held the patronage right over the Hungarian church. During the reign of King Matthias Corvinus and his followers, several legates even became bishops in the country and could have utilized the resources of the individual benefices.[162] This is, however, a specific circumstance, which cannot be regarded as the regular income of the legates. Local bishops also occasionally became legates or nuncios with the power of legaes *de latere*. It is not known, unfortunately, whether their financing was in any way adjusted. The revenues of the benefices and of the cardinals' chamber were not part of the central income from the *Camera Apostolica*. The remaining possibilities for financing are, however, directly linked to the resources of the central Apostolic Chamber.

The criticism of the procurations necessarily brought about some further changes in the system of financing the legations of papal legates *de latere* and

158. Eubel, *Hierarchia catholica*, vol. 2, pp. 29-30.

159. *Ibid.*, pp. 38, 42.

160. *Ibid.*, pp. 30-31; Bourgin, "Les cardinaux", p. 289.

161. For example, the *familiares* of Ausias Despuig in 1479, see ASV, Reg. Vat. 680, fol. 147r-148r.

162. For example, Gabriele Rangoni became Bishop of Alba Iulia (1472) and later Bishop of Eger (1475); Giovanni d'Aragona, Archbishop of Esztergom (1479/1484); Baldassare Turini, Bishop of Srem (1479); Pietro Isvalies, Bishop of Veszprém (1503).

other papal representatives. Apart from the income of the College of Cardinals, there were other resources of the central financial system that were to be used. Even if the sources of the money may have varied, it was always the income of the Chamber that was redistributed. The revenues could come from annates, services, subsidies, further taxes, but also from indulgences, the crusading fund, Turkish war support, etc.[163] Thus, it could still have been the province itself that paid for the stay of the legate; no longer, however, with the procurations, even if there were still some isolated references to them in the early fifteenth century.[164] Such revenues were usually gathered by the papal collectors, who could then redistribute the money on the spot and supply it to the legates.[165] The most important result of the reconstruction of the financing of the legates was that there were now standard salaries granted to the individual representatives of the pope. In 1422, for example, Cardinal Branda Castiglione, a legate to Bohemia with the task of organising the crusade against the Hussites, was assigned a salary of 200 florins per month drawn from the Apostolic Chamber. He was, however, still entitled to receive procurations.[166] The organisation and the amount of the salary developed during the early fifteenth century and had been clarified and stabilised by the second half of that century.[167]

3.3.3. *The salary of the legate*

Legates *de latere* were assigned as a rule a salary of 500 florins per month in the second half of the fifteenth and early sixteenth centuries. This salary was extremely high, even in comparison with other high dignitaries of the Church. For a comparison, the annual income of almost all Italian bishoprics was much lower than this monthly payment.[168] A cardinal, who fulfilled his task as a legate, had to surpass all the church hierarchy in the parts to which he was sent, and also – when possible – outmatch secular dignitaries including the king or the emperor. While the amount of salary was usually clear, there were more complicated problems involving getting hold of the money and securing sufficient resources for such a costly undertaking.

The payments of the Apostolic Chamber must have come from the central budget, which was, however, not yet (or only very occasionally and without detailed analysis) planned in advance in the later Middle Ages.[169] Receiving a salary from the resources of the Chamber might have been consequently problematic, especially in the case of the *ad hoc* papal legates, whose expenditures could not be arranged and

163. Lunt, *Papal Revenues*, vol. 1, pp. 57-136; Partner, "Papal Financial Policy"; Thomson, *Popes and Princes*, pp. 78-94; Maleczek, "Die päpstlichen Legaten", p. 52.

164. *Ibid.*, p. 50.

165. Schuchard, *Die päpstliche Kollektoren*, pp. 66-68.

166. Eršil, ed., *Acta Martini*, pt. 1, p. 380, no. 924; Maleczek, "Die päpstlichen Legaten", p. 50.

167. For the payments in relation to the crusade see, Weber, *Lutter contre le Turcs*, pp. 266-276.

168. Hay, *The Church*, pp. 110-117.

169. Partner, "Papal Financial Policy", pp. 32-39.

accounted for in advance. A means of transmitting the desired financial support to the legate (or his procurator) must have nevertheless been devised. In this case, four possibilities may have occurred: (1) receiving money directly from the Apostolic Chamber, which would mean a direct transfer in Rome; (2) using bank services, which might be problematic in the areas without bank systems and Italian financial structures; (3) securing income on the basis of revenues due to the Chamber in the regions; and finally (4) investing private personal money in the undertaking and then negotiating with the Chamber for reimbursement.

First, as the legate planned his departure from Rome, he was given the first payment, which – in this period – usually equalled to the salary for the first four months, i.e. 2,000 florins. This practice is attested to by a number of sources and a number of individual legates. A special case is mentioned by Giacomo Gherardi da Volterra in his *Roman diary:* he speaks about the legatine creation of Cardinal Giovanni Battista Cibo (the future Pope Innocent VIII) in 1481 and about his later rejection of the legation. "It is rumoured that the reason for renouncing the legation of the *Melfitensis* [the cardinal was also the bishop of Molfetta, close to Bari] was that the two thousand florins that were given to him seemed to him too little. They were estimated as being insufficient for the long lasting legation, but hardly for leaving Rome".[170] The legate was replaced by another one, a nuncio with the power of the legate *de latere* Orso Orsini, who undoubtedly did not spend as much money. It is apparent, however, that the 2,000 florins were not to be spent on the entire legation, but were instead a cash advance for the first four months.

The cash payment was only one way of financing the legations. The rest was usually in the hands of the legate, who spent the local revenues of the Chamber or his own financial resources. The legates were usually (*ut moris est*) assigned 500 florins per month, as, for example, in the case of Cardinal Bessarion in 1460.[171] For further illustration, the Chamber paid 6,000 florins to Didacus de Vayas, a canon of Ávila and procurator of Cardinal Juan Carvajal, the legate in Hungary, in a series of instalments between September 1458 and July 1459 to provide for twelve months salary in total.[172] As stated above, this was the standard amount in the second half of the fifteenth century and still in the early sixteenth, before the introduction of permanent nuncios. The advance payment of 2,000 florins at the start of the legation was usually the only money the legates received directly from the Apostolic Chamber before or during the legation; although we should note the above-mentioned cases of Cardinals Juan Carvajal and Bessarion. Ready money was thus a problem, as demonstrated by the larger loan (600 florins) obtained by Cardinal Bessarion in Vienna in 1461, which he promised to pay back in Venice.[173] A few cases may be examined here to illustrate the system.

170. Gherardi da Volterra, *Il diario romano*, pp. 36-37.

171. ASV, Cam. Ap., Div. Cam. 29, fol. 98r, "... Et ut moris est idem sanctissimus dominus noster statuit, quod ipse legatus habeat pro sua provisione omni mense de pecuniis camere apostolice quingentos floren. auri de camera ...".

172. ASV, Cam. Ap., Intr. et Ex. 440, fol. 84r, 126r, 130v, 132r, 136r.

173. Maleczek, "Die päpstlichen Legaten", p. 51; Mohler, *Kardinal Bessarion*, vol. 3, pp. 507-508, no. 47.

In December 1471, Pope Sixtus IV created five legates, who left Rome to all parts of Europe in support of the crusade that the new Pope planned against the Ottoman Turks. One of the legates was Cardinal Bessarion, who was an experienced legate following his earlier obligations in Germany and in Venice. In 1460, as stated above, he had spent some time in Vienna and there are references to his receiving 2,000 florins in advance and then five payments of 1,000 florins each in the registers of the mandates of the Chamber.[174] This was not enough, however, since his legation lasted for twenty-two months in total and he was due to obtain some 11,000 florins from the Chamber. As a general rule, after returning to Rome, the legate was obliged to present his accounts in the Chamber. Cardinal Bessarion did so in the form of a little paper booklet (*in quodam parvo quinterno papireo*) in December 1461 and the accounts were approved with the Chamber being still a debtor (*debetrix*) to the Cardinal of 3,000 gold florins of the Chamber.[175] The records of the Chamber attest to 7,000 florins plus the debt of 3,000. If these numbers are correct, the accounts of the cardinal might have justified 1,000 florins at most. The *exitus* of the Chamber mentions the payment of 5,250 florins as late as the beginning of the pontificate of Sixtus IV, which was still paying off debts owed to the legate from the legations in Germany and Venice.[176] Bessarion soon became a legate again and spent almost seven months on legation to France before he died in Ravenna. He had left Rome on 20 April 1472 and the registers of the Chamber show that he was paid two sums of 1,041 florins and 36 or 48 bolognini respectively before he departed from Rome, which equals 2,000 florins.[177] He was given 2,000 florins as an advance payment before he started his legation for both the major legations. The further salary was then 500 florins per month at least in the first case. The legation to France ended in total failure and finally in his death before he was able to return to Rome.

Another of the legates of 1471, Cardinal Marco Barbo, left Rome on 22 February 1472 and returned on 26 October 1474, that is after more than thirty-two months; thus the salary was to be 16,000 florins. Cardinal Barbo was initially paid 2,083 florins and 24 solidi through the Medici bank a week before he left Rome.[178] During his absence on legation there are no references in the Chamber's registers, but for a few payments to the legate. In February 1473, Cardinal Barbo was paid 100 florins as revenues from the Chamber for January 1472, when he still resided in Rome; it is not related, however, to his legation.[179] Two months later, he received 766 florins from the papal collector in Poland and in July 100 florins from the Chamber.[180] Finally, in April and August 1474 two payments of

174. *Repertorium Germanicum*, vol. 8/1, no. 513.

175. ASV, Cam. Ap., Div. Cam. 29, fol. 235v-236r.

176. ASV, Cam. Ap., Intr. et Ex. 487, fol. 103v.

177. ASV, Cam. Ap., Intr. et Ex. 487, fol. 164v, 166v; compare with Eubel, *Hierarchia catholica*, vol. 2, p. 38.

178. ASV, Cam. Ap., Intr. et Ex. 487, fol. 152r; cf. AS Roma, Camerale I, Mandati della Camera Apostolica, vol. 845, fol. 87v.

179. AS Roma, Camerale I, Mandati della Camera Apostolica, vol. 845, fol. 186r.

180. AS Roma, Camerale I, Mandati della Camera Apostolica, vol. 845, fol. 202r; vol. 846, fol. 5v.

541 and 1,000 florins respectively are attested to in the *exitus*,[181] and the legate received a further payment of 1,000 florins in October.[182] It is, thus, quite clear that the legate must have used much of his own money to finance the legation. Only after he arrived back in Rome was the salary properly administered by the Apostolic Chamber. As in the case of Cardinal Bessarion, the legate would have had to present the accounts of his legation, which were used for the settlement of the expenses of the legation. Cardinal Barbo presented his accounts[183] and the final settlement of the Chamber was issued more than a year after his return to Rome, on 15 December 1475. The *camerlengo* Cardinal Latino Orsini signed a mandate which stated that Marco Barbo was still a creditor to the Chamber for 4,825 florins; 1,000 florins of which were accounted for from the Chamber. Cardinal Orsini assigned the outstanding debt of 3,825 florins to the revenues of the March of Ancona, but it was impossible to draw more than 700 florins from those revenues and a new assignment was made in the land of Soriano nel Cimino near Rome, for a total of 3,125 florins (he, however, had to share the revenues of Soriano with other beneficiaries).[184] The account book of Marco Barbo could have revealed much more than is available in the records of the Chamber, which come to only 11,416 florins.[185] This means that Barbo's accounts should have shown the origin of further income of more than 4,500 florins. These could have come (at least in part) from the benefices in the province, since Cardinal Marco obtained a faculty to extract the revenues due to the Chamber, including the payment of the census, Peter's pence and the annates. The legate must have accounted for the collecting of such money.[186] One such example (even though outside the legatine

181. ASV, Cam. Ap., Intr. et Ex. 488, fol. 158r; 490, fol. 83v. For the first one cf. AS Roma, Camerale I, Mandati della Camera Apostolica, vol. 846, fol. 66r.

182. AS Roma, Camerale I, Mandati della Camera Apostolica, vol. 846, fol. 115v.

183. The accounts of the legation of Marco Barbo were still present in the chamber in 1485. After a cleric of the chamber Antonio da Forlì died in that same year, the book of Marco Barbo's accounts was returned to the office from the cleric's home together with eighty other books including the accounts of other five legates and nuncios. An inventory of the cleric's books in ASV, Cam. Ap., Div. Cam. 44, fol. 96r-97v; edited by Göller, "Untersuchungen", pp. 233-236. The inventory mentions the accounts as "Computa reverendissimi domini cardinalis sancti Marci in partibus Germanie et Ungarie legati".

184. ASV, Cam. Ap., Div. Cam. 39, fol. 50r-51r. See also Schlecht, *Andrea Zamometić*, p. 152, with some inconsistencies; for other payments from Soriano Marco Barbo had to respect, see AS Roma, Collezione acquisiti e doni, b. 26, no. 1, fol. 171v-172v.

185. Apart from the above-mentioned places see also ASV, Cam. Ap., Intr. et Ex. 490, fol. 106r, when Barbo received 1,000 florins. It is not clear, however, whether this sum is the one mentioned in Latino Orsini's mandate. If so, the sum accounted for in the records of the chamber would be 10,416 florins.

186. ASV, Reg. Vat. 680, fol. 56r, "… et cum inibi quam plurime pecuniarum summe tam ipsorum annuorum censuum, quam denarii sancti Petri, necnon annatorum ocasione ac etiam aliter camere apostolice debeantur. Nos cupientes, ut de dictis pecuniarum summis prefate camere quam tocius satisfiat, circumspectioni tue omnes et singulas pecuniarum summas huiumodi eidem camere premissorum, vel alia quacumque occasione in natione Germania provinciis civitatibus terris locis necnon regnis predictis debitas a quibusvis personis cuiuscumque dignitatis status gradus ordinis vel preeminentie fuerint, eciam si archiepiscopali

province of Marco Barbo) could be drawn from the records of the Chamber. Cardinal Latino wrote to the papal collector in Venice who was supposed to pay money to the messengers and couriers of Marco Barbo in March 1473. The accounts from November 1472 to June 1473 indicate total expenditures of 64 florins.[187] The case of Marco Barbo clearly exposes the system of financing from the Apostolic Chamber, including the tendency of the papacy towards temporal revenues in the second half of the fifteenth century.[188] The problem of identifying, however, the sources of a large part of the salary remains.

The third of the five legates appointed in 1471 was sent to Naples. The case of Cardinal Oliviero Carafa was special since he was destined to lead the papal fleet, and thus the Chamber paid within a few months a larger sum of money for the costs of the navy. The Chamber disbursed in total almost 70,000 florins, including four months salary of the legate.[189] The study of the other two legates of 1471 does not add any further information, but examples of yet other legates of the period may help to elucidate the financial strategies of the Apostolic Chamber.

Similarly as in the case of Marco Barbo, Cardinal Pietro Isvalies still had to settle the expenses of his legation a long time after he returned to Rome. His legation lasted for thirty-five months and he returned to the City in October 1503. It was only in May 1505 that the Chamber, in the person of *camerlengo* Cardinal Raffaele Riario Sansoni, confirmed its debts to Cardinal Pietro. An agreement explicitly mentions the total number of months and the monthly payment of 500 florins. The cardinal was supposedly paid 2,000 florins upon leaving Rome and then three payments of 1,000 florins, which he received in Hungary. The income of the Jubilee and the confessionals, which went to the servants of the legate, is mentioned as the source of one of the latter payments. Otherwise, the Chamber remained in debt to the cardinal to the enormous sum of 11,500 florins.[190]

Cardinal Ausias Despuig was one of the three legates sent from the court of Sixtus IV in 1479. His legation to Germany lasted for six and a half months, as he returned on 1 December 1479. His case is even more informative than that of Cardinal Marco Barbo, since at least short accounts of his travels have been preserved in the records of the Chamber.[191] The accounts were presented by

episcopali vel alia quavis dignitate prefulgeant exigendi et levandi necnon personas ipsas per excommunicationis et alias sentencias censuras et penas, de quibus tibi videbitur, quas aggravare et reaggravare possis et valeas, ad illarum solucionem cogendi et compellendi ac de receptis nostro et dicte camere nomine etiam in forma autentica quitandi et absolvendi certaque omnia et singula facienda gerendi disponendi et ordinandi, que circa premissa tibi visa fuerint oportuna plenam et liberam tenore presentium facultatem concedimus et etiam potestatem…".

187. ASV, Cam. Ap., Div. Cam. 37, fol. 218rv.

188. Thomson, *Popes and Princes*, pp. 82-83.

189. ASV, Cam. Ap., Intr. et Ex. 487, fol. 163r-183v passim. Platina (Gaida, ed., *Platynae historici Liber*, p. 405) mentioned 65,000 florins; and he also confirmed that 500 florins were assigned to each legate as monthly payment (p. 404), "… singulis enim legatis singulis mensibus quingenti aurei nummi assignati sunt".

190. ASV, Cam. Ap., Div. Cam. 57, fol. 140v-142v.

191. ASV, Cam. Ap., Div. Cam. 40, fol. 71r-72r; edited in Göller, "Zur Geschichte", pp. 239-240; summarised also in ASV, Cam. Ap., Div. Cam. 40, fol. 62v.

the secretary of the legate before the Apostolic Chamber and agreed on by the clerics of the Chamber. The accounts show the same situation: he had been given 2,000 florins when leaving the City and was able to draw income from annates and collation of benefices worth 87 ducats, the new Chamber gold coins, and 67 Rhenish guilders. He was therefore owed 1,114 ducats and 18 bolognini by the Chamber. A later mandate of *camerlengo* Cardinal Guillaume d'Estouteville (May 1480) only stipulated that the debt should be paid from the revenues of the Chamber, but does not identify the specific resources.[192] In the same year, Cardinal Giovanni d'Aragona was sent as legate *de latere* to Hungary. As in other cases, the Chamber is confirmed to be the *debitrix* to the legate after he returned and presented his accounts to the clerics of the Chamber. The legate should have been paid 6,000 florins, but the accounts attest the receipt of only 3,208 florins and 22 solidi; thus, the Chamber still owed 2,791 florins and 28 solidi.[193]

The accounts of the legates and the individual settlements with the Apostolic Chamber indicate that larger amounts of money must have been invested by the legates to sustain themselves in their legatine tasks, even if they did not need to spend all 500 florins per month. The actual expenditures and outlays of the legates, cannot be ascertained, however, on the basis of the available sources.

3.3.4. *The salary of the nuncio*

The salaries of the papal nuncios with the power of legates *de latere* were naturally much smaller than those of the legates. They had a lesser need for display; their retinue and chancery were much smaller. Their monthly income in the second half of the fifteenth century usually amounted to between 100 and 200 florins; no clear rule, however, existed. Thus, Rudolf of Rüdesheim (as *legatus missus cum potestate legati de latere* or *nuncius*), for example, was assigned 65 florins of the revenues of the Apostolic Chamber per month in 1465.[194] Papal nuncio Lorenzo Roverella, his companion and partner in organising the crusade against King George of Bohemia, was able to obtain a sum of 150 florins per month from the *Depositeria della crociata* during the period of May to December 1467.[195] His salary came from the special fund for organising crusades, which was predominantly used against the Ottoman Turks, although the Hussites (Utraquists) of Bohemia and the heretical King George also received their share of attention. It meant, however, that the Chamber was able to use other resources of financial support. Several years later, in 1475, papal nuncio to Germany, Hungary, Poland and Bohemia Baldassare Turini da Pescia was entitled to a salary of 80 florins per month with a retinue of eight horses.[196] A year later, papal nuncio Domenico Camisati with the same commission could extract a salary

192. ASV, Cam. Ap., Div. Cam. 40, fol. 94v-95r.
193. ASV, Cam. Ap., Div. Cam. 40, fol. 216rv.
194. ASV, Cam. Ap., Intr. et Ex. 459, fol. 109v.
195. AS Roma, Camerale I, Depositeria della crociata, vol. 1235, fol. 82r, 135r, 145v, 146r; Beneš, "Depositeria", pp. 747, 749.
196. AS Roma, Camerale I, Mandati della Camera Apostolica, vol. 846, fol. 216v, 218v.

of 200 florins per month.[197] A special situation may be observed in the case of the frequently-mentioned Angelo Pecchinoli in 1488. The Apostolic Chamber had an individual agreement with the nuncio, who was to receive 100 florins per month as a salary from the Chamber, or 120 florins from the revenues of the church of Kalocsa, whose archbishop Péter Váradi was imprisoned at the time.[198] When easier, the nuncios would be assigned the revenues with which the Chamber had certain problems.

As the above-mentioned inventory of accounting books transferred to the Apostolic Chamber in 1485 indicates, the nuncios were also obliged to present the accounts of their missions.[199] A settlement of the expenses of a nuncio was preserved in the case of Antonio Grassi, who was dispatched to the Roman Emperor in 1478. Antonio Grassi accounted for the expenses incurred by himself and ten persons (with horses) in his retinue; in total, he should have been paid one thousand one hundred and fifty-six and two-thirds florins, representing 100 florins per month. The Chamber had paid 450 florins and thus 706 florins remained to be accounted for. Due to the deaths of horses and some other losses, however, the total debt of the Chamber was in fact 800 florins and the sum of 720 florins was later to be paid through the Florentine banks of the Ricasoli and the Arabatti families.[200]

Some further individual documents, which were transcribed in the registers of the Apostolic Chamber, reveal the sources of revenue that the nuncios could draw on for their activities. Bartolomeo Maraschi, for example, in 1484 issued a receipt (*quitantia*) to the collector of Mainz Konrad Tues, which confirmed he had received 120 Rhenish guilders from the revenues of the Chamber.[201] Similarly, in the same year, but a few months earlier, papal nuncio Angelo Geraldini received 200 florins from the same papal collector. The collector was even asked to assist Angelo by a direct *breve* from the pope.[202] Not only the collectors, however, but also individual church institutions may have been approached by the legates or nuncios with requests for assistance. The papal nuncio Alexander Numai, for example, in 1475 obtained 20 Rhenish guilders from the annates of a female convent in Cologne.[203] Last but not least, the case of yet another legate dispatched from Rome at the start of the pontificate of Sixtus IV, Cardinal Roderigo Borja (the future Alexander VI), who was sent to the Iberian kingdoms, shows that the most highly-ranking legates *de latere* would also do the same as nuncios, that is, collect money from local church institutions and issue receipts. He collected 50 florins as half of the annates from the canonry of Seville.[204] As mentioned above, the legates as well as nuncios

197. ASV, Cam. Ap., Div. Cam. 38, fol. 207r.
198. ASV, Cam. Ap., Div. Cam. 46, fol. 188v, 195rv.
199. Cf. an edited report of nuncio *cum potestate legati de latere* in Poland Battista Enrici from 1448, Kowalski, "Baptysty Enriciego", pp. 585-588.
200. ASV, Cam. Ap., Div. Cam. 40, fol. 61v-62r and fol. 95v-96r.
201. ASV, Cam. Ap., Div. Cam. 46, fol. 239v.
202. ASV, Cam. Ap., Div. Cam. 46, fol. 240rv, 241rv.
203. ASV, Cam. Ap., Div. Cam. 39, fol. 21v.
204. ASV, Cam. Ap., Div. Cam. 39, fol. 15v.

could have carried special faculties, which enabled them to collect almost any payment due to the Apostolic Chamber, or direct briefs to the local collectors, who could then help them.

3.3.5. *Further resources*

The legates and nuncios had still further opportunities for financial support. The legatine chancery produced a number of letters and charters that were to be paid for by the recipients. It was entitled to publish such charters in the same way as the Papal Chancery, as mentioned in the previous section (§ 3.2.2.). This income could be high, but difficult to identify. The chancery could earn considerable money when it was large enough and the legate had at his disposal a high number of faculties. A legate's *ordo* for running of the chancery written in 1482/1483 and based on Francesco Todeschini Piccolomini's legation in 1471 identified, in contrast, even the treasurer of the legate's chancery. He was responsible for listing all the income both from publishing the charters and from annats and collecting the money in a chest with a lock. Moreover, the income should be counted every month and money earned with taxes for the charters divided in two: one half for the legate, one for the clerks of the chancery, who do not receive any share in the annats. This *ordo* mentioned a significant number of people writing supplications and the price for a charter being one florin, nevertheless the income of the chancery cannot be ascertained, as accounts and registers of letters are generally missing. Further research is thus needed to evaluate the possibilities for the legate's chancery to support itself.[205]

There was naturally the possibility of receiving gifts and presents on the spot. It was, however, forbidden to the legates to accept gifts, as stipulated by the legatine ceremonial drafted by Cardinal Francesco Todeschini Piccolomini. It is clear, however, that this regulation was not always observed. Only food, drink and fodder were gifts which could be accepted.[206] Such a situation is attested to by local sources for a number of legates and nuncios. Cardinal Marco Barbo, for example, accepted gifts in Wrocław only to the degree permitted. The efforts of the Wrocław burghers to give him more were, in his eyes, related to the devoutness of the burghers rather than an attempt to bribe the legate.[207] Similarly, papal nuncio Lorenzo Roverella accepted just "three measures of oats, one quarter of white beer and one wineskin of malmsey" in Wrocław.[208] Jan Długosz, the Polish chronicler of the later fifteenth century, even told the story of the papal legate (or nuncio) Rudolf of Rüdesheim, to whom Casimir, the King of Poland, offered very generous gifts when the legate was leaving Toruń, including forty florins, four silver dishes, two bowls and various beautiful pieces of clothing, etc. The legate, however, "with his celebrated modesty, refused to accept them, so that he would not come into disgrace." The chronicler even mentioned that such gifts

205. For the *ordo* see Dendorfer, "Ein kurialer Ordo".
206. Wasner, "Fifteenth-Century Texts", p. 329.
207. Kronthal and Wendt, eds., *Politische Correspondenz*, vol. 1, p. 106, no. 145.
208. Eschenloer, *Geschichte*, p. 763.

were forbidden by the Apostolic See.[209] Thus, it is clear that the rules had a general validity, which was known outside the Curia.

Cases of legates (or nuncios) accepting lavish presents may be identified, however, in the sources as well. Girolamo Lando, the papal legate (but not a cardinal legate) was given many presents by King George of Bohemia, as well as by the burghers of Wrocław, who were in opposition to the King. In the latter case, financial gifts were also given to other members of the legate's retinue.[210] Similarly, Achille Grassi, a nuncio with the powers of a legate *de latere*, accepted large and generous presents from Casimir, King of Poland, when leaving the royal court in 1510.[211] As in the case of the resources of the local benefices, these cannot be regarded as the regular and standard revenues of the legates.

All the cases reveal a standardised procedure in accounting for the financial needs of the papal legates and nuncios in the second half of the fifteenth and early sixteenth centuries. It is clear that the financing of the papal legations had changed substantially compared to the twelfth and thirteenth century *procuratio canonica*, which had come under criticism in the fourteenth century and obviously was not enough to meet the changing needs of the cardinal legates. The financial support of the legates was always a special expense of the Apostolic Chamber and only with the use of nuncios for permanent representation did the financial system begin to change.[212]

The legates could have utilised the resources of their legatine provinces. Instead of procurations, however, these were the regular (annates, services, spoils, etc.) as well as extraordinary (crusade money, indulgence, Jubilee, etc.) revenues of the Chamber. A detailed accounting of all the income received from these sources was required from the legates after they returned to Rome. Generally, a salary of 500 florins per month was typical for the legates *de latere*, i.e. the cardinal legates, who must have used their own money to support themselves during their legations. It seems that in the 1460s, the legates were sent more money in more instalments in addition to the first advance payment for four months (2,000 florins) before their departure. In the later periods, however, the Apostolic Chamber was unable to pay further instalments to the legates during their legations. As a rule, the legates became the creditors of the Chamber. The debt was then redeemed from the revenues of the Chamber, very often from its temporal income.

The period of the second half of the fifteenth and early sixteenth centuries also represents a transitional period for the financial organisation of the legations. The financial needs, which were taken up by the Apostolic Chamber, to alleviate the burden of the province, could, however, contribute to a change in the system, as they clearly became unbearable for the papal budget. Permanent nuncios became the rule in the sixteenth century and the system gradually developed. The nuncios, then, were better suited to the needs of a planned budgetary policy. The *ad hoc* legates *de latere*, who remained in their legations for three years or more, became history during the substantial changes of the sixteenth century.

209. *Joannis Dlugossii Annales*, 1462-1480, pp. 168-169.
210. Eschenloer, *Historia*, p. 98; idem, *Geschichte*, p. 300.
211. Smołucha, *Papiestwo a Polska*, p. 115.
212. Cf. Partner, "Papal Financial Policy".

4. Politics and diplomacy

From the "how" we can now move to the "why". Why did the legates visit their province? Why did they leave Rome at all? Why did the popes sent them? With such a large number of legates, naturally, a large number of reasons appear. In general, papal legates *de latere* were sent out of Rome or out of the Curia for causes related to the Church government, as is clear from the above text, or for political and church-political matters of the period and of the region. This part of the book will focus on general theoretical reasons for legations with actual examples.

As Innocent III remarked, a man could not be simultaneously in diverse places, neither could he quickly fly to such a place, when trying to avoid a delay in action, and thus a pope needs his legates or judges delegate.[1] Legates were then sent out of the Curia to solve various problems of the Church government in the local setting and support the politics and intentions of the papacy. The actual reasons for sending a legate are definitely varied and difficult to describe in detail, as each situation would require some individual study. In order to obtain some kind of overview, one might focus on general political and church-political causes. The legates led negotiations for supporting papal policy within the regions they visited. In the later Middle Ages, the popes no longer attempted to acquire secular rule over the whole of Christendom, but on European level were instead arbiters of regional political problems and struggles, as well as organisers of larger projects, especially the crusades. For Central Europe, where most of the examples are drawn, the crusades were ever present in the period due to the two major challenges to western Christendom in the fifteenth century, namely the Bohemian Hussites and the Ottoman Turks. Bohemia attracted the attention of papal policy due to the Hussite movement in the 1420s and 1430s. Several crusades were organised at this time, as well as in the later period in the late 1460s and early 1470s. After a short break at the beginning of the fifteenth century, the Turkish crusades were again a repeated issue for papal policy as of the 1440s. Both these problems led legates to the German lands and Hungary most importantly, but also to other parts of the region of Central Europe and even the entire continent. The crusades represent the most crucial problem of the period and is to some extent central to all the legations, as they combine

1. Cf. Müller, "The Omnipresent Pope", p. 199.

matters of both an ecclesiastical and secular nature. Legates came to the regions to solve matters of both the ecclesiastical and secular substance. Other such matters that the legates dealt with concerned the general situation of the local churches and the bishoprics and the bishops of the region, whereas problems of secular politics were mostly related to the question of peace between the local lords (and thus linked to the crusade).

4.1. *Papal legates and the crusades*

Legates were present on expeditions from the very beginning of the crusading movement during the pontificate of Pope Urban II. Bishop Adhémar of Le Puy was appointed legate to the army in 1096, commissioned to promote the crusade and be one of the leaders of the armies in Europe as well as in the far-off Holy Land.[2] His position was not only based on his personal abilities, but it was conceived as an office: after Adhémar's death he was replaced by other prelates who also held legatine powers.[3] He had thus established a precedent for later crusades: legates were usually present and influential in the leadership of a crusade.

What was the role of legates in the later crusades? What capacity did legates hold upon entering the field of crusading activity? Did they continue personally to wield the sword against their enemies and lead crusading armies? The role of papal legates is traditionally described according to the afore-mentioned model, but both the office of papal legates and their operational roles evolved in different settings and times. Legates and nuncios were concerned with two specific forms of crusade in the fifteenth century: one against the advancing Ottoman Turks, the other against the first successful heretics, the Hussites of Bohemia. The Ottoman Turks had set foot on the European continent in the mid-fourteenth century and by the end of it had managed to conquer large parts of the south-eastern tip of Europe. Although their advance was halted by Timur Lenk and subsequent internal conflicts, the issues raised by their expansion resurfaced in the 1420s and 1430s, featuring in the texts of popes, scholars as well as popular preachers for centuries to come. The Hussites were, in contrast, successful in their revolt and managed to exert control over most of Bohemia and Moravia in the 1420s and early 1430s. Constant civil war and occasional struggle against external intruders led to a split within Czech society and to the creation of the Utraquist church (from communion in both kinds, *sub utraque specie*), which incorporated a number of the main ideas of the Hussite revolution. The country later became problematic once again and a crusade was proclaimed not only in the first stage of the revolt, but also in the later 1460s.[4]

2. Cf. Runciman, *A History*, vol. 1; Riley-Smith, *The First Crusade.*
3. *Ibid.*, 80.
4. This section is based on two other book chapters of mine (Kalous, "The Papacy and the Czech Lands" and "Papal Legates and Crusading Activity").

4.1.1. *Papal legates and the Hussite crusade*

Crusading activity in Central Europe is related to the 'heretical' movement of the Czech Hussites of Bohemia and Moravia. A brief overview of the Hussite crusades and the legatine involvement in them will help to illustrate the role of the legates. The Bohemian preacher and reformer Jan Hus was burned at the stake in July 1415; liturgical reforms designed by his followers began to develop even prior to his death at the Council of Constance. It was only in 1418, after Pope Martin V was elected by the council, that the first legates were dispatched to the region. The new Pope intended to use the traditional papal powers and authority in terms of crusades and organise the fight against the dangerously spreading Hussites in Bohemia. In cooperation with the King of the Romans and of Hungary, Sigismund, he wanted to subdue the rising heresy.[5] Declaring crusades and dispatching legates seemed to be a clear strategy tested already in the case of the thirteenth-century Albigensians. Although these events do not fall into the post-conciliar period which is studied by this book, the use of legates in the crusade against the Hussites defined to some extent what followed.

This strategy began with the personages of Cardinal Giovanni Dominici (Banchini), who had previously worked as a legate to Hungary and Germany and was appointed on 10 July 1418,[6] and Fernando de Palacios, the bishop of Lugo in Galicia, both of whom worked out of the court of King Sigismund. Following Dominici's death at Buda in June 1419, it was de Palacios who actively administered the organization of the first crusade against the Hussites. Cardinal Dominici was, thus, replaced by Fernando de Palacios, who had arrived in Central Europe in the cardinal's retinue. De Palacios took part in the political negotiations of Sigismund, being present in December at the discussions between the King and the Prague delegation in Brno, and using his authority to declare an interdict on the city due to the presence of the heretics. He went to Wrocław in the train of King Sigismund, where on 17 March 1420, he officially declared a crusade against the heretical Czechs on the basis of the papal bull *Omnium plasmatoris domini* from 1 March.[7] The nuncio (sometimes termed *legatus missus*) actively cooperated with King Sigismund in military actions and possible disputations and reconversion to Catholicism. As the representative of the papacy, however, he was strongly criticised by the Hussites.

As he did not enjoy great success, the nuncio was replaced by the legate *de latere* Cardinal Branda Castiglione (who like Giovanni Dominici previously went on a legation in Hungary and Germany). His commission from 13 April 1421 applied to Bohemia, Moravia and Meissen, the lands affected by the Wycliffite and Hussite heresy. Cardinal Branda operated in Central Europe until

5. Studt, "Legationen"; eadem, *Papst Martin V.*, pp. 478-704; Šmahel, *Die Hussitische Revolution*, vol. 2-3, pp. 1007-1560. See also, Heymann, "The Crusades".

6. Eršil, ed., *Acta Martini*, pt. 1, pp. 149-152, 154, no. 325-328, 333; Cracco, "Banchini".

7. The bull in Eršil, ed., *Acta Martini*, pt. 1, pp. 247-249, no. 565; Šmahel, *Die Hussitische Revolution*, vol. 2, pp. 1071-1073.

his return to Rome on 27 October of the same year. He left Rome on 17 March 1422 with a new commission and returned more than three years later.[8] Not even the second crusade was a success, however. After Cardinal Branda left, the new organiser of the crusade was to be Cardinal Giordano Orsini, appointed legate *de latere* for Hungary and Bohemia in January, and for all the kingdoms of the King of the Romans in February 1426.[9] He believed it was impossible to negotiate with the Hussites: they had to be eliminated. He tried to persuade the Nuremberg *Reichstag* of this in early May 1426. Here he learned of the Catholic army's defeat at Ústí nad Labem, which only made him organise further attempts at subduing the Czechs, only to fail again.

As the conflict was still unresolved, Pope Martin V found a new proponent for the crusade in the person of Henry Beaufort, Bishop of Winchester, who had been created cardinal in May 1426. His commission as legate was published on 18 March 1427 and the province included Germany, Hungary and Bohemia. His main task was to root out the Hussite heresy. Cardinal Beaufort received the cardinal's hat on 25 March 1427 in Calais, and in spite of the fact that he had already set out on his journey to Germany, it was mid-June before he formally agreed to his appointment. The Pope then called upon him to proceed with haste. After the defeat at Tachov, he continued to organise the army against the Hussites at the *Reichstag* in Frankfurt, to which the Pope's financial support was meant to contribute. The money was insufficient and the legate also left the region. He moved to England and the French parts controlled by the English, where he gathered support for the next crusade that the Pope planned. An English army to campaign against the Hussites was to be created, but due to the events in the Anglo-French conflict in 1429, Beaufort provided the army, mustered using papal money (from the Apostolic Chamber, for indulgences in England and from the annual tithes for the crusade from October 1427), for the French war.[10] Thus, yet another legate failed in organising a crusade against Bohemia.

Pope Martin V found a new legate in the person of the capable diplomat, former Padua professor and secretary to Cardinal Castiglione during his legation in Bohemia and Hungary, Giuliano Cesarini. The Pope chose Cesarini for two difficult tasks. He was appointed legate for the territory of Bohemia, Moravia and Meissen on 1 January 1431, and immediately after this his legatine province was expanded to include Germany, Hungary and Poland so that he could operate effectively in the organisation of the fifth crusade against the heretics. The Pope also appointed him his legate at the council in Basel on 1 February.[11] In the spring and summer, Cesarini, now confirmed in his mission by Pope Eugenius

8. Picotti, "Castiglione, Branda da"; Eršil, ed., *Acta Martini*, pt. 1, pp. 310-314, 316, 350, 362, 380, no. 732-736, 740, 837, 875, 924; Eršil, ed., *Acta Martini*, pt. 2, pp. 549-550, no. 1363.

9. *Ibid.*, pp. 605-606, 614, no. 1516-1520, 1545-1546; basic info König, *Kardinal Giordano Orsini*; Celenza, "Orsini, Giordano".

10. Eršil, ed., *Acta Martini*, pt. 2, pp. 680-682, 704-705, no. 1757-1760, 1837; in detail see, Holmes, "Cardinal Beaufort".

11. Eršil, ed., *Acta Martini*, pt. 2, pp. 828-829, 831-832, 835-836, no. 2234, 2235, 2240, 2241, 2252; Strnad and Walsh, "Cesarini, Giuliano".

IV, focused with great energy on starting a new crusade to Bohemia, recruiting the army in Germany. The expedition to Bohemia began from Nuremberg, but ended in fiasco. On 14 August 1431, the problematically organised crusader army fled from Domažlice even before there was a direct fight with the Hussite troops. Cesarini's failure (he even lost the bull of Eugenius IV that declared the crusade) was celebrated with great joy in Bohemia.

What kind of involvement of these papal legates can be identified in the first phase of the Hussite crusades? Did they really imitate Bishop Adhémar? In this context, the papal legates had a number of functions related to the crusade. They were first the agents of the Pope in proclaiming the crusade and preaching the cross. Cardinal Branda was well-known for spreading the word throughout Germany, especially during his second legation to Germany, when he was also commissioned to advance the cause of reform.[12] In the case of the crusade, he was able to utilize not only the bull of the crusade and faculties for condemning the Wycliffites and Hussites, but also mandates for granting indulgences and disseminating an anti-Hussite liturgy. It is clear, however, that Cardinal Branda was not directly leading the crusade, for he confined his involvement to political negotiations with local rulers: he even brought a military banner for King Sigismund, consecrated by the Pope, for the fight against the heretics. Others, however, did try to stand at the head of the crusading army.

Papal nuncio Fernando de Palacios, for example, was fiercely criticized by the Hussite manifestos as "not a legate of Christ, who is the author of peace and salvation, but rather a nuncio of the Antichrist, who like Behemoth maintains himself with forged weapons and shields, vaunts himself and grows with bloodshed, murder, pestilence and the oppression of innocent saints". He was, they continued, not ashamed to take up the cross against the Czechs in Wrocław, to assemble large numbers of troops and cast away all justice.[13] This text naturally illustrates the opposing side's criticism of the active leadership of the crusade. The same can be said about the other proponents of the crusade. They were heavily criticized by the Hussites, naturally, and praised by the Catholic side. Even from the Catholic side, however, the praise was not unanimous, because the crusades failed to bring about positive outcomes. Thus the Pope was driven to search for more effective substitutes for his legates, a search which explains the above-mentioned sequence of cardinals, each of whom failed and was replaced. Normally, a legate would return to Rome after achieving the goals of his legation. In this case, however, the permanent mission which needed to be accomplished required a series of legates *de latere*.

The organizational role of the legates was thus the key one. Although they were unsuccessful and did not manage to eliminate the Hussite heresy, both their

12. Studt, "Legationen", pp. 426-437.

13. Palacký, ed., *Urkundliche Beiträge zur Geschichte des Hussitenkrieges*, vol. 2, pp. 487-494, no. 2, at p. 489, "Et super hoc quemdam Fernandum, praetensum episcopum Lucensem, incentorem et auctorem sceleris et stimulum suae damnationis, ad nostras partes missum legatum quidem non Christi, qui totus auctor est pacis et salutis, sed nuntium Antichristi, qui more Vehemot in armis scutisque fusilibus fovere (sic), gloriaturque et crescit in sanguine, nece, peste et sanctorum oppressione innocentum, sibi adhibuit et adjunxit".

intention and the volume and range of their activity were quite clear. All the legates gathered money as well as troops to lead the war in Bohemia. Giuliano Cesarini's other obligation was to preside over the Council of Basel and it was the council that took over the initiative in dealing with the Hussites. It was clear that the latter could not be subdued by force and negotiations began. The legates of the council were no longer interested in crusading, but in discussions. The struggle between the council and the Pope clearly constituted a hindrance to the crusade, and even to further negotiations. That is why it was not until the 1450s that negotiations with the Pope recommenced.

The role of the legates in the struggle against the Hussites, or Utraquists as they were generally called, began to change in the mid-fifteenth century. It entailed substantially more negotiations than previously. Discussions between the council and the Czechs in the 1430s shaped later communication with the Pope and the representatives of the Papal Curia. The end of the Hussite wars coincided with renewed interest in the Ottoman Turks and papal activity in this direction. It did not mean, however, that the Pope neglected the battlefields of Central Europe. At the end of the 1440s, Cardinal Juan Carvajal was the man who initiated discussions with the 'heretical' Czechs. The Czech embassy, representing the land diet of Bohemia, appeared in Rome in 1447, but arrived too late to deliver obedience to Pope Eugenius IV. It was Nicholas V or rather his cardinals, who began to talk to the Czechs: their crucial topic was always the question of the Compacts, the agreement with the Council of Basel that allowed communion in both kinds in Bohemia and Moravia, and of the possible confirmation of the new Archbishop of Prague. Cardinal Juan Carvajal led the talks in Rome and at this point it was already clear that he was earmarked to go to Central Europe as legate *de latere.* He there managed to conclude the Concordat of Vienna with Frederick III, but in Prague he was unsuccessful. There was no sign, however, of a renewed crusade.[14] It seemed that the crusade was to be confined to the Ottoman Turks. Giuliano Cesarini, as leader of the crusade against Sultan Murad II, fell at Varna in 1444 together with Wladislas, the king of Poland and Hungary.[15] Cesarini, who had first-hand experience with the battlefields of Bohemia, also led a crusade against the Ottoman Turks, but as will shortly become apparent, he was not the last prelate to connect the two most urgent crusades of the fifteenth century.

When one considers the involvement of papal legates and nuncios in Hussite, or rather Utraquist, affairs in the second half of the fifteenth century, there is no longer much debate about crusade. Nicholas of Cusa planned to hold negotiations with the Utraquists, but never entered Bohemia when on legation in Germany, despite having been commissioned to go there.[16] The King of Bohemia, George of Poděbrady, installed in 1458 with limited and even questionable papal backing, at first enjoyed the grudging support of Pope Pius II, who had met him personally when in Bohemia and viewed him as the only person capable of

14. Odložilík, *The Hussite King*, pp. 44-50; Gómez Canedo, *Don Juan*, pp. 99-121.
15. Setton, *The Papacy*, vol. 2, pp. 82-107.
16. Cusa, *Writings*, pp. 356-428; Kalous, *Plenitudo potestatis*, pp. 185-186.

reconciling the quarrelling Czechs. Pius also counted on George for the crusade against the Ottoman Turks. The negotiations of the archbishop of Crete and papal nuncio Girolamo Lando and his colleague Francesco da Toledo did not, however, bring positive results.[17]

The embassy sent to Rome by the King in 1462 to offer obedience was the start of the clash between the Pope and King George. The fatal blow to the King's plans was the Pope's abolition of the Compacts when this royal embassy was actually present in Rome. As recounted by Pius II in his *Commentaries*, Fantino della Valle, the papal nuncio and former diplomat of King George, was imprisoned following his speech on his return to the royal court at Prague, and an argument with the King. George then firmly supported the idea of the redeeming function of communion in both kinds.[18] The organization of a new crusade was at hand, but it was only the successor to Pius II, the Venetian Pope Paul II, who embarked on the road leading to a new anti-Hussite, or more properly anti-George, crusade. After unsuccessful dealings with the Emperor and the King of Poland, Matthias Corvinus, King of Hungary, and former son-in-law of King George, offered his cooperation. King Matthias promised to fight both against the Ottoman Turks and the heretics (i.e. the Utraquists), thereby once more connecting the two struggles.[19]

The war only began in 1468, but the preparation, coordination and communication with King George's opposition was largely a task for papal diplomacy: the Pope himself wrote to the Catholic powers of Central Europe, but more importantly a papal legate (*legatus missus*) Rudolf of Rüdesheim operated in the region. It was Lorenzo Roverella, as a nuncio *cum potestate legati de latere*, who was eventually commissioned to proclaim war against the heretical King. He was dispatched to reinforce the activity of Rudolf together with another papal representative, Gabriele Rangoni, a greatly energetic Franciscan friar who later became one of the crucial supporters of Matthias Corvinus in Rome. These three men actively organized the fight against King George, dealing with conflicting interests and constructing support for the crusade.[20]

One example of their activity was discussion about possible neutrality. Lorenzo Roverella was open to discussion, confirming, for example, the compromising neutral position of České Budějovice, a strongly Catholic royal town in southern Bohemia.[21] Rudolf, on the other hand, was not willing to hear anything at all about neutrality and political (which effectively entailed doctrinal) compromise. According to the Wrocław chronicler, Peter Eschenloer, Rudolf remarked to the town's envoys "if you are able to find a middle way between God and the Devil,

17. Odložilík, *The Hussite King*, pp. 106-107; Heymann, *George of Bohemia*, pp. 232-234.

18. *Pii Secundi Pontificis Maximi Commentarii*, pp. 439-445.

19. Fraknói, ed., *Mátyás király levelei*, vol. 1, pp. 113-114, no. 78, summarized in Heymann, *George of Bohemia*, pp. 476-477; Kalous, *Matyáš Korvín*, pp. 122-126; Housley, *Crusading and the Ottoman Threat*, pp. 88-91.

20. Odložilík, *The Hussite King*, pp. 204-209; for the crusading bull see ASV, Reg. Vat. 528, fol. 180r-181v, for the commission for Lorenzo Roverella *ibid.*, fol. 209rv.

21. Beneš, "Postoj Českých Budějovic", pp. 64-65; Pletzer, "České Budějovice", pp. 20-23.

it would be better for you to stay in the middle between the lords and the heretics, but since it is not possible, you will have to choose between the Devil and God".[22] So while the religiously divided inhabitants of Bohemia and Moravia were in some instances attempting to continue with cohabitation and toleration – which they knew, from personal experience in the first round of the crusades against the Hussites, was the only way to survive – the opposition league was formed and in 1468 King Matthias of Hungary joined it in order to lead the crusade.

The position of the legates was changing, however, as Rudolf was appointed bishop of Wrocław and began to be less involved in the crusade itself. His inactivity was noticed and even criticized by the other nuncios, especially Gabriele Rangoni.[23] The crusade itself was entrusted to the secular arm, that is King Matthias, who organized it in close cooperation with the local opposition. The nuncios Lorenzo Roverella and Gabriele Rangoni, who were present at the court of Matthias Corvinus, gained financial support, and organized political negotiations with allies as well as with opponents (one example being the meeting between King George's sons and King Matthias in Olomouc in April 1469).[24]

The papal representatives (legates or nuncios) thus had three basic functions in the crusading activity directed by King Matthias against King George. In the first place, they were organizers of the crusade, though not in the sense of the earlier crusades against the Hussites. In this instance they were not leaders of the military actions, but rather organizers in the background, remaining absent from the battlefields; for the most part they confined their activities to the court of Matthias Corvinus, the city of Wrocław or some equally safe spot. Secondly, they were organizing the collection of financial support for the warring King. It was through Lorenzo Roverella that papal support reached the King of Hungary, and at the same time Roverella organized the collection of money from crusading indulgences in the region.[25] Thirdly, they represented papal policy in the region, which had always to be adapted to the circumstances. For example, even while disagreeing and lacking a direct commission by the Pope, Lorenzo Roverella was forced by Matthias to confirm his election as King of Bohemia (he was elected by the Catholic estates in May 1469 in Olomouc). That happened after the death of King George and the election of another candidate, the first-born son of the King of Poland, Wladislas, as King of Bohemia in 1471 by the election land diet in Kutná Hora.[26]

Even prior to King George's death, another legate *de latere*, Francesco Todeschini Piccolomini, was dispatched as a representative of the Pope in the *Reichstag* held at Regensburg. In reaction to the mission of the Saxon envoys in Rome, who tried

22. Eschenloer, *Geschichte*, pp. 690-691, "kőnden sie czwischen got vnd dem tewfil ein mittil finden, so were wol, das sie in mittil der herren vnd des keczirs rweten, adir das mőchte nicht gesein, sunder műsten bey dem tewfil adir bey got bleiben".

23. Drabina, "Działalność dyplomatyczna legata apostolskiego Rudolfa", pp. 222-224; Eschenloer, *Geschichte*, pp. 730-731; Markgraf, ed., *Politische Correspondenz*, vol. 2, p. 286, no. 409; pp. 290-291, no. 414.

24. Palacky, ed., *Urkundliche Beiträge zur Geschichte Böhmens*, pp. 571-582.

25. Cf. Fink, "Der Kreuzablaß".

26. Theiner, ed., *Vetera monumenta Hungariae*, vol. 2, pp. 422-423, no. 603.

to exonerate King George, he was expressly commissioned not to deal with the heretical King or to attempt any cooperation with the heretics. The crusade against the Ottoman Turks was again emphasised, even if Paul II never abandoned the idea of the crusade against the Utraquists. The settlement of the conflict came only later, with the King's death acting only as a tentative first step.[27]

The policy of the Papacy changed considerably with the death of Paul II and the accession of Sixtus IV. He continued to support King Matthias, but did not consider the Bohemian struggle to be as important as his predecessor had. Like Paul, Sixtus wished to launch a crusade against the Ottoman Turks, but unlike Paul strove for internal peace in Central Europe. The legates sent to the region were supposed to act accordingly. Politically the situation had also changed: Wladislas, King of Bohemia, elected at the diet in Kutná Hora, was a Catholic, even though he was not yet confirmed as King by either the Pope or the Emperor.

The papal legate *de latere* who arrived in Central Europe immediately after Sixtus's accession to the throne was Cardinal Marco Barbo. He was dispatched from Rome together with four other legates to facilitate preparations for the crusade. The Central European legate was destined to go to the courts of the Emperor and the kings of Hungary and Poland. He was coming as *angelus pacis* with a commission of halting the war between the two kings, who were in conflict for the Bohemian crown. Cardinal Marco not only enjoyed the typical *facultates* of papal legates *de latere*, he also had at his disposal special mandates for negotiation, with two alternative outcomes. One was the excommunication of the King of Poland as well as his son and their supporters and also, should the peace negotiations prove unsuccessful, Matthias's confirmation as King of Bohemia. The other was the division of the Bohemian Crown lands into two parts, this being the precondition for bringing about a compromise solution.[28] The political division of the lands was first mentioned in 1472 and finally occurred in 1478/79, though it resulted not from the activity of Cardinal Marco Barbo, but from discussions between the representatives of the two kings (and kingdoms). In Italy, at least, peace was viewed as a success for papal diplomacy.[29]

From this point onwards the heretical Czechs were not really viewed in crusading terms. Only at the end of 1483, when there was an Utraquist uprising in Prague and the second defenestration occurred, did Pope Sixtus call for organised Central European action against the heretics. He wrote to the nuncio in place, Bartolomeo Maraschi and the legate *de latere*, Giovanni d'Aragona, to the kings of Poland and Hungary, to the neighbouring German bishops and princes and to the administrator of the Prague archdiocese.[30] The crucial person in this list was, however, Matthias Corvinus, the King of Hungary and Bohemia,

27. ASV, Arm. XXXIX 12, fol. 129v-133r; BAV, Vat. lat. 10637, fol. 588r-611v; Macek, "K zahraniční politice", pp. 37-48; cf. Strnad, "Francesco Todeschini-Piccolomini", pp. 226-248; Kalous, *Plenitudo potestatis*, pp. 237-243.

28. ASV, Reg. Vat. 680, fol. 65r-69r (Theiner, ed., *Vetera monumenta Hungariae*, vol. 2, pp. 431-434), 80rv.

29. Montefeltro, *Lettere*, pp. 14-15, no. 14.

30. ASV, Arm. XXXIX 16, fol. 89v-93r.

as the Pope still did not recognize Wladislas II Jagiellonian as King of Bohemia (that would happen only in 1487). The Pope requested that Matthias deal with the heretics, acting as "always the hammer of infidels and heretics" (*semper malleus infidelium et hereticorum*), but without mentioning a crusade. That was now reserved for another theatre, the south-east. The kingdom of Bohemia returned to negotiations for union with the Roman Church, which acquired new urgency with the arrival of the German Reformation.[31]

4.1.2. *The Ottoman crusades*

As a logical consequence of the geographical advance of the Ottoman Turks, Central Europe represented a key region for the Turkish crusade during the fifteenth and sixteenth centuries. The papal legates and nuncios (usually with the powers of the legate *de latere*) had specific roles to play within the evolving process of the Papacy's programme. The Cardinals' College also functioned as a centre for organising the war against the Ottomans, as Cardinal Bessarion presided in the 1450s and 1460s over the papal commission for the promotion of the holy war that was constituted of Cardinals d'Estouteville, Trevisan, Capranica, Orsini and Barbo. The help of the cardinals lay not only in the work for the Curia itself at the centre, but also in the activities they should follow up on in the day-to-day work in the field, namely as papal legates outside the centre of Rome.[32]

In the broadest terms, what can be seen is a sequence of general European-wide crusade projects launched by individual popes during the second half of the fifteenth century and the early 1500s. The intention was that papal legates would play a decisive role in such projects, which placed severe demands on the European sovereigns in terms of their coordination and cooperation. Active cooperation would represent participation in the crusade, but there was also passive cooperation in ensuring general peace between all Christian monarchs and countries. In this sense the papal legates were negotiators and facilitators of the crusade all over Europe rather than direct leaders and organizers.

Four larger projects were launched during this period, which had their predecessor in the project of Pope Eugenius IV, which ended unsuccessfully at Varna in 1444 (organised by the cardinal legates, Giuliano Cesarini on land and Francesco Condulmer on sea). Pope Calixt III sent four papal legates *de latere* out from Rome in 1455 to various parts of Europe and one as general of the papal fleet; in 1471 Pope Sixtus IV dispatched as many as five cardinals as legates, one of them also related to the fleet. This practice was followed in 1500 by Pope Alexander VI who confined himself to three legates, and finally, in 1518 Pope Leo X commissioned four cardinals to act on his behalf as papal legates. It may be useful here to refer back to Table 1 (p. 92) for an overview of legatine provinces in papal crusading projects.

31. See Kalous, "The Politics of Church Unification".

32. Mureşan, "Kardinálské kolegium"; Setton, *The Papacy*, vol. 2, p. 168. A vast body of literature covers the late medieval crusades and crusading projects, see at least Housley, Pellegrini, Setton in bibliography.

Without going overly into detail on the individual legates at this point, these cases illustrate the distribution of legates around Europe, the division of Europe into large legatine provinces and the representation of individual popes by papal legates. The legates must have been created with the consent of the other cardinals, as the requirements of the election capitulations of the popes usually specified that legates could be sent on a mission only with the consent of other cardinals and under no false pretence.[33] Crusades, then, were always justifiable in front of the cardinals and even part of their interests. As can be seen from the table, there was always an interest in the area of Germany and its eastern neighbours, because this was the crucial area for a military expedition against the Ottoman Turks. Central and east-Central Europe was the border region of the advancing Ottoman Turks and needed to be internally organized and externally supported if it was to withstand the pressure of the south-eastern superpower. In the historiography of the subject, the positions of Hungary and to a lesser extent Poland have been emphasized.[34] The treatment of these two countries in papal policy is highly revealing for Rome's overall strategy.

First, however, the cluster of attempts at dispatching multiple legates calls for comment. Pope Calixt III actually began this tradition: he named a number of legates, whose job was to prepare the road for the crusade itself.[35] He did not create them on the same day, as the other popes did in the other instances of 1471, 1500 and 1518. Consecutively, he was bringing in more people to get involved in the process of focusing on the crusade. There were two legates assigned and destined to the wider region of Hungary and its southern borderland. Cardinal Dionysius Szécsi, the archbishop of Esztergom and primate of Hungary and Cardinal Juan Carvajal, who was also – just like Calixt III – of Spanish origin (from Extremadura), even though he had no warlike past in Spain. Dionysius (or Dénes) Szécsi, a Hungarian prelate, had been active in internal politics for some time already. He even held the title of *legatus natus* as explained earlier, but was not all that active in organising the crusade itself in Hungary and later, in 1457, when he was supposed to proceed with the organisation, he was even called into doubt by Pope Calixt III (and defended by Juan Carvajal).[36]

In 1455 and 1456 the floor was actually given to Cardinal Juan Carvajal, who travelled around the country and was active in Germany as well. He was preaching the cross, but also trying to organise the army and explain the crusading plans of the papacy to the land diet in Buda on 6 February 1456 (he explained about the fleet, about the possible involvement of Alfonso V of Aragon and Philip of Burgundy, who promised to help, and offered plenary indulgence to every participating soldier). A week later, he even bestowed a consecrated cross sent by

33. Cf. chapter four, § 4.3.

34. See, e.g., Veszprémy, "The State and Military Affairs"; Housley, *Crusading and the Ottoman Threat*, pp. 107-119.

35. See, e.g., Setton, *The Papacy*, vol. 2, pp. 138-160; individual chapters in Housley, ed., *Crusading in the Fifteenth Century.*

36. Theiner, ed., *Vetera monumenta Hungariae*, vol. 2, pp. 311-312, no. 480 (14 Mar 1458).

the Pope on John of Capistrano as well as a papal brief allowing him to preach the crusade, as the friar himself reported in a letter to the Pope.[37]

In a sense, however, the legate was entering into a process that was already happening. There were the anti-Turkish imperial diets (*Reichstage*) organised in Regensburg and Frankfurt in 1454 and Wiener Neustadt in 1455. Friar John of Capistrano was, as it is well known, active in the last two diets.[38] Similarly, Bishop Giovanni da Castiglione was active in Germany and particularly in the imperial diets as a representative of the Pope with the power of nuncio.[39] Cardinal Nicholas of Cusa was present in Regensburg in 1454 before he returned to the Curia only to be dispatched from Rome in 1455 as a part of the wider project of Calixt III.[40] Giovanni da Castiglione was re-sent to Central Europe in June 1456 as nuncio *cum potestate legati de latere* to the Roman Empire and the Emperor and to the King of Hungary and Bohemia Ladislaus Posthumous, so that he could actively contribute to the organisation of the army in 1456 as the threat of the Ottoman attack on Hungary became more acute.[41]

Apart from the independent agents, representatives of the pope, there were a number of people in the retinue of Cardinal Juan Carvajal. The legate's chancellor, bishop of Assisi Francesco Oddi, was very active, for example, in communication with Italian states and actual organisation of the crusading troops.[42] He had sent a number of crusaders to Belgrade on 3 July, before the siege of the fortress began. Capistrano even asked him to write to the legate that he should work day and night with the king and barons to bring help and subsidies to the battlefields against the Turks.[43] What is interesting is that while the cardinal legate himself was sitting in Buda (trying to organise an official army and communicating with the King), John of Capistrano vigorously took part in the battles at Belgrade and the legate's chancellor actively raised troops for the help of the soon-to-be besieged Belgrade somewhere along the Danube, in Petrovaradin. This only illustrates the changes in the role of the legates: apart from the fleet, the legates were no longer leading the crusading armies themselves; not all *exempla trahunt*, and especially not the one of Giuliano Cesarini at Varna.

Belgrade was freed from the Ottoman siege and was celebrated as a great success on the part of the Christians. It was not the end, however, of the crusading efforts: the activity of the legates and nuncios continued. The activities of Juan Carvajal and Giovanni da Castiglione, who left the region for Rome only after he was created cardinal in the beginning of 1457, are known, however.[44] There were other papal representatives active in the region and the example of Franciscan

37. Setton, *The Papacy*, vol. 2, p. 173.
38. Hofer, *Johannes Kapistran*, vol. 2, pp. 303-312, 321-334.
39. Nowak, *Ein Kardinal*, pp. 175-208.
40. Wolff, "Päpstliche Legaten", p. 28; Setton, *The Papacy*, vol. 2, p. 165; Smołucha, *Polityka kurii rzymskiej*, pp. 98, 102.
41. Nowak, *Ein Kardinal*, pp. 283-298.
42. Setton, *The Papacy*, vol. 2, pp. 174-175.
43. Thallóczy and Áldásy, eds., *Magyarország*, pp. 465-467, no. 801.
44. Nowak, *Ein Kardinal*, pp. 305-311.

Mariano da Siena who visited Dubrovnik in 1457 as *nuncius et collector apostolicus* is worthy of mention. He received faculties, which entitled him (among other things) to preach a crusade in Hungary, Bosnia, Serbia and adjacent places. As he was of minor status, he had to have his commission confirmed by Cardinal Carvajal, whose legatine province he had entered.[45] He collected a larger sum of money in Dubrovnik. The money was then contested, as the King of Hungary wanted to use it for his purposes as well. The Pope, however, sent over another papal nuncio only after the people of Dubrovnik learned about the death of the King of Hungary in the autumn of 1457. In their eyes, the King of Hungary would have definitely used it much more efficiently, as they were interested in land protection, rather than the sea.[46] The money was supposed to be used for the support of the fleet of Lodovico Trevisan, the cardinal, who was largely responsible for the election of Pope Calixt III, but after losing his favour, tried to regain it in the service of the papal crusading project as the commander of the fleet.[47] Fra Mariano, as many others, was sent back to the region to preach the crusade by Pius II in 1459,[48] who wanted to continue the efforts of his predecessor, keeping his legates and nuncios in the area even after the success of Belgrade. Cardinal Juan Carvajal, for example, was instructed to congratulate Matthias Corvinus on his election as King of Hungary and incite him to continue in the crusading zeal against the Ottoman Turks, just like the other legate in the region, Dionysius Szécsi, archbishop of Esztergom.[49]

The idea of the crusade, naturally, was central to all the popes, including Pius II and Paul II. One of the first acts, for example, of Paul II as Pope was promoting the crusade through Girolamo Lando, who was already constituted in Hungary by his predecessor.[50] In 1464, it was the third mission of Girolamo Lando. The previous ones had the crusade in the background, but this one was even related directly to the financial and ideological support of the King of Hungary. Lando's mission was even financed by the *Depositeria della crociata* (like Roverella's in 1467), a budget that was based on the income of the alunite mine in Tolfa (for the alum production) and was solely reserved for matters of the crusade.[51] It is impossible here to name all the papal representatives that

45. Theiner, ed., *Vetera monumenta Hungariae*, vol. 2, p. 298, no. 467; cf. also pp. 298-299, no. 468. Cf. the decretal X 1.30.8.

46. Setton, *The Papacy*, vol. 2, p. 169, n. 34.

47. *Ibid.*, p. 169.

48. Theiner, ed., *Vetera monumenta Hungariae*, vol. 2, p. 327, no. 501 (9 May 1459).

49. *Ibid.*, p. 309-312, no. 479-480. Apart from the legates, the Pope wrote to many other people, including the King himself, his mother and uncle, and the Hungarian barons.

50. *Ibid*, vol. 2, pp. 398-399, no. 572 (29 Sep 1464).

51. AS Roma, Camerale I, Depositeria della crociata (1463-1490), vol. 1234, fol. 216r; vol. 1235, fol. 121v (3 Oct 1464), "... reverendo in Christo patri domino Jeronimo archiepiscopo Cretensi in Ungariam a prelibato domino nostro misso floren. sexcenos pro suo salario et provisione ...", also fol. 127r (23 May 1465); cf. Beneš, "Depositeria", pp. 742-743, no. 2. On the Tolfa money, see Gottlob, *Aus der Camera Apostolica*, pp. 278-305; Weber, *Lutter contre les Turcs*, pp. 315-324; idem, "L'alun"; Gilbert, *The Pope, His Banker, and Venice*, esp. pp. 72-85.

were actively searching support for the crusade in the region. Let us focus, however, on the wider plans with the use of legates. Although both Pius II and Paul II showed significant interest in the crusade against the Ottoman Turks, a new general proposition with the use of a number of legates created on the same day and other papal representatives in the region came from their successor.

Pope Sixtus IV's attempt to organize a crusade in 1471 constituted one of the first acts of his pontificate, through which he hoped to consolidate his position in Christendom. A papal diplomat and Dalmatian bishop, Nicholas of Modruš, described in his *Defensio ecclesiastice libertatis* the struggle against the Ottoman Turks and in particular its organization by papal legates and nuncios. After Cesarini and Carvajal, and all the legates and nuncios of Pius II, including himself, he came to Sixtus IV with the following words: "Now I hasten to Sixtus, who sitting on the throne sent legates with enormous power all around the world to invoke help against the common enemy of the Christians".[52] Sixtus's efforts were viewed as a decisive step for the crusade after the fall of Negroponte and the legatine nominations became one of the central parts of Platina's account of Sixtus IV in his *Liber de vita Christi ac omnium pontificum*.[53]

The involvement of the top cardinals is also quite telling: Cardinal Bessarion, for example, was an ardent supporter of the crusade for the liberation of his homeland. He wanted to work in France, but his mission was a complete failure, due to the suspicions of the King against Bessarion, as the Pope remarked in 1478 when corresponding with the Emperor.[54] Similarly, even though Roderigo Borja was a native of the Iberian peninsula, where he was destined to go, his mission did not present a positive image in the eyes of other cardinals. Both Bessarion and Borja were heavily criticized by Giacomo Ammannati Piccolomini in a letter to Francesco da Toledo written on 20 October 1473. Cardinal Ammannati mentioned Bessarion's criticism of the Pope and his promotion of nephews to cardinals, but then focused on his enthusiasm for the French legation (to be precise, he was sent to France, Burgundy and England). The Greek cardinal, however, had to wait two months to be admitted by the King, and when he finally was, "there was no time or place to explain the faculties". The vice-chancellor of the church, Roderigo Borja – who induced the Pope to create him legate *artibus et corruptelis suis* – proved to be equally unsuccessful in Aragon, Castile and Portugal, as he was not welcome in the first place and returned to Rome "with the hatred of the princes and the people". Moreover, his entourage had suffered a serious blow when two of his ships collided and one sank, taking with it all the people aboard.[55] Not only did Cardinal Ammannati criticize both the legates after their return, but he had discerned a problem in the legations

52. BAV, Vat. lat. 8092, fol. 62r, "Ad Sixtum festino, qui vix dum in sedem collocatus ex templo per universum orbem ad implorandam adversus comunem hostem Christianorum opem, magna cum potestate mittit legatos".

53. Gaida, ed., *Platynae historici Liber*, pp. 404-417.

54. Bachmann, ed., *Urkundliche Nachträge*, p. 448.

55. Ammannati Piccolomini, *Lettere*, vol. 3, pp. 1750-1752, no. 686. Cf. chapter on travelling (§ 3.2.1.).

even before they set out. On 1 January 1472 he communicated to the same addressee his fears that "their legations will bring more confusion than profit" and criticized the decision to send the respective legates to western countries, including Italy and the papal fleet. The only hope he could see lay in Hungary, "if it is decided to send money with the legate;" the legate *de latere* to Hungary being the frequently mentioned Cardinal Marco Barbo.[56]

Although Ammannati Piccolomini was inconsistent in his criticism, given that he personally encouraged Bessarion to go to France, he did make a crucial point in one of his letters. There was hope in Hungary and Central Europe. Sending legates to Central Europe might have meant that they would succeed, to the benefit of the future crusade. Even Marco Barbo, whom Ammannati praised to the skies, proved unsuccessful in his efforts to make peace in Central Europe to facilitate the crusading activities of its Christian princes: as we have seen, it was only later that peace was secured there.

Europe was divided into three main parts in 1500: Germany and the regions to the east and to the west. Germany was perceived as central in the new crusade, which – with its crusading indulgences – was connected to the Jubilee of 1500.[57] The attempt to organise a crusade was equally unsuccessful as the previous one.

Certain tendencies can be discerned, however, in the projects. In his attention to Hungary, Giacomo Ammannati Piccolomini agreed with the papal master of ceremonies Paride Grassi, who described in detail Leo X's creation of his four legates in 1518. Grassi recounted the discussion he had with Leo after he learned that no legate would be sent to Hungary and Poland. For him, it was natural to send an extra legate to the region of Hungary and Poland, as he deemed the legate, who was present in the region, as not particularly useful. He had in mind Tamás Bakóc, whom Pope Leo X considered part of the project, whereas Paride Grassi completely rejected his participation, as in his eyes the legate rather served the King than the Pope.[58]

In general, the papal court viewed the role of Hungary and Poland as crucial in the event of war against the Ottoman Turks. The fact that the two countries

56. *Ibid.*, pp. 1484-1485, no. 512.

57. Setton, *The Papacy*, vol. 2, pp. 531-533.

58. Grassi, *Diarium*, pp. 402-404, "Et cum dicerem pape, quare etiam non faceret alium legatum ad regem Hungarie et Polonie, respondit mihi, quod ibi esset cardinalis Strigoniensis, ut legatus destinatus iam diu ab ipso super hac materia. Replicavi, per ipsum Strigoniensem non esse utilem legatum, quia cum sit de natione et tanquam regis Hungarie creatura, non se gerit tanquam legatum, sed tanquam capellanum regis; nam cum deberet esse tanquam legatus apostolicus supra regem, non solum non est supra regem, sed sub illo et in omnibus regi defert tanquam minor … Et papa respondit, quod hoc idem a pluribus aliis de hoc Strigoniensi cardinali intellexit, qui se male habet cum honore, imo cum dedecore sedis apostolice et quod ille esset male aut parum nationi acceptus et parum existimatus, unde volebat providere. Desuper dixi bonum fore, si sanctitas sua etiam illuc destinaret unum prelatum tanquam nuncium, qui simul cum legato provideret, ut reges illi duo potentissimi venirent ad expeditionem istam contra Turcas. Et papa mihi respondit, quod non esset de his duobus regibus dubitandum, quia ipsi quotidio papam interpellabant, cum diversis nunciis et litteris super hac expeditione, quia in primo periculo sunt, si Turcus christianitatem petit". For Bakóc, see Fraknói, *Erdődi Bakócz*; Tompa, *Cardinal Thomas*.

were left without a legate, who would organize the crusade, alarmed the master of ceremonies. Pope Leo X, in contrast, believed that no legate was needed: the attempt by Tamás Bakóc, the cardinal and archbishop of Esztergom, to organize a crusade in 1513 and 1514 ended in a peasant uprising with a consequent diminishing of the legate's role in papal planning. Leo's creation of legates in 1518, then, did not entail much for Central Europe. It was in reality little more than the continuation of the struggle between the major Christian powers, including the Papacy, as can be seen from the later nomination of *collegati* in the case of England and Germany, where the ministers or "creations of the kings" (*creatura regis*, the term Paride Grassi reserved for Tamás Bakóc) – Thomas Wolsey for England and Matheus Lang for Germany – were officially to accompany the legates who were originally named.[59]

In general, legates primarily charged with the organisation of the crusade carried the same faculties and had the same role as other legates. They brought spiritual benefits normally entrusted to the Sacred Penitentiary, could impose ecclesiastical bans and – most importantly – they had the authority to distribute indulgences, as is clear both from the cases mentioned above and from the well-known career of Raymund Peraudi (Perault).[60]

It is obvious from the afore-mentioned cases that, in the second half of the fifteenth century, legates and nuncios became rather observers. The role of the nuncios began to resemble the system of papal nunciatures of the sixteenth century. A few nuncios can be singled out for the informative reports, which they sent back to Rome. In 1483-1485 the above-mentioned Bartolomeo Maraschi was sent to Central Europe as a nuncio *cum potestate legati de latere.* He spent several months at the royal court in Buda and passed on remarks concerning King Matthias's views of the crusade. When reporting on his talks with the King, he noted the frequent references to Sultan Djem, whom the King wanted to acquire for his crusading plans.[61] Maraschi also described the visit of the Ottoman ambassadors to the royal court, where they concluded a truce with Matthias.[62] Even more detailed are the reports of Angelo Pecchinoli, likewise a nuncio *cum potestate legati de latere.* He spent roughly two years in Central Europe and recounted a number of discussions with King Matthias. In addition to the recurrent topic of Sultan Djem, in his first report he mentioned one of Matthias's proud proclamations: "lord legate, I tell you that if our lord insists on this war against the Turks, which I greatly desire in order to gain entry to paradise, it is my wish to drive the Turks away within two years, beyond the sea and their lands…"[63] The papal nuncio, who was present

59. ASV, Arch. Concist., Acta Vicecanc. 2, fols 67v, 69r, 74v; Setton, *The Papacy*, vol. 3, pp. 172-197.

60. Gottlob, "Der Legat"; Paulus, 'Raimund Peraudi"; Housley, "Indulgences"; Kalous, *Plenitudo potestatis*, pp. 336-343.

61. On Djem, who appears in many contemporary sources, see Thuasne, *Djem-Sultan*; Fisher, *The Foreign Relations*, pp. 21-50; İnalcık, "A Case Study".

62. BMV, Lat. X 174 (=3621), fol. 110v.

63. BAV, Vat. lat. 5641, fol. 242rv, "Ego dico vobis, domine legate, quod si dominus noster intendit ad istum bellum contra Turchos, quod ego tantum desidero, sic ire ad paradisum, quod in duobus annis ego volo expellere Turchum ultra mare et terras suas …"

at the court, was not to play any role in the military measures themselves: his function was simply to observe and transmit information that the King wanted to share with the Pope and the Pope with the King.

Before the system of nunciatures officially and fully developed, nuncios would come to Central Europe to report on the local political situation, on the gains made by the Reformation as well as by the Ottoman Turks. In 1518, no nuncio was dispatched to assist the organization of the general crusade east of Germany. Later, however, Giovanni Antonio Buglio barone di Burgio remained in the region for more than two years, and was present during the decisive period of the mid-1520s. His vast amount of letters are stored in the Vatican archives and library. Most of the letters have been edited, but among other documents relating to his mission one can find detailed information on Hungary's land diets, reports on the negotiations with the Bohemian Utraquists, on military preparations against the Ottomans as well as on their advance in the Balkans.[64] One of the most remarkable documents is a depiction of the order of the Hungarian army when ceremonially leaving Buda on 20 July 1526, led by King Louis II towards Mohács, where the decisive battle would take place more than a month later.[65] The author of the outline was in all probability another man in papal service, namely Giovanni Verzelio, a papal messenger, who brought money for Burgio.[66] According to the drawing, Burgio (called *il signor Barone* by Verzelio) was following the King and his guard accompanied by Elek Thurzó, master of the treasury, and László Szalkai, archbishop of Esztergom. Thus, the nuncio took part in a solemn departure for war that was not organized by the Papal Curia, though it did enjoy its support. The Curia itself was informed about what happened in detail by the nuncio and other people in its service. This was no more than a ceremonial participation in the campaign; otherwise, the nuncio remained detached from the host and reported from Buda (see fig. 1).[67]

One observation, that stems from the documents the legates were given and the tasks they were charged with, is that the crusade – as crucial and the most significant part of the papal policy of the period – provided the legates with an extra authority and rights to carry out their commissions. It will be apparent from the next chapter that legates were charged with various tasks, however, in their faculties the Curia never forgot to mention the crusade. This

64. For Burgio's letters see Fraknói, ed., *Relationes oratorum*; Wojtyska, ed., *Acta*, vol. 2, pp. 149-224; Kalous, *Plenitudo potestatis*, pp. 382-406; on Burgio, Rill and Scichilone, "Burgio, Giovanni Antonio Buglio barone di".

65. BAV, Vat. lat. 3924, fol. 257r; the drawing published in Kalous, "Elfeledett források", p. 607 and idem, "The Last Medieval King", p. 520; facsimile in Hermann, ed., *Kis magyar hadtörténet*, p. 59; on the papal legates and nuncios in Hungary in the 1520s (up to 1526), Nemes, "Pápai követek".

66. Fraknói, ed., *Relationes oratorum*, p. 424, no. 114, "Mando a Vostra Reverendissima Signoria la uscita del Re da Buda aponcto, con che ordine è andato. Saranno un poco più o meno gente, di quello io pongo, chè non gli ho aponto noverati. In verità furono molti Signori bene in ordine, con bellisimi fornimenti et richi, et pennache sino in terra bellissimi".

67. See Fraknói, ed., *Relationes oratorum*; Wojtyska, ed., *Acta*, vol. 2, pp. 149-224.

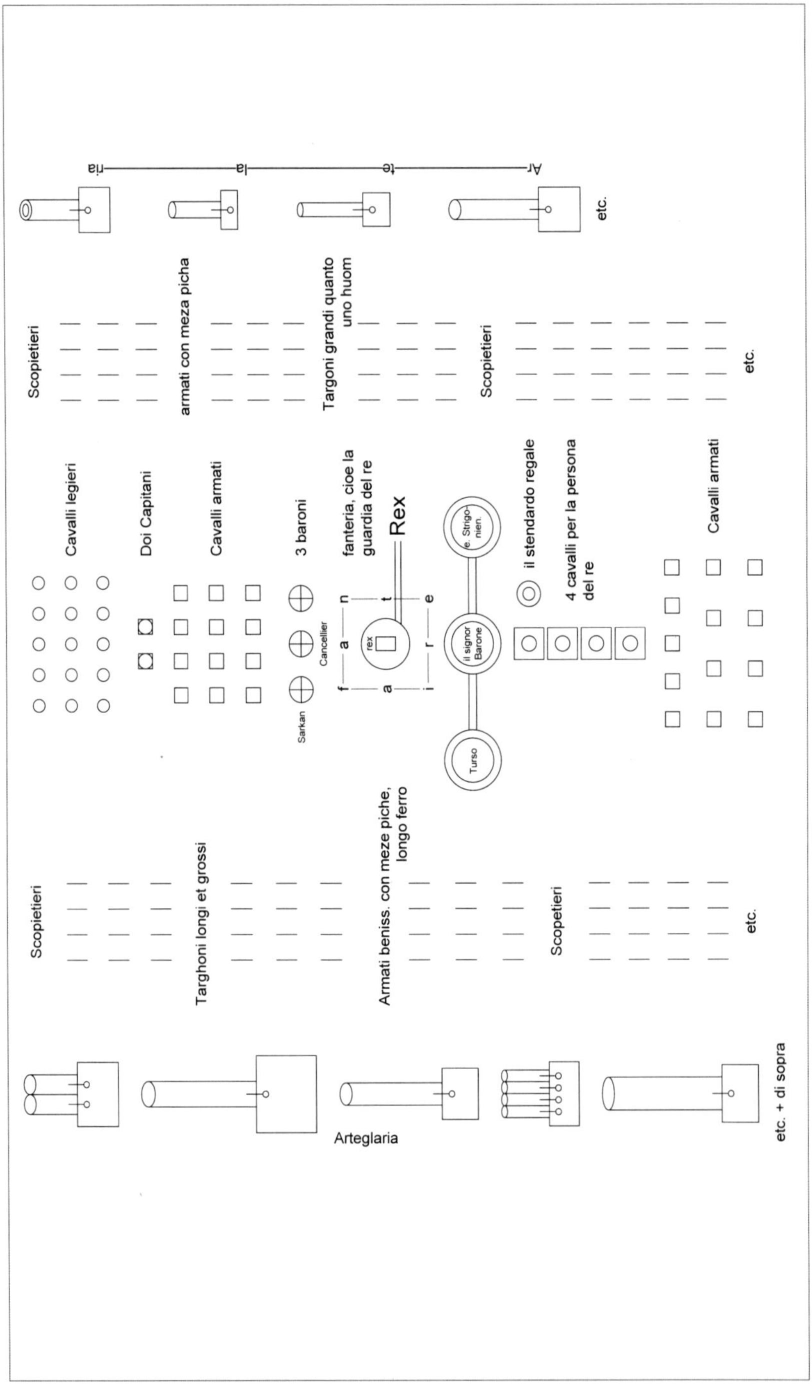

Fig. 1. Depiction of the royal army leaving Buda on 20 July 1526 in the direction to Mohács.

was a general goal of papal diplomacy of the period and this was an argument no one could possibly refuse or disagree with. The legates and nuncios also had at their disposal an extra argument for supporting their authority; apart from the commissions from the Pope, they had a higher right to conduct their activities with reference to the holy war against the enemy of Christendom.

All the examples make it clear that the fifteenth century initiated a change in the system of organising the crusades. The task of organising a crusade was one of the first ones that was related to legatine activities since the eleventh century. It is apparent that individual papal legates *de latere*, necessarily cardinals, played a crucial role in organizing the sequence of crusades against the Hussites, in raising money for the campaigns as well as mobilizing support from secular Christian leaders. The same can be said about the crusades directed in Central and east-Central Europe against the Ottoman Turks. One notable example, applying to both cases, is Giuliano Cesarini who personally led a crusade against the Hussites and another crusade against the Ottomans. Both crusades failed and in the latter the cardinal lost his life. Gradually, legates as well as other papal representatives (in the fifteenth century frequently nuncios *cum potestate legati de latere*) began to shift their duties towards organization, preaching and communication with Rome. In the first instance, they gave up the role of military leaders and their presence in crusading armies was no longer needed. Later, legates and nuncios became primarily involved in raising money through crusading indulgences and – most importantly – in reporting to the Papal Curia. Central Europe, as the region most endangered by the Ottoman advance, was never omitted from plans for crusading, but the fact that the region's kingdoms had such a strong vested interest in their own defence caused a steady shrinking of the Curia's organisational role, leaving military obligations exclusively to individual rulers. The role of papal representatives thus evolved from acting as the agents of crusading to being its promoters and finally its observers.

4.2. Angeli Pacis

Central Europe might serve as another example for a crucial part of the activities of legates, namely, the political negotiations that the legates conducted and the often related matters of the local churches, which – in the case of Bohemia and Moravia – could not be solved with simple directives from the centre, but rather with negotiations as well. The political negotiations reflected the political interests of the papacy in the region and were often aimed at stabilising the internal situation of the countries as well as at pacifying the warring nature of local rulers and most importantly at bringing peace to the region, which constituted the most crucial background for the wars against the advancing Ottoman Turks. The ecclesiastical talks presented an extension of the strategy of dealings with the Hussites, later known as the Utraquists. Overall, the papacy tried to fulfil the role it acquired after the fall of the idea of world theocracy, when the popes found themselves in a clash with the King of France from the point they resided in Avignon. Within the framework of international diplomacy, popes strived to bring peace to the warring parties, which respected their position and status and respected their diplomats, legates and nuncios. Popes thus acted as "arbitrators" with an "international authority".[68] As in Western Europe in the fourteenth century, when this role of the papacy stabilised, there were protracted conflicts in the region of Central Europe. The struggle over the Kingdom of Bohemia and the conflicts between the King of Hungary and the Holy Roman Emperor occupied a large part of the second half of the fifteenth century.

Political negotiations were conducted by a number of legates since the beginning of the office. The Anglo-French conflict of the fourteenth century brought about the need for the above-mentioned international authority which would not become involved in the conflict from the position of power, but rather from the position of commonly shared values and a commonly accepted respect. Papal diplomacy was then vital in the conflict and for bringing the war to negotiations, even though papal mediation was naturally crucial mostly outside Italy, as on the Apennine peninsula popes had their territorial claims even in the later Middle Ages. The role of legates and nuncios in the Hundred Years' War was briefly mentioned in earlier chapters. In the context of the Hundred Years' War it may have been crucial that cardinals accepted the status of nuncios not to paralyse the negotiations with the highest position of legates.[69] In other settings, however, no such considerations were brought forth. In Central Europe, then, legates and nuncios came as needed for the papal politics within the region.

The political constellation of the region was a three- or four-fold situation with the Kingdoms of Bohemia, Hungary and Poland and the Holy Roman Empire, represented by the hereditary lands of the Habsburg family, the Austrian lands. The borders were more or less stabilised, although troubles and conflicts still appeared, especially at the times of selecting a new king. The fifteenth century began with the rule of Sigismund of Luxembourg in Hungary, Bohemia and in the Empire. Being closely connected, the rulers of these countries, along with Poland, paid attention to any chance of change on the thrones of these kingdoms. In the kingdoms of Hungary and Bohemia, the situation after the death of Albert, Sigismund's heir, was not particularly favourable. The complex problems of Central Europe became even more complicated with the ascension to the thrones of Ladislaus the Posthumous, son of Albert, and more importantly by his early death. Both countries had problems which needed to be addressed: in the first one it was the danger of the advancing Ottoman Turks, in the latter the unresolved situation of the Utraquists. Papal legates could therefore play a crucial role in stabilising the internal conditions of the countries.

As high church representatives, papal legates played the role of political arbiters and negotiators, as was propagated by the revived papacy in the fifteenth century. The interests of the papacy in local contexts were many, differing and varying, however, in every situation. In relation to the political developments of the countries, popes and papal policy in general became involved in solving

68. Southern, *Western Society*, pp. 147-150.
69. Cf. chapter one, § 1.1.

troublesome conditions and circumstances. It is impossible, however, to differentiate between political and ecclesiastical matters completely, as they were often interconnected: the interests of local or national churches represented to a certain extent the interests of the entire country or of political representation, be it kings and sovereigns or estates and other representatives of the individual lands. Only a few examples focused on the explication of the role of legates and nuncios will be introduced here, as following all the activities of these papal representatives even in a limited region would entail the writing of several volumes. These are also often treated in the national histories, or specialised works on various political problems of the period as well as in the biographies of the potentates.

4.2.1. *International and internal conflicts*

Papal diplomacy focused on two points in conflicts between individual countries. First of all, acting as an angel of peace, i.e. legates were expected to bring peace in situations of fighting. Secondly, the legates' other objective was often related to the fact that papacy was not impartial. Thus, papal diplomats tried to achieve the pope's goals in the region. As in the case of the Hundred Years' War and the conflict between England and France, Central Europe was faced with long-standing struggles between independent countries. Writing on the activities of legates in a certain area and certain time would surely involve writing about the political history of the place in general. Legates became involved in the most significant and crucial events and dealings of the time as exponents of papal policy in the region. A generalised treatise is almost impossible, so once again, examples that will be explained and analysed will illustrate the role of legates, without going into extensive detail on political history.

4.2.1.1. *Poland and the Teutonic Knights*

As an isolated case, the struggle of the Kingdom of Poland and the Teutonic Knights might be singled out. The "Thirteen Years' War" could serve as an example. The unstable position of the Order in the region, its defeat in the war with the Kingdom of Poland-Lithuania in the war of 1409-1411 and constant conflicts with the Kingdom of Poland resulted in an open rebellion of the Prussian estates in 1454, who revolted against the rule of the Order and wanted to be accepted under the government of the King of Poland. The king's "act of incorporation," a charter published on 6 March 1454, newly united the areas of Pomerania and Prussia with the Kingdom of Poland and launched another conflict with the Order that lasted up until 1466, the Peace of Toruń.[70] The problem of Prussia and its rebellion was even discussed at the *Reichstag* in Regensburg in 1454 and the participants of the convention (including Cardinal Nicholas of Cusa) asked Pope Nicholas V to send a legate to a planned mediatory congress in Wrocław scheduled for 1 September of that year. They asked for Cardinal Nicholas of Cusa to be the legate *de latere*. Further negotiations in Rome led to a number

70. For the first war, Kuczyński, *Wielka wojna*; on the Thirteen Year's War a basic study is Biskup, *Trzynastoletnia wojna*.

of possibilities for solution of the problem, however, representatives of both parties tried to influence the decision of the Pope. Clearly, the first task was to understand the problem and search for a possible way out. The Pope established a commission of two members, Cardinal Juan Carvajal, the Pope's compatriot and a specialist for Central European matters, and Cardinal Guillaume-Hugues d'Estaing. A procurator of the Order in Rome, Jodocus Hohenstein, tried to influence all the decision-making process before any steps were taken in the region. The Pope published a bull that ordered King Casimir to refrain from any further steps against the Order and focus on the defence of Christendom: again, the crusade was a cornerstone of all the negotiations. Nicholas of Cusa was chosen to be the legate *de latere*; however, the Polish embassy protested, as he was very favourable towards the Order at the *Reichstag* in Regensburg. The Polish achieved, then, a change in plans and Cusa was named a legate for Prussia, whereas authority over Poland was given to Cardinal Juan Carvajal. This was only a partial success for the Order's procurator, as Marian Biskup wrote. Not even this materialised, however, as the negotiations and preparations were hindered by the illness and death of Pope Nicholas V.[71]

Although the result was not final, this is a very telling situation. The conflict between the Teutonic Order and the King of Poland had just begun and although the Knights attempted to secure the support of the Pope through papal legates, their interests were hindered by the intentions and interventions of King Casimir and by the Pope's interest in the crusade. This nevertheless demonstrates how even the persons of legates were a matter of discussion for regional politics. The Order was successful in its intentions only with the new Pope, Calixt III, who excommunicated the Prussian Estates and their collaborators and launched a greater crusading project in 1455 with legates sent all around Europe. Polish matters were assigned to Cardinal Juan Carvajal, while Cardinal Nicholas of Cusa was sent to Germany and England.[72]

Pope Calixt III remained firm in his positions towards the Prussian problem and the pleas of King Casimir; he supported the Teutonic Knights up until the end of his days. It was only his successor, Pope Pius II, who attempted to facilitate projects for appeasement and ending of the war. The mediation of papal nuncio *cum potestate legati de latere* Girolamo Lando and his fellow nuncio Francesco da Toledo, however, did not work out in 1460, as King Casimir did not allow either of the papal envoys into his kingdom.[73] To make this come about, the Pope even suspended the excommunication of the Prussians and their allies. Other news from the Congress in Mantua reached the King, however, before the nuncios arrived in Poland and he instead accepted the offer for mediation by Albert, Duke of Austria. Reportedly, Girolamo even stated, after being rejected, that the Pope would lead

71. *Ibid.*, pp. 242-245.

72. *Ibid.*, pp. 393-396; Setton, *The Papacy*, vol. 2, pp. 161-168.

73. *Joannis Dlugossii Annales*, 1445-1461, p. 340, "Sed is illos ad se (iam enim quales viri essent, didicerat, Venetus enim ex mercatura noviter in sacerdocium translatus eciam aput suos propter quoddam scelus censebatur infamis, Hispanus pluribus ante annis Rome causas Cruciferorum adiuvabat) venire, velut sue parti suspectos, vetuit".

a crusade against Poland.[74] The Polish chronicler Jan Długosz even mentioned as a reason for the royal rejection that Girolamo was a Venetian merchant known for crimes and Francesco helped the cause of the Order in Rome some years ago.[75] In this case, the papal commission and authority could not bring about the acceptance of the nuncios, as it was too clear to the King that papal policy of that time was supporting the positions of the Teutonic Order and was not impartial. Although Pope Pius II still wanted to organise the crusade, the conflicts between the King of Poland and the Teutonic Knights could not be overcome by nuncios with whatever concessions for making negotiations possible.

After an unsuccessful mediation by Albert of Austria and another one organised by the north-Hungarian magnate Jan Jiska z Brandýsa, the King assented to yet another attempt at mediation by a papal diplomat. It was once again, however, nuncio *cum potestate legati de latere* Girolamo Lando, whose name was not particularly popular in Poland. This time, Girolamo entered the kingdom and joined the diet in Piotrków in November 1462. After travelling between the Poles and the Teutonic Knights, the nuncio was able to bring them together in May 1463 in Brześć Kujawski. The talks, however, were unsuccessful once again, as the two parties did not respect each other. After the Poles celebrated the news of military success of one of their captains, the nuncio left the city and even Poland for Wrocław.[76] The negotiations failed and the papal diplomacy was unable to solve the clash between the warring parties, as the relationship with one of them, namely the Teutonic Order, was too close. The intended arbiter and mediator of international politics was unsuccessful.

The final stage of the war and of the political negotiations came only with Pope Paul II. The papacy under the new Venetian pope had a different agenda. The Ottoman crusade was still at the forefront of papal thoughts, however, the struggle in Central Europe against King George of Bohemia had no less importance. Peace in Poland was very much desired and new mediation should have been able to enforce it. A new legate (who termed himself *legatus missus*), bishop Rudolf of Rüdesheim, was dispatched from Rome in 1465 to facilitate the peace talks between King Casimir and the Order. The King and the Poles were eager to advise the legate to proceed differently than his predecessor; even the land diet in Piotrków in March 1466 expressed concern about the legation and asked the King to ensure that the legate would behave differently. The King send his advisor and chronicler Jan Długosz to meet Rudolf in Wrocław. Długosz himself reported on the discussion with Rudolf and expressed his hopes that he would not be the same as Girolamo.[77] When the actual peace talks took place in Toruń in September 1466, the legate first assured the King that he, as mediator, would be impartial and would work for the peace.[78] Rudolf then travelled between the

74. Szujski, ed., *Codex epistolaris*, vol. 2, pp. 192-193, no. 172 (the papal lifting of the excommunication); Biskup, *Trzynastoletnia wojna*, pp. 566-570.

75. *Joannis Dlugossii Annales*, 1445-1461, p. 340.

76. *Joannis Dlugossii Annales*, 1462-1480, pp. 61-63.

77. *Ibid.*, pp. 133-135.

78. *Ibid.*, pp. 154-155.

King and the grand-master of the Order and finally also facilitated the talks of the representations of both sides. He even signed the peace treaty of Toruń between the King of Poland and the Teutonic Order.[79] Rudolf of Rüdesheim, who was also instrumental in the peace talks between the Emperor Frederick III and King of Hungary Matthias Corvinus in 1463, made the peace between Poles and Teutonic Knights possible. It may be inferred that more than one element influenced the results of the mediation. Even if the papal policy and general attitude was the most significant of these, the person of the legate/nuncio crucially influenced the possible results. Skilful diplomats were naturally welcome.

4.2.1.2. *Central Europe, 1460s-1480s*

Central Europe here entails the Kingdoms of Hungary, Poland and Bohemia as well as the eastern parts of the Empire. Legates and nuncios usually came with commissions for the entire region and dealt with political and ecclesiastical matters for the whole area. Conflicts which occupied a number of papal diplomats stemmed from the troublesome situation within the kingdoms of the late Ladislaus Posthumus. As King of Hungary and Bohemia, he left behind after his death (1457) countries that needed stabilisation in the form of a new strong king, who would settle problems of internal as well as international standing in the lands. It is impossible to recount the national political histories here, so only a few hints, which should serve to elucidate the work of legates and nuncios in the reconciliation process, will be introduced. The role of legates and nuncios in the crusades has already been mentioned and it is impossible to dissociate this role from their other tasks involving bringing peace to the region. All of their tasks were often interconnected and they had a role in political negotiations which either led to peace on the one hand or war on the other. Crucial conflicts came about between Matthias Corvinus, the King of Hungary an heir to the heroic tradition of his father John Hunyadi, and his neighbours. In order to elucidate the functioning of legates and nuncios in political negotiations, the situation in the 1460s (with overlapping on both sides) in Central Europe between four powers, the Emperor and the Kings of Hungary, Poland and Bohemia, can be viewed as an example. The entire area became a great theatre of diplomatic activity on the part of the papacy, which hoped to turn this region into a platform for the crusade.

Conflicting situations in Central Europe endangered the peace among Christian princes which was needed for a successful campaign against the Ottoman Turks. Papal diplomacy organised and supported crucial negotiations between King Matthias Corvinus and Emperor Frederick III, who also longed for the Hungarian throne. The first agreement between the two monarchs came about only five years after the election of Matthias Corvinus and the counter-election of Frederick as Kings of Hungary. This brought out war and conflicting situations which also involved other potentates in the regions (most importantly King George of Bohemia, who changed sides several times). Negotiations in 1460 were led by two papal representatives, namely two legates *de latere*, Cardinal

79. In detail about the talks, Biskup, *Trzynastoletnia wojna*, pp. 701-717.

Juan Carvajal and directly in Vienna by Cardinal Bessarion. Cardinal Bessarion was created legate *de latere* on 2 January 1460 and left Rome in February. He had planned to leave his mission earlier due to failures in the negotiations between Frederick III and Matthias Corvinus, but did not receive permission from the pope and the cardinals. He only returned to Rome on 20 November 1461.[80]

The talks were not successful, however, in all probability due to the counter-actions of Bohemian diplomats, who did not desire peace between the Emperor and the King of Hungary.[81] The peace treaty was only concluded in 1463 in the presence, and through the mediation, of the nuncios (or *legati missi*) with the power of legate *de latere*, the above-mentioned Girolamo Lando, archbishop of Crete, Domenico Dominici, bishop of Torcello and Rudolf of Rüdesheim, provost of Freising.[82] Their names are explicitly mentioned in the peace treaties which were concluded *in presencia* of these papal representatives. Due to his knowledge of the region, Pius II was personally involved. He confirmed the treaties and even mentioned the cooperation of Domenico Dominici with Rudolf of Rüdesheim in his *Commentaries*.[83] This first stage of wars between the two monarchs was crucial for the general acceptance of Matthias Corvinus, as (following the peace treaty) St Stephen's Holy Crown came back to Hungary which enabled him to be crowned in Székesfehérvár, the traditional coronation city of the Kings of Hungary. Conflicts between the King of Hungary and the Holy Roman Emperor, however, continued for the rest of the lifetime of Matthias Corvinus.

Among the papal representatives, Rudolf of Rüdesheim seems to have been one of the most active nuncios, later nuncio or *legatus missus cum potestate legati de latere*, who successfully worked in the region of Central Europe. He was involved not only in the negotiations between the King of Poland and the Teutonic Knights, between Matthias and Frederick, but also in the talks in connection with the Bohemian problem, that is the dialogue with and later crusade against King George of Bohemia. The initial stage of negotiations, however, was led by another of these prelates, namely the Archbishop of Crete, Girolamo Lando, who, like Rudolf of Rüdesheim, embodied papal diplomacy in the region in the 1460s. First, however, the dialogue did not limit itself to the conflicting situation. Papal diplomats negotiated with King George about his possible turning to the Roman side, against

80. About the legation to Germany Mohler, *Kardinal Bessarion*, vol. 1, pp. 292-303; Meuthen, "Zum Itinerar"; P. K. Enepekides, "Die Wiener Legation"; Setton, *The Papacy*, vol. 2, pp. 216-219. Cf. Smołucha, *Polityka kurii rzymskiej*, pp. 202-215; about Carvajal's legation, Gómez Canedo, *Don Juan*, pp. 205-216.

81. Kalous, "Služba Boskovických", pp. 85-86; idem, "Boskovice urai", p. 378; Bessarion even reported back to Rome about the bishop of Olomouc Prothasius of Boskovice, who supposedly ruined all the positive results, Bachmann, ed., *Urkundliche Nachträge*, pp. 3-4.

82. Nehring, *Matthias Corvinus*, pp. 20-23, text editions of the peace treaties, pp. 202-217.

83. *Pii Secundi Pontificis Maximi Commentarii*, p. 585, "Oportune circa idem tempus Torcellanus episcopus aliis de causis in Germaniam missus imperatorem adierat. Hunc sibi Rudulfus in tam difficili ac propemodum desperato pacis negocio socium ascivit, nec recusavere partes ob reverentiam Primę Sedis. Ambo concordię summis conatibus operas navavere – alter ad eam rem missus, alter admissus …".

the Utraquism that was professed by him as an heir to the Hussite tradition in the internal struggles. Enea Silvio Piccolomini had already designated George of Poděbrady as a particularly able man, who could unite the Bohemians.[84] In his later *Historia Bohemica* (written in 1458), he reported on the election of George as King of Bohemia and surprisingly did not defame him, but admitted that George was not lacking in a certain prudence which would benefit him as King.[85]

It is true that at first the papacy believed King George could have been used in the wars against the Ottomans. Pope Calixt III contemplated congratulating George on his election, but due to other political pressures abandoned the idea, as he specified in a letter to Cardinal Juan Carvajal, the legate *de latere* in the region at the time.[86] Cardinal Carvajal was instrumental, however, in the acceptance of George, as he even commissioned two Hungarian bishops to carry out the coronation, with the condition that on the eve of the coronation the King would sign a coronation vow that he would respect the Pope and protect the Catholic faith.[87] Cardinal Carvajal, kept in the region as legate *de latere* for a relatively long period of time, was instructed by the Pope to act in the best possible way, not only in the question of the crusade, but also in guiding the political events of the kingdoms with the newly elected rulers.[88] Although the Pope instructed Carvajal to work for the conversion of the Bohemian heretics to the true faith, it was Girolamo Lando who actively operated in the region for the appeasement of the internal conflicts within the Kingdom of Bohemia that arose after the election of King George.

Girolamo Lando first came to Bohemia in 1459 with faculties published on 16 September together with Francesco da Toledo, who was the theologian for the negotiation team.[89] Lando, in contrast, was supposed to negotiate concerning political matters within the region. The above-mentioned mission to appease the situation between the King of Poland and the Teutonic Knights was only one task of his legation. In the Bohemian lands, it was predominantly the attempt to prevent the internal conflict between King George and the Silesian towns represented by the city of Wrocław, which refused to pay homage to the new King of Bohemia.[90] Both the nuncios reached Prague in October and Lando, after their arrival, gave a long speech before the King and other officials of the kingdom, which explained

84. Wolkan, ed., *Der Briefwechsel*, vol. 3/1/1, pp. 22-57, no. 12 (here p. 36).

85. Piccolomini, *Historia Bohemica*, p. 254.

86. ASV, Arm. XXXIX 7, fol. 172v, "Eidem electo in regem Boemie cogitabamus scribere, prout videbis in copia introclusa, postea tamen, quod intelleximus alios in eiusmodi re pretendere interesse habere et precipue dux Saxonie, qui nobis et toti collegio valde querelando scripsit et se missuris oratores ad nos super hoc, deliberavimus non scribere".

87. Theiner, ed., *Vetera monumenta Hungariae*, vol. 2, pp. 405-406, no. 580.

88. ASV, Arm. XXXIX 7, fol. 171v-172v.

89. Urbánek, *České dějiny*, vol. 3/3, pp. 567-594; Drabina, "Działalność dyplomatyczna Hieronima Lando", pp. 149-155; idem, "Kontakty Wrocławia z Piusem II", pp. 518-519; Smołucha, *Polityka kurii rzymskiej*, pp. 191-198.

90. ASV, Arm. XXXIX 9, fol. 97r-98r (10 Jan 1460) (ed. Filip and Borchardt, *Schlesien*, pp. 214-215, no. 15).

the reasons for their coming to Bohemia.[91] Similarly, Lando gave a long speech in Wrocław, where they arrived in November, in order to persuade the burghers to subdue to the King of Bohemia. Peter Eschenloer noted in his historical writings the discussions the burghers had with the nuncios at their solemn entry.[92] Although the entry of the nuncio was a huge ceremony, the results were not particularly positive. The burghers pushed through a three-year postponement of the obligation to swear an oath to the King of Bohemia and the nuncios returned to Prague. Francesco da Toledo then visited Wrocław once more and came back to Prague with the delegation of the Wrocław burghers. The negotiations were to some extent successful, as the imminent conflict was averted.[93] The Pope reminded both of them in December that they should proceed to Poland and work on the other agenda.[94]

After the failure in Poland, both of them returned to Rome via Wrocław, but Lando was sent back to the region in December 1461.[95] He was commissioned to work for the crusade which did not involve the organisation of the crusade as such, but rather preparing the ground, appeasing and solving local conflicts and campaigning for the crusade itself. This was the crusade against the Ottoman Turks once again, which seemed to be the driving force behind the steps taken by nuncio Girolamo Lando. He led the talks with the Emperor and, as noted above, was present at the concluding of peace treaties between the Emperor and the King of Hungary, although his primary tasks were in Bohemia and Poland. After briefly visiting Hungary and negotiating once again in the Empire, Girolamo set off for Wrocław, then to Poland and again to Wrocław where he found himself in a fierce conflict with the bishop (Jošt of Rožmberk), who had no intention of publishing papal bulls because of the threat of open conflict in Bohemia.[96] His

91. Bachmann, ed., *Urkunden und Actenstücke*, pp. 287-294, no. 208.

92. On their presence in the city, see Eschenloer, *Geschichte*, pp. 292-350; idem, *Historia*, pp. 63-100.

93. Urbánek, *České dějiny*, vol. 3/3, p. 594; idem, *České dějiny*, vol. 3/4, pp. 337-342

94. ASV, Arm. XXXIX 9, fol. 96v-97r (23 Dec 1459).

95. His faculties in ASV, Reg. Vat. 518, fol. 18v-21r, 37r-44v, 50v-58v, 81v-86r, 157v-158v, 197r.

96. Eschenloer, *Geschichte*, pp. 399-400, "Der legat Cretensis gebot dem bischoff Jost, er sulde ken Breslow komen, vnd gab jm mit der stat sicher gleite, ane das er nicht wolt komen, vnd Jost brochte mit jm die czwene brudere herczuge zur Olssen. Am montag noch Trinitatis [6 Jun 1463] quomen sie zum legaten in seine herberge, vnd hatten vil rede mitenander vnd disputirunge. Cretensis gebot dem Josten gehorsam zu sein bebstlichen geboten, vnd die processus wider Girsik lossen awsgeen vnd den beisteen. Bischoff Jost sagte, es tőchte nicht, vnd wűrden nicht andirs denn crige doruß entsteen. Cretensis slug ab alle sache vnd gebot jm gehorsam zusein. Bischoff Jost appelliret vor den bobist, vnd vorczalte vil sache als eynir, der gerne der lande frid gesehen hette. Also kiffleten sie sich swerlichen mitenander, das zu leczte Cretensis sagte zu Jodoco: 'Du bist ein gifft dis vatirlandis vnd ein stein der schande'. Doruff antwortet jm Jost den spruch Sand Pauls 'Die Cretenn sint alleczeit lűgener, bőse tire, vnd tregis bawchs' [Tit 1,12] etc. Do stunt vff Cretensis in czornn vnd slug mit der hand noch Jost. Die fűrsten filen do czwischen vnd redten nichtis, sunder die ratmanne vndirstunden ferrer, das do nichtis geschah, vnd bestalten das haws, das kein geschrey doruß quőme, wan der Sweidnicz keler (a renowned inn in Wrocław) nahent dobey vnd am obend was. ... Die fűrsten vnd die gancze Slesia stunde bey bischoff Jost, vnd woren alle dem legaten gram ...".

mission did not attain, however, any fundamental success. The struggles between the King of Poland and the Teutonic Knights continued and the conflict situation between Wrocław and the King of Bohemia also remained unsolved,[97] despite Girolamo having left behind one member of his retinue, Baldassare Turini as a *subdelegatus*.[98] Girolamo Lando arrived in Central Europe once more in the commission of Pope Paul II, who sent him to Hungary with the task of organising the crusade and supporting the king of Hungary. In the meantime, however, additional papal envoys participated in the negotiations.

The above-mentioned Rudolf of Rüdesheim, a German-born who studied in Heidelberg, knew the situation in Germany and the region relatively well, even after his involvement as secretary at the Council of Basel.[99] He continuously worked in Central Europe for the improvement of the internal relations of the individual sovereigns as well as issues between some bishoprics. After the failed negotiations of Cardinal Bessarion, he together with Domenico Dominici tried to appease the conflict between the King of Hungary and the Emperor.[100] He supported the crusade preparations in 1463-1464 with another commission and was finally sent by Pope Paul II in the beginning of 1465 to the region as a papal envoy to Wrocław, the city which was endangered by a conflict with its King, George of Bohemia. Baldassare Turini remained in Wrocław at this time, but not much is known about his activities. He was definitely replaced by Rudolf in the capacity of papal envoy.[101]

After taking part in the negotiations between the Emperor and the King of Hungary, he arrived in order to solve additional political struggles in the region. He was involved in the talks between the King of Poland and the Teutonic Knights, but also in the Bohemian matters; the Pope commissioned him to negotiate at the imperial court and involve Frederick III in these problems.[102] When he arrived in Wrocław on 9 November 1465, after staying in Austria and Germany for some time, Rudolf began to cooperate with the Catholic opposition against King George and even threatened the opponents with an interdict. Rudolf's strict position in relation to the 'heretics' was welcomed by the Wrocław burghers, who even supported him against the Pope, who wanted to recall him immediately after his arrival at the Silesian city. Strangely enough, the Pope planned to keep Baldassare Turini, whereas Rudolf was to be sent back. The burghers, however,

97. Cf. Urbánek, *České dějiny*, vol. 3/4, passim; Drabina, J.: *Działalność dyplomatyczna Hieronima Lando*, pp. 156-164; and in the most detail, Smołucha, *Polityka kurii rzymskiej*, pp. 224-315; Kalous, *Plenitudo potestatis*, pp. 196-202.

98. Eschenloer, *Geschichte*, pp. 432-434; Palacky, ed., *Urkundliche Beiträge zur Geschichte Böhmens*, pp. 324-325, no. 314; Markgraf, ed., *Politische Correspondenz*, vol. 2, pp. 74-76, nos. 249, 250.

99. Radziszewska, "Działalność dyplomatyczna".

100. Katona, ed., *Historia critica*, vol. 7, pp. 601-604 (4 and 5 May 1463).

101. Drabina, *Kontakty Wrocławia z Rzymem*, pp. 164-165.

102. Markgraf, ed., *Politische Correspondenz*, vol. 2, pp. 108-109, no. 272; on the legation see Drabina, "Działalność dyplomatyczna legata apostolskiego Rudolfa"; Radziszewska, "Działalność dyplomatyczna", pp. 16-43; Odložilík, *The Hussite King*, passim; Heymann, *George of Bohemia*, passim.

opposed the Pope's decision and pointed to the imminent dangers. The pope confirmed Rudolf's position once again in February 1466.[103] This all led to a new crusade against the King of Bohemia, as is apparent from the fact that his stay was sponsored from the *Depositeria generale della crociata.*[104]

In the meantime, he organised the Polish-Teutonic matters, only to return to Wrocław in December 1466, where he shaped the anti-George opposition and began to preach the crusade on 27 April 1467. In order to have a higher authority, he was named nuncio *cum potestate legati de latere* three weeks later by the Pope.[105] His position and stay in the city was so important to the city council that they even wrote a supplication to Pope Paul II to appoint him to the newly vacant bishopric of Wrocław. The right to elect the bishop belonged to the chapter, which followed the same line and nominated him as well. While maintaining the position of nuncio *cum potestate legati de latere*, Rudolf became the bishop of Wrocław, which strengthened his position even further.[106]

103. Drabina, "Działalność dyplomatyczna legata apostolskiego Rudolfa", pp. 214-215; Radziszewska, "Działalność dyplomatyczna", p. 19; Markgraf, ed., *Politische Correspondenz*, vol. 2, pp. 146-147, no. 310 (17 Dec 1465); pp. 155-156, no. 315 (28 Jan 1466); p. 164, no. 317 (27 Feb 1466), "... Intelleximus introitum tuum ad Wratislaviam et diligenciam quam ibi facere studes in rebus commissis, et quod populus ille non parvam consolacionem ex accessu tuo habuit, in omnibus laudantes diligenciam tuam. Committimus tibi et mandamus, quod non obstantibus quibuscunque litteris nostris quibus scripsimus quod festinares ad nos, ut ex te de his que ibi facta sunt et per te gesta pro negocio contra Georgium consumando cerciorem informacionem haberemus, remaneas in dicta civitate ...".

104. AS Roma, Camerale I, Depositeria della crociata, vol. 1235, fol. 135r; cf. Beneš, "Depositeria", pp. 743-744.

105. Eschenloer, *Geschichte*, pp. 607-608; Markgraf, ed., *Politische Correspondenz*, vol. 2, pp. 233-236, no. 365 (15 May 1467), "... hac itaque fiducia et consideracione ducti te in Polonie et Bohemie regnis necnon ducatibus marchionatibus comitatibus et aliis dominiis ad ea spectantibus et pertinentibus ac eciam in Prussie Livonie et Misnensibus partibus auctoritate apostolica tenore presencium nuncium nostrum cum potestate legati de latere constituimus et deputavimus ac ad effectum execucionis predicte sentencie [versus Georgium, alias Jersicum Pogiebrat] tantum plenam et liberam eidem fraternitati tue concedimus facultatem". His powers are enumerated in a manuscript of the chancery of King George, cf. *ibid.*, pp. 228-229, no. 360; he could collect money for the crusade, use tithes and received some more faculties, *ibid.*, p. 236-240, no. 366-370. On preaching the new crusade against the Hussites, Soukup, "Crusading against Christians", pp. 98-110.

106. Drabina, "Działalność dyplomatyczna legata apostolskiego Rudolfa", pp. 221-222; Markgraf, ed., *Politische Correspondenz*, vol. 2, pp. 250-251, no. 379 (27 Dec 1467). Confirmed as bishop of Wrocław on 27 Apr 1468 (see, *ibid.*, pp. 271-272, no. 394), and newly confirmed as nuncio because of the change of bishoprics, so that there are no doubts, see Theiner, ed., *Vetera monumenta Poloniae*, vol. 2, pp. 158-159, no. 195, "Cum nos... te in Polonie et Boemie regnis necnon ducatibus, marchionatibus, comitatibus et aliis dominiis ad ea spectantibus, ac in Pruscie, Livonie et Misne partibus auctoritate apostolica nuntium nostrum cum potestate legati de latere constituerimus et deputaverimus, tibique tunc Laventino, nunc vero Wratislaviensi Episcopo, ad obviandum perditionis filio Georgio... diversas concesserimus facultates, et postmodum te licet absentem a vinculo, quo ecclesie Laventine, cui tunc preeras, tenebaris, de fratrum nostrorum consilio et potestatis apostolice plenitudine absolventes, te ad ecclesiam Wratislaviensem tunc pastoris solatio destitutam duxerimus auctoritate predicta transferendum: Nos ne propter translationem huiusmodi de

It is apparent here that the nuncio, the organiser of the negotiations, turned into an organiser and preacher of a crusade. There were also others who played this double role at the end of the 1460s. The crucial papal envoys were Lorenzo Roverella, bishop of Ferrara and from January 1468 nuncio *cum potestate legati de latere*, and Gabriele Rangoni, a Franciscan colleague of John of Capistrano in the early 1450s and later the vicar and organiser of the Franciscan province in Central Europe, *inquisitor heretice pravitatis* against the Hussites and Wycliffites of Bohemia and later a papal nuncio (from 1470 at the latest). Both of them were instrumental in the organisation of the crusade, as briefly mentioned in the previous section. Both of them also contributed essentially to the good relations between the papacy and King Matthias of Hungary, who was chosen to be the leader of the crusade.[107] Additional papal envoys, who contributed to the political negotiations of the time, included Francesco Todeschini Piccolomini, who was sent to the *Reichstag* in Regensburg in 1471. He also had commissions to negotiate and not allow any compromise with the 'heretics', even after the death of King George.[108] Cardinal Francesco embodied the highest representative of the Church in the negotiations. The name of Peter Wimars of Erkelenz, who cooperated with Nicholas of Cusa previously and knew the region relatively well, was on the other side of the scale. He was charged in 1467 with the task of helping Gabriele Rangoni in his negotiations in Kraków with the King of Poland, whom they wanted to persuade to take part in the fight against King George. Like others, he was financed from the *Depositeria generale della crociata*.[109] All these envoys were also instructed to communicate amongst themselves in order to harmonise their activities and advance. Rudolf was supposed to be in contact with Lorenzo Roverella, whereas Lorenzo was informed of the activities of Baldassare Turini, Francesco Todeschini Piccolomini and Fabiano de Montepulciano, another nuncio in the region.[110]

These papal envoys institutionalised their position in the region, clearly focusing on negotiations and then, even more so, on the crusade. Their political

iuribus facultatum huiusmodi hesitetur, facultatum ipsarum tenores, ac si de verbo ad verbum inserti forent, etiam si de illis eorumque totis tenoribus specialis et expressa mentio habenda esset, presentibus pro expressis habentes, tibi motu proprio, non ad cuiusvis instanciam, sed ex certa scientia auctoritate predicta concedimus et volumus, quod facultatibus predictis libere uti possis et debeas, ac si dicte ecclesie Laventine preesses, et de illa ad ipsam Wratislaviensem ecclesiam translatus non fuisses".

107. Odložilík, *The Hussite King*, passim; Heymann, *George of Bohemia*, passim; on Gabriele Rangoni, Hlaváček, *Die böhmischen Franziskaner*, pp. 135-151.

108. Macek, "K zahraniční politice", pp. 37-48; Strnad, "Francesco Todeschini-Piccolomini", pp. 226-248.

109. Beneš, "Depositeria", pp. 746-749; Eschenloer, *Geschichte*, pp. 645-656, "Sieben wochen bleben dise legaten zu Cracow vnd teglichen arbeiten, wie sie hetten mőgen den konig dorein fűren, das er hette das reich zu Behemen vffgenomen". Cf. also *Joannis Dlugossii Annales*, 1462-1480, p. 190; Kaprinai, ed., *Hungaria diplomatica*, pt. 2, pp. 591-592, anonymous narrative 1458-1469.

110. Markgraf, ed., *Politische Correspondenz*, vol. 2, pp. 256-257, no. 384; ASV, Arm. XXXIX 12, fol. 30rv, 129v-130v.

involvement in local matters also brought about an involvement with local powers. Baldassare Turini, Lorenzo Roverella and Gabriele Rangoni had specifically close relations with the King of Hungary. The King, having the patronage right over the Hungarian Church, even appointed Gabriele Rangoni bishop of Transylvania in 1472 and Baldassare Turini bishop of Srem, in 1479. The relationship with the local power could not have been more obvious. Both of them were also later closely connected to Matthias Corvinus; Baldassare as *nuncius et orator* in 1475-1482, when he actively influenced the on-going conflict between the Kings of Hungary and Poland and reported to Rome on the events of Central Europe and the Turkish wars. He actively supported King Matthias Corvinus, when he even excommunicated the King of Poland and his son. First residing at the royal court in Buda, he later moved to Wrocław again with the burghers even complaining to the King of Hungary about Baldassare's strict advance against the Polish (which was problematic in commercial terms). He stayed in Wrocław at the King's expense, who even sent letters of support to Wrocław and to Olomouc (in Moravia). All these details show that Baldassare actually served the King, even though he was still papal nuncio and used such authority.[111] Gabriele Rangoni represented an even more useful ally for the King, as when he became a cardinal, he moved to Rome in 1479 and functioned as a kind of unofficial protector of the interests of the King.[112]

Lorenzo Roverella's position was not improved by any such office given to him by the King, but it is clear that he cooperated with him very closely. Apart from the conflict when the King pressured him to confirm his title of King of Bohemia (immediately after the official election land diet at Kutná Hora elected King Wladislas) in Jihlava in May 1471,[113] the relationship did not suffer from any problems. This was even the case when the King learned about the possibility of a new legate being sent to his court and he advised his envoy in Rome to express concerns about this decision. The King's envoy, Miklós Nyújtódi Székely, bishop of Knin, was instructed to state that Matthias was very much surprised and disturbed when he learned about the new legate, who would surely not understand the situation to the extent that the bishop of Ferrara, Lorenzo Roverella, did. The King viewed him a fitting and convenient partner for political negotiations. He emphasised, for example, that changing the legate might result in strengthening the arguments of the other side, the Poles, who might twist the Pope's decision in order to support their claims that Lorenzo's actions were not supported by the papacy, and was therefore recalled.[114]

111. Baczkowski, "Nieznane listy"; Eschenloer, *Geschichte*, p. 1030, "Jn disem jore lag zu Breslow ein bebstlicher sendebot Baltazar von Piscia, doctor decretorum vff konigs Mathie czerunge"; complains of the burghers, Kronthal and Wendt, eds., *Politische Correspondenz*, vol. 1, pp. 257-259, no. 305; supporting letters, for Wrocław, cf. *ibid.*, p. 257, no. 305, for Olomouc, Land archives Opava, branch Olomouc, Metropolitan chapter Olomouc, Listiny, sign. A IV c 12 (12 Aug. 1477). Cf. also Kalous, *Plenitudo potestatis*, pp. 215-217.

112. E.g. Paschini, ed., *Il carteggio*, p. 72.

113. Theiner, ed., *Vetera monumenta Hungariae*, vol. 2, pp. 422-423, no. 603 (and previous section).

114. Roma, Biblioteca Angelica, ms. 1077, fol. 36v-38v; the instructions published and analysed in Kalous, "King Matthias Corvinus and the Papacy".

Although the King's interests were clearly voiced, they did not change the decision of the new Pope Sixtus IV, who created five legates for the organisation of the crusade in late 1471. As mentioned earlier, Cardinal Marco Barbo was designated to go to Central Europe. He was one of the greatest prelates who visited the region following, for example, the personality of Cardinal Juan Carvajal; as Peter Eschenloer remarked, "no one saw such a prelate in Wrocław before".[115] The previously mentioned negotiations in Rome must have occurred in late 1471 or very early 1472, as Marco Barbo left the City on 22 February 1472. Despite being new to Central Europe, he could have benefited from certain informal instructions,[116] as well as from the presence of the Hungarian envoy in his company while travelling to Hungary. Similarly, his predecessor Lorenzo Roverella travelled to Central Europe in 1468 in company with Hilarius Litoměřický (of Litoměřice), administrator of the archbishopric of Prague and canon of the Prague chapter, who went to Rome to ask for stricter steps against King George of Bohemia.[117]

Marco Barbo held a large number of faculties (some of them giving him powers in political matters, he could use excommunications or interdicts following the development of the talks) and his main task was organising the crusade, and even persuading the warring parties in Central Europe of its greater importance than fighting against heretics in Bohemia. His instructions spoke about concluding peace between the Kings of Hungary and Poland and he was commissioned to solve the Polish-Teutonic problem.[118] He had organised negotiations between the two kings (with representatives on both sides and envoys going back and forth) and the individual parties, but did not achieve a final peace. He described his activities in a report preserved among his correspondence, as well as in several letters. In this case, actual negotiations are apparent: the legate described his arrival at the royal court of Poland and his talks there. After departing, he was in contact with both the Hungarian and the Polish courts through his or royal envoys and in this manner held talks, for example, about prolonging of the truce, freeing captives and organising congresses in Silesia for solving the conflict.[119] Although the peace talks only achieved success

115. Eschenloer, *Geschichte*, p. 903. On Marco Barbo, see Gualdo, "Barbo, Marco"; Paschini, ed., *Il carteggio*, pp. 1-12; idem, "I benefici ecclesiastici"; Fletcher, "The Making"; eadem, "Cardinal Marco Barbo"; Bullard, "Renaissance spirituality"; on the legation, Fraknói, *Magyarország egyházi és politikai összeköttetései*, vol. 2, pp. 142-145; Drabina, "Misja dyplomatyczna"; idem, "Legaci apostolscy", pp. 264-268; Baczkowski, *Walka Jagiellonów*, pp. 59-84; Macek, "Prag und Rom", pp. 395-397; idem, *Víra a zbožnost*, pp. 242-244; Kalous, "Papežský legát Marco Barbo"; idem, *Plenitudo potestatis*, pp. 245-284.

116. Rome, Biblioteca Angelica, ms. 1077, fol. 21r-24r.

117. Hejnic and Polívka, *Plzeň*, p. 14.

118. ASV, Misc., Arm. II 30, fol. 38r-41r (Theiner, ed., *Vetera monumenta Hungariae*, pp. 436-439, no. 622; Artner, ed., *"Magyarország"*, pp. 142-143, no. 119; Teleki, ed., *Hunyadiak kora*, vol. 11, pp. 459-465, no. 535); additional instructions, ASV, Misc., Arm. II 30, fol. 41r-42r.

119. BAV, Vat. lat. 5641, fol. 201r-208v (ed. Kalous, *Plenitudo potestatis*, pp. 264-284).

after he left the region, his activity initiated a longer process that ended in the general truce of 1474-1475 and the peace treaty of 1478-1479.[120]

The conflict between the Emperor and the King of Hungary revived in the late 1470s. Papal legates and nuncios participated in the peace negotiations between the King of Hungary and the Emperor and his son Maximilian in later years: first, after 1477 and the second war between them, and then in the 1480s after the third war broke out. Substantial negotiations were conducted by Raymund Peraudi towards the end of the life of King Matthias (1489-1490).[121] One episode of these relations attracts attention. This was in 1479 when three legates were created by the Pope in order to help organise the crusade in Europe against the Ottoman Turks. Cardinal Ausias Despuig went to Germany, while Cardinal Giovanni d'Aragona, brother-in-law to King Matthias Corvinus, was assigned the region east of Germany, specified as Hungary, Bohemia and Poland.[122] King Matthias was well informed about the whereabouts of Cardinal Giovanni even before he entered his legatine province, as the King even sent a bishop to meet and accompany him on his way to Hungary.[123] Giovanni had many political tasks to deal with, but also importantly connected the King with other legates and nuncios, for even after he returned to Rome in August 1480, the King asked him for help.

It is apparent that once the legates and nuncios visited certain kings they were, on the one hand, considered specialists in the regions and, on the other hand, remained in touch with the locals. It was shown previously how King Matthias involved the legates and nuncios in the matters of his kingdom. He did not stop, however, with them. He asked Marco Barbo to be the protector of the Paulines, the Hungarian eremitic order,[124] and Marco Barbo also remained in touch with further papal envoys in the region (papal nuncio Angelo Pecchinoli sent him his report in 1489 and Barbo was in all probability involved in drafting further instructions for the nuncio).[125] The King then tried to make use of his brother-in-law. Cardinal Giovanni was another contact person at the Papal Curia and, together with the afore-mentioned Gabriele Rangoni, who became a cardinal in 1479, was crucial for the King when he tried to influence papal decisions, even concerning nuncios in the region.

Prospero Caffarelli was sent to the Emperor and the King of Hungary in March 1480 with the task of solving conflicts between the two sovereigns in order to improve the chances for a general crusade against the Ottoman Turks,

120. Kalous, *Matyáš Korvín*, pp. 142-153, 179-185.

121. Nehring, "Quellen"; idem, *Matthias Corvinus.*

122. The extensive faculties of both of them are preserved in ASV, Reg. Vat. 680.

123. Fraknói, ed., *Mátyás király levelei*, vol. 1, pp. 455-456, no. 308 (end Oct 1479), "Acceptis hodie litteris paternitatis vestre, postquam intelleximus illam Landrotham applicuisse, civitatem illustrissimi ducis Bavarie, ibique maximo cum honore et letitia susceptam, gratulati fuimus et e vestigio expedivimus reverendum patrem dominum Ioannem episcopum Waradiensem, quem jussimus ire crastino in occursum reverendissime paternitatis vestre usque Pathaviam. Is accepit a nobis in mandatis, ut se paternitati vestre associet, et via commodiori conducat ...".

124. Fraknói, ed., *Mátyás király levelei*, vol. 1, pp. 315-316, no. 222 (15 Jun 1475).

125. BAV, Vat. lat. 5641, fol. 237r-247v; 96r-99v.

especially after the loss of Otranto.[126] His mission was from its very beginning, however, criticised by King Matthias, who even asked Cardinal Gabriele to voice his request that the papal diplomacy should stay out of the business between him and the Emperor.[127] After his stay at the imperial court, Prospero arrived in Buda and Matthias again informed Cardinal Gabriele about the talks and told him what to report in case Prospero would not accurately relate about the talks.[128] The King did not trust the nuncio at all and wanted change. He asked that another legate be sent who could lead negotiations, for in his eyes Prospero was too inactive.[129] Despite this fact, the King respected him, called him his friend and corresponded with him.[130] The call for a new legate was only partially successful. The Pope created a new legate in January 1481 in the person of Cardinal Giovanni Battista Cibo. As mentioned earlier, he first accepted the mission and the task to visit the *Reichstag* in Nuremberg and appease the Emperor and the King of Hungary, but soon rejected the legation and a new nuncio had to be chosen.[131] The papal nuncio Orso Orsini, bishop of Teano, was charged with the task of negotiating peace between Emperor Frederick III and the King of Hungary Matthias. The King communicated again with Prospero and about him even with Cardinal Giovanni d'Aragona.[132] Matthias then found Prospero more suitable for the talks than the new nuncio. He even asked the Pope not to give the negotiations over to Orso

126. Zapperi, "Caffarelli, Prospero"; see also, Schlecht, *Andrea Zamometić*, pp. 165-166; Fraknói, *Magyarország egyházi és politikai összeköttetései*, vol. 2, pp. 167-170.

127. Fraknói, ed., *Mátyás király levelei*, vol. 2, p. 31, no. 21 (Spring 1480), "… Quare rogamus paternitatem vestram, velit sanctissimum dominum admonere, ne aliquos hoc tempore tractatores deputet, donec experiamur utrum nos ipsi aliquam possumus cum ipso cesare viam pacis et concordie reperiri. Si enim id facere non poterimus, nos ipsi petemus, et sanctissimum dominum nostrum admonebimus quid facto in huiusmodi rebus opus erit".

128. *Ibid.*, pp. 42-45, no. 30 (Aug 1480), "… ob eam copias ipsas ad paternitatem vestram misimus, ut is orator apostolicus aliter de hiis ad pontificem scriberet, sciter paternitas vestra honorem nostrum defendere et causam nostram iustificae ubi opus foret".

129. *Ibid.*, pp. 65-70, no. 43 (6 Nov 1480), "… Quantum vero ad imperatorem Romanorum attinet, cum quo hortatur nos sanctitas vestra ad pacem et subiungit missuram se legatum apostolicum, si placeat, esse vero hic reverendissimum dominum patrem episcopum Asculanum oratorem apostolicum, cuius nos opera tuto et fideliter uti possumus etc.; respondemus sanctitati vestre profecto ipsum dominum Asculanum videri nobis hominem doctum et prudentem ac optime expertum ad res gerendas sanctitatis vestre; verum id possumus affirmare de illo, quod dicitur in evangelio salvatorem nostrum dixisse de se ipso: Discite, inquit a me, quia mitis sum et humilis corde. Si ipse aliquantulum severior esset et aggrederetur rem ipsam animo maiore, vel si alium talem legatum mitteret sanctitas vestra, iudicio nostro melius conduceret istis rebus, quia ut intelligat sanctitas vestra mores imperatoris, ipse omni conatu refuti, quandocumque videt se trahi ad hoc, quod iustum est. Vellemus, talem legatum mitteret sanctitas vestra, qui videret, cognosceret, palparet et diffiniret negotium differentiarum inter nos, et utra pars justo et honesto nollet acquiescere, non curato favore cuiuslibet partis, cogeret partem contravenientem ad parendum iusto per censuras. …"

130. *Ibid.*, pp. 117-118, no. 65 (11 Mar 1481).

131. Pellegrini, "Innocenzo VIII"; on the nomination as legate, Gherardi da Volterra, *Il diario romano*, pp. 34-37.

132. Fraknói, ed., *Mátyás király levelei*, vol. 2, pp. 119-120, no. 67 (end of March 1481).

Orsini and tried to use both his contacts in Rome to push through this demand.[133] The King then focused on restoring the activity of Prospero Caffarelli. He wanted him to be sent there instead of Orso and even urged Prospero to go there. After the Nuremberg diet, he even implored the original nuncio to try and influence the unfavourable results of the convention. In his letter the King also mentioned the troubles of communication, as one boy (*puer*), who was supposed to carry a previous letter was imprisoned by the Emperor and the letter intercepted.[134] The activities of Prospero Caffarelli culminated, however, at the end of 1481, as the nuncio informed the King early the following year from Rome.[135]

Orso Orsini represented the Pope at the *Reichstag* in Nuremberg.[136] King Matthias strongly disagreed, however, with the results of the diet and criticised in particular the nuncio, whose activity he viewed as the reason for his failure. The King even called the nuncio his enemy and complained to Rome, as Giovanni Lorenzi reported in August 1481.[137] Matthias also informed his envoy to the Pope, John Vitéz the Younger, about the activity of nuncio Orsini, whom he actually held responsible for the fact that the imperial army levied in Germany against the Turks attacked Hungary instead.[138] This does not seem to be the case, however, as the cardinals in Rome did not know anything about this and when discussing the case, they thought it necessary to write to both the nuncios (Orsini and Caffarelli) and to both the potentates (the Emperor and the King of Hungary). Unfortunately, in a letter to the Pope they did not mention expressly what was supposed to be done.[139] In the meantime, Matthias still asked the Pope to recall the nuncio and send a cardinal in his place.[140] Orso Orsini visited Buda and attempted to organise some peace talks,

133. *Ibid.*, pp. 126-128, no. 72 (4 Apr 1481); p. 129, no. 73 (13 Apr 1481); pp. 131-132, no. 75 (May 1481).

134. *Ibid.*, p. 391, no. 248 (1481); pp. 144-145, no. 80 (13 Jul 1481).

135. *Ibid.*, pp. 206-207, no. 111.

136. Bachmann, ed., *Urkundliche Nachträge*, pp. 462-467, no. 444; pp. 467-468, no. 445 (Feb 1481); cf. Schlecht, *Andrea Zamometić*, pp. 165-167.

137. Fraknói, ed., *Mátyás király levelei*, vol. 2, pp. 134-135, no. 77 (13 Jul 1481); Paschini, ed., *Il carteggio*, p. 37, no. 11, (17 Aug 1481), Lorenzi wrote in a letter to Marco Barbo, "Rex Ungarie litteras pontifici scripsit iracundie plenas et stomachi, in quibus gravissime de Theanen. conqueritur; appellatque eum, ut accepi, hostem suum, vultque ut omnino revocetur".

138. MZK Brno, ms. sign. Mk 9, fol. 257v, "Ad quae tibi respondemus, quod non fuisset opus suae sanctitati de ipso Theanensi et in dieta Norimbergae egerit et etiam scripserit sanctissimo domino nostro. Extat apud nos scriptum sui secretarii prepositi Constantiensi, qui nobis significavit ipsum dominum Theanensem scripsisse pontifici, qualiter gentes illae, quae alius nobis contra Turcos per imperialis promissae fuerant, iam caesari in subsidium contra nos sint promissae. Super hoc autem in suis litteris quaesivit ipse dominus Theanensis a pontifice informari, utrum voluntas suae sanctitatis sit, quod gentes illae caesari in subsidium decretae contra nos convertantur, vel si quid aliud sua sanctitas velit ipsum edoceat ...". It is clear from the letter that Matthias demanded recalling the nuncio even before: "quae nobis de actis tuis et responso pontificis ad suplicationem nostram de revocatione domini Theanensi rescripsisti, intelleximus ..."

139. BMV, Lat. X 174 (=3621), fol. 158rv (18 Sep 1481).

140. Fraknói, ed., *Mátyás király levelei*, vol. 2, pp. 164-166, no. 95 (4 Sep 1481), "... revocatoque domino Theanensi, aliquem magis idoneum, et si fieri posset, quod nos summopere optaremus, unum ex reverendissimis sancte Romane ecclesie cardinalibus ad ipsos principes

but was unsuccessful and after the outbreak of the new war between the King and the Emperor, he retired from all the negotiations and returned to Rome.[141]

After these developments, the Pope actually sent a letter to the Emperor in reaction to the Nuremberg diet, most openly manifesting the reasons for papal diplomacy. The Pope claimed that if he thought it useful before, he would have sent a legate *de latere.* If the envoys of both the parties met again with sufficient mandates to complete this struggle and controversy and if a new diet with imperial princes was organised and envoys of the King of Hungary let in, then, the Pope stated, "we will send a legate *de latere* not suspected of service to either of the parties, who would by our right bring the parties to peace and confirm the treaties with our apostolic authority".[142] The legates and papal diplomacy should be impartial when dealing with Catholic princes.

The legates and nuncios in 1480-1482 had a number of problems to solve. These events may serve as an example of possible involvement of papal diplomacy in secular political matters on the one hand, and the involvement of secular rulers into papal diplomacy on the other. The above-mentioned clearly indicates that it was not only the Pope, who influenced his diplomats, but also the local sovereigns. In this case, Matthias Corvinus tried to attract the important prelates and legates to his side with appointments and offices. When he had the cooperation of Cardinals Marco Barbo and especially Giovanni d'Aragona and Gabriele Rangoni (his strongest supporter at the Curia), he did not hesitate to communicate with them about his problems. He wrote to the Pope directly and then attempted to influence the decisions through his friends and supporters. Requesting a change in the decision of the Pope was very different with these allies than without them in late 1471 with only his envoy Miklós Nyújtódi Székely. Second, it was possible to see that when the King was not content with the actual legates or nuncios, he tried to do everything possible to change the situation. Although Pope Sixtus IV was in general favourable to King Matthias, a nuncio who did not convene with the King's ideas might have been quite dangerous to the King's plans.

destinare, qui semoto favore et odio causam utriusque cognosceret et insuper pro subsidio contra Turcas promisso fideliter laboraret".

141. Fraknói, *Magyarország egyházi és politikai összeköttetései*, vol. 2, pp. 170-171; idem, ed., *Mátyás király levelei*, vol. 2, pp. 765-766, no. 108.

142. Rome, Biblioteca Angelica, ms. 1077, fol. 18v, "Ita enim cordi continuo heret hec tanta contentio tamquam periculosa concertatio, ut iam pridem legatum quempiam de latere nostro misissemus, si invitati ad id fuissemus, vel si id expedire putavissemus. Verum regi gravitatem et animorum obstinationem considerantes utilius fore, iudicamus rem ipsam cum oratoribus utriusque partis bene instructis et pleno mandato suffultis per nos et sacrum senatum tractare cognoscere et sine debito terminare, quod si magis placet tue celsitudinis conducibiliusque videtur rem tractari per imperii principes in aliquo conventu per tuam maiestatem indicendo, in quo regis oratores tuto esse possint, mittemus et nos legatum aliquem de latere neutri partium merito suspectum, qui iure nostra partes suas paci et concordie interponat confirmetque conventa nostra apostolica auctoritate, nullos labores nullasque impensas recusabimus, dum modo concordia quam tantopere concupivimus consequi possit".

Disagreement with a legate, whose job was to settle arguments between conflicting parties, must have been a common occurrence. Girolamo Lando in Poland or Prospero Caffarelli and Orso Orsini in Hungary are only a few examples; the conflicts stemmed from the papal policy. When the Pope clearly supported one side, the legates and nuncios also made it clear with their activities. The cardinal legates, such as Marco Barbo, acted in a way to be respected by both the sides. As a cardinal and legate *de latere*, he was supposed to bring peace to all, even if reached with compromises. This was possibly the reason King Matthias Corvinus suggested that the Papal Curia send a cardinal legate instead of a nuncio, Prospero Caffarelli. The Pope himself even stressed the impartiality of the future legate. Such attempts to suggest the person of a legate to be sent to a particular region were not uncommon. The King of France, for example, did not accept Cardinal Bessarion in 1472, but asked for Cardinal Guillaume d'Estouteville as legate *de latere.* The King "hoped that Cardinal d'Estouteville would do those things, which Cardinal Bessarion refused to do", even though the Pope had first refused to send him. (His legation did not even begin, even though he had been selected and confirmed by the consistory).[143] The same informer, namely Luka Tolentić, bishop of Šibenik and nuncio at the court of Burgundy, reported a year later that the duke wanted the new Burgundian cardinal Philibert Hugonet, bishop of Mâcon, to be sent as legate to confirm the agreements between the duke and the Emperor.[144]

The problem of respecting lower status envoys also appeared in the last round of peace negotiations between the Emperor (and the King of the Romans) and King Matthias. A nuncio was sent to the Emperor, in order to make peace possible, in 1489. Raymund Peraudi, apart from collecting money for a crusade and issuing a number of confessional letters in print, attempted to organise peace talks between the two rulers.[145] According to Angelo Pecchinoli, who visited the court of Matthias Corvinus, Raymund Peraudi asked the King for a letter of safe conduct, *salvus conductus*, to visit his court. This outraged the King and he complained that despite having always respected the Curia and its envoys, this had clearly stated that he was the King's enemy. Why else would he need safe conduct? The King even told Angelo that he could not sleep for two nights as he was so very upset.[146] Although nuncios were supposed to carry credentials, they normally did not need a letter of safe conduct, as they were usually protected by the authority of their lord and master, the Pope. This behaviour, which Angelo Pecchinoli ascribed to the other nuncio's simplicity, or French mores,[147] could undermine the credibility of the nuncio, who could be viewed as someone who did not trust the King and even feared for his own security. It should only be

143. Ljubić, ed., *Dispacci*, pp. 31-32.

144. *Ibid.*, pp. 34-35.

145. On Peraudi see Gottlob, "Der Legat"; Paulus, "Raimund Peraudi"; Höflechner, *Die Gesandten*, pp. 229-232; Schmid, "Der päpstliche Legat"; and on negotiations in Austria particularly Nehring, "Quellen".

146. BMV, Lat. X 175 (=3622), fol. 124r.

147. BMV, Lat. X 175 (=3622), fol. 124v.

added that just as King Matthias in a few cases distributed bishoprics to papal envoys, Maximilian, King of the Romans, nominated Raymund Peraudi to the bishopric of Gurk.[148]

4.2.2. *Communication*

Papal legates conducted negotiations and worked at bringing peace to various conflicts. Their tasks, were, however, often connected with the internal matters of individual countries. They represented popes at local conventions and diets and referred back to Rome about these events. Their sphere of activity was not only limited to the royal courts, but they would frequently visit the imperial diets and attempted to shape not only the situation in the Empire, but through these conventions in all of Europe and certainly in relation to the crusade against the Ottomans or the struggle against the 'heretics' in Bohemia.[149] Examples of these kinds of efforts include Domenico Dominici, who took part in the diet in Nuremberg in 1463 with the intention of helping organise a crusade. In 1471, a great legation of Cardinal Francesco Todeschini Picollomini was directed to the *Reichstag* in Regensburg, where he attempted to organise the advance against the Bohemians and where nuncio Lorenzo Roverella also actively worked in the war against Bohemia. Orso Orsini and Prospero Caffarelli have been mentioned in previous paragraphs. Even later in the 1520s, Antonio Burgio took part in the land diets of Hungary, as the country was of prime interest to Rome because of the fight against the Turks. He sent reports back to Rome, including the conclusions concerning the diets which later became royal decrees (even in various versions concluded at consecutive conventions of the estates). He also collected additional documents related to the developments in the individual countries of his authority.[150]

In general, standards of communication, talks and negotiations of papal legates did not differ substantially from the diplomatic practice of the period, which has been thoroughly described by historians.[151] In this sense, the legates and especially the nuncios were diplomatic agents who had to report back to the Curia. Although the papal diplomacy adopted the system of permanent nuncios more slowly than certain other Italian states, some papal representatives may be labelled as such: e.g. Luka Tolentić in Burgundy, Alexander Numai at the Emperor's court, Angelo Pecchinoli or Antonio Burgio at the King of Hungary's court. Nevertheless, even the non-stable nuncios and legates followed the standard mode of conduct as seen previously, and sent reports including speeches or even

148. BMV, Lat. X 178 (=3625), fol. 175r, Raymund wrote to pope, "… sicuti etiam me nominavit ad episcopatum Gurcen. propter honorem vestre sanctitatis, de quo plurimas et humillimas graciarum actiones refero vestre sanctitati…"; fol. 14r, Frederick III wrote to the cardinals about Raymund as *electus Gurcensis* on 21 Jan 1491.

149. Cf. for example, Wolff, "Päpstliche Legaten"; Schmid, "Der päpstliche Legat".

150. BAV, Vat. lat. 3924, passim.

151. Cf. at least the basic work of Mattingly, *Renaissance Diplomacy*; and some more recent analyses Mallett, "Ambassadors"; Lazzarini, *Communication and Conflict*; de Vivo, "Archives of Speech"; on the system of legatine communication most recently, Untergehrer, "'Diligenter se informet'".

personal interviews; their reports reached the consistory where they were handled publicly or secretly according to their content.

The legatine reports and letters elucidate these talks in a particularly rich manner. One of the few whose reports are preserved in larger numbers was Angelo Pecchinoli, nuncio *cum potestate legati de latere* to the lands of King Matthias Corvinus, who provided detailed accounts on what happened during his meetings with the King, the Queen and other members of the royal court.[152] Pecchinoli even included the words of the talks in direct speech, as it was common in the Italian diplomatic practice.[153] He was always addressed by the King and others as "domine legate". He often mentioned that he was present at the audience of other envoys, displaying a particular interest in the envoys of the Sultan and the envoys of the Roman Emperor and the King of the Romans. Upon one occasion, for example, he expressly mentioned that the King did not allow him to be present at the audience of the imperial envoy, nor was Raymund Peraudi present at the hearing of the Hungarian envoy by the King of the Romans Maximilian. Nevertheless, the King later recounted what was said. This typical practice meant that the nuncio related to the King what he obtained from Rome and on certain occasions even showed him the papal letters. Once, in a case involving a contradictory situation as to what had been reported and what the King did, he showed his report to the King and had it confirmed and agreed on by him, so as to prevent any possible confusion. The nuncio behaved as a diplomatic agent of the period and in this sense did not differ much from other envoys, staying at the court he visited. The legates, however, must have followed much more the ceremonial that belonged to them (and which was described previously).

The instructions are an example of additional sources which reveal a great deal about the political communications and even provide limits to the possibilities of legatine talks. In these, as it was mentioned earlier, legates and nuncios could be instructed to use certain powers entrusted to them under certain conditions. The Curia even planned the course of their mission, asked them to visit certain rulers first and only then proceed to others. These kinds of unofficial instructions are also preserved in manuscripts. At some point in 1471 or 1472, general instructions, or rather informal guidance, were given to a legate dispatched from Rome with tasks of solving problems in Bohemia, Hungary and Germany. The text was in all probability drafted for Cardinal Marco Barbo, who received these directions informing him about the situation in Bohemia and the contesting parties (including their leaders), about the main political figures in Hungary and the crucial fractions in the Empire. To a certain extent, they shared previously gathered knowledge about the region to the new legate, who needed to be introduced to the situation in order to be able to judge it appropriately and solve the problems on the spot.[154] This kind of knowledge was passed on either in script or orally by former legates and other envoys to the region, or by locals who visited Rome. It is apparent, then,

152. Their overview in chapter one, § 1.2., I am currently working on their edition.
153. De Vivo, "Archives of Speech", p. 522.
154. Rome, Biblioteca Angelica, ms. 1077, fol. 21r-24r.

that the legates needed to prepare themselves not only for the ecclesiastical part of their legation, but also for the political one. They had to be briefed about all the problems they had on their agenda and ideally this was done before they left the City. Such a briefing should have prevented criticism on the part of the locals that the new legates did not understand the problems of the region.

Political negotiations and diplomacy were one of the primary tasks of the legates and nuncios and they have naturally left a great number of sources. Political events were influenced by papal policy that needed its exponents and envoys all over Europe. To a great extent these envoys respected the standards of diplomatic practice of the late Middle Ages, but their position was special to a great degree. Particularly the legates *de latere* used their status as cardinals to their advantage in case of problematic political negotiations in royal courts. As specified in the section on ceremonial, they also required a specific position in festivities and special dignity even when meeting secular rulers. Their political activities were then governed by the popes and authority and legitimacy were granted to them not only by the simple fact that they represented the head of the Christendom, but also, as it becomes clear from all the above-mentioned examples, by the fact that they supported their position with reference to a crusade. Most of the legates and nuncios of the period carried in their letters a direct reference to organising a crusade, which gave them a higher authority and purpose in all other political matters. Apart from that, however, they engaged in all sorts of political negotiations usually as intermediaries, who were supposed to help with concluding peace and bringing solutions to problems, but sometimes as supporters of one of the two sides. Their position varied on the basis of papal interests in the region and on their status. Their acceptance was, however, influenced by their personal skills and abilities as well as their particular affinities. Personal relations to individual secular rulers might have played a role, but they are difficult to trace in the sources. Only indirectly. Legates were present in individual courts and were given gifts or benefices along with other offices. Their actions were not therefore only motivated by papal policy, although they would not have rejected the general directions of the Papal Curia.

4.3. *Church politics and policy*

Legates not only represented the Pope as the head of Christendom and in order to carry out all possible tasks for the protection of Christendom against external or internal enemies, but also represented the Pope as the head of the Church. In the later Middle Ages this office was no longer contested and legates had full powers in terms of governing the Church for their lord and master. The local church had its head in the person of the bishop, so the bishop could solve all its problems, except for cases reserved to the Pope. As has been stated above, inhabitants of distant regions often had to rely on the connection to Rome in terms of the spiritual benefits that stemmed from the authority and powers of the Pope; or they could be transported to them in the form of legates who represented the supreme pontiffs. The legates did not only have, however, powers in spiritual matters, but could also wield all the powers that were given to them in special mandates. They could even have power over bishops, leading not only political negotiations, but also negotiating in matters of the Church. Papal legates were essential in correcting and governing the church of the later medieval period. Church policy towards local churches, however, could be complemented with the church politics in Rome. This concerned not only the general policies of the Church, but also the individual nominations of cardinals and bishops and the papal intentions as concerns the presence of cardinals at the Curia.

4.3.1. *Outside Rome*

The majority of the tasks of the papal legates described earlier obviously had a spiritual or church administrative character. Nevertheless, there are always specific cases and individual problems that the papal legates were asked to solve. These situations were not generally predicted by the canon law or could not be part of the general office of the legate. The pope in his commissions to the legates must have reacted to the current affairs of the church in the regions and through legates tried to propose and support his policies relevant for the problems. The list of such situations would be endless, so in this section, I will focus on the general situation of the local church and the problems of the bishoprics on the one hand and on church politics in Rome on the other.

Although the papacy restored its position as the head of the Church in the second half of the fifteenth century, the theocratic ambitions of the thirteenth century could no longer stand as viable policy. This period is the era of concordats, which were concluded between the papacy and many European countries. Indeed, matters of national churches were on the edge between the secular and ecclesiastical politics and papal legates focused on these negotiations as well.[155] The Concordat of Vienna in 1448 designed for Germany formed the relations between the papacy and the local church, and it was concluded by Cardinal Juan Carvajal during his legation to the court of the King of the Romans.[156]

Traditionally, legates were active in organising local synods and proposing the canons of the synods which concerned the entire church of a country, or an (arch)diocese. Presiding over synods was one of the tasks entrusted to legates since the times of the reform papacy under Pope Gregory VII. In the period of the second half of the fifteenth and early sixteenth centuries, however, not much was found in terms of such synods and the activity of individual legates. Isolated cases can be presented here, for example, the great reform legation of Cardinal Nicholas of Cusa in Germany. A provincial synod of Mainz in 1451 promulgated its canons by the power of the archbishop, whereas the synod of Cologne published the canons by the legate Cardinal Nicholas of Cusa with

155. On concordats in general, see Pellegrini, *Il papato*, pp. 177-182; Thomson, *Popes and Princes*, pp. 181-200.

156. See Gómez Canedo, *Don Juan*, pp. 109-111; Toews, "Pope Eugenius IV", pp. 178-194; for the wider context, Meyer, "Das Wiener Konkordat".

the Archbishop of Cologne consenting.[157] Roderigo Borja, cardinal and legate *de latere*, presided over a provincial synod in Madrid in 1473[158] and Nicolao Franco, bishop of Treviso and an experienced nuncio, published canons of the synod of Treviso in 1491 as *legatus apostolicus cum potestate legati cardinalis de latere per universum Venetorum dominium*.[159] In provincial synods, these legates worked at pushing through the idea of reform of the Church, but most importantly presided over the synods representing the Pope. These reforms cannot be compared, however, with the eleventh and twelfth centuries. The role of legates, who did not have the office of a local bishop (as in the last case mentioned) in the fifteenth century, is rather ceremonial and representative. Local churches were under the power of local rulers to a greater extent.[160]

Reform of the Church may be represented in the matters of individual monasteries that could be reformed by legates, and often were. As mentioned earlier, legates frequently acquired faculties that enabled them to authorise changes in individual monasteries and friaries, usually bringing in stricter and more reformed branches of existing orders. Faculties in general provided these powers and in some cases the actual changes might be attested from other sources. Angelo Pecchinoli, for example, took part in publishing a charter concerning the reform of all monastic orders in Hungary, but interestingly enough, the charter was published by the King of Hungary with the assistance of the nuncio.[161] Moreover, he frequently mentioned the reform of friaries of Friars Minor (Conventuals), who should have been replaced by the Observant Franciscans, according to the will of the King. The nuncio even conducted a visitation to a nunnery, that was under the administration of the Conventuals. They also should have been replaced by a stricter branch of their order.[162]

More grave and complicated matters were related to the crucial ecclesiastical conflict of the later Middle Ages in Central Europe, namely the Hussite revolution and the Utraquist Church that originated from Hussitism. The events were mentioned several times together with various solutions to the problem. The Church tried to solve the dissent as heresy and reacted by organising crusades against Bohemia. This approach did not prove successful, however, and negotiations began between the Council of Basel and Bohemian representation and resulted in several concessions to the Bohemians, which were called *compactata*, or the Compacts. According to these agreements, those who professed communion in both kinds could continue until the end of their lives. This idea was understood

157. Mansi, *Sacrorum conciliorum*, vol. 32, col. 113-146 (Mainz), 145-154 (Cologne).

158. *Ibid.*, col. 381-382, 403-404.

159. Mansi, *Sacrorum conciliorum*, vol. 35, col. 1543.

160. For the "downgrading" of the power of the Church in favour of secular rulers, see e.g. Decaluwe, *A Successful Defeat*, pp. 337-348.

161. Pongrácz and Rezner, eds., *A Pannonhalmi főapátság története*, vol. 3, pp. 540-542, no. 87, "Mathias dei gracia Hungarie, Bohemie rex etc. … assistente nobis reverendissimo in Christo patre domino Angelo, episcopo Ortensi, sancte sedis apostolice cum plena potestate legati de latere ad predicta regna legato in infrascripta capitula et reformacionis et correccionis ordines decrevimus …"

162. BMV, Lat. X 175, fol. 144v, 112r; visitation, 113rv.

somewhat differently, however, by the population of the country as well as by the political representatives, who basically took it for granted that such a practice would be allowed and would continue forever. The acceptance of such a solution caused numerous problems and also the fact that it was the Council that confirmed this agreement. The Pope actually never confirmed it and when the authority of the Council wavered and popes took over, the agreements made by the Council also lost the basis of their validity. Thus, Pope Pius II even officially abolished the Compacts in 1462, even though attempts to solve the situation had begun much earlier. The role of papal legates in these matters smoothly alternated between the above-mentioned crusade and negotiations.[163]

As explained earlier, two rounds of crusades were organised against 'heretical' Bohemia. These phases of the conflict could not last for long and the crusading ideology faded away. First, it was the failure of the first round of crusades and agreements with the Council, and then the introduction of the new Catholic king, who ascended the throne in 1471 and the inability of Matthias Corvinus to defeat the Bohemians and conquer the land by force. The Utraquist church, however, flourished in Bohemia (and to some extent in Moravia) throughout the fifteenth century which naturally brought increased legatine activity in attempts to bring the Utraquists back to the Roman Church. This was a protracted problem of the Church that only lost its significance with the advance of the German Reformation.

From the papal side (unlike the conciliar part), the negotiations began with the legation of Cardinal Juan Carvajal in 1447-1449, who after a successful sojourn in Vienna arrived in Prague. Both parties had high expectations. He had been preparing for the mission in Rome, and had already there with the Bohemian embassy. Nevertheless, already at that point the Utraquists were aware of his stricter position in the question of reconciliation with Rome: he even said he would come to Bohemia to teach them the proper ways of the faith.[164] In Prague the legate received a glorious and solemn procession which introduced him to the city, but the mission itself did not bring success in negotiations. He was even attacked, when trying to take away the charters of agreements between the Bohemians and the Council of Basel.[165] To some extent Juan Carvajal then became a specialist on the Bohemian question, as he led further negotiations in the question during his second legation to Central Europe (1455-1461) and took part in Roman talks in 1462, when another Bohemian embassy tried to have the Compacts and the Archbishop of Prague confirmed once again.[166] Since the first mission of Carvajal, several missions of legates and nuncios occurred, including Nicholas of Cusa, Girolamo Lando and Francesco da Toledo and Fantino della Valle in the first round of negotiations. After a brief intermission with the second round of Bohemian crusades, negotiations about a possible union began again and intensified only in the 1520s with the start of the German Reformation. More subtle negotiations

163. Kalous, "The Politics of Church Unification"; idem, "Cardinal legate Tamás Bakóc".

164. In a travel report of Bohemian envoys, *Výbor z české literatury*, vol. 2, pp. 240-242.

165. On his mission, Gómez Canedo, *Don Juan*, pp. 112-121.

166. *Výbor z české literatury*, vol. 2, pp. 243-250.

only began again after the death of King Matthias Corvinus, when Wladislas II Jagiellonian of Bohemia became King of Hungary as well in 1490. Prior to this date, only Bartolomeo Maraschi and Angelo Pecchinoli are worthy of mention, having been charged to conduct union talks, although no sources actually prove they did so. Nicholas Cola, Orso Orsini, Pietro Isvalies, Tamás Bakóc, Lorenzo Campeggi and Antonio Burgio were involved after 1490.

Apart from the general commission of organising the crusade or rather preparing the path for it, the legates and nuncios were charged with the task of organising the union talks with the Bohemians. They tried to prepare for the argumentation and negotiations in advance, as can be seen in the case of Juan Carvajal. Girolamo Lando and Francesco da Toledo even took separate roles. Lando tried to negotiate the political agreement, whereas Francesco da Toledo was the theologian of the two, who was supposed to evaluate the theological questions. When they arrived in 1459, however, there was very little discussion about the actual Church union.[167] Reaching an actual negotiation was extremely difficult. Several attempts were made to solve the troubling situation between the two camps, but no actual solution was reached concerning the split in the Church.

A certain Nicholas Cola actively worked in Bohemia in 1493 and Czech narrative sources even mention meetings between the estates and the "legate" Cola in Buda. Leaving aside the fact that he was never officially a legate, no results were actually reached. At the same time a certain Franciscan representative travelled in Bohemia and insulted the Czechs in the land diet by stating that at the Roman Curia all refer to them as "heretics".[168] The land representation (estates), which was much more active in this sense than the King who now resided in Buda in Hungary, even wrote before Christmas 1493 to Pope Alexander VI that they planned to dispatch an embassy that would discuss a possible union.[169] In the meantime (Autumn 1493), the bishop of Teano Orso Orsini left Rome as a papal nuncio *cum potestate legati de latere* with the commission to solve the situation, but was also unable to understand the complexity of the problem. In his reports to Rome, he described the talks of the land diet, efforts to send an embassy to Rome, even though he himself urged the estates to send an embassy that would submit to the Pope unconditionally and admit their errors. For the Bohemians, however, the *conditio sine qua non* was still the confirmation of the *compactata*, as, for example, proclaimed by the estates' embassy to the nuncio in Buda in May 1494.[170] Although the two sides carried on some negotiations, they were still firm in their respective demands.

A papal legate *de latere* came to Central Europe once again in 1500. Cardinal Pietro Isvalies was instructed to help organise a crusade, but apart from

167. Urbánek, *České dějiny*, vol. 3/3, pp. 567-594; Drabina, "Działalność dyplomatyczna Hieronima Lando", pp. 149-155; idem, *Kontakty Wrocławia z Piusem II*, pp. 518-519; Smołucha, *Polityka kurii rzymskiej*, pp. 191-198.

168. Šimek and Kaňák, eds., *Staré letopisy*, pp. 306-308; Dvorský, ed., "Dopisy", p. 17, no. 30.

169. BMV, sign. Lat. X 178 (=3625), fol. 32r, 34r.

170. BMV, sign. Lat. X 178 (=3625), fol. 121r, 27rv

that was supposed to focus on the Bohemian matters. Apart, however, from his involvement in the "Olomouc matters", i.e. disputations between the Unity of Brethren and the Dominicans, he did not participate in any attempts to unify the Church again.[171] Further efforts are not known. Only Cardinal Tamás Bakóc was dispatched with a commission from the Pope and the Fifth Lateran Council to renew the negotiations and bring the Utraquists back to the bosom of the Church in 1513. Although Cardinal Tamás Bakóc left Rome that same year with two crucial commissions, i.e. the crusade and the Bohemian question, no talks came about in the end. Contemporary reports make mention of a number of theologians and doctors, whom he brought from Rome to be able to discuss the subtle matters of theology with the Bohemian Utraquists. No sources confirm, however, any actual talks with the Bohemians, although there is positive proof from local sources that those *doctores* left Rome and came to Hungary.[172]

Apart from having the theologians with him, Cardinal Tamás was well prepared and informed about the development of the problem. A bull that introduced this task first mentioned and emphasised the crusade as a critical part of the legation. In a general way, then, the Pope declared that the state of affairs in Bohemia and Moravia should no longer be neglected. Just as the one lost sheep was pursued by the good shepherd, the Bohemians, who were condemned at the Councils of Constance and Basel, needed to be brought back. Tamás was supposed to employ all his efforts to achieve this goal and to restore the kingdom in its original pristine form. Moreover, if and when they were brought back, the Bohemians due to their warlike nature were to be used against the Tartars in Poland and the Turks in Hungary. Practically, those who wanted to return to the Roman Church, should abjure heresy and take an oath that they would not do anything like that again. They would then receive absolution in the usual form of the Church. The cardinal could even choose people who would lead the negotiations and conclude a final treaty.[173]

Another bull published a few days later depicted Tamás Bakóc as an "angel of peace" to Bohemia (*ad partes Bohemie*) as the Pope and other cardinals had decided to commission him with the task of uniting the erring Bohemians with the Roman Church. The bull with the commission went into a great deal of detail. It mentioned the Council of Constance, which condemned the forty-five articles of John Wycliffe and thirty of Jan Hus and which decided that the lay population should commune in one kind, and the Council of Basel, which led the discussions with the Bohemians about their Four Articles.[174] These were then recounted in detail. First, the traditional ways of the Church should be preserved as for the communion *sub utraque specie*. In secret dealings with the Bohemians, it was

171. Kalous, "The Politics of Church Unification", p. 185.

172. Fekete Nagy, Kenéz, Solymosi and Érszegi, eds., *Monumenta rusticorum*, passim; cf. Minnich, "The Closing", pp. 28-35; Kalous, "Cardinal legate Tamás Bakóc". For the conciliar bull, see Minnich, ed., *Concilium Lateranense V*, pp. 1365-1368.

173. ASV, Reg. Vat. 1006, fol. 56v-59r; 1007, fol. 134r-136v (Theiner, ed., *Vetera monumenta Hungariae*, vol. 2, pp. 608-610, no. 806).

174. Discussed in a number of places in detail, cf. e.g. Kaminsky, *A History*, pp. 369-375; Šmahel, *Die Hussitische Revolution*, vol. 1, pp. 636-674.

concluded that the lay communion would be allowed, but only under the condition that they believed that all of Christ was contained in all kinds of communion, which should also be emphasised by the present council (i.e. the Fifth Lateran Council). Children should not take communion at all, due to the danger of disrespect. There were also added instructions for the legate: it is not prudent to concede in the matter of the Eucharist, they should rather be encouraged to abandon this practice completely. Second, public mortal sins should be punished whatever the status of the sinners - a matter that was discussed in length by the Council of Basel. The punishment should only be administered by those who hold jurisdictional authority and not by private persons. Third, as for the free preaching of the word of God, it should be done, according to the Council of Basel, by appropriate priests who have been examined by their superiors. The fourth article, then, was the most complex one and required that church property be limited. The Council of Basel concluded that the clerics and the Church can have possessions and temporal dominion. The clerics were only, however, administrators of the property as they administered it for their own good but also for the good of others; appropriation was not allowed and was punished as sacrilege. This article was even treated as the most problematic and the cardinal was advised to proceed with utter care and vigilance. If the Bohemians were persuaded in this matter, they would be more easily united in others. If an agreement was reached, they would be able to gather an army of ten or five thousand against the Ottomans. The bull even suggested that the money and the property that was taken from the Church could be used for this purpose. They should also in the future believe that the Church and its institutions can have property. They could remain in possession of some property which they had taken from church institutions, but not as owners but rather as feudal holders. The agreement, when reached, had to be confirmed by the Lateran Council. Finally, in other cases, Bohemians should be treated as other Catholics, i.e. no special rights were possible, but they could receive the same dispensations and indults as other believers.[175] These were the basic powers and instructions Tamás Bakóc held when leaving the Eternal City, but like his predecessors, he was unable to celebrate success in the complicated matter.[176]

Only one more attempt for the reconciliation of the Utraquist Church was made before the full spreading of the German Reformation, and it was in the hands of legates once again, these being Cardinal Lorenzo Campeggi, an experienced papal diplomat, and Antonio Burgio, who held a role of a standing envoy at the court of Louis, King of Hungary and Bohemia.[177] Although talks actually occurred and meetings were held in Buda at the royal court as well as in Prague and even though a number of local figures of the highest significance were involved the efforts were in vain again. The first attempts followed the

175. ASV, Reg. Vat. 1007, fol. 137r-141r; Theiner, ed., *Vetera monumenta Hungariae*, vol. 2, pp. 610-612, no. 807.

176. In detail see Kalous, "Cardinal legate Tamás Bakóc".

177. Idem, "The Politics of Church Unification"; idem, "Elfeledett források"; Nemes, "Pápai követek"; for Campeggi, Skalweit, "Campeggi, Lorenzo"; for Burgio, Rill and Scichilone, "Burgio, Giovanni Antonio Buglio barone di".

Prague Utraquist uprising of 1523 and the main *spiritus agens* was the then bishop of Eger and later archbishop of Esztergom László Szalkai. From the Bohemian side a number of noblemen, members of the estates, were involved, as well as the leaders of the Utraquist party of the country (Duke Charles of Münsterberg, grand-son of George of Poděbrady) and of Prague. A possible union between the Utraquists and the Catholics was mentioned for the first time in February 1525.[178] Further talks took place in Buda in May and June 1525, but still no agreement appeared as the legate could not confirm what even the Pope and the College of Cardinals were unable to confirm. A Czech report even spoke about a possible council in the future.[179] The talks failed again after the legate wanted the representatives to reject all their "heretical" teachings and after it was clear the delegation did not have full powers to reach a decision.[180] It seems that individual personal interests constituted the greatest problem in the negotiations. Personal differences between the leaders of the Catholic side (between Archbishop László Szalkai and the legate Lorenzo Campeggi) also contributed to the failure of the project, and the King then – when writing to Pope Clement VII – could only write about *magna impedimenta.*[181] The legate thus observed, that he did not find enthusiasm for the true Christian faith and neither Christian charity, but rather individual hatreds, passions and interests.[182]

A longer narration about the attempts to solve the problems of the Utraquists illustrates that legates were not always successful, even in matters of the Church. Some tasks entrusted to legates seemed impossible. Bringing about a Church unification between divided Christians created numerous problems and not even the personal interest and personal efforts of legates brought about positive results. They prepared for their missions in advance, as in the case of political matters, but when a special situation arose, as in the case of the Bohemian Utraquists, when the Church matters were strongly interlinked with the political system of the country, not even legates were able to bring about positive results. They could not solve the church struggles that began in the fifteenth and culminated in the following century bringing about the division of medieval western Christendom.

On a less general level, only the Pope had the powers to deal with the matters of bishops, to depose, restore and transfer bishops; the Pope could also split or

178. Fraknói, ed., *Relationes oratorum*, p. 148, no. 40; p. 149, no. 41; cf. Palacký, *Geschichte von Böhmen*, vol. V/2, pp. 537-539.

179. Šimák, *Fontes*, vol. 6, p. 154, 324; for the negotiations, see *ibid.*, p. 152-157, 322-326; Fraknói, ed., *Relationes oratorum*, passim. For detailed studies, Fraknói, *Magyarország egyházi és politikai összeköttetései*, vol. 2, p. 355-361; Balogh, *Szalkay László*, pp. 47-52; Skýbová, "Česká šlechta", pp. 93-107; Eberhard, *Konfessionsbildung*, pp. 182-193; Nemes, "Elszalasztott lehetőségek".

180. Kalous, "The Politics of Church Unification", p. 187-188.

181. Bessenyei, ed., *Lettere*, p. 33, no. V/1; p. 37, no. V/3.

182. Fraknói, ed., *Relationes oratorum*, pp. 197-198, no. 52, "Ma Monsignor mio, per le molte difficultà chio vedo in questo negocio, io dubito assai di buona conclusione, perchè vedo che non per zelo de la fede, nè per charità christiana, ma per particolari odii, passioni et interesse siano mossi, temendo che da la potentia de Pichardi non fusseno oppressi. Dio linspiri qualche più santa intentione, si che si possa fare bene".

unite bishoprics, as specified in canon law.[183] Even the legates *de latere* needed a special mandate to exercise their powers over bishops, however, they frequently carried out tasks connected to bishops and their bishoprics. As representatives of the pope, they were the only ones who could solve such problems on the spot.

In his dissertation, Wolfgang Untergehrer gave a list of conflicts over bishoprics in the German lands in the second half of the fifteenth century that the legates came to solve in one way or another. These were the conflicts for the archbishoprics of Mainz (1459-1463), Cologne (1472-1480), Salzburg (1478-1482), and the bishoprics of Liège (1464, 1467/8), Constance (1474-80) and Passau (1479-1482).[184] The list could obviously be enlarged with a number of examples from other regions, which might include the bishopric of Warmia (1467-1479) or the bishopric of Olomouc (1482-1497).

In the case of Warmia, two candidates to the bishop's throne contested the bishopric. While Wincenty Kiełbasa, the candidate of the King, retired from the conflict, Nicholas von Tüngen continued to fight for his right, as a candidate elected by the chapter of Warmia and supported by the chief enemy of King Casimir, namely Matthias Corvinus, King of Hungary. A final agreement only in the year 1479 made it clear that it would be the chapter who was to elect bishops, but only to the liking of the kings of Poland. Tüngen kept the bishopric, but had to pay homage to the king. The involvement of legates was primarily manifested in the person of Rudolf of Rüdesheim, who initiated the negotiations as concerns the bishopric, as he actively participated in the talks concerning the conflict between the Teutonic Knights and the King of Poland.[185] Cardinal Marco Barbo was also supposed to solve the matters and as papal legate was charged to support the case of Nicholas von Tüngen. Similarly, as in previous cases, the legate was well informed about the previous developments of the situation as his report clearly shows.[186] The negotiation between the two kings did not restrict itself to political matters only, but also concerned the bishop of Warmia, as the King of Hungary supported his claims.

The contested bishopric of Olomouc provided subject for discussions for the papal nuncio Angelo Pecchinoli. As in other cases, it was the person of the bishop that was problematic. The chapter, undoubtedly influenced by Matthias Corvinus, King of Hungary and Bohemia, elected Jan Filipec, bishop of Várad (Oradea). Although he had spent some time in Rome in 1483, i.e. in the year of his election to the bishopric of Olomouc, the Pope never confirmed him in this position and Filipec never received a dispensation from the canonical obstacle that he could not have two benefices with *cura animarum*. At a later point, another Hungarian bishop, John Vitéz, bishop of Srem, was supported by the King, but lost the support quite soon after. When he was transferred to Veszprém, the Olomouc bishopric was considered vacant by the Pope, who

183. Cf. above § 2.1.

184. Untergehrer, *Die päpstlichen nuntii und legati*, pp. 357-361.

185. Schmauch, "Der Kampf"; Drabina, "Działalność dyplomatyczna legata apostolskiego Rudolfa"; Radziszewska, "Działalność dyplomatyczna".

186. BAV, Vat. lat. 5641, fol. 201v-206v (ed. Kalous, *Plenitudo potestatis*, pp. 267-77).

first appointed Cardinal Ardicino della Porta and later, after his death, Cardinal Giovanni Borgia, the Pope's nephew. The bishopric received a new shepherd in the person of Stanislas Thurzo finally in the year 1497.[187] This complicated issue and the person of Jan Filipec appeared many times in the reports of Angelo Pecchinoli. The bishop was even charged with the accusation of heresy as, reportedly, his parents were of the Utraquist belief (he came from the Moravian town of Prostějov). Taking any action against the bishop, however, was extremely difficult and virtually impossible for the nuncio, even though he had met Filipec personally. He described him as a very obstinate man, who even had royal support because the King needed him as a capable diplomat for negotiations in Silesia. Although the accusation was not lifted, the bishop even celebrated vespers at the royal court. With the royal backing, the bishop was safe and the nuncio could not initiate any kind of trial.[188]

Similarly, with secular backing and support, other bishops could avoid the papal will manifested through papal legates or nuncios. Andrea Jamometić, archbishop of Krajina, who criticised Pope Sixtus IV as an imperial envoy in Rome and whom the Pope even imprisoned, moved to Basel after his release and there tried to organise a new Council of Basel.[189] At precisely that same time, the bishop of Santorini (basically a titular bishop on a Greek island), Agostino Luciani, ran away from Italy, where he had been present at the court of Mirandola, to Utraquist Bohemia. There he held the functions of bishop for the Utraquists, as the archbishopric of Prague became vacant after the Hussite revolution.[190] Both of them secured the protection of secular powers; the first in Basel, the latter in Prague and Kutná Hora. When Jamometić was taken captive by the city council of Basel, he was not handed over to papal diplomats but ended his life himself in prison. A number of papal envoys were dispatched from Rome with the commission to capture the archbishop and bring him back to Rome, including two nuncios *cum potestate legati de latere*, Angelo Geraldini and Bartolomeo Maraschi. Agostino Luciani, in contrast, lived in Prague and Kutná Hora in Bohemia and the nuncios could not even get close enough. First, they did not know who the Italian bishop in Prague was, as a letter addressed to him by Bartolomeo Maraschi indicates.[191] Later, although they were in contact, papal nuncios were unable to proceed against him due to the strong position of Utraquism in Bohemia.

Angelo Pecchinoli also held a commission to undertake a completely opposite task. The King of Hungary imprisoned the archbishop of Kalocsa and Bács Péter Váradi, whom another nuncio described as "the right eye of the

187. In detail, Kalous, "Spor o biskupství olomoucké".

188. In many places in reports of the nuncio, BMV, Lat. X 175, fol. 129r-131r, 112v; Lat. X 178, fol. 167v.

189. Schlecht, *Andrea Zamometić*; Petersohn, *Ein Diplomat des Quattrocento*; idem, ed., *Diplomatische Berichte*; idem, *Kaiserlicher Gesandter*; Daniels, "Die italienische Mächte".

190. Cf. Del Re, "Agostino Luciani"; Macek, *Víra a zbožnost*, pp. 118-131.

191. BMV, Lat. X 174, fol. 112rv, addressed "Ignoto cuidam episcopo inter Boemos erranti atque agenti etsi catholicus est. Reverendo michi patri etc. In Praga".

King".[192] The archbishop was kept under lock and key as he was ready and willing to reveal all the King's secrets, as Matthias Corvinus stated to the nuncio. Here once again, although the King at first promised to transfer Váradi into Pecchinoli's hands as it was required by the Pope, he postponed it as long as he could and the nuncio only managed to have the archbishop transferred from the Orava castle to a more hospitable place at Visegrád. He was only finally freed after the King's death and actively took part in the succession negotiations.[193] The legates and nuncios held power over bishops when they had special mandates at their disposal. Not even such a papal charter could, however, enable them to perform such difficult tasks which would lead them against the interests of secular power or even in conflict with local rulers.

Once again the *relationes* of Angelo Pecchinoli reported on capturing one *ciaratanus*, i.e. a priest who falsely distributed indulgences in the name of the Hospital of Santo Spirito in Rome. These kinds of problems with clerics within the Church were therefore clearly not limited to only bishops, but to all who seriously broke obedience and canon law.[194]

In the local church, the legates actually functioned as an extended arm of papal jurisdiction and government in general. Even if the major problems of conflicts with the Church could not be solved, administering the papal will was one of the key elements of the legatine activity in the field of local bishoprics and monasteries. Moreover, the end of the fifteenth century was a period when *libertas ecclesiastica* came to the attention of the popes and thus also the legates and nuncios.[195] Again, the example of Angelo Pecchinoli might be introduced here: he was asked several times in the instructions to protect the ecclesiastical liberty, namely in the cases of imprisoned prelates (the Archbishop of Kalocsa, but also his brother, the provost of Esztergom and another provost of Pécs), appropriated Church property of a bishopric and even the papal city of Ancona that wanted to accept King Matthias as its lord. He was even asked to promote the idea of protecting *libertas ecclesiastica* to the King's son, who was at that point the strongest candidate to succeed his father.[196] When the nuncio returned to Rome, he received two letters of recommendation: one from Hungarian prelates and one from the newly crowned King Wladislas. Both of them praised the nuncio and stated that he was most diligent and hardworking in terms of protecting *libertas ecclesiastica* (even the King wrote this to the Pope).[197] Matters of the Church in the local context had to be guarded, this being the job of legates and nuncios with a similar authority.

192. BMV, Lat. X 174, fol. 110r, "...qui regis oculus est dexter..." (Bartolomeo Maraschi).

193. BMV, Lat. X 175, fol. 127v-128v, 141v-142v, 111v-112r, 116r.

194. ASV, Misc., Arm. II 56, fol. 190r, 191v (Theiner, ed., *Vetera monumenta Hungariae*, vol. 2, p. 529-530).

195. On *libertas ecclesiastica* in this period, see Pennington, "Ecclesiastical Liberty".

196. ASV, Misc., Arm. II 56, fol. 163v, 164r, 168r, 201r.

197. BMV, sign. Lat. X 178 (=3625), fol. 99r; AS Venezia, Collezione Podocataro, busta 8, no. 604.

4.3.2. *Rome*

A brief consideration concerning the personalities of the individual legates and their acceptance in the regions would be relevant at this point. First and foremost, they represented the popes. Although they received one of the highest honours from the popes, this did not necessarily mean that all the cardinals wanted such an honour and that all people in the regions received them with such honour. The legations did not constitute permanent offices, as the nunciatures did later in the sixteenth century. This did not mean, however, that they were not asked to come and that they were not required by the local rulers.

The selection of the legates was definitely influenced by all the characteristics of the legation itself, as well as by the cardinals, who received this honour. Church politics in Rome played a decisive role. Papal legates in Rome can be followed and viewed not only through the pageants and ceremonies, but also through the eyes of Church politics and 'tactical' negotiations among the pope, the cardinals and the Papal Curia itself. In Rome, the position of the popes was – after the conciliar crisis – shaken and at that same time, the status of the College of Cardinals as a corporation increased.[198]

Matters concerning internal struggles within the Roman Curia are, however, highly questionable and uncertain. In many cases they can be only speculated and conjectured upon rather than clearly confirmed by the sources. It is nevertheless worth considering the following lines when judging the papal policy on dispatching legates from the Curia. As stated above, leaving Rome had clear consequences for individuals. Unless they had a special mandate, the cardinals could not participate in the incomes of the Chamber of the Sacred College. When out of Rome, the cardinals had no way of influencing the policy of the papacy, they did not take part in the decision-making process and most importantly, in the case of a death of a pope, could not be present in the conclave. The pope, on the other hand, could control the cardinals' presence in the City by distributing the tasks of legations. Although no bad intentions or two-faced decisions can be proven or shown in the sources related to actual situations, generalised sources would seem to indicate that such circumstances were possible.

The papal election capitulations consist of documents that lucidly and plainly speak about the possible side effects of legatine nominations and even the possible hidden intentions of the popes. These were drafted by the cardinals in conclave and represent their aims and objectives when they were still equal as cardinals and candidates to the pope. They were meant to limit the powers of the Pope or rather to direct papal policies after the new Pope was elected. At the same time, the articles of the election capitulations attempted to preserve or confirm certain

198. On cardinals, cardinal creations and the politics of the Sacred College in the later fifteenth and early sixteenth century, Dendorfer and Märtl, "Papst und Kardinalskolleg", esp. pp. 361-372; Pellegrini, "A Turning-Point"; idem, "Das Kardinalskolleg", esp. pp. 414-434; idem, "Il sacro collegio cardinalizio"; DeSilva, "Senators or Courtiers"; in the context of factions and Roman cardinals, Rehberg, "Die Kardinäle".

rules, regulations and privileges of the cardinals and the Sacred College.[199] One of the articles of the election capitulation of 1484 conclave expressly stated:

> Moreover, since by some it is asserted that certain cardinals of the Holy Roman Church, fearing that the Roman Pontiff may compel them to depart from the Roman Court, on the pretext of some legation, have sometimes abstained, and do abstain from freely discussing in the consistory, those things which they deem it advisable to discuss, and it is of importance to the Roman Church and to the Apostolic See, that the mind of the said cardinals should be free to discuss, and that all fear and timidity in the expression of their views should cease to exist, I likewise vow, swear, and promise that, against his will, I will not send any cardinal on any legation (unless it be truly and unfeignedly necessary to send him), but only in accordance with his desire and express consent, nor will I, indirectly, in any way, force him to express desire and consent by any sinister means.[200]

This article did not appear in election capitulations before, but appeared in later capitulations of the conclaves which elected Popes Alexander VI and Pius III. It could be argued, then, that it was introduced after the period of strong nepotism of Pope Sixtus IV.[201] Out of, however, the thirty-six legations of cardinals during the pontificate of Pope Sixtus IV one was taken by a cardinal created by Eugenius IV (plus one when Guillaume d'Estouteville after first accepting, rejected the legation), two by a cardinal created by Calixt III, seven by cardinals of Pius II and five by cardinals created by Paul II. All the rest, i.e. twenty-one legations, were assigned to cardinals created by Sixtus IV. It is therefore impossible to prove that the pope would send away cardinals who he did not want to be present at the Curia.

The text of the election capitulation does not speak directly of specific situations, but it clearly tries to limit the Pope's liberty to send cardinals away from the centre of church politics. In several cases, cardinals refused to go on a legation. Guillaume d'Estouteville's legation in 1472 to France never happened, for example, even though he was created legate in the consistory.[202] The case is even more interesting, as the conflict between France and Burgundy required some arbitration from the side of papal diplomacy. Luka Tolentić, who remained in the region as a permanent nuncio, reported about the unsuccessful Cardinal Bessarion

199. On election capitulations, see at least Krüger, "Überlieferung"; Ullmann, "The legal validity".

200. Burchard, *The Diary*, vol. 1, p. 30; Celani, ed., *Johannis Burckardi Liber*, vol. 1, p. 34, "Item, quum a nonnullis asseratur quosdam s. r. E. cardinales, timentes ne romanus pontifex eos, sub colore alicujus legationis, compellat a romana curia secedere, nonnumquam abstinuisse et abstinere a libere consultando in consistorio ea que eis videntur, intersitque romane Ecclesie et apostolice sedis quod ipsorum cardinalium animus sit in consulendo liber et cesset in consiliorum eorumdem exhibitione omnis formido omnisque timor, pari modo, juro, voveo et promitto non mittere aliquem cardinalem invitum in aliquam legationem, nisi necessitas mittendi vera et non ficta, sed dumtaxat volentes et expresse consentientes, nec eos indirecte ad volendum et consentiendum per aliqua mala media quoquo modo inducere". The original election capitulation, BAV, Vat. lat. 12518, fol. 12r-17r (*capitula publica*), 21r-29r (*capitula privata*), the discussed article, fol. 24v.

201. BAV, Vat. lat. 6200, fol. 32v-33r, 59rv; cf. Pellegrini, "Das Kardinalskolleg", pp. 416-419.

202. Eubel, *Hierarchia catholica*, vol. 2, p. 38.

and most crucially about the supplications of the King of France, who wanted Cardinal d'Estouteville to be sent as legate to France. Supposedly, he would have been able to accomplish things which Bessarion could not.[203] However, a new cardinal of Burgundy, Philibert Hugonet, bishop of Mâcon was created on 7 May 1473, and the Duke of Burgundy asked for his involvement as legate *de latere* in confirming the agreements between the duke and the emperor.[204]

Cardinal Giovanni Battista Cibo, whom the cardinals elected Pope in 1484 (as Innocent VIII) actually refused a legation to Germany only three years before his election. Cardinal Cibo was created a legate *de latere* to Emperor Frederick III and to King Matthias of Hungary and to the Imperial diet in Nuremberg to appease conflicts between the two sovereigns (which was briefly described in the previous section) on 19 January 1481. First, Cardinal Cibo accepted the legation and was accompanied by all the cardinals to his house. Later, however, on 7 February, he refused the office with his substitute being the above-mentioned Orso Orsini. The reason for this refusal was in all probability the 'small' sum of money legates received as an advance payment (2,000 fl.), as we learn from the Roman diary of Giacomo Gherardi da Volterra.[205] The same source described the original nomination of the legate, where in the discussion Cardinal Marco Barbo reportedly stated, that none of the cardinals should reject the duty, except for three of them, who were physically unable to travel.[206]

These reports indicate that such situations could be a matter of discussion even in their day. On the one hand, the cardinals tried to protect their positions in Rome, while on the other, the legation was still regarded as a duty, a means of service to the Church and the Pope, and most crucially as a highest honour. Refusing a legation could be as telling as sending a cardinal on an invented mission. Cardinal Cibo accepted a legation to Rome in 1476 during the absence of Pope Sixtus IV and to Tuscany two years later. In 1481, however, he managed to stay in Rome, which proved useful for the 1484 election, in which he also made use of the strong support of Giuliano della Rovere.[207]

The above-mentioned Cardinal Marco Barbo accepted his legation in December 1471, two months later went to Germany and Central Europe and spent there almost three years. Marco became a cardinal under his uncle Pietro Barbo, as Pope Paul II, in 1467. When Pope Sixtus IV ascended the papal throne soon after, he sent the nephew of his predecessor away from the Curia. A few months earlier, Paul II also sent the predecessor's nephew for a legation beyond the Alps: this was Francesco Todeschini Piccolomini, who was created cardinal by his uncle Pius II in 1460. When looking for false pretence, these nominations might seem suspicious. It can never be proven, however, from the sources, as the legations aimed at solving problems of highest importance for the papacy. The name of Cardinal Giuliano della Rovere can be used as an example of cardinal-nephews used as legates by their

203. Ljubić, ed., *Dispacci*, pp. 31-32.
204. *Ibid.*, pp. 34-35.
205. Gherardi da Volterra, *Il diario romano*, pp. 34-37.
206. *Ibid.*, p. 34.
207. Cf. also Pellegrini, "Innocenzo VIII".

papal relatives. He was created cardinal at the first instance of Sixtus IV's cardinal creations in December 1471 and sent as legate *de latere* to the Marches (1473), to France and Avignon (1476) and to his great legation to France (with the province also including the Low Countries, England and Scotland) in 1480-1482.[208]

One case, however, may illustrate the influence of Church politics in Rome. The election of Pope Alexander VI could not be called easy. Individual factions of cardinals supported individual candidates, the strongest being Ascanio Maria Sforza, Jorge da Costa, Oliviero Carafa, Ardicino della Porta, but also Roderigo Borja and Giuliano della Rovere. In the beginning of 1491, two main parties developed, namely those of Ascanio Sforza and Giuliano della Rovere. In August 1492, the situation changed slightly and the negotiations in the conclave revealed the impossibility of the election of both of these. The strongest candidates at the beginning of the conclave, Jorge da Costa and Oliviero Carafa, could not be elected and allegiance shifted – especially with promises of benefices, offices and property from the side of Roderigo Borja. Six legates were created twenty days after the election and five days after the new Pope's coronation, but only to Italy and the lands of the Church. One of the legates was Ascanio Sforza and other two belonged to his party: they received a number of benefices and offices, including these legations to Bologna (Ascanio), Spoleto (Giovanni Battista Savelli) and the Marches (Giovanni Battista Orsini). Additional legates included Giuliano della Rovere himself and two others, who like Giuliano, could not be persuaded by gifts. Giuliano was sent to Avignon, Paolo Fregoso to Campania and Giovanni de' Medici to the Patrimony of St Peter. Clearly, Italian legations did not entail a long absence, but rather a source of income; the main opponent, Cardinal Giuliano, received a legation to Avignon, close to the King of France, where he had worked before.[209] The legations, then, might function as a reward, but also as a means of dispatching anyone from the centre of political happenings and deprive them of any political power at the Curia.

What might be questioned here is not the reason for the legation, but the selection of the individuals, of the individual cardinals for a specific legation. For Sixtus IV the creation of cardinals in 1471 began a huge campaign for organising a crusade as five legates *de latere* headed to various parts of Europe. These five legates (Marco Barbo, Bessarion, Angelo Capranica, Roderigo Borja, Oliviero Carafa) ranked among the most influential cardinals at the Curia. It can be argued, on the one hand, that the new Pope wanted them out of the way from Rome, on the other hand, however, their power and authority supported the weight of their missions and the new Pope's plans. The argumentation might sway both ways. It is difficult therefore to prove that the assertion of certain cardinals (mentioned in the election capitulation of 1484), that they might be sent away from the Roman Curia, was actually founded upon real situations and particular cases. It should still, however, be taken into account as a possibility. One such example with the certain

208. Cf. Pastore, "Giulio II"; cf. also Labande, *Avignon.*

209. A summary of the events with references to many sources, see Pastor, *Geschichte*, vol. 3/1, pp. 339-361, vol. 3/2, pp. 1049-1056; cf. Tommasini, ed., *Diario della Città di Roma di Stefano Infessura*, pp. 279-282. Burckard's diary is unfortunately interrupted for this period; cf. Celani, ed., *Johannis Burckardi Liber*, vol. 1, p. 371.

desired side effects of the legatine nomination seems to be the creation of Cardinal Tamás Bakóc as legate *de latere* to Hungary in 1513. Cardinal Tamás, who arrived in Rome in 1512 with pomp and ostentation which surpassed any papal pageant, entered the conclave as one of the strong candidates for the papacy. After receiving a considerable number of votes in the first round, however, he did not succeed and the victorious Giovanni de' Medici created him legate four months later.[210] In the case of Cardinal Tamás Bakóc, however, he undoubtedly as a born Hungarian met very well the demands on someone who would organise a crusade in Hungary and with his power and authority support the papal plans there.

From the point of view of a cardinal, the legation meant leaving Rome for a longer period of time and thus less influence in the City. This entailed leaving the structures in Rome and within the College of Cardinals and also leaving the offices at the Curia. Cardinal Giovanni Arcimboldi, for example, was created a legate to Perugia on 15 November 1483, while he held the function of *camerarius* of the college. He had left for his legation only after he left the office.[211] Cardinal Marco Barbo left the office of a *camerlengo* of the Apostolic Chamber in July 1471 and was created a legate *de latere* in December of that year. Pope Paul II died in the meantime, however, and Sixtus IV was elected, which also changed the situation. Cardinals in essential offices were not sent to legations, however, or left these positions before leaving Rome.

Popes selected the legates with the consent of other cardinals. The remaining cardinals were still involved in the process and accompanied their colleagues in the Roman processions after the creation and when they left the City. Cardinal legates were also supposed to visit all the cardinals who remained behind between these two occasions. They obviously had friends and closer colleagues among the other cardinals and they provided one other with mutual support. When Cardinal Antonio Ferrero left the papal palace as a legate *de latere* for Perugia, as mentioned earlier, in 1506, he was accompanied by all the cardinals only half way towards the gate. Four "more friendly cardinals" joined him, however, up to the *Porta del Popolo*.[212] Cardinal Giacomo Ammannati Piccolomini wrote several times to Marco Barbo while he was on legation in Central Europe, that he should return to Rome.[213] The very same cardinal criticised, in contrast, other legates of the period.

210. Fraknói, *Erdődi Bakócz*, pp. 137-142.

211. Eubel, *Hierarchia catholica*, vol. 2, pp. 46-48.

212. BAV, Vat. lat. 4739, fol. 203v-205v (ed. Kalous, "Through the Gates", pp. 42-44).

213. Ammannati Piccolomini, *Lettere*, vol. 3, p. 1577, no. 569 (28 Jul 1472), "Si tam longe inter Hungarum et Polonum sunt pactae indutiae, si Turco a novo hoste Cassano grande exhibetur negotium, si vacas, si denique per commodum rei publicae decedere provincia potes, redi, mi Aquilegiensis, ad nos"; pp. 1805-1806, no. 712 (14 Mar 1474), "Non eris hic minus quam in Germania necessarius, ubi iam legationes nostrae magis ad probandam Romanae Sedis potestatem, quam ad praestandam salutem, celebres sunt. Ita ubique caritas refricuit et in nos reverentia. Sunt tibi apud nos sacerdotia, in senatu sententia. Multa decernuntur quotidie, in quibus tam opus est constantia tua, quam magna est multorum facilitas. Expetunt haec omnia suo iure reditum peregrinantis iam biennio patris, expetimus et nos tui amantes tecumque peculiari benivolentia in Domino iuncti. Itaque redi unoque consilio publicis prospice et privatis".

Going on a legation not only meant leaving Rome, but also increasing the cardinal's influence in the countries of destination. Cardinal Bessarion, in the words of Cardinal Ammannati Piccolomini, desperately wanted to go for a legation to France in 1472 and persuaded the Pope to dispatch him. Cardinal Roderigo Borja even used tricks to obtain the legation to the Iberian peninsula.[214] When cardinals left Rome the situation in the City and at the Curia changed both for the Pope and for the rest of the cardinals.

Even after stating all the problems and conflicts, the office of a legation has to be viewed as an honour, as it surely was by the cardinals who accepted the task. As mentioned above, Marco Barbo declared in 1481 that none of the cardinals should reject the legation, unless physically unable to go abroad. He himself, on a legation in Central Europe in 1472, stated clearly that although there were some (the above-mentioned Cardinal Ammannati Piccolomini and possibly others), who called him back to Rome, he was going to keep the office and overcome all the troubles of the duty: "I will turn my eyes to the Lord, from where help will come to me, and he will make sure I will not waver. Do believe me, that trusting only in Him, I will not divert from the right way… Those, who want, may invent, shout and tear, but I will not leave my office, even if the indignation of almost the whole world should arise".[215] Such a proclamation demonstrates the involvement and dedication that individual cardinals might have had.

Cardinals were a renowned group of prelates that can be traced with their family background and ties to one another. When researching the legates, however, the nuncios and especially the nuncios with the power of legates *de latere* had to be taken into consideration, and there it becomes more difficult. When looking at a list of these nuncios, one can only say that they were exclusively bishops and almost exclusively curial bishops who had some experience with the functioning of the Papal Curia and even with certain diplomatic tasks before. As a group, they are more difficult to trace in the Roman sources, because cardinals were much more closely watched and their whereabouts recorded, their ceremonial entries or leavings mentioned, as it had also legal and financial consequences. In the case of curial bishops, information is often lacking about the exact dates of their absence from Rome, when they left exactly and when they returned. Apart from special cases, help only comes from documents published for the nuncios when they left, namely faculties, instructions and other letters. Concerning individual personalities, Bartolomeo Maraschi, bishop of Città di Castello, for example, entered the service of Francesco Gonzaga as a tutor in 1458 and stayed as master of Gonzaga's household when he became cardinal in 1461. As of 1468, he began acquiring various curial offices, and only left the service of Francesco Gonzaga in 1469. David Chambers wrote about him:

214. See the section on crusading; Ammannati Piccolomini, *Lettere*, vol. 3, pp. 1750-1752, no. 686 (20 Oct 1473).

215. BAV, Vat. lat. 5641, fol. 175r-176r (25 Oct 1472), "Convertam igitur et dirigam oculos meos ad dominum unde veniet auxilium mihi, et ipse sua pietate a dextris erit ne commovear. Credite credite in ipso solo confidens non divertam a via recta… Fingant, clament, lanient, qui velint, non deseram oficium meum, eciam si totius mundi pene indignatio subeunda foret".

> Bartolomeo Marasca was one of those figures of secondary importance who are too easily overlooked; if not one of the most distinguished prelates making his career in Rome in the 1460s, he appears to have been a striking case of the officious and self-tormented cleric, and deserves his own niche in the social history of the Church.[216]

Chambers did not study his later career, but has already demonstrated that Bartolomeo became one of the crucial prelates at the Curia for the earlier period. He received certain missions as a nuncio even with legatine powers, most notably, a mission to the Emperor, to Sigismund, archduke of Austria, to other parts of the Empire and to the King of Hungary in 1483-1485.[217] The frequently mentioned Angelo Pecchinoli is not so well known before his mission to the King of Hungary, but he held the bishopric of Orte (and Cività Castellana, as the two dioceses united in 1437) a bishopric that was traditionally used as a bishopric for curial bishops[218] – one of his successors in this office was, for example, Johannes Burckard. Orso Orsini, when replacing Cardinal Cibo in 1481, was described as "bishop of Teano, an educated man, best skilled in public matters and a prelate of a completely honest life".[219] Legates and nuncios had to meet certain standards of position within the Church hierarchy as well as suitability in their way of life.

The title of *nuncius cum potestate legati de latere* was usually used in this period. This was an innovation, as already mentioned above. One of the explanations may be related precisely to the nominations of individuals. Cardinals did not always want to leave Rome and nuncios needed more powers, especially those related to the government of the local churches. Providing bishops with the powers of cardinal-legates (although without the requirements for the ceremonial) meant a broadening of the pool of possible candidates for legatine office and made it possible to send a larger number of legates to various parts of Europe without dispatching too many cardinals and, as stated above, this was much cheaper as well.

A table of cardinal legates and nuncios with the power of legates *de latere* for the region of Germany and Central Europe (the region is vaguely defined as the Kingdoms of Bohemia, Hungary and Poland) has been added as an illustration. Table 2 demonstrates the involvement of cardinals as legates (in bold letters) in the region and their substitutes, the nuncios *cum potestate legati de latere.* The simple nuncios have been left out,[220] which can cause some misinterpretations. Namely, it is in the later period, as was specified in earlier chapters, where papal envoys left Rome as simple nuncios, but at the same time were endowed with a number of faculties that would normally be held by legates or nuncios with the power of legates. Secondly, a number of persons appeared in papal service as envoys even before they appear in this table. Rudolf of Rüdesheim, for example,

216. Chambers, "Bartolomeo Marasca", p. 265.

217. Scharf, "Maraschi (Marasca, de Maraschis), Bartolomeo"; Kalous, *Plenitudo potestatis*, pp. 314-334; Untergehrer, *Die päpstlichen nuntii und legati*, pp. 450-458.

218. Mastrocola, *Note storiche*, pp. 67-89, not even this biography tells us more about his previous activities.

219. Gherardi da Volterra, *Il diario romano*, pp. 36-7.

220. For more details see Kalous, *Plenitudo potestatis* and Untergehrer, *Die päpstlichen nuntii und legati.*

bore the title of nuncio several times before 1467, when he was named nuncio with the power of a legate. The table still reveals, however, the temporal frame of activities of papal envoys with the highest possible authority and commission as well as the service of cardinals in the office.

Table 2. Papal legates and nuncios with the power of legates in Germany and Central Europe (1447-1525)

LEGATE/NUNCIO	YEARS	OFFICE	PROVINCE
Juan Carvajal	1447-1449	*legatus de latere*	Germania, Hungaria, Bohemia
Battista de' Errici	1448	*nuntius cum plenae legationis officio*	Polonia
Nicholas of Cusa	1450-1453	*legatus de latere*	Germania, Bohemia
Luis Pires	1450-1451	*nuntius cum potestate legati de latere*	Prussia
Enea Silvio Piccolomini	1452-1455	*nuntius cum potestate legati de latere*	Bohemia, Moravia, Silesia, Aquileia, Saltzburg, Austria, Styria, Carinthia, Carniola; Hungaria
Giovanni di Castiglione	1453-1455	*nuntius cum potestate legati de latere*	Austria, Hungaria, Moravia
Dionysius Szécsi	1455-1465	*legatus de latere*	Hungaria
Juan Carvajal	1455-1461	*legatus de latere*	Germania, Hungaria, Polonia
Giovanni di Castiglione	1456-1457	*nuntius cum potestate legati de latere*	Germania
Girolamo Lando	1459-1460	*nuntius cum potestate legati de latere*	Bohemia, Polonia
Bessarion	1460-1461	*legatus de latere*	Germania
Girolamo Lando	1461-1464	*nuntius cum potestate legati de latere*	Germania, Hungaria, Bohemia, Polonia, Prussia
Domenico Dominici	1463-1464	*legatus missus cum potestate legati de latere*	Germania
Girolamo Lando	1464-1465	*orator (cum potestate legati de latere)*	Hungaria
Lorenzo Roverella	1467	*nuntius cum potestate legati de latere*	Germania
Peter von Schaumberg	1467-1469	*legatus de latere*	Germania

LEGATE/NUNCIO	YEARS	OFFICE	PROVINCE
Rudolf of Rüdesheim	1467-1482	*nuntius cum potestate legati de latere*	Germania, Bohemia, Polonia, Prussia etc.
Lorenzo Roverella	1468-1472	*nuntius cum potestate legati de latere*	Germania, Hungaria, Bohemia
Francesco Todeschini-Piccolomini	1471	*legatus de latere*	Germania
Marco Barbo	1471-1474	*legatus de latere*	Germania, Hungaria, Bohemia, Polonia; Datia, Norvegia, Svetia
Gabriel Rangoni	1474-1479	*nuntius cum potestate legati de latere*	Hungaria, Bohemia
Alexander Numai	1474-1483	*nuntius cum potestate legati de latere*	Germania
Domenico Camisati	1476	*nuntius cum potestate legati de latere*	Germania, Hungaria, Bohemia, Polonia
Giovanni Arcimboldi	1477	*legatus de latere*	Germania, Hungaria, Bohemia (legation did not happen)
Ausias Despuig	1479	*legatus de latere*	Germania
Giovanni d'Aragona	1479-1480	*legatus de latere*	Hungaria, Bohemia, Polonia
Giovanni Battista Cibo	1481	*legatus de latere*	Germania, Hungaria (legation did not happen)
Orso Orsini	1481-1482	*nuntius cum potestate legati de latere*	Germania, Hungaria
Angelo Geraldini	1482-1484	*nuntius cum potestate legati de latere*	Germania, Bohemia, Polonia, Datia
Bartolomeo Maraschi	1483-1485	*nuntius cum potestate legati de latere*	Germania, Hungaria, Bohemia, Polonia, Datia
Giovanni d'Aragona	1483-1484	*legatus de latere*	Hungaria, Bohemia
Ladislaus Geréb of Vingárt	1484-1488	*legatus cum potestate legati de latere*	Hungaria, Bohemia
Angelo Pecchinoli	1488-1490	*nuntius cum potestate legati de latere*	Germania, Hungaria, Bohemia, Polonia
Raymund Peraudi	1488-1491	*nuntius cum potestate legati de latere*	Germania
Orso Orsini	1493-1495	*nuntius cum potestate legati de latere*	Hungaria, Bohemia, Polonia

LEGATE/NUNCIO	YEARS	OFFICE	PROVINCE
Raymund Peraudi	1500-1505	*legatus de latere*	Germania
Pietro Isvalies	1500-1503	*legatus de latere*	Hungaria, Bohemia, Polonia
Mariano Bartolini	1504-1506	*nuntius cum potestate legati de latere*	Germania
Achille Grassi	1510	*orator cum potestate legati de latere*	Germania, Hungaria, Polonia
Tamás Bakóc	1513-1519	*legatus de latere*	Hungaria, Bohemia, Polonia
Roberto Latino Orsini	1516	*nuntius cum potestate legati de latere*	Hungaria (legation did not happen)
Alessandro Farnese	1518	*legatus de latere (sine fac.)*	Germania (legation did not happen)
Tommaso De Vio	1518-1519	*legatus de latere (sine fac.)*	Germania
Mattheus Lang	1518-1519	*legatus de latere (sine fac.)*	Germania
Pompeo Colonna	1523	*legatus de latere*	Hungaria, Polonia (legation did not happen)
Tommaso De Vio	1523-1524	*legatus de latere*	Hungaria, Polonia, Bohemia
Lorenzo Campeggi	1524-1525	*legatus de latere*	Germania, Hungaria, Bohemia, Polonia

4.4. *Acceptance of legates*

Willing or not, cardinals left their positions in Rome and carried out the wishes of the pope. How were they accepted in the individual lands? What was their position there? We know that legates departed from the Curia because of *nonnullis nostris et Romane ecclesie arduis negotiis*, i.e. because of certain difficult tasks and negotiations of the Pope and the Roman Church; they were dispatched in accordance with the will of the Pope and with the consent of the cardinals. They were to be supported by the region and especially by the Church. The oath sworn by the Patriarch of Aquileia to Pope Gregory VII in 1079 was mentioned several times. The Patriarch promised to "treat the Roman legate honourably when he departs and when he returns and [to] assist him with his needs".[221] A similar text of the oath or profession appeared in the twelfth century, only adding that the archbishop would support and assist the legate, "whom [he]

221. Robinson, "The institutions", p. 406; for the context of the conflicts with episcopal power, see idem, "'Periculosus Homo'".

will recognise as the proper legate".[222] Such a condition consequently appeared in the thirteenth-century oaths of archbishops, and even more specifically bishops and abbots who should even protect the legate. These kinds of texts of the oaths were used also in the later period, and as stated above, were one of the foundations for the *procuratio canonica* as a form of support to the legate in his province.[223] To demonstrate the importance of the legates for the popes, tax exemptions for the Hospitallers or the Templars never actually included financial support for the legates.[224] These oaths clearly expressed the idea of the papal government of the Church and the papal claims for authority over bishops.

Legates, however, did not only come to their province in order to invade the episcopal authority. As demonstrated above, they, on the one hand, governed the local church, and, on the other hand, provided a number of spiritual benefits for the province as well as authority for political negotiations. To change the perspective, however: did the province need a legate? Was he expected or waited for or even asked for? In general, the answers must stem from the benefits that could be given to the province with the presence of a legate or nuncio with the power of a legate. The locals could have asked the Pope to send a legate because of the political situation, as they were used to having some kind of papal backing. Legates *de latere* could then support their cause with the papal authority. The burghers of Wrocław, for example, asked Pope Pius II to send a legate *de latere* in 1463, who would have even higher authority than the nuncio with the power of a legate Girolamo Lando, who was residing in Wrocław at the time. The new legate should have had the authority to publish indulgences in support of a crusade against the Ottomans and the plea was also motivated by the fact that the bishop of Wrocław at the time, according to the burghers, sided with the Bohemian heretics.[225]

Several cases of requesting a legate were related to the activities of King Matthias Corvinus. Apart from the reasons motivated by the political negotiations, there were others related to other benefits for the land. In 1484, for example, he had asked for a legate, or rather for the office of legation, that would be presented to a Hungarian bishop. The motive for such a request was the simple reason that no legate resided in the country. The Pope recounted the request of the King in his breve to Ladislaus Geréb, bishop of Transylvania, on 8 November 1484 and even mentioned that the King himself proposed the nomination of Ladislaus to the Pope.[226] A year later, the King even asked for the enlargement of the legatine province of Ladislaus to all the lands under his rule.[227] The King suggested his own person (Ladislaus was actually a cousin of the king) who would hold the legatine powers in the country. The person of this *legatus cum potestate legati de latere*, as he was called, worked with royal support, as can even be seen from the instructions of Angelo Pecchinoli, who came to Hungary in 1488. His

222. Andrieu, *Le pontifical romain*, vol. 1, p. 290.
223. Tangl, *Die päpstliche Kanzleiordnungen*, pp. 50-52, no. 18, 19.
224. Bronstein, *The Hospitallers and the Holy Land*, p. 117.
225. Markgraf, ed., *Politische Correspondenz*, vol. 2, pp. 25-26, no. 205.
226. Theiner, ed., *Vetera monumenta Hungariae*, vol. 2, pp. 500-501, no. 688.
227. ASV, Arm. XXXIX 19, fol. 26rv (7 Oct 1485).

instructions specified that he carried with himself papal letters which gave him the power to annul and terminate all the faculties of previous nuncios and orators and "especially the bishop of Transylvania". He also carried, however, letters, which enabled him to reinstate the legate after leaving the province, should the King desire so.[228] Having a legate in one's lands definitely meant papal support and benefits that could only be offered by papal authority.

Have a legate with papal authority on your side! That was a piece of advice given even to the 'heretical' King George of Bohemia. Pavel Židek, a scholar and Catholic priest in Utraquist Prague, wrote a series of suggestions to the King entitled *Spravovna.* He based the welfare of the kingdom on thirty basic assumptions, the first ones being related to the proper religion and obedience to the Pope. Number eight stated that for the well being of the kingdom, the King should ask for a "wise cardinal legate" who would stay for a year or two at the royal court and (apart from fulfilling certain tasks of a bishop, as the Archbishopric of Prague was vacant) increase the King's legitimacy. All other princes would "eat out of his hand". With the help of the legate, moreover, the King could establish agreement about the faith with other princes.[229] The reasons for wanting a legate in the country or even at the royal court were once again the authority legates could provide for the prince who hosted them. This advice, even though it was given to King of Bohemia, to some sense explains the actions of King Matthias Corvinus, who clearly realised that collaborating with a legate was crucial in order to obtain the respect of other princes.

Pavel Židek added one more reason for having a legate in connection with the special case of the Kingdom of Bohemia. The archbishopric of Prague was vacant as of 1431 and he suggested that the King find an appropriate person who would fill the position. As he could not find anyone apt for the job, he eventually advised the King that: "It is better to take a wise legate for a few years, so that he would, in place of the archbishop, with at least ten doctors, administer all the clergy with God's and your advice…".[230] In a way, Židek wanted to use a legate to fill the empty space of an Archbishop of Prague. He could have known from experience that this is possible, as Philibert de Montjeu, bishop of Coutances and legate of the Council of Basel to Bohemia proved in 1436-1439 with his stay in the Kingdom.[231]

One more example can serve to demonstrate how the legates and their faculties were viewed in the lands beyond the Alps. Matters of politics and political capital were only mentioned. The King of Poland asked Pope Leo X in 1520 to increase the powers of the existing Nuncio Zacharia Ferreri. He was a simple *nuncius*, but still had faculties at his disposal. Their usage was, however, limited to other countries, namely Lithuania and Muscovy, where some of his tasks resided. King Sigismund asked the Pope to make these faculties available for Poland as well, as they were not so useful for those lands anyway because of the large number of people of "the Greek rite". He also added: "It will be

228. ASV, Misc., Arm. II 56, fol. 162v-163r.
229. Tobolka, ed., *M. Pavla Židka Spravovna*, pp. 9-10.
230. *Ibid.*, p. 10.
231. Zilynská, "Biskup Filibert"; Kleinert, *Philibert de Montjeu*, pp. 408-416.

a matter uncommonly pleasing and useful to my subjects, as they would be able to receive at home those things, they so far have asked from Rome or from Hungary". The king referred to spiritual benefits and various licences, dispensations and absolutions which the legates (and also this nuncio) could distribute in their legatine provinces when having at their disposal proper faculties. It should only be added here, that the King's plea was successful and the validity of the faculties was extended to the Kingdom of Poland as well.[232]

King Sigismund was not the only one, of course, who wished to have such benefits available for his subjects. A very similar plea, motivated by the same ideas, was sent by King Henry VII of England in July 1488. He asked the Pope to provide Giovanni Gigli, collector in England, with faculties for various dispensations (as the previous collectors used to have), so that the inhabitants would not have to suffer the hardships of the road to Rome.[233] Legates brought many benefits for the province, which is confirmed not only by the benefits themselves, and by the kings asking for legates in their province because of their subjects, but also by the observations of the members of a legate's retinue. Antonio Romagnano served as an auditor at the legation of Cardinal Francesco Todeschini Piccolomini in 1471 and in his description of the legate's chancery, observed that "because of the low payments all the inhabitants of the province gathered to the chancery of the legate disregarding even their ordinary judges, as flies gather to honey".[234]

The spiritual benefits and especially indulgences (or confessional letters) the legates could distribute represented one of the most demanded and required articles they carried and could offer to the province. This is why false legates appeared in the region: one is known, for example, in the 1480s. Richardus Pontanus published in 1485 a number of printed confessional letters that are still preserved in local archives.[235] Nothing seems problematic from the point of view of the prints, however, an activity against the "false legate" is recorded elsewhere. Angelo Pecchinoli reported on 25 June 1489 that there were some fake distributors of indulgences, "ciaratani, qui portant falsas indulgentias". Later, in the same relation, he even reported that he caught one such false priest of the name Antonius de Ponte, who published indulgences for the benefit of the

232. Wojtyska, ed., *Acta*, vol. 2, pp. 48-49, no. 18, "... Erit haec res mihi non vulgariter grata et subditis meis utilis, cum ea, quae isthinc ex Urbe aut ex Hungaria peteretur, hic domi haberi possint"; pp. 70-71, no. 28.

233. AS Venezia, Collezione Podocataro, busta 7, no. 422 (16 Jul 1488), "... Rogavimus insuper eandem vestram sanctitatem, ut cum ex subditis nostris complures essent, qui vestra et istius sacrosancte sedis ope in plurium rerum dispensationibus egerent, nec omnibus Romam eundi aut mittendi ob itineris longitudinem et graves sumptus facultates suppeterent idonee̜, eidem domino collectori facultates illas gratiose concedere vellet, quibus alii ut primum sedis apostolice̜ collectores hoc in regno antehac sunt perfuncti, quin immo ex uberiore gratia aliquid addere super et ampliare tum virtute viri, tum nostra intercessione dignaretur, nostroque oratori domino Limiricensi mandavimus, ut apud vestram sanctitatem ea in re nomine nostro instaret".

234. Dendorfer, "Ein kurialer Ordo", pp. 80, 91.

235. *Einblattdrucke des XV. Jahrhunderts*, p. 322, no. 1202.

Hospital of *Santo Spirito in Sassia* (just like Richardus Pontanus in 1485).[236] An undated concept of a papal breve addressed to the Archbishop of Magdeburg and a number of other archbishops, bishops and secular rulers of a large part of Europe (the Emperor, kings of Hungary, Poland, England, Denmark and princes of the Empire) even mentioned Richardus Pontanus as someone who had published indulgences for over two years as well as other disobedient clerics. The Pope asked the addressees to assist in capturing him before he dispatched someone from Rome.[237] A legate with such powers, then, was welcome in the provinces as he could provide the believers with the indulgences they longed for.

Thus, on the one hand, the legates and nuncios were accepted as those who brought "celestial gifts" and made life and especially salvation easier for the inhabitants of their province. On the other hand, they were welcome as diplomatic agents representing the pope as the head of one of the Italian states, but more significantly, as the organiser and leader of western Christendom, *res publica christiana.* As diplomats, they fulfilled their role following the then typical system of diplomatic representation and were accepted as part of the diplomats at a certain court. Bartolomeo Maraschi even reported on his visit to the royal palace of Buda (typically in Italy, diplomatic agents were shown into the palace to observe the prince's display of power),[238] and also on his dinner at the royal palace of Buda in the presence of the royal couple, István Bátori, voyvode of Transylvania, Jan Filipec, the above-mentioned bishop of Várad and the ambassador of the King of Naples.[239] Diplomacy interlinked European courts including the papal Curia, which was a diplomatic hub in itself, but diplomatic negotiations on the spot and reports from trustworthy and reliable agents became a must even for the pope.

Taking into consideration these and many other examples, it is clearly apparent that local princes wanted and needed to cooperate with papal legates. During wartime the cooperation was particularly close and apparent to external observers, when they were on the same side. Legates participated in the crusades or helped organise them and also took part in political negotiations. When siding with one of the parties in conflicts or political talks, legates and nuncios could cause problems for their opponents, as it was believed that, at least concerning persons who were not accused of heresy, papal diplomacy should be impartial. Peaceful cooperation was, however, also part of the agenda of kings, especially in relation to the local church. Cooperation with a legate could give one's rule an extra legitimacy, especially in cases like King George or King Matthias, both of whom won the kingship with no royal lineage in their background. Legates and nuncios carried extremely high authority, although without any actual judicial or other decisive power outside ecclesiastical matters.

236. ASV, Misc., Arm. II 56, fol. 190r, 191v.

237. AS Venezia, Coll. Podocataro, b. 1, no. 196.

238. ASV, Misc., Arm. II 56, fol. 350v-351r, "... a quodam amico invitatus sim ad inspiciendum palatium regis..."; cf. Martines, *Power and Imagination*, pp. 221-234.

239. ASV, Misc., Arm. II 56, fol. 355r.

Concluding remarks

The last section of the previous chapter could have served as a sort of conclusion. The acceptance of legates *de latere* was crucial for their activities. If not accepted and respected, their powers would be useless, however, their position was linked to that of the papacy of the later Middle Ages. When no one questioned the leading role of the popes, few dared to question the authority of their legates. Since the reform of the papacy in the eleventh and twelfth centuries, legates were responsible for a large part of spreading the common features of papal government in the High Middle Ages. The role, position and authority of legates in the later period did not change much, however, the system itself needed to be adjusted to current developments within the Church and society. The most crucial challenges to the authority of legates were those that refused to accept the rights and powers of the papacy: the rise of national states and churches and the Reformation. The first would lead towards the limitations of powers of legates within the context of secular powers on the one hand and the episcopal authority on the other. The second problem undermined the system completely in regions that no longer recognised the pope as the head of Christendom. This is also why the system of papal representation changed in that period substantially.

The 1520s and 1530s finally brought general changes of European diplomatic service to papal diplomacy as well. The system of papal nuncios developed and spread throughout Europe, with a well-defined organisation and archive keeping. With the introduction of permanent papal nuncios, the legations became less frequent and more special. Papal legates, however, did not disappear, but represented the pope mostly in ceremonial matters or in matters of the papal states. Thus, although the system of papal legation did not disappear in the Middle Ages, in later periods it was to some extent limited. Even the *Codex iuris canonici* of 1983 still defines papal legates, but does not mention the office of the legation (*officium legationis*), but rather the function of a legate (*munus*), in canon 358, and the cardinal who is entrusted with such a task "has competence only over those things which the Roman Pontiff commits to him". Furthermore, the text only mentions "the office of representing the Roman Pontiff". This is the greatest change from the medieval legation: the legates do not hold an office to which certain specific powers and privileges belong.

Late medieval papal legation is not a simple matter. Historians cannot focus only on the office and its innate powers. Even though the medieval legation may be studied in the context of the official and institutional history of the Church, it belongs to all other aspects of medieval studies. The legation offers a further wide range of possibilities, e.g. history of diplomacy, crusades, travelling, political and diplomatic history of individual states and countries, the field of communication and representation, but also – apart from Church history in general – religious and social history. After dealing mostly with the aspects of the office, the actual procedure and major tasks of legations, a few features deserve to be singled out.

First, as legates largely appealed not only to the highest strata of medieval society, but also to much lower individuals, especially with their penitentiary faculties, historians could access individuals or groups of people on various social levels. Papal legates were often the closest people could get in the Middle Ages to the pope. As they travelled around Europe with all their powers and privileges, in a way they constituted small travelling 'curias'. Like the Papal Curia in Rome, they could be accessed by all. Judging from some of the reactions to the presence or absence of legates in a kingdom, this aspect crucially defined the understanding of the office. Second, the office of legation constituted a strong political tool both for the advancement of the political goals of the papacy in individual regions, but also within the Papal Curia. The nominations of individual cardinals to legations could have had crucial effects on the situation at the papal court before the unprecedented creation of thirty-one cardinals at one time by Pope Leo X. The legation meant leaving Rome, but also increased personal prestige. All these elements, however, had implications for changes that reformed the system of papal diplomacy and representation at the start of the Early Modern era.

This book took a general European perspective on the problem, even though most of the situations and individual legations are taken from the context of Central Europe. Such a limitation is not so typical in literature that focuses on general problems of western Christendom, although Central Europe was always a part it. It is equally legitimate as studying the problem in detail in France, Germany or Spain, as the system was standardised and centralised in Rome. Legates and nuncios with the power of legates forwarded the ideas of papal authority and ecclesiastical liberty equally in France as in Hungary. It is only the local context that prepared different situations for the legates and a need to solve them according to their powers. To some extent it may even be argued that Central Europe proved to be crucial for the crusade organisation in the late medieval period.

Such a study is necessarily based mostly on original sources produced by the Papal Curia, by individual papal legates and nuncios and by almost anyone in the specific regions. This might be one of the greatest obstacles to the research, i.e. collecting and analysing all possible materials requires concentrated and painstaking efforts. It should be emphasised that late-medieval papal legates encompassed the whole of Europe and thus their office and activity in its multiplicity and complexity can contribute to general European history. There is a great amount of work and research that still can and should be done. Even the simple lists of papal envoys of the period have been a *desideratum* of the research for some time. The creation of a database would then enable historians to proceed with some additional statistical and prosopographic research, which would further elucidate the particularities of the office. Listing all the faculties (done by Wolfgang Untergehrer and to some extent by Janusz Smołucha) together with the names and destinations also explains the possible activities of individuals. Topics for research in this respect are numerous, however, even publishing documents for individual legations might hugely contribute not only to the study of the medieval papal legation as such, but also to wider areas of research ranging from political to general Church and religious history. Especially the reports of the legates and nuncios, which – for nuncios – have been systematically published for the Early Modern period, need to be published and made available for further research.

These brief notes show that research into medieval papal legation still needs a great deal of attention and historians should dedicate their efforts to a number of issues connected to the general theme. This volume tries to further the discussion and draw some more attention to the late medieval legates as they represent a basic tile in the mosaic of late medieval ecclesiastical, religious, political, social and cultural history.

Bibliography

Abbreviations

ANP	*Acta nuntiaturae Polonae* (see Wojtyska)
AS	Archivio di Stato
ASV	Archivio Segreto Vaticano, Città del Vaticano
AT	*Acta Tomiciana*
BAV	Biblioteca Apostolica Vaticana, Città del Vaticano
BMV	Biblioteca Nazionale Marciana, Venezia
DBI	*Dizionario biografico degli Italiani*. Roma 1960-
DRMH	*Decreta regni mediaevalis Hungariae*
FRA	*Fontes rerum Austriacarum* (see Bachmann, Fuchs, Palacky, Pangerl, Schroll)
FRB	*Fontes rerum Bohemicarum* (see Šimák)
MDE	*Magyar diplomácziai emlékek*
MGH	*Monumenta Germaniae Historica*
MHH	*Monumenta Hungariae Historica*
MKL	*Mátyás király levelei, külügyi osztály*
MNL	Magyar nemzeti levéltár, Budapest
MVH	*Monumenta Vaticana historiam regni Hungariae illustrantia* (see Pór, Fraknói)
MZK	Moravská zemská knihovna, Brno
NA	Národní archiv, Praha
OL DL	Országos levéltár Diplomatikai levéltára (collection of charters from before 1526)
OSzK	Országos Széchényi Könyvtár
QFIAB	*Quellen und Forschungen aus italienischen Archiven und Bibliotheken*
RPG	*Repertorium poenitentiariae Germanicum*
RIS	*Rerum Italicarum Scriptores*
SOkA	Státní okresní archiv
SRP	*Scriptores rerum Polonicarum* (see Szujski)
SRS	*Scriptores rerum Silesiacarum* (see Eschenloer, Markgraf, Kronthal)
VKOL	Vědecká knihovna, Olomouc

Primary sources

Archival sources

Archivio di Stato di Roma

Camerale I, Depositeria della Crociata (1463-1490), vol. 1233-1237
Camerale I, Mandati della Camera Apostolica, vol. 845, 846
Collezione acquisti e doni, b. 26, n. 1; b. 27, n. 1

Archivio di Stato di Venezia

Collezione Podocataro

Archivio Segreto Vaticano

Archivio Concistoriale, Acta Vicecancellarii (Arch. Concist., Acta Vicecanc.), vol. 1, 2, 3
Archivio Concistoriale, Acta Miscellanea (Arch. Concist., Acta Misc.), vol. 6
Armadio XXXI (Arm. XXXI), vol. 52
Armadio XXXIX (Arm. XXXIX), vol. 7, 9, 12, 15, 16, 16A, 18, 19, 20, 21, 22, 28
Armadio XL (Arm. XL), vol. 1
Armadio XLIV (Arm. XLIV), vol. 5
Camera Apostolica, Introitus et Exitus (Cam. Ap., Intr. et Ex.), vol. 440, 459, 487, 488, 490
Camera Apostolica, Diversa Cameralia (Cam. Ap., Div. Cam.), vol. 29, 37, 38, 39, 40, 44, 46, 57
Instrumenta Miscellanea (Instr. Misc.), no. 4151
Miscellanea, Armadio II (Misc., Arm. II), vol. 7, 20, 30, 53, 56
Miscellanea, Armadio VI (Misc., Arm. VI), vol. 39
Registra Vaticana (Reg. Vat.), vol. 518, 519, 528, 531, 549, 655, 679, 680, 734, 779, 1006, 1007
Segretaria di Stato, Germania (Segr. Stato, Germania), vol. 53, 55

Biblioteca Angelica, Roma

ms. 1077

Biblioteca Apostolica Vaticana

Chigiani (Chig.) L I 22
Vaticani latini (Vat. lat.) 3922, 3924, 4739, 5641, 6200, 6351, 8092, 10637, 12273, 12285, 12348, 12518, 13451, 13454

Biblioteca Nazionale Marciana, Venezia

Cod. Lat. IX 42 (=3483), Lat. X 174 (=3621), Lat. X 175 (=3622), Lat. X 176 (=3623), Lat. X 177 (=3624), Lat. X 178 (=3625), Lat. XIV 99 (=4278), Lat. XIV 100 (=4279)

Esztergomi Prímási és Főkáptalani Levéltár, Esztergom (Hungary)

Haus-, Hof- und Staatsarchiv, Wien (HHStA) (www.monasterium.net)

Magyar nemzeti levéltár, Budapest (MNL Budapest) (see also, http://mol.arcanum.hu/dldf)
Országos levéltár diplomatikai levéltára (OL DL)

Moravská zemská knihovna, Brno (MZK Brno)
Ms. sign. Mk 9

Národní archiv, Praha (NA Prague) (www.monasterium.net)
Archivy českých klášterů zrušených za Josefa II (1115-1760). ŘP Chotěšov (AZK, ŘP Chotěšov)
Augustiniáni obutí - provincialát a konvent, Praha (1285-1510) (ŘA)
Františkáni Praha (1283-1524) (ŘF)
Křižovníci s červenou hvězdou - generalát a konvent, Praha (1233-1872) (I-ŘKř)
Maltézští rytíři - české velkopřevorství (1085-1526) (ŘM)
Premonstráti - klášter Strahov (1192-1921) (NACR/I-ŘP) (ŘP)

Státní okresní archiv Jihlava (SOkA Jihlava)
Archiv města Jihlavy, Listiny

Státní okresní archiv, Olomouc (SOkA Olomouc)
Archiv města Olomouce, Sbírka listin

Státní okresní archiv, Znojmo (SOkA Znojmo)
Archiv města Znojma, Listiny

Vědecká knihovna, Olomouc (VK Olomouc)
Sign. II 39012

Zemský archiv Opava, branch Olomouc
Metropolitní kapitula Olomouc, Listiny

Published sources

Acta Tomiciana, vols. 1-8, ed. Stanislaus Gorski, Poznań, 1852-1876.

Ammannati Piccolomini, Iacopo, *Lettere (1444-1479)*, 3 vols., ed. Paolo Cherubini, Roma 1997.

Andrieu, Michel, ed., *Le pontifical romain au moyen-age*, 3 vols., Città del Vaticano, Biblioteca Apostolica Vaticana, 1938-1940.

Artner, Edgár, ed., *"Magyarország mint a nyugati keresztény művelődés védőbástyája": A Vatikáni Levéltárnak azok az okiratai, melyek őseinknek a Keletről Európát fenyegető veszedelmek ellen kifejtett erőfeszítéseire vonatkoznak (cca 1214-1606)*, Roma and Budapest, Pázmány Péter Katolikus Egyetem Egyháztörténeti Kutatócsoportja, 2004.

Bachmann, Adolph, ed., *Urkunden und Actenstücke zur österreichischen Geschichte im Zeitalter Kaiser Friedrichs III. und König Georgs von Böhmen (1440-1471)*, Wien, Carl Gerold's Sohn, 1879 (FRA, II/42).

——, ed., *Briefe und Acten zur österreichisch-deutschen Geschichte im Zeitalter Kaiser Friedrich III.*, Wien, Carl Gerold's Sohn, 1885 (FRA, II/44).

——, ed., *Urkundliche Nachträge zur österreichisch-deutschen Geschichte im Zeitalter Kaiser Friedrich III.*, Wien, F. Tempsky, 1892 (FRA, II/46).

Barbaro, Ermolao, *De coelibatu. De officio legati*, ed. Vittore Branca, Firenze, Leo S. Olschki, 1969.

Battioni, Gianluca, ed., *Camera Apostolica. Documenti relativi alle diocesi del Ducato di Milano*, vol. 2, *I "libri annatarum" di Sisto IV (1471-1484)*, Milano, Edizioni Unicopli, 2000.

Beneš, František, "Depositeria generale della crociata", *Československý časopis historický*, 14 (1966), pp. 738-757.

Bernardi Papiensis Summa Decretalium, ed. Ern. Ad. Theod. Laspeyres, Regensburg, Manz, 1860 (rpt. Graz, Akademische Druck- und Verlagsanstalt, 1956).

Bessenyei, József, ed., *Lettere di principi: Litterae principum ad papam / Fejedelmi levelek a pápának (1518-1578)*, Roma and Budapest, Római Magyar Akadémia Fraknói Vilmos Történeti Intézete and OSzK, 2002.

Bonfinis, Antonio de, *Rerum Ungaricarum Decades*, 5 vols., ed. I. Fógel, B. Iványi, L. Juhász, M. Kulcsár, P. Kulcsár, Leipzig and Budapest, Teubner, Egyetemi Nyomda and Akadémiai Kiadó, 1936-1976.

Bónis, György, *Szentszéki regeszták: Iratok az egyházi bíráskodás történetéhez a középkori Magyarországon*, A szerző hátrahagyott kéziratát gondozta és szerkesztette Balogh Elemér, Budapest, Püski, 1997.

Bretholz, Bertold, ed., *Die Chronik der Böhmen des Cosmas von Prag*, Berlin, Weidmannsche Buchhandlung, 1923 (MGH, SRG, n.s. 2).

Brewer, J.S., ed., *Letters and Papers, Foreign and Domestic, Henry VIII*, vol. 2, *1515-1518*, London, Her Majesty's Stationery Office, 1864 (http://www.british-history.ac.uk/letters-papers-hen8/vol2).

Burchard, John, *The Diary of John Burchard of Strasburg*, trans. Arnols Harris Mathew, London, Francis Griffiths, 1910.

Castellano, Alberto, *Liber sacerdotalis*, Venezia, Melchior Sessa et Petrus de Ravanis, 1523.

Celani, Enrico, ed., *Johannis Burckardi Liber Notarum ab anno MCCCCLXXXIII usque ad annum MDVI*, 2 vols., Città di Castello, S. Lapi, 1907-1942.

Chmel, Joseph, ed., *Actenstücke und Briefe zur Geschichte des Hauses Habsburg im Zeitalter Maximilian's I.*, 3 vols., Wien, 1854-1858 (Monumenta Habsburgica I/1-3.).

Cusa, Nicholas of, *Writings on Church and Reform*, ed. and trans. Thomas M. Izbicki, Cambridge, Mass., Harvard University Press, 2008.

Decreta regni Hungariae / Gesetze und Verordnungen Ungarns 1301-1457, ed. Franciscus Döry, Georgius Bónis and Vera Bácskai, Budapest, Akadémiai Kiadó, 1976.

Decreta regni Hungariae / Gesetze und Verordnungen Ungarns 1458-1490, ed. Franciscus Döry, Georgius Bónis, Geisa Érszegi and Susanna Teke, Budapest, Akadémiai Kiadó, 1989.

Decreta Regni Mediaevalis Hungariae / The Laws of the Medieval Kingdom of Hungary, vol. 4, *1490-1526*, ed. and trans. Péter Banyó, Zsolt Hunyadi, Martyn Rady and János M. Bak, Budapest and Idyllwild, CA, Department of Medieval Studies, CEU and Charles Schlacks, 2010.

Deutsche Reichstagsakten unter Kaiser Friedrich III., vol. 8, pt. 1, *1468-1470*, ed. Ingeborg Most-Kolbe, vol. 8, pt. 2, *1471*, ed. Helmut Wolff, Göttingen, Vandenhoeck & Ruprecht, 1973-1999.

Durantis, Wilhelm (Guillaume Durand), *Speculum iudiciale illustratum et repurgatum a Giovanni Andrea et Baldo degli Ubaldi*, Basel, Frobenius, 1574 (rpt. Aalen, Scientia Verlag, 1975).

Dvorský, František, ed., "Dopisy pana Viléma z Pernšteina z let 1480-1521", in *Archiv český*, vol. 16, Praha, Bursík & Kohout, 1897, pp. 1-72.

Dykmans, Marc, ed., *L'oeuvre de Patrizi Piccolomini ou le cérémonial papal de la première renaissance*, 2 vols., Città del Vaticano, Biblioteca Apostolica Vaticana, 1980, 1982.

——, ed., *Le cérémonial papal de la fin du moyen âge à la renaissance*, vol. 2, *Du Rome en Avignon ou le cérémonial de Jacques Stefaneschi*, Bruxelles and Roma, Institut Historique Belge de Rome, 1981.

——, ed., *Le cérémonial papal de la fin du moyen âge à la renaissance*, vol. 4, *Le retour à Rome ou Le cérémonial du patriarche Pierre Ameil*, Bruxelles and Roma, Institut Historique Belge de Rome, 1985.

Dyson, R.W., ed., *Giles of Rome's On Ecclesiastical Power: A Medieval Theory of World Government*, New York, Columbia University Press, 2004.

Emler, Josef, ed., *Fontes rerum bohemicarum*, vol. 7, *Drobnější kroniky a zprávy k dějinám českým*, Praha, Grégr a Ferd. Dattel, s.d.

Eršil, Jaroslav, ed., *Acta Martini V. pontificis Romani (1417-1431)*, 3 parts, Praha, Academia, 1996-2001 (Monumenta Vaticana res gestas Bohemicas illustrantia VII/1-3).

Eschenloer, Peter, *Historia Wratislaviensis*, ed. Hermann Markgraf, Breslau, Josef Max, 1872 (SRS, 7).

——, *Geschichte der Stadt Breslau*, 2 vols., ed. Gunhild Roth, Münster, New York, München and Berlin, Waxmann, 2003.

Fekete Nagy, Antonius, Victor Kenéz, Ladislaus Solymosi and Geisa Érszegi, eds., *Monumenta rusticorum in Hungaria rebellium anno MDXIV*, Budapest, Akadémiai Kiadó, 1979.

Fink, Karl August, "Der Kreuzablaß gegen Georg Podiebrad in Süd- und Westdeutschland", *QFIAB*, 24 (1932-1933), pp. 207-243.

Fraknói, Vilmos, ed., *Relationes oratorum pontificiorum / Magyarországi pápai követek jelentései 1524-1526*, Budapest, Franklin-Társulat, 1884 (rpt. 2001) (Monumenta vaticana Hungariae, II/1).

——, ed., *Mathiae Corvini Hungariae regis Epistolae ad Romanos pontifices datae et ab eis acceptae / Mátyás király levelezése a római pápákkal 1458-1490*, Budapest, Franklin-Társulat, 1891 (rpt. 2000) (Monumenta vaticana Hungariae, I/6).

——, ed., *Mátyás király levelei, külügyi osztály*, 2 vols., Budapest, Magyar tudományos akadémia, 1893-1895.

Friedberg, Aemilius, ed., *Corpus Iuris Canonici*, pt. 1, *Decretum magistri Gratiani*, Leipzig, Tauchnitz, 1879 (rpt. Graz, Akademische Druck- und Verlagsanstalt, 1956).

——, ed., *Corpus Iuris Canonici*, pt. 2, *Decretalium collectiones*, Leipzig, Tauchnitz, 1881 (rpt. Graz, Akademische Druck- und Verlagsanstalt, 1959).

——, ed., *Quinque compilationes antique*, Leipzig, Tauchnitz, 1882 (rpt. Graz, Akademische Druck- und Verlagsanstalt, 1956).

Fuchs, Adalbert Franz, ed., *Urkunden und Regesten zur Geschichte des Benedictinerstiftes Göttweig*, vol. 3, *1468-1500*, Wien, Carl Gerold's Sohn, 1902 (FRA, II/55).

Gaida, Giacinto, ed., *Platynae historici Liber de vita Christi ac omnium pontificum (AA. 1-1474)*, Città di Castello, S. Lapi, s.d (RIS, 3,1).

Ganzer, Klaus ed., *Concilium Tridentinum, 1545-1563*, in *Conciliorum Oecumenicorum Generaliumque Decreta. Editio critica*, vol. III, ed. Klaus Ganzer, Giuseppe Alberigo and Alberto Melloni, Turnhout, Brepols, 2010, pp. 1-178.

García y García, A. and A. Melloni, eds., *Concilium Lateranense IV, 1215*, in *Conciliorum Oecumenicorum Generaliumque Decreta. Editio critica*, vol. II/1, ed. Giuseppe Alberigo and Alberto Melloni, Turnhout, Brepols, 2013, pp. 149-204.

Gherardi da Volterra, Jacopo, *Il diario romano dal VII settembre MCCCCLXXIX al XII agosto MCCCCLXXXIV*, ed. Enrico Carusi, Città di Castello, S. Lapi, 1904-1906 (RIS, 23,3).

Grassi, Paris de, *Diarium Curiae Romanae*, in *Nova scriptorum ac monumentorum ... collectio...*, ed. Christ. Godofredus Hoffmannus, 2 vols., Leipzig, Haeredes Lanckisiani, 1731-1733, vol. 1, pp. 361-500.

——, *Il diario di Leone X*, ed. Pio Delicati and Mariano Armellini, Roma, F. Cuggiani, 1884.

Hrabar, Vladimir E., ed., *De Legatis et Legationibus Tractatus Varii*, Dorpati Livonorum [Tartu], 1905.

[Hug, Johannes], *Quadruvium Ecclesie: Quatuor prelatorum officium quibus omnis status tum secularis tum vero ecclesiasticus subiicitur*, Argentina (Strasbourg), Iohannes Grüninger, 1504.

Iványi, Béla, *Bártfa szabad királyi város levéltára, 1319-1526*, vol. 1, *1319-től 1501-ig*, Budapest, Magyar Tudományos Akadémia, 1910.

Joannis Dlugossii Annales seu Cronicae incliti regni Poloniae. Liber duodecimus, 1445-1461, ed. Krzysztof Baczkowski et al., Kraków, Akademia Umiejętności, 2003.

Joannis Dlugossii Annales seu Cronicae incliti regni Poloniae. Liber duodecimus, 1462-1480, ed. Krzysztof Baczkowski et al., Kraków, Akademia Umiejętności, 2005.

Johannes Andreae, *Novella in sextum*, Venezia, 1499 (rpt. Graz, Akademische Druck- und Verlagsanstalt, 1963).

Kaprinai, Stephanus, ed., *Hungaria diplomatica temporibus Mathiae de Hunyad regis Hungariae*, part 2, Wien, Joannes Thomas, 1771.

Katona, Stephanus, ed., *Historia critica regum Hungariae stirpis mixtae*, tom. 7-12, Buda 1792-1793.

Kronthal, Berthold and Heinrich Wendt, eds, *Politische Correspondenz Breslaus im Zeitalter des Königs Matthias Corvinus*, 2 vols., Breslau, Josef Max, 1893, 1894 (SRS, 13, 14).

Larson, Atria A. and Kenneth Pennington, eds, *Concilium Lateranense III, 1179*, in *Conciliorum Oecumenicorum Generaliumque Decreta. Editio critica*, vol. II/1, ed. Giuseppe Alberigo and Alberto Melloni, Turnhout, Brepols, 2013, pp. 115-147.

Ljubić, Simeone, ed., *Dispacci di Luca de Tollentis vescovo di Sebenico e di Lionello Cheregato vescovo di Traù, nunzi apostolici in Borgogna e nelle Fiandre, 1472-1488*, Zagreb, Tipografia sociale, 1876.

Lukcsics, Josephus, ed., *Monumenta Romana Episcopatus Vesprimiensis / A veszprémi püspökség római oklevéltára*, vol. 3, *1416-1492*, Budapest, Franklin, 1902, vol. 4, *1492-1526*, Budapest, Franklin, 1907.

Markgraf, Hermann, ed., *Politische Correspondenz Breslaus im Zeitalter Georgs von Podiebrad*, 2 vols., Breslau, Josef Max, 1873, 1874 (SRS, 8, 9).

McGready, William D., *The Theory of Papal Monarchy in the Fourteenth Century: Guillaume de Pierre Godin, Tractatus de causa immediata ecclesiastice potestatis*, Toronto, Pontifical Institute of Medieval Studies, 1982.

Mansi, Johannes Dominicus, *Sacrorum conciliorum nova et amplissima collectio*, vol. 32, 35, Paris, Hubert Welter, 1902.

Mátyás király levelei, külügyi osztály, ed. Vilmos Fraknói, 2 vols., Budapest, 1893-1895 (MKL).

Meuthen, Erich, ed., *Acta Cusana: Quellen zur Lebensgeschichte des Nikolaus von Kues*, vol. 1, pt. 3a: *1451 Januar-September 5*, vol. 1, pt. 3b: *1451 September 5-1452 März*, Hamburg, Felix Meiner, 1996.

Minnich, N., ed., *Concilium Lateranense V, 1512-1517*, in *Conciliorum Oecumenicorum Generaliumque Decreta. Editio critica*, vol. II/2, ed. Giuseppe Alberigo and Alberto Melloni, Turnhout, Brepols, 2013, pp. 1317-1455.

Monaco, Michele, ed., *Il De officio collectoris in regno Angliae di Pietro Griffi da Pisa (1469-1516)*, Roma, Edizioni di storia e letteratura, 1973.

Montefeltro, Federico da, *Lettere di stato e d'arte (1470-1480)*, ed. Paolo Alatri, Roma, Edizioni di storia e letteratura, 1949.

Nanni, Luigi, ed., *Epistolae ad Principes*, vol. 1, *Leo X - Pius IV (1513-1565)*, Città del Vaticano, Archivio Segreto Vaticano, 1992.

Nehring, Karl, "Quellen zur ungarischen Aussenpolitik in der zweiten Hälfte des 15. Jahrhunderts", *Levéltári Közlemények*, 47 (1976), pp. 87-120, 247-268.

Opll, Ferdinand and Richard Perger, eds, *Kaiser Friedrich III. und die Wiener 1483-1485: Briefe und Ereignisse während der Belagerung Wiens durch König Matthias Corvinus von Ungarn*, Wien, Franz Deuticke, 1993.

Palacký, Franz (František), ed., *Urkundliche Beiträge zur Geschichte Böhmens und seiner Nachbarländer im Zeitalter Georg's von Podiebrad (1450-1471)*, Wien, 1860 (FRA, II/20).

——, ed., *Urkundliche Beiträge zur Geschichte des Hussitenkrieges in den Jahren 1419-1436*, 2 vols., Praha, Friedrich Tempsky, 1873.

——, ed., *Staří letopisové čeští od roku 1378 do 1527*, in *Dílo Františka Palackého*, vol. 2, ed. Jaroslav Charvát, Praha, L. Mazáč, 1941.

Paschini, Pio, ed., *Il carteggio fra il card. Marco Barbo e Giovanni Lorenzi (1481-1490)*, Città del Vaticano, Biblioteca Apostolica Vaticana, 1948.

Patrizi Piccolomini, Agostino and Johannes Burckard, *[Pontificalis liber]*, Roma, Stephanus Plannck, 1485.

Patrologia latina: Patrologiae Cursus completus, vol. 54, ed. J. P. Migne, Paris, 1846.

Petersohn, Jürgen, ed., *Diplomatische Berichte und Denkschriften des päpstlichen Legaten Angelo Geraldini aus der Zeit seiner Basel-Legation 1482-1483*, Stuttgart, Franz Steiner, 1987.

Piccolomini, Enea Silvio, *Historia Bohemica / Historie česká*, ed. Dana Martínková, Alena Hadravová and Jiří Matl, Praha, KLP, 1998.

Pii Secundi Pontificis Maximi Commentarii, 2 vols., ed. Ibolya Bellus and Iván Boronkai, Budapest, Balassi Kiadó, 1993.

Pór, Antal, ed., *Acta legationis cardinalis Gentilis / Gentilis bíbornok magyarországi követségének okiratai 1307-1311*, Budapest, Franklin-Társulat, 1885 (rpt. 2000) (MVH, I/2).

Ransanus, Petrus, *Epithoma Rerum Hungararum*, ed. Petrus Kulcsár, Budapest, Akadémiai Kiadó, 1977.

Repertorium Germanicum, 9 vols., ed. Emil Göller et al., Berlin and Tübingen, Weidmann and Niemeyer, 1916-2004.

Repertorium poenitentiariae Germanicum, 10 vols., ed. Ludwig Schmugge et al., Tübingen, Max Niemeyer and Berlin and Boston, De Gruyter, 1996-2016.

Sanudo, Marino, *I Diarii*, vol. 17, ed. Federico Stefani, Guglielmo Berchet and Nicolò Barozzi, Venezia, Visentini, 1886.

Schmitz-Kallenberg, Ludwig, ed., *Practica Cancellariae apostolicae saeculi XV. exeuntis*, Münster, Coppenrath, 1904.

Smolinsky, Heribert, ed., *Domenico de' Domenichi und seine Schrift "De potestate pape et termino eius"*, Münster, Aschendorff, 1976.

Stieber, J., ed., *Concilium Basiliense, 1431-1449*, in *Conciliorum Oecumenicorum Generaliumque Decreta. Editio critica*, vol. II/2, ed. Giuseppe Alberigo and Alberto Melloni, Turnhout, Brepols, 2013, pp. 667-1157.

Stieber, J., F. Lauritzen, J. Uhlich, and H. Suermann, eds, *Concilium Ferrariense - Florentinum - Romanum, 1438-1445*, in *Conciliorum Oecumenicorum Generaliumque Decreta. Editio critica*, vol. II/2, ed. Giuseppe Alberigo and Alberto Melloni, Turnhout, Brepols, 2013, pp. 1159-1316.

Storm, Gustav, et. al, eds, *Diplomatarium Norvegicum*, vol. 17, *Romerske Oldbreve*, Christiania, Aktie-Bogtrykkeriet, 1902-1913.

Szujski, Josephi, ed., *Codex epistolaris saeculi decimi quinti*, vol. 2, *1444-1492*, Kraków, Akademia Umiejętności, 1876.

Šimák, Josef V., ed., *Fontes rerum bohemicarum / Prameny dějin českých*, vol. 6, Praha, Bursík a Kohout, 1907.

Šimek, František, ed., *Staré letopisy české z vratislavského rukopisu*, Praha, Historický spolek, 1937.

Šimek, František and Miloslav Kaňák, eds, *Staré letopisy české z rukopisu křižovnického*, Praha, Státní nakladatelství krásné literatury, hudby a umění, 1959.

Tangl, Michael, ed., *Die päpstlichen Kanzleiordnungen von 1200-1500*, Innsbruck, Wagner, 1894.

Teleki, József, ed., *Hunyadiak kora Magyarországon*, vols. 10-12, Pest, Emich Gusztáv, 1853, 1855, 1857.

Thallóczy, Lajos and Antal Áldásy, eds, *Magyarország melléktartományainak oklevéltára*, vol. 2, *A Magyarország és Szerbia közti összeköttetések oklevéltára, 1198-1526*, Budapest, Magyar tudományos akadémia, 1907 (MHH, I/33).

Theiner, Augustinus, ed., *Vetera monumenta historica Hungariam Sacram illustrantia maximam partem nondum edita ex tabulariis Vaticanis deprompta collecta ac serie chronoligica disposita*, vol. 2, *Ab Innocentio PP. VI. usque ad Clementem PP. VII., 1352-1526*, Roma, Typis Vaticanis, 1860.

——, ed., *Vetera monumenta Poloniae et Lithuaniae gentiumque finitimarum historiam illustrantia*, vol. 2, *Ab Ioanne PP. XXIII. usque ad Pium PP. V., 1410-1572*, Roma, Typis Vaticanis, 1861.

Thuasne, Louis, ed., *Johannis Burchardi Diarium sive rerum urbanarum commentarii (1483-1506)*, 3 vols., Paris, Ernest Leroux, 1883-1885.

Thurocz, Johannes de, *Chronica Hungarorum*, vol. 1, *Textus*, ed. Elisabeth Galántai and Julius Kristó, Budapest, Akadémiai Kiadó, 1985.

Tobolka, Zdeněk, ed., *M. Pavla Židka Spravovna*, Praha, Česká akademie císaře Františka Josefa, 1908.

Tommasini, Oreste, ed., *Diario della Città di Roma di Stefano Infessura scribasenato*, Roma, Istituto storico italiano, 1890.

Tractatus universi iuris = Tractatus illustrium in utraque tum pontifici, tum caesarei iuris facultate iurisconsultorum, De potestate ecclesiastica, vol. 13/2, Venezia, 1584.

Tusor, Péter and Gábor Nemes, eds, *Consistorialia documenta pontificia de Regnis Sacrae Coronae Hungariae (1426-1605)*, Budapest and Roma, Pázmány Péter Katolikus Egyetem Egyháztörténeti Kutatócsoportja, 2011.

Valentinelli, Joseph, ed., *Regesten zur deutschen Geschichte aus den Handschriften der Marcusbibliothek in Venedig*, 2 vols., München, Verlag der k. Akademie, 1864 (rpt. Nendeln, Kraus Reprint, 1976).

Výbor z české literatury doby husitské, vol. 2, ed. Bohuslav Havránek, Josef Hrabák, Jiří Daňhelka et al., Praha, Nakladatelsví ČSAV, 1964.

Wojtyska, Henricus Damianus, *Acta nuntiaturae Polonae*, vol. 1, *De fontibus eorumque investigatione et editionibus. Instructio ad editionem. Nuntiorum series chronologica*, Roma, Institutum historicum polonicum Romae, 1990.

——, ed., *Acta nuntiaturae Polonae*, vol. 2, *Zacharias Ferreri (1519-1521) et nuntii minores (1522-1553)*, Roma, Institutum historicum polonicum Romae, 1992.

Wolkan, Rudolf, ed., *Der Briefwechsel des Eneas Silvius Piccolomini*, section 3, *Briefe als Bischof von Siena*, vol. 1, *Briefe von seiner Erhebung zum Bischof von Siena bis zum Ausgang des Regensburger Reichstages (23. September 1450-1. Juni 1454)*, pt. 1, Wien, Alfred Hölder, 1918.

Zombori, István, ed., *Krzysztof Szydłowiecki kancellár naplója 1523-ból*, Budapest, METEM, 2004.

Secondary literature

Alberzoni, Maria Pia and Claudia Zey, eds, *Legati e delegati papali: Profili, ambiti d'azione e tipologie di intervento nei secoli XII-XIII*, Milano, Vita e pensiero, 2012.

Andretta, Stefano, Stéphane Péquignot and Jean-Claude Waquet, eds, *De l'ambassadeur: Les écrits relatifs à l'art de négocier du Moyen Âge au début du XIXe siècle*, Roma, École Française de Rome, 2015.

Baczkowski, Krzysztof, *Walka Jagiellonów z Maciejem Korwinem o koronę czeską w latach 1471-1479*, Kraków, Uniwersytet Jagielloński, 1980.

——, "Nieznane listy Baltazara z Piscii do papieża Sykstusa IV z lat 1476-1478 ze zbiorów weneckich", in *Zeszyty naukowe Uniwersytetu Jagiellońskiego, prace historyczne*, 89 (1989), pp. 239-251.

Balogh, István, *Szalkay László esztergomi érsek (+1526)*, Kassa, Szent Erzsébet nyomda, 1942.

Barbiche, Bernard, "Les 'diplomates' pontificaux du moyen âge tardif à la première modernité: Office et charge pastorale", in *Offices et papauté (XIVe-XVIIe siècle): Charges, hommes, destins*, ed., Armand Jamme and Olivier Poncet, Roma, École Française de Rome, 2005, pp. 357-370.

——, *Bulla, Legatus, Nuntius: Études de diplomatique et de diplomatie pontificales (XIIIe-XVIIe siècle)*, Paris, École des chartes, 2007.

Barraclough, Geoffrey, *Medieval Papacy*, London, Thames & Hudson, 1968.

Baumgarten, Paul Maria, *Untersuchungen und Urkunden über die Camera Collegii Cardinalium für die Zeit von 1295 bis 1437*, Leipzig, Giesecke & Devrient, 1898.

Baumgärtner, Ingrid, *Martinus Garatus Laudensis: Ein italienischer Rechtsgelehrter des 15. Jahrhunderts*, Köln and Wien, Böhlau, 1986.

Beattie, Blake R., *Angelus Pacis: The Legation of Cardinal Giovanni Gaetano Orsini, 1326-1334*, Leiden and Boston, Brill, 2007.

——, "The Cardinals and Diplomacy in the Fourteenth Century", in *Die Kardinäle des Mittelalters und der frühen Renaissance*, ed. Jürgen Dendorfer and Ralf Lützelschwab, Firenze, Sismel - Edizioni del Galuzzo, 2013, pp. 167-183.

Behrens, Betty, "Treatises on the Ambassador Written in the Fifteenth and Early Sixteenth Centuries", *English Historical Review*, 51 (1936), pp. 616-627.

Beneš, František, "Postoj Českých Budějovic ke králi Jiřímu z Poděbrad v letech 1465-1471", *Jihočeský sborník historický*, 37 (1968), pp. 57-75.

Benson, Robert L., "Plenitudo Potestatis: Evolution of a Formula from Gregory IV to Gratian", *Studia Gratiana*, 14 (1967), pp. 193-217.

Bentley, Jerry H., *Politics and Culture in Renaissance Naples*, Princeton, N.J., Princeton University Press, 1987.

Berger, Adolf, *Encyclopedic Dictionary of Roman Law*, Philadelphia, American Philosophical Society, 1953 (Transactions of the American Philosophical Society, new series, vol. 43, pt. 2).

Bertram, Martin, ed., *Stagnation oder Fortbildung? Aspekte des allgemeinen Kirchenrechts im 14. und 15. Jahrhundert*, Tübingen, Max Niemeyer, 2005.

Biskup, Marian, *Trzynastoletnia wojna z Zakonem Krzyżackim, 1454-1466*, Oświęcim, NapoleonV, 2014 (orig. 1967).

Black, Anthony, *Council and Commune: The conciliar movement and the fifteenth-century heritage*, London, Burns & Oates, 1979.

——, "The conciliar movement", in *The Cambridge History of Medieval Political Thought c. 350-c. 1450*, ed. J. H. Burns, Cambridge, Cambridge University Press, 1988, pp. 573-587.

——, *Church, State and Community: Historical and Comparative Perspectives*, Aldershot, Variorum, 2003.

Black, Jane, *Absolutism in Renaissance Milan: Plenitude of Power under the Visconti and the Sforza 1329-1535*, Oxford, Oxford University Press, 2009.

Blet, Pierre, *Histoire de la Répresentation Diplomatique du Saint Siège des origines à l'aube du XIXe siècle*, Città del Vaticano, Archivio Vaticano, 1982.

Bölling, Jörg, *Das Papstzeremoniell der Renaissance: Texte - Musik - Performanz*, Frankfurt am Main, Peter Lang, 2006.

Bónis, György, *A jogtudó értelmiség a Mohács előtti Magyarországon*, Budapest, Akadémiai Kiadó, 1971.

Borsa, Gedeon, "Bakócz Tamás nyomtatott búcsúlevele az 1514. évi keresztes hadjárat hirdetéséhez", *Magyar Könyvszemle*, 93 (1977), pp. 213-221.

——, "Bakócz Tamás újabb nyomtatott búcsúlevele", *Magyar Könyvszemle*, 95 (1979), pp. 400-408.

Bourgin, Georges, "Les cardinaux français et le diaire caméral de 1439-1486", *Mélanges d'archéologie et d'histoire*, 24 (1904), pp. 277-319.

Bronstein, Judith, *The Hospitallers and the Holy Land: Financing the Latin East, 1187-1274*, Woodbridge, Boydell Press, 2005.

Brundage, James A., *Medieval Canon Law*, London and New York, Longman, 1995.

Bullard, Melissa Meriam, "Renaissance spirituality and the ethical dimensions of church reform in the age of Savonarola: the dilemma of Cardinal Marco Barbo", in *The World of Savonarola: Italian élites and perceptions of crisis*, ed. Stella Fletcher and Christine Shaw, Aldershot, Ashgate, 2000, pp. 65-89.

Burns, J.H., "Angelo da Vallambrosa and the Pisan Schism", in *The Church, the Councils, and Reform: The Legacy of the Fifteenth Century*, ed. Gerald Christianson, Thomas M. Izbicki and Christopher M. Bellitto, Washington, D.C., The Catholic University of America Press, 2008, pp. 194-211.

Celenza, Christopher S., "Orsini, Giordano", in *DBI*, vol. 79, Roma, Istituto della Enciclopedia Italiana, 2013, pp. 657-662.

Chambers, D.S., "Bartolomeo Marasca, master of Cardinal Gonzaga's household (1462-1469)", *Aevum*, 63 (1989), pp. 265-283.

——, *Renaissance Cardinals and their Worldly Problems*, Aldershot, Variorum, 1997.

Cherubini, Paolo, "Fasolo, Angelo", in *DBI*, vol. 45, Roma, Istituto della Enciclopedia Italiana, 1995, pp. 249-254.

——, "L'intensa attività di un notaio di Camera: Gaspare Biondo", in *Dall'archivio segreto vaticano: Miscellanea di testi, saggi e inventari*, vol. 2, Città del Vaticano, Archivio Segreto Vaticano, 2007, pp. 25-145.

Christianson, Gerald, Thomas M. Izbicki and Christopher M. Bellitto, eds, *The Church, the Councils, and Reform: The Legacy of the Fifteenth Century*, Washington D.C., The Catholic University of America Press, 2008.

Cracco, Giorgio, "Banchini, Giovanni di Domenico", in *DBI*, vol. 5, Roma, Istituto della Enciclopedia Italiana, 1963, pp. 249-252.

Cushing, Kathleen G., *Reform and the Papacy in the Eleventh Century: Spirituality and Social Change*, Manchester and New York, Manchester Univesity Press, 2005.

Daniels, Tobias, "Die italienische Mächte und der Basler Konzilsversuch des Andreas Jamometić", *Zeitschrift der Savigny-Stiftung für Rechtsgeschichte: Kanonistische Abteilung*, 100 (2014), pp. 339-367.

Davies, Clifford S.L., "Bishop John Morton, the Holy See, and the Accession of Henry VII", *English Historical Review*, 102 (1987), pp. 2-30.

De Poli, Francesca, *Inventario della collezione Podocataro*, Ariccia, Aracne, 2015.

De Vivo, Filippo, "Archives of Speech: Recording Diplomatic Negotiation in late Medieval and Early Modern Italy", *European History Quarterly*, 46 (2016), pp. 519-544.

Decaluwe, Michiel, *A Successful Defeat: Eugene IV's Struggle with the Council of Basel for Ultimate Authority in the Church, 1431-1449*, Bruxelles and Roma, Institut Historique Belge de Rome, 2009.

Del Re, Niccolò, "Agostino Luciani, apostata hussita", *Rivista di storia della chiesa in Italia*, 1 (1947), pp. 418-428.

——, *Monsignor governatore di Roma*, Roma, Libreria editrice vaticana, 1972.

Dendorfer, Jürgen, "Ein Kurialer Ordo über die Kanzlei und das Gefolge eines *legatus de latere* (1482/83)", in *Päpste, Privilegien, Provinzen: Beiträge zur Kirchen-, Rechts- und Landesgeschichte: Festschrift für Werner Maleczek zum 65. Geburtstag*, ed. Johannes Gießauf, Rainer Murauer and Martin P. Schennach, Wien, Böhlau, 2010, pp. 77-92.

Dendorfer, Jürgen and Ralf Lützelschwab, eds, *Geschichte des Kardinalats im Mittelalter*, Stuttgart, Anton Hiersemann, 2011.

——, eds, *Die Kardinäle des Mittelalters und der frühen Renaissance*, Firenze, Sismel - Edizioni del Galluzzo, 2013.

Dendorfer, Jürgen and Claudia Märtl, "Papst und Kardinalskolleg im Bannkreis der Konzilien – von der Wahl Martins V. bis zum Tod Pauls II. (1417-1471)", in *Geschichte des Kardinalats im Mittelalter*, ed. Jürgen Dendorfer and Ralf Lützelschwab, Stuttgart, Anton Hiersemann, 2011, pp. 335-397.

——, eds, *Nach dem Basler Konzil: Die Neuordnung der Kirche zwischen Konziliarismus und monarchischem Papat (ca. 1450-1475)*, Münster, Lit Verlag, 2008.

DeSilva, Jennifer Mara, "Senators or Courtiers: Negotiating Models for the College of Cardinals under Julius II and Leo X", *Renaissance Studies*, 22 (2008), pp. 154-173.

Drabina, Jan, "Działalność dyplomatyczna Hieronima Lando na Śląsku i w Polsce w latach 1459-1464", in *Acta Universitatis Wratislaviensis*, 126, *Historia* 19, Wrocław, Uniwersytet Wrocławski, 1970, pp. 149-169.

——, "Kontakty Wrocławia z papieżem Pawłem II", *Śląskie Studia Historyczno-Teologiczne*, 5 (1972), pp. 131-150.

——, "Misja dyplomatyczna kardynała Marka Barbo w Polsce i jego działalność na Śląsku w latach 1472-1473", *Colloquium Salutis, Wrocławskie Studia Teologiczne*, 5 (1973), pp. 125-144.

——, "Legaci apostolscy na Śląsku w latach 1471-1479", *Śląskie Studia Historyczno-teologiczne*, 6 (1973), pp. 257-276.

——, "Działalność dyplomatyczna legata apostolskiego Rudolfa z Rüdesheimu na Śląsku", in *Acta Universitatis Wratislaviensis* 195, *Historica* 23, Wrocław, Uniwersytet Wrocławski, 1974, pp. 205-229.

——, "Kontakty Wrocławia z Piusem II i kurią rzymską w latach 1458-1464", *Kwartalnik historyczny*, 83 (1976), pp. 513-530.

——, "Kontakty Wrocławia z legatem papieskim, kardinalem Pietrem Isvali w pierwszych latach XVI wieku", *Studia historyczne*, 21 (1978), pp. 529-544.

——, *Kontakty Wrocławia z Rzymem w latach 1409-1517*, Wrocław, Zakład Narodowy im. Ossolińskich, 1981.

Dragoun, Michal, *Soupis středověkých rukopisů Knihovny Národního muzea: Doplňky ke katalogům F. M. Bartoše, J. Vašici a J. Vajse*, Praha, Scriptorium and National museum, 2011.

Dykmans, Marc, "Paris de Grassi", *Ephemerides liturgicae*, 96 (1982), pp. 407-482; 99 (1985), pp. 383-417; 100 (1986), pp. 270-333.

Eberhard, Winfried, *Konfessionsbildung und Stände in Böhmen 1478-1530*, München and Wien, Oldenbourg, 1981.

Einblattdrucke des XV. Jahrhunderts: ein bibliographisches Verzeichnis, Halle, E. Karras, 1914.

Enepekides, Polychronis K., "Die Wiener Legation des Kardinals Bessarion in den Jahren 1460-1461: Unter Berücksichtigung der neuentdeckten urkundlichen Quellen in Wien", in *Miscellanea marciana di studi bessarionei (a coronamento de V Centenario della donazione nicena)*, ed. Rino Avesani, Padova, Editrice Antenore, 1976, pp. 69-82.

Erdő, Péter, "The Papacy and the Kingdom of Hungary during the reign of Sigismund of Luxemburg (1387-1437)", in *A Thousand Years of Christianity in Hungary: Hungariae Christianae Millenium*, ed. István Zombori, Pál Cséfalvy and Maria Antonietta De Angelis, Budapest, Hungarian Catholic Episcopal Conference, 2001, pp. 63-68.

Erfle, Bernd, *Alexander Numai, Bischof von Forlì, als Diplomat in Diensten von Papst und Kaiser (1470-1483)*, PhD Dissertation, Marburg, 2002.

Eubel, Conradus, *Hierarchia catholica medii aevi*, vol. 2, 1431-1503, Münster, Libraria Regensbergiana, 1914.

Eubel, Conradus and Ludovicus Schmitz-Kallenberg, *Hierarchia catholica medii et recentioris aevi*, vol. 3, *Saeculum XVI ab anno 1503 complectens*, Münster, Libraria Regensbergiana, 1923.

Feldkamp, Michael F., *La diplomazia pontificia: Da Silvestro I a Giovanni Paolo II, un profilo*, Milano, Jaca Book, 1998.

Figueira, Robert C., *The Canon Law of Medieval Papal Legation*, PhD Dissertation, Cornell University, 1980.

——, "The Classification of Medieval Papal Legates in the *Liber Extra*", *Archivum Historiae Pontificiae*, 21 (1983), pp. 211-228.

——, "Decretalists, Medieval Papal Legation, and the Roman Law of Offices and Jurisdiction", *Res Publica Litterarum*, 9 (1986), pp. 119-135.

——, "'Legatus apostolice sedis': The Pope's 'Alter Ego' According to Thirteenth-century Canon Law", *Studi medievali*, 3d ser., 27 (1986), pp. 527-574.
——, "Papal Reserved Powers and the Limitations on Legatine Authority", in *Popes, Teachers, and Canon Law in the Middle Ages*, ed. James Ross Sweeney and Stanley Chodorow, Ithaca, Cornell University Press, 1989, pp. 191-211.
——, "Subdelegation by Papal Legates in Thirteenth-Century Canon Law: Powers and Limitations", in *In Iure Veritas: Studies in Canon Law in Memory of Schafer Williams*, eds Steven Bowman and Blanche Cody, Cincinnati, Univesity of Cincinnati, 1991, pp. 56-79.
——, "The Medieval Papal Legate and His Province: Geographical Limits of Jurisdiction", in *Plenitude of Power: The Doctrines and Exercise of Authority in the Middle Ages. Essays in Memory of Robert Louis Benson*, ed. Robert C. Figueira, Aldershot, Ashgate, 2006, pp. 73-105.
Filip, Václav and Karl Borchardt, *Schlesien, Georg von Podiebrad und die römische Kurie*, Würzburg, Verein für Geschichte Schlesiens, 2005.
Fisher, Sidney Nettleton, *The Foreign Relations of Turkey, 1481-1512*, Urbana, University of Illinois Press, 1948.
Fletcher, Stella, "The Making of a Fifteenth-century Venetian Cardinal", *Studi Veneziani*, n.s. 31 (1996), pp. 27-49.
——, "Cardinal Marco Barbo as Protector of English Interests at the Roman Curia in the Late Fifteenth Century", *The Downside Review*, 118 (2000), pp. 27-44.
——, *Cardinal Wolsey: A Life in Renaissance Europe*, London, Continuum, 2009.
Foa, Anna, "Chiericati, Leonello", in *DBI*, vol. 24, Roma, Istituto della Enciclopedia Italiana, 1980, pp. 682-689.
Fosi, Irene, "*'Parcere subiectis, debellare superbos'*: L'immagine della giustizia nelle cerimonie di possesso a Roma e nelle legazioni dello stato pontificio nel cinquecento", in *Cérémonial et rituel à Rome (XVIe-XIXe siècle)*, ed. Maria Antonietta Visceglia and Catherine Brice, Roma, École Française de Rome, 1997, pp. 89-115.
——, "Court and City in the Ceremony of the Possesso in the Sixteenth Century", in *Court and Politics in Papal Rome, 1492-1700*, ed. Gianvittorio Signorotto and Maria Antonietta Visceglia, Cambridge, Cambridge University Press, 2002, pp. 31-52.
Fragnito, Gigliola, "Carvajal, Bernardino Lopez de", in *DBI*, vol. 21, Roma, Istituto della Enciclopedia Italiana, 1978, pp. 28-34.
Fraknói, Vilmos, *Erdődi Bakócz Tamás élete*, Budapest, Méhner Vilmos, 1889.
——, *Pecchinoli Angelo: Pápai legátus Mátyás udvaránál (1488-1490)*, Budapest, Athenaeum, 1898 (Offprint from *Katholikus Szemle*, 12, 1898).
——, *Magyarország egyházi és politikai összeköttetései a Római szent-székkel*, vol. 2, *1418-1526, A konsztanczi zsinattól a mohácsi vészig*, Budapest, Szent-István-Társulat, 1902.
Frenz, Thomas, *Die Kanzlei der Päpste der Hochrenaissance (1471-1527)*, Tübingen, Max Niemeyer, 1986.
——, *Papsturkunden des Mittelalters und der Neuzeit*, 2nd ed., Stuttgart, Franz Steiner, 2000.
——, *Das Papsttum im Mittelalter*, Köln, Weimar and Wien, Böhlau, 2010.

Fubini, Riccardo, "L'ambasciatore nel XV secolo: due trattati e una biografia (Bernard de Rosier, Ermolao Barbaro, Vespasiano da Bisticci)", *Mélanges de l'Ecole française de Rome. Moyen-Âge*, 108 (1996), pp. 645-665.

Gardi, Andrea, "Parole di negoziatori? La trattatistica sul legato pontificio in età moderna", in *De l'ambassadeur: Les écrits relatifs à l'ambassadeur et à l'art de négocier du Moyen Âge au début du XIXe siècle*, ed. Stefano Andretta, Stéphane Péquignot and Jean-Claude Waquet, Roma, École Française de Rome, 2015, pp. 199-226.

Gilbert, Felix, *The Pope, His Banker, and Venice*, Cambridge, Mass. and London, Harvard University Press, 1980.

Goering, Joseph, "The Internal Forum and the Literature of Penance and Confession", in *The History of Medieval Canon Law in the Classical Period, 1140-1234: From Gratian to the Decretals of Pope Gregory IX*, ed. Wilfried Hartmann and Kenneth Pennington, Washington, D.C., The Catholic University of America Press, 2008, pp. 379-428.

Göller, Emil, "Aus der Kanzlei der Päpste und ihrer Legaten", *QFIAB*, 10 (1907), pp. 301-324.

——, "Zur Geschichte des päpstlichen Legationswesens im Ausgehenden 15. Jahrhundert", in *Festschrift Für Felix Porsch*, Paderborn, Ferdinand Schöningh, 1923, pp. 234-240.

——, "Untersuchungen über das Inventar des Finanzarchivs der Renaissance Päpste (1447-1521)", in *Miscellanea Francesco Ehrle*, vol. 5, Roma, Biblioteca Apostolica Vaticana, 1924, pp. 227-272.

Gómez Canedo, Lino, OFM, *Don Juan de Carvajal, cardenal de Sant'Angelo legado en Alemania y Hungria (1399?-1469): Un español al servicio de la Sante Sede*, Madrid, Instituto Jeronimo Zurita, 1947.

Gottlob, Adolf, "Der Legat Raimund Peraudi", *Historisches Jahrbuch*, 6 (1885), pp. 438-461.

——, *Aus der Camera Apostolica des 15. Jahrhunderts: Ein Beitrag zur Geschichte des päpstlichen Finanzwesens und des endenden Mittelalters*, Innsbruck, Wagner, 1889.

Graf, Karl, "Der Straßburger Gelehrte Johannes Hug und sein vergessenes Werk *Quadruvium ecclesiae* (Straßburg: Johann Grüninger 1504)", in *Humanisten am Oberrhein: Neue Gelehrte im Dienst alter Herren*, ed. Sven Lembke and Markus Müller, Leinfelden-Echterdingen, DRW-Verlag, 2004, pp. 175-187.

Gualdo, Germano, "Barbo, Marco", in *DBI*, vol. 6, Roma, Istituto della Enciclopedia Italiana, 1964, pp. 249-252.

Gualandi, Maria Letizia, "*Roma resurgens:* Fervore edilizio, trasformazioni urbanistiche e realizzazioni monumentali da Martino V Colonna a Paolo V Borghese", in *Roma del Rinascimento*, ed. Antonio Pinelli, Roma, Editori Laterza, 2001, pp. 123-160.

Hallman, Barbara McClung, *Italian Cardinals, Reform, and the Church as Property*, Berkeley, Los Angeles and London, University of California Press, 1985.

Hartmann, Wilfried and Kenneth Pennington, eds, *The History of Medieval Canon Law in the Classical Period, 1140-1234: From Gratian to the Decretals of Pope Gregory IX*, Washington D.C., The Catholic University of America Press, 2008.

Harvey, Margaret, *England, Rome and the Papacy, 1417-1464: A study of a Relationship*, Manchester and New York, Manchester University Press, 1993.

Hay, Denys, *The Church in Italy in the Fifteenth Century*, Cambridge, Cambridge University Press, 1977.

Hejnic, Josef and Miloslav Polívka, *Plzeň v husitské revoluci: Hilaria Litoměřického "Historie města Plzně", její edice a historický rozbor*, Praha, Academia, 1987.

Herbers, Klaus, Fernando López Alsina and Frank Engel, eds, *Das begrenzte Papsttum: Spielräume päpstlichen Handelns: Legaten - delegierte Richter - Grenzen*, Berlin and Boston, De Gruyter, 2013.

Hermann, Róbert, ed., *Kis magyar hadtörténet*, Budapest, Zrínyi Kiadó, 2013.

Heymann, Frederick G., *George of Bohemia: King of Heretics*, Princeton, N.J., Princeton University Press, 1965.

——, "The Crusades against the Hussites", in *A History of the Crusades*, ed. Kenneth M. Setton, vol. 3, *The Fourteenth and Fifteenth Centuries*, ed. Harry W. Hazard, Madison, University of Wisconsin Press, 1975, pp. 586-646.

Hlaváček, Petr, *Die böhmischen Franziskaner im ausgehenden Mittelalter: Studien zur Kirchen- und Kulturgeschichte Ostmitteleuropas*, Stuttgart, Franz Steiner, 2011.

Hledíková, Zdeňka, "Die Prager Erzbischöfe als ständige päpstliche Legaten. Ein Beitrag zur Kirchenpolitik Karls IV.", *Beiträge zur Geschichte des Bistums Regensburg*, 6 (1972), pp. 221-256.

Hofer, Johan, *Johannes Kapistran: Ein Leben im Kampf um die Reform der Kirche*, 2 vols., 2nd ed., Roma and Heidelberg, Editiones Franciscanae and F.H. Kerle Verlag, 1964-1965.

Höflechner, Walter, *Die Gesandten der europäischen Mächte, vornehmlich des Kaisers und des Reiches 1490-1500*, Wien, VÖAW, 1972 (Archiv für österreichische Geschichte, 129).

Holmes, G.A., "Cardinal Beaufort and the Crusade against the Hussites", *The English Historical Review*, 88 (1973), pp. 721-750.

Horst, Ulrich, *Autorität und Immunität des Papstes: Raphael de Pornassio OP und Julianus Tallada OP in der Auseinandersetzung mit dem Basler Konziliarismus*, Paderborn, Ferdinand Schöningh, 1991.

Housley, Norman, *The Later Crusades, 1274-1580: From Lyons to Alcazar*, Oxford, Oxford University Press, 1992.

——, *Religious Warfare in Europe, 1400-1536*, Oxford, Oxford University Press, 2002.

——, "Giovanni da Capistrano and the Crusade of 1456", in *Crusading in the Fifteenth Century: Message and Impact*, ed. Norman Housley, Basingstoke, Palgrave Macmillan, 2004, pp. 94-115.

——, "Indulgences for Crusading, 1417-1517", in *Promisory Notes on the Treasury of Merits: Indulgences in Late Medieval Europe*, ed. R. N. Swanson, Leiden and Boston, Brill, 2006, pp. 277-307.

——, *Crusading and the Ottoman Threat, 1453-1505*, Oxford, Oxford University Press, 2012.

——, ed., *Crusading in the Fifteenth Century: Message and Impact*, Basingstoke, Palgrave Macmillan, 2004.

——, ed., *The Crusade in the Fifteenth Century: Converging and competing cultures*, London and New York, Routledge, 2017.
——, ed., *Reconfiguring the Fifteenth-century Crusade*, London, Palgrave Macmillan, 2017.

Ilardi, Vincent, "Fifteenth-Century Diplomatic Documents in Western European Archives and Libraries (1450-1494)", *Studies in the Renaissance*, 9 (1962), pp. 64-112.
İnalcık, Halil, "A Case Study in Renaissance Diplomacy: the Agreement between Innocent VIII and Bayezid II on Djem Sultan", *Journal of Turkish Studies*, 3 (1979), pp. 209-223.
Izbicki, Thomas M., "Papalist Reaction to the Council of Constance: Juan de Torquemada to the Present", *Church History*, 55 (1986), pp. 7-20.

Jaritz, Gerhard, Torstein Jørgensen and Kirsi Salonen, eds, ... *et usque ad ultimum terrae: The Apostolic Penitentiary in Local Contexts*, Budapest, New York and Roma, Central European University, Department of Medieval Studies, Central European University and Hungarian Academy in Rome, 2007.

Kalous, Antonín, "Elfeledett források a mohácsi csatáról. Antonio Burgio pápai nuncius jelentései, és azok hadtörténeti jelentősége", *Hadtörténelmi Közlemények*, 120 (2007), pp. 603-621.
——, "Služba Boskovických u Matyáše Korvína", in *Sborník prací historických XXI. Acta Universitatis Palackianae Olomucensis, Facultas philosophica, Historica*, 33 (2007), pp. 83-99.
——, "Spor o biskupství olomoucké v letech 1482-1497", *Český časopis historický*, 105 (2007), pp. 1-39.
——, "Boskovice urai Mátyás király diplomáciai és politikai szolgálatában", *Századok*, 141 (2007), pp. 375-389.
——, "Papežský legát Marco Barbo, angelus pacis střední Evropy", in *Rituál smíření: Konflikt a jeho řešení ve středověku*, ed. Martin Nodl and Martin Wihoda, Brno, Matice moravská, 2008, pp. 159-171.
——, "Bohemians and Moravians in the Court of Matthias Corvinus", in *Matthias Corvinus, the King: Tradition and Renewal in the Hungarian Royal Court 1458-1490. Exhibition catalogue*, ed. Péter Farbaky, Enikő Spekner, Katalin Szende and András Végh, Budapest, Budapest History Museum, 2008, pp. 65-75.
——, *Matyáš Korvín (1443-1490): Uherský a český král*, České Budějovice, Veduta, 2009.
——, "The Politics of Church Unification: Efforts to Reunify the Utraquists and Rome in the 1520s", in *Friars, Nobles and Burghers. Sermons, Images and Prints: Studies of Culture and Society in Early-Modern Europe. In Memoriam István György Tóth*, ed. Jaroslav Miller and László Kontler, Budapest and New York, Central European University Press, 2010, pp. 179-197.
——, *Plenitudo potestatis in partibus? Papežští legáti a nunciové ve střední Evropě na konci středověku (1450-1526)*, Brno, Matice moravská, 2010.
——, "Tři týdny slávy, tři roky šťastného manželství: Beatrix a Matyáš", in *Manželství v pozdním středověku: Rituály a obyčeje*, ed. Paweł Kras and Martin Nodl, Praha, Filosofia, 2014, pp. 187-205.

——, "Středovýchodní Evropa na konci středověku: vývoj mezi konfliktem a integrací", in *Hledání nové Evropy: Projekt krále Jiřího*, ed. Jaroslav Boubín, Praha, Historický ústav, 2015, pp. 257-272.

——, "Financing a Legation: Papal Legates and Money in the Later Middle Ages", in *Money and Finance in Central Europe during the Later Middle Ages*, ed. Roman Zaoral, Basingstoke, Palgrave Macmillan, 2016, pp. 205-221.

——, "Late Medieval Nuptial Rites: Paride Grassi and the Royal Wedding of Székesfehérvár (Hungary) in 1502", *Questions Liturgiques / Studies in Liturgy*, 97 (2016), pp. 51-64.

——, "The Last Medieval King Leaves Buda", in *Medieval Buda in Context*, ed. Balázs Nagy, Martyn Rady, Katalin Szende and András Vadas, Leiden and Boston, Brill, 2016, pp. 513-25.

——, "The Papacy and the Czech Lands between Reform and Reformation (1417-1527)", in *The Papacy and the Czech Lands: A History of Mutual Relations*, ed. Tomáš Černušák, Roma and Praha, Institute of History and Istituto Storico Ceco di Roma, 2016, pp. 115-146.

——, "Papal Legates and Crusading Activity in Central Europe: The Hussites and the Ottoman Turks", in *The Crusade in the Fifteenth Century: Converging and Competing Cultures*, ed. Norman Housley, London, Routledge, 2017, pp. 75-89.

——, "Through the Gates and the Streets of the City: Cardinals and their Processions in Rome in the Late Fifteenth and Early Sixteenth Centuries", in *Ritualizing the City: Collective Performances as Aspects of Urban Construction from Constantine to Mao*, ed. Ivan Foletti and Adrien Palladino, Roma, Viella, 2017, pp. 29-44.

——, "King Matthias Corvinus and the papacy in early 1472: Miklós Nyújtódi Székely in Rome", *Povijesni prilozi*, 36, vol. 52 (2017), pp. 7-27.

——, "Cardinal legate Tamás Bakóc and the Utraquists", in *V Concilio Lateranense*, ed. Nelson Minnich, in print.

Kaminsky, Howard, "Pius Aeneas Among the Taborites", *Church History*, 28 (1959), pp. 281-309.

——, *A History of the Hussite Revolution*, Berkeley and Los Angeles, University of California Press, 1967.

Kipling, Gordon, *Enter the King: Theatre, Liturgy, and Ritual in the Medieval Civic Triumph*, Oxford, Clarendon Press, 1998.

Kleinert, Christian, *Philibert de Montjeu (ca. 1374-1439): Ein Bischof im Zeitalter der Reformkonzilien und des Hundertjährigen Krieges*, Ostfildern, Jan Thorbecke, 2004.

Koller, Alexander, ed., *Kurie und Politik: Stand und Perspektiven der Nuntiaturberichtsforschung*, Tübingen, Max Niemeyer, 1998.

König, Erich, *Kardinal Giordano Orsini († 1438): Ein Lebensbild aus der Zeit der großen Konzilien und des Humanismus*, Freiburg im Breisgau, Herder, 1906.

Kowalski, Marek Daniel, "Baptysty Enriciego z Rzymu, biskupa Camerino, legacja do Polski w 1448 roku", in *Memoria viva. Studia historyczne poświęcone pamięci Izabeli Skierskiej (1967-2014)*, Warsaw and Poznań, Instytut Historii Polskiej Akademii Nauk, 2015, pp. 573-588.

Krofta, Kamil, "Kurie a církevní správa zemí českých v době předhusitské", *Český časopis historický*, 10 (1904), pp. 15-36, 125-152, 249-275, 373-391; 12 (1906), pp. 7-34, 178-191, 274-298, 426-446; 14 (1908), pp. 18-34, 172-196, 273-287, 416-435.

Krüger, Thomas Michael, "Überlieferung und Relevanz der päpstlichen Wahlkapitulationen (1352-1522): Zur Verfassungsgeschichte von Papsttum und Kardinalat", *QFIAB*, 81 (2001), pp. 227-255.

Kubinyi, András, *Főpapok, egyházi intézmények és vallásosság a középkori Magyarországon*, Budapest, METEM, 1999.

——, "The Hungarian State and the Papacy during the Reign of Jagello Kings (1490-1526)", in *A Thousand Years of Christianity in Hungary: Hungariae Christianae Millenium*, ed. István Zombori, Pál Cséfalvy and Maria Antonietta De Angelis, Budapest, Hungarian Catholic Episcopal Conference, 2001, pp. 79-85 (Hung. version with notes, see Kubinyi, *Főpapok*, pp. 107-121).

——, *Matthias Rex*, Budapest, Balassi Kiadó, 2008.

Kuczyński, Stefan M., *Wielka wojna z Zakonem Krzyżackim w latach 1409-1411*, Warszawa, Wydawnictwo Ministerstwa obrony narodowej, 1955 (with many later editions).

Kühne, Hartmut, "Raimund Peraudi und der Türkenkreuzzugsablass in Deutschland: Zwei unbekannte Drucke", in *Alltag und Frömmigkeit am Vorabend der Reformation in Mitteldeutschland*, ed. Enno Bünz and Hartmut Kühne, Leipzig, Universitätsverlag, 2015, pp. 429-470.

——, "Magdeburg und der Ablass am Vorabend der Reformation", in *Magdeburg und die Reformation*, vol. 1, *Eine Stadt folgt Martin Luther*, ed. Maren Ballerstedt, Gabriele Köster and Cornelia Poenicke, Halle, Mitteldeutscher Verlag, 2016, pp. 23-55.

Kuttner, Stephan, "Cardinalis: The History of a Canonical Concept", *Traditio*, 3 (1945), pp. 129-214.

——, *The History of Ideas and Doctrines of Canon Law in the Middle Ages*, London, Variorum Reprints, 1980.

——, "The Revival of Jurisprudence", in *Renaissance and Renewal in the Twelfth Century*, ed. Robert L. Benson, Giles Constable and Carol D. Lanham, Cambridge, Mass., Harvard University Press, 1982, pp. 299-323.

Kyer, Clifford Ian, "*Legatus* and *nuntius* as used to denote papal envoys, 1245-1378", *Medieval Studies*, 40 (1978), pp. 473-477.

——, *The Papal Legate and the "Solemn" Papal Nuncio 1243-1378: The Changing Pattern of Papal Representation*, PhD Dissertation, University of Toronto, 1979.

——, "The legation of Cardinal Latinus and William Duranti's 'Speculum legatorum'", *Bulletin of Medieval Canon Law*, n.s. 10 (1980), pp. 56-62.

Labande, Léon-Honoré, *Avignon au XVᵉ siècle: Légations de Charles de Bourbon et du cardinal Julien de La Rovère*, Marseille, Laffitte reprints, 1975 (orig. 1920).

Landau, Peter, *Jus Patronatus: Studien zur Entwicklung des Patronats im Dekretalenrecht und der Kanonistik des 12. und 13. Jahrhunderts*, Köln and Wien, Böhlau, 1975.

Lazzarini, Isabella, *Communication and Conflict: Italian Diplomacy in the Early Renaissance, 1350-1520*, Oxford, Oxford University Press, 2015.

Lesage, Georges-L., "La titulature des envoyés pontificaux sous Pie II (1458-1464)", *Mélanges d'archéologie et d'histoire*, 58 (1941), pp. 206-242.

——, "Note sur les envoyés pontificaux sous Paul II (1464-1471)", *Mélanges d'archéologie et d'histoire*, 58 (1941), pp. 243-247.

Lunt, William E., *Papal Revenues in the Middle Ages*, 2 vols., New York, Columbia University Press, 1934 (rpt. New York, Octagon Books, 1965).

Lützelschwab, Ralf, *Flectat cardinales ad velle suum? Clemens VI. und sein Kardinalskolleg: Ein Beitrag zur kurialen Politik in der Mitte des 14. Jahrhunderts*, München, Oldenbourg, 2007.

Macek, Josef, "K zahraniční politice krále Jiřího", *Československý časopis historický*, 13 (1965), pp. 19-48.

——, "Prag und Rom am Ende des 15. Jahrhunderts: Zum Verhältnis der päpstlichen Kurie zur böhmischen Reformation", in *Historische Blickpunkte: Festschrift für Johann Rainer. Zum 65. Geburtstag dargebracht von Freunden, Kollegen und Schülern*, ed. S. Weiss, Innsbruck, AMOE, 1988, pp. 391-403.

——, *Víra a zbožnost Jagellonského věku*, Praha, Argo, 2001.

Maciejewski, Jacek, *Adventus Episcopi: Pozaliturgiczne aspekty inauguracji władzy biskupiej w Polsce średniowiecznej na tle europejskim*, Bydgoszcz, Wydawnictwo Uniwersytetu Kazimierza Wielkiego w Bydgoszczy, 2013.

Maleczek, Werner, "Die päpstlichen Legaten im 14. und 15. Jahrhundert", in *Gesandtschafts- und Botenwesen im spätmittelalterlichen Europa*, ed. Rainer C. Schwinges and Klaus Wriedt, Ostfildern, Jan Thorbecke, 2003, pp. 33-86.

Mallett, Michael, "Ambassadors and their audiences in Renaissance Italy", *Renaissance Studies*, 8 (1994), pp. 229-243.

Mályusz, Elemér, *Das Konstanzer Konzil und das königliche Patronatsrecht in Ungarn*, Budapest, Akadémiai Kiadó, 1959.

Margaroli, Paolo, *Diplomazia e stati rinascimentali: le ambascerie sforzesche fino alla conclusione della Lega italica (1450-1455)*, Firenze, La Nuova Italia, 1992.

Martines, Lauro, *Power and Imagination: City-States in Renaissance Italy*, Baltimore, The Johns Hopkins University Press, 1988 (orig. 1979).

Märtl, Claudia, "Zwischen Habitus und Repräsentation: Der kardinalizische Ornat am Ende des Mittelalters", in *Die Kardinäle des Mittelalters und der frühen Renaissance*, ed. Jürgen Dendorfer and Ralf Lützelschwab, Firenze, Sismel - Edizioni del Galuzzo, 2013, pp. 265-300.

Mastrocola, Mario, *Note storiche circa le diocesi di Civita C., Orte e Gallese*, part 3, *I Vescovi dalla Unione delle Diocesi alla fine del Concilio di Trento (1437-1564)*, Civita Castellana, Pian Paradisi, 1972.

Mattingly, Garrett, "The First Resident Embassies: Mediaeval Italian Origins of Modern Diplomacy", *Speculum*, 12 (1937), pp. 423-439.

——, *Renaissance Diplomacy*, Harmondsworth, Penguin, 1965 (orig. 1955).

Meuthen, Erich, "Zum Itinerar der deutschen Legation Bessarions (1460-1461)", *QFIAB*, 37 (1957), pp. 192-221.

——, "Die deutsche Legationsreise des Nikolaus von Kues 1451/1452", in *Lebenslehren und Weltentwürfe im Übergang vom Mittelalter zur Neuzeit*, ed. H. Boockmann, B. Moeller and K. Stackmann, Göttingen, Vanderhoeck & Ruprecht, 1989, pp. 421-499.

——, "Das Itinerar der deutschen Legationsreise des Nikolaus von Kues 1451/1452", in *Papstgeschichte und Landesgeschichte: Festschrift für Hermann Jakobs zum 65. Geburtstag*, ed. Joachim Dahlhaus and Armin Kohnle, Köln, Weimar and Wien, Böhlau, 1995, pp. 473-502.

Meyer, Andreas, "Das Wiener Konkordat von 1448. Eine erfolgreiche Reform des Spätmittelalters", *QFIAB*, 66 (1986), pp. 108-152.

——, "The Curia: The Apostolic Chancery", in *A Companion to Medieval Papacy*, ed. Keith Sisson and Atria A. Larson, Leiden and Boston, Brill, 2016, pp. 239-258.

Miller, Maureen C., "The Florentine Bishop's Ritual Entry and the Origins of the Medieval Episcopal Adventus", *Revue d'Histoire Ecclesiastique*, 98 (2003), pp. 5-28.

Minnich, Nelson H., "The Closing of the Fifth Lateran Council (1512-1517)", *Archivum Historiae Pontificiae*, 45 (2013), pp. 17-58.

Mohler, Ludwig, *Kardinal Bessarion als Theologe, Humanist und Staatsmann*, vol. 1, *Darstellung*, Paderborn, Ferdinand Schöningh, 1923; vol. 3, *Aus Bessarions Gelehrtenkreis: Abhandlungen, Reden, Briefe*, Paderborn, Ferdinand Schöningh, 1942.

Monaco, Michele, "The Instructions of Alexander VI to his Ambassadors Sent to Louis XII in 1498", *Renaissance Studies*, 2 (1988), pp. 251-257.

Morris, Colin, *The Papal Monarchy: The Western Church from 1050 to 1250*, Oxford, Clarendon Press, 1989.

Mortier, Daniel Antonin, *Histoire des maitres généraux de l'ordre des frères prêcheurs*, vol. 4, *1400-1486*, Paris, Alph. Picard, 1909.

Müller, Harald, "The Omnipresent Pope: Legates and Judges Delegate", in *A Companion to Medieval Papacy*, ed. Keith Sisson and Atria A. Larson, Leiden and Boston, Brill, 2016, pp. 199-219.

Müller, Heribert, ed., *Das Ende des konziliaren Zeitalters (1440-1450): Versuch einer Bilanz*, München, Oldenbourg, 2012.

Mureşan, Dan Ioan, "Girolamo Lando, titulaire du Patriarcat de Constantinople (1474-1497), et son rôle dans la politique orientale du Saint-Siège", *Annuario dell'Istituto Romeno di Cultura et Ricerca Umanistica di Venezia*, 8 (2006), pp. 153-258.

——, "Kardinálské kolegium jako "generální štáb": Křižácké plány z let 1464-1469 a kardinál Bessarion", in *Křížové výpravy v pozdním středověku: Kapitoly z dějin náboženských konfliktů*, ed. Pavel Soukup and Jaroslav Svátek, Praha, Nakladatelství Lidové noviny, 2010.

Nehring, Karl, *Matthias Corvinus, Kaiser Friedrich III. und das Reich: Zum hunyadisch-habsburgischen Gegensatz im Donauraum*, 2nd ed., München, Oldenbourg, 1989.

Nemes, Gábor, "Elszalasztott lehetőségek: VII. Kelemen pápa és II. Lajos országainak belpolitikája (1523-1526)", *Egyháztörténeti Szemle*, 15, no. 4 (2014), pp. 3-19.

——, "Pápai követek a Mohács előtti Magyarországon", *Századok*, 150 (2016), pp. 369-385.

Nörr, Knut Wolfgang, "Institutional Foundations of the New Jurisprudence", in *Renaissance and Renewal in the Twelfth Century*, ed. Robert L. Benson, Giles Constable and Carol D. Lanham, Cambridge, Mass., Harvard University Press, 1982, pp. 324-338.

Nowak, Jessika, *Ein Kardinal im Zeitalter der Renaissance: Die Karriere des Giovanni di Castiglione (ca. 1413-1460)*, Tübingen, Mohr Siebeck, 2011.

Oakley, Francis, *The Conciliarist Tradition: Constitutionalism in the Catholic Church 1300-1870*, Oxford, Oxford University Press, 2003.

Odložilík, Otakar, *The Hussite King: Bohemia in European Affairs, 1440-1471*, New Brunswick, N.J., Rutgers University Press, 1965.
Ollendiek, Hans, *Die päpstlichen Legaten im deutschen Reichsgebiet von 1261 bis zum Ende des Interregnums*, Freiburg, Universitätsverlag, 1976.
Opll, Ferdinand, "Das Archiv eines päpstlichen Legaten aus der zweiten Hälfte des 15. Jahrhunderts: Ein Bestand im Wiener Stadt- und Landesarchiv", in *Städtische Wirtschaft im Mittelalter: Festschrift für Franz Irsigler zum 70. Geburtstag*, ed. Rudolf Holbach and Michel Pauly, Köln, Weimar and Wien, Böhlau, 2011.

Palacky, Franz, *Geschichte von Böhmen*, 5 vols., Praha, Kronberger, later Friedrich Tempsky, 1836-1867.
Paravicini-Bagliani, Agostino, *The Pope's Body*, trans. David S. Peterson, Chicago and London, University of Chicago Press, 2000.
Paro, Gino, *The Right of Papal Legation*, Washington, D.C., The Catholic University of America Press, 1947.
Partner, Peter, *The Lands of St. Peter: The Papal State in the Middle Ages and the Early Renaissance*, Berkeley, University of California Press, 1972.
——, "Papal Financial Policy in the Renaissance and Counter-Reformation", *Past and Present*, 88 (1980), pp. 17-62.
——, *The Pope's Men: The Papal Civil Service in the Renaissance*, Oxford, Oxford University Press, 1990.
Paschini, Pio, *Leonello Chieregato: Nunzio d'Innocenzo VIII e di Alessandro VI*, Roma, Facultas theologica pontificii Athenaei seminarii Romani, 1935.
——, *Roma nel Rinascimento*, Bologna, Licinio Cappelli, 1940.
——, "I benefici ecclesiastici del cardinale Marco Barbo", *Rivista di storia della chiesa in Italia*, 13 (1959), pp. 335-354.
Pastor, Ludwig, *Geschichte der Päpste seit dem Ausgang des Mittelalters*, vols. 1-4, Freiburg im Breisgau, Herder, 1923-1925.
Pastore, Alessandro, "Giulio II", in *Enciclopedia dei papi*, vol. 3, S.l., Istituto della Enciclopedia Italiana, 2000, pp. 31-42.
Paul, Herman, "A Weberian medievalist: Hayden White in the 1950s", *Rethinking History*, 12 (2008), pp. 75-112.
Paulus, Nikolaus, "Raimund Peraudi als Ablaßkommissar", *Historisches Jahrbuch*, 21 (1900), pp. 645-682.
Pavloff, George G., *Papal Judge Delegates at the Time of the Corpus Iuris Canonici*, Washington, D.C., The Catholic University of America Press, 1963.
Pellegrini, Marco, "Pio II", in *Enciclopedia dei papi*, vol. 2, S.l., Istituto della Enciclopedia Italiana, 2000, pp. 663-685.
——, "Innocenzo VIII", in *Enciclopedia dei papi*, vol. 3. S.l., Istituto della Enciclopedia Italiana, 2000, pp. 1-13.
——, "A Turning-Point in the History of the Factional System in the Sacred College: The Power of Pope and Cardinals in the Age of Alexander VI.", in *Court and Politics in Papal Rome, 1492-1700*, ed. Gianvittorio Signorotto and Maria Antonietta Visceglia, Cambridge, Cambridge University Press, 2002, pp. 8-30.
——, *Il papato nel Rinascimento*, Bologna, il Mulino, 2010.

——, "Das Kardinalskolleg von Sixtus IV. bis Alexander VI. (1471-1503)", in *Geschichte des Kardinalats im Mittelalter*, ed. Jürgen Dendorfer and Ralf Lützelschwab, Stuttgart, Anton Hiersemann, 2011, pp. 399-445.

——, *Le crociate dopo le crociate: Da Nicopoli a Belgrado (1396-1456)*, Bologna, il Mulino, 2013.

——, "Il sacro collegio cardinalizio tra rinascimento e controriforma: Orientamenti tematici e bibliografici", in *Die Kardinäle des Mittelalters und der frühen Renaissance*, ed. Jürgen Dendorfer and Ralf Lützelschwab, Firenze, Sismel - Edizioni del Galuzzo, 2013, pp. 321-356.

——, *La crociata nel Rinascimento: Mutazioni di un mito 1400-1600*, Firenze, Le lettere, 2014.

Pennington, Kenneth, "Johannes Teutonicus and Papal Legates", *Archivum Historiae Pontificiae*, 21 (1983), pp. 183-194.

——, *Pope and Bishops: The Papal Monarchy in the Twelfth and Thirteenth Centuries*, Philadelphia, University of Pennsylvania Press, 1984.

——, *Popes, Canonists and Texts, 1150-1550*, Aldershot, Variorum, 1993.

——, "The Canonists and Pluralism in the Thirteenth Century", *Speculum*, 51 (1976), pp. 35-48.

——, "Ecclesiastical Liberty on the Eve of the Reformation", *Bulletin of Medieval Canon Law*, 33 (2016), pp. 185-207.

Perrin, John W., "Legatus, the Lawyers and the Terminology of Power in Roman Law", *Studia Gratiana*, 11 (1967), pp. 461-489.

——, "'Legatus' in Medieval Roman Law", *Traditio*, 29 (1973), pp. 357-378.

Persico, Tommaso, *Diomede Carafa: Uomo di stato e scrittore del secolo XV*, Napoli, Luigi Pierro, 1899.

Petersohn, Jürgen, *Ein Diplomat des Quattrocento: Angelo Geraldini (1422-1486)*, Tübingen, Max Niemeyer, 1985.

——, *Kaiserlicher Gesandter und Kurienbischof: Andreas Jamometić am Hof Papst Sixtus IV. (1478-1481)*, Hannover, Hahnsche Buchhandlung, 2004.

Petrucci, Franca, "Carafa, Diomede", in *DBI*, vol. 19, Roma, Istituto della Enciclopedia Italiana, 1976, pp. 524-530.

Picotti, Giovanni Battista, "Castiglione, Branda da", in *DBI*, vol. 22, Roma, Istituto della Enciclopedia Italiana, 1979, pp. 69-75.

Pillinini, Giovanni, *Il sistema degli stati italiani, 1454-1494*, Venezia, Libreria universitaria, 1970.

Pletzer, Karel, "České Budějovice za Matyáše Korvína (1468-1490)", in *Minulost a současnost Českých Budějovic. Studie a materiály I*, České Budějovice, 1969, pp. 17-56.

Pongrácz, Sörös and Tibold Rezner, eds, *A pannonhalmi főapátság története*, vol. 3, *Az uralkodók reformáló törekvései a pannonhalmi apátságnak főapátsággá való szervezése, 1405-1535*, Budapest, Stephaneum, 1905 (A pannonhalmi szent-Benedek-rend története, 3).

Queller, Donald E., "Thirteenth-Century Diplomatic Envoys: *Nuncii* and *Procuratores*", *Speculum*, 35 (1960), pp. 196-213.

——, *The Office of the Ambassador in the Middle Ages*, Princeton, NJ, Princeton University Press, 1967.

Radziszewska, Julia, "Działalność dyplomatyczna Rudolfa von Rüdesheim", *Prace historyczne*, 1 (1964), pp. 7-44.

Rapp, Francis, *L'Église et la vie religieuse en Occident à la fin du Moyen âge*, Paris, Presses Universitaires de France, 1971.

Rehberg, Andreas, "Die Kardinäle aus Rom und die Macht der Klientelbeziehungen (1277-1527)", in *Die Kardinäle des Mittelalters und der frühen Renaissance*, ed. Jürgen Dendorfer and Ralf Lützelschwab, Firenze, Sismel - Edizioni del Galuzzo, 2013, pp. 55-109.

——, ed., *Ablasskampagnen des Spätmittelalters: Luthers Thesen von 1517 im Kontext*, Berlin and Boston, De Gruyter Mouton, 2017.

Rennie, Kriston R., *The Foundations of Medieval Papal Legation*, Basingstoke, Palgrave Macmillan, 2013.

——, "The 'Injunction of Jeremiah': papal politicking and power in the Middle Ages", *Journal of Medieval History*, 40 (2014), pp. 108-122.

Richard, P., "Origines de la nonciature de France: Nonces résidants avant Léon X, 1456-1511", *Revue des questions historiques*, 40, tome 78 (1905), pp. 103-147.

——, "Origines de la nonciature de France: Débuts de la représentation permanente sous Léon X, 1513-1521", *Revue des questions historiques*, 41, tome 80 (1906), pp. 112-180.

Richardson, Carol M., *Reclaiming Rome: Cardinals in the Fifteenth Century*, Leiden and Boston, Brill, 2009.

Righi, Davide, *Il "sacerdotale" di Alberto da Castello e le sue numerose edizioni (1523-1603): Analisi delle edizioni e della struttura del "Liber sacerdotalis". Una introduzione allo studio del testo e delle fonti*, Tesi per il conseguimento della Licenza in Sacra Teologia, Istituto di Liturgia pastorale, Padova, 2013.

Riley-Smith, Jonathan, *The First Crusade and the Idea of Crusading*, London and New York, Continuum, 2003 (orig. 1986).

Rill, Gerhard and Giuseppe Scichilone, "Burgio, Giovanni Antonio Buglio barone di", in *DBI*, vol. 15, Roma, Istituto della Enciclopedia Italiana, 1972, pp. 413-417.

Rivière, Jean, "In partem sollicitudinis… evolution d'une formule papale", *Revue des Sciences Religieuses*, 5 (1925), pp. 210-231.

Rizzi, Marco, "'Plenitudo potestatis': dalla teologia politica alla teoria dello stato assoluto", in *Images, cultes, liturgies: Les connotations politiques du message religieux / Immagini, culti, liturgie: Le connotazioni politiche del messaggio religioso: Actes du premier atelier international du projet Les vecteurs de l'idéel. Le pouvoir symbolique entre Moyen Âge et Renaissance (v. 1200-v. 1640)*, ed. Paola Ventrone and Laura Gaffuri, Roma and Paris, École Française de Rome and Publications de la Sorbonne, 2014, pp. 49-60.

Robinson, Ian Stuart, "'Periculosus Homo': Pope Gregory VII and Episcopal Authority", *Viator*, 9 (1978), pp. 103-131.

——, "Church and Papacy", in *The Cambridge History of Medieval Political Thought c. 350-c. 1450*, ed. J.H. Burns, Cambridge, Cambridge University Press, 1988, pp. 252-305.

——, *The Papacy, 1073-1198: Continuity and Innovation*, Cambridge, Cambridge University Press, 1990.

——, "Reform and the Church, 1073-1122", in *The New Cambridge Medieval History*, vol. 4, c. 1024-c. 1198, pt. 1, ed. David Luscombe and Jonathan Riley-Smith, Cambridge, Cambridge University Press, 2004, pp. 268-334.

——, "The institutions of the church, 1073-1216", in *The New Cambridge Medieval History*, vol. 4, c. 1024-c. 1198, pt. 1, ed. David Luscombe and Jonathan Riley-Smith, Cambridge, Cambridge University Press, 2004, pp. 368-460.

Rollo-Koster, Joëlle, *Avignon and Its Papacy, 1309-1417: Popes, Institutions, and Society*, Lanham, MD, Rowman and Littlefield, 2015.

Ruess, Karl, *Die rechtliche Stellung der päpstlichen Legaten bis Bonifaz VIII.*, Paderborn, Ferdinand Schöningh, 1912.

Runciman, Steven, *A History of the Crusades*, 3 vols., Cambridge, Cambridge University Press, 1988 (orig. 1951-1954).

Ryan, Christopher, ed., *The Religious Roles of the Papacy: Ideals and Realities 1150-1300*, Toronto, Pontifical Institute of Mediaeval Studies, 1989.

Salmon, Pierre, *Les manuscrits liturgiques latins de la Bibliothèque vaticane*, vol. 3, *Ordines Romani, pontificaux, rituels, cérémoniaux*, Città de Vaticano, Biblioteca Apostolica Vaticana, 1970.

Salonen, Kirsi, *The Penitentiary as a Well of Grace in the Late Middle Ages: The Example of the Province of Uppsala 1448-1527*, Saarijärvi, Academia Scientiarum Fennica, 2001.

——, "The Curia: The Apostolic Penitentiary", in *A Companion to Medieval Papacy*, ed. Keith Sisson and Atria A. Larson, Leiden and Boston, Brill, 2016, pp. 259-275.

——, "The Curia: The Sacra Romana Rota", in *A Companion to Medieval Papacy*, ed. Keith Sisson and Atria A. Larson, Leiden and Boston, Brill, 2016, pp. 276-288.

——, *Papal Justice in the Later Middle Ages: The Sacra Romana Rota*, London and New York, Routledge, 2016.

Salonen, Kirsi and Jussi Hanska, *Entering a Clerical Career at the Roman Curia, 1458-1471*, Farnham, Ashgate, 2013.

Salonen, Kirsi and Ludwig Schmugge, *A Sip from the "Well of Grace": Medieval Texts from the Apostolic Penitentiary*, Washington, D.C., The Catholic University of America Press, 2009.

Savettieri, Chiara, "Lo spettacolo del potere: i luoghi, i simboli, le feste", in *Roma del Rinascimento*, ed. Antonio Pinelli, Roma, Editori Laterza, 2001, pp. 161-198.

Sayers, Jane E., *Papal Judges Delegate in the Province of Canterbury 1198-1254: A Study in Ecclesiastical Jurisdiction and Administration*, Oxford, Oxford University Press, 1971.

Scharf, Gian Paolo, "Maraschi (Marasca, de Maraschis), Bartolomeo", in *DBI*, vol. 69, Roma, Istituto della Enciclopedia Italiana, 2007, pp. 439-442.

Schimmelpfennig, Bernhard, *Die Zeremonienbücher der römischen Kurie im Mittelalter*, Tübingen, Max Niemeyer, 1973.

——, *The Papacy*, New York, Columbia University Press, 1992 (orig. 1984).

Schlecht, Joseph, *Andrea Zamometić und der Basler Konzilsversuch vom Jahre 1482*, Paderborn, Ferdinand Schöningh, 1903.

Schmauch, Hans, "Der Kampf zwischen dem ermländischen Bischof Nikolaus von Tüngen und Polen oder Der Pfaffenkrieg (1467-1479)", *Zeitschrift für die Geschichte und Altertumskunde Ermlands*, 25 (1935), pp. 69-186.

Schmid, Peter, "Der päpstliche Legat Raimund Peraudi und die Reichsversammlungen der Jahre 1501-1503: Zum Prozeß der Entfremdung zwischen Reich und Rom in der Regierungszeit König Maximilians I.", in *Reichstage und Kirche*, ed. Erich Meuthen, Göttingen, Vanderhoeck & Ruprecht, 1991, pp. 65-88.

Schmugge, Ludwig, *Kirche, Kinder, Karrieren: Päpstliche Dispenze von der unehelichen Geburt im Spätmittelalter*, Zürich, Artemis und Winkler, 1995.

Schmugge, Ludwig, Patrick Hersperger and Béatrice Wiggenahuser, *Die Supplikenregister der päpstlichen Pönitentiarie aus der Zeit Pius' II. (1458-1464)*, Tübingen, Max Niemeyer, 1996.

Schumann, Otto, *Die päpstlichen Legaten in Deutschalnd zur Zeit Heinrichs IV. und Heinrichs V. (1056-1125)*, Marburg, Joh. Aug. Koch, 1912.

Schmutz, Richard Antone, *The Foundations of Medieval Papal Representation*, PhD Dissertation, University of Southern California, 1966. [microfilm: Ann Arbor, Michigan 1967]

——, "Medieval Papal Representatives: Legates, Nuncios, and Judges-delegate", *Studia Gratiana*, 15 (1972), pp. 441-463.

Schuchard, Christine, *Die päpstliche Kollektoren im späten Mittelalter*, Tübingen, Max Niemeyer, 2000.

Schwinges, Rainer C. and Klaus Wriedt, eds, *Gesandtschafts- und Botenwesen im spätmittelalterlichen Europa*, Ostfildern, Jan Thorbecke, 2003 (Vorträge und Forschungen, Bd. 60).

Setton, Kenneth M., *The Papacy and the Levant (1204-1571)*, 4 vols., Philadelphia, The American Philosophical Society, 1976-1984.

Shaffern, Robert W., *The Penitents' Treasury: Indulgences in Latin Christendom, 1175-1375*, Scranton and London, University of Scranton Press, 2007.

Shogimen, Takashi, "The Relationship between Theology and Canon Law. Another Context of Political Thought in the Early Fourteenth Century", *Journal of the History of Ideas*, 60 (1999), pp. 417-431.

——, *Ockham and Political Discourse in the Late Middle Ages*, Cambridge, Cambridge University Press, 2007.

Sisson, Keith and Atria A. Larson, eds, *A Companion to the Medieval Papacy: Growth of an Ideology and Institution*, Leiden and Boston, Brill, 2016.

Skalweit, Stephan, "Campeggi, Lorenzo", in *DBI*, vol. 17, Roma, Istituto della Enciclopedia Italiana, 1974, pp. 454-462.

Skýbová, Anna, "Česká šlechta a jednání o povolení kompaktát r. 1525", *Acta Universitatis Carolinae, Philosophica et Historica*, 1 (1976), pp. 81-108.

Šmahel, František, *Die Hussitische Revolution*, 3 vols., Hannover, Hahnsche Buchhandlung, 2002.

Smolinsky, Heribert, "Dominici, Domenico (Domenico de' Domenichi)", in *DBI*, vol. 40, Roma, Istituto della Enciclopedia Italiana, 1991, pp. 691-695.

Smołucha, Janusz, *Papiestwo a Polska w latach 1484-1526. Kontakty dyplomatyczne na tle zagrożenia tureckiego*, Kraków, Societas Vistulana, 1999.

——, *Polityka kurii rzymskiej za pontyfikatu Piusa II (1458-1464) wobec Czech i krajów sąsednich. Z dziejów dyplomacji papieskiej w XV wieku*, Kraków, Księgarnia Akademicka, 2008.

Soukup, Pavel, "Crusading against Christians in the Fifteenth Century: Doubts and Debates", in *Reconfiguring the Fifteenth-Century Crusade*, ed. Norman Housley, London, Palgrave Macmillan, 2017, pp. 85-122.

Southern, R.W., *Western Society and the Church in the Middle Ages*, London, Penguin, 1970.

Stein, Peter, *Roman Law in European History*, Cambridge, Cambridge University Press, 1999.

Stinger, Charles L., *The Renaissance in Rome*, Bloomington and Indianapolis, Indiana University Press, 1998.

Stöve, Eckehart, "Ferreri, Zaccaria," in *DBI*, vol. 46, Roma, Istituto dell'Enciclopedia Italiana, 1996 (http://www.treccani.it/enciclopedia/zaccaria-ferreri_(Dizionario-Biografico)\).

Strnad, Alfred A., "Francesco Todeschini-Piccolomini. Politik und Mäzenatentum im Quattrocento", *Römische historische Mitteilungen*, 8/9 (1964/65-1965/66), pp. 104-425.

Strnad, Alfred A., and Katherine Walsh, "Cesarini, Giuliano", in *DBI*, vol. 24, Roma, Istituto della Enciclopedia Italiana, 1980, pp. 188-195.

Studt, Birgit, "Legationen als Instrumente päpstlicher Reform- und Kreuzzugspropaganda im 15. Jahrhundert", in *Formen und Funktionen öffentlicher Kommunikation im Mittelalter*, ed. Gerd Althoff, Stuttgart, Jan Thorbecke, 2001, pp. 421-453 (Vörträge und Forschungen, Bd. 51).

——, *Papst Martin V (1417-1431) und die Kirchenreform in Deutschland*, Köln, Weimar and Wien, Böhlau, 2004.

——, "Anspruch und Wirklichkeit: Der Wandel von Handlungsspielräumen und Reichweite päpstlicher Diplomatie im 15. Jahrhundert", in *Aus der Frühzeit europäischer Diplomatie: Zum geistlichen und weltlichen Gesandtschaftswesen vom 12. bis zum 15. Jahrhundert*, ed. Claudia Zey and Claudia Märtl, Zürich, Chronos, 2008, pp. 85-118.

Sullivan, Donald, "Nicholas of Cusa as Reformer: the Papal Legation to the Germanies, 1451-1452", *Medieval Studies*, 36 (1974), pp. 382-428.

Swanson, R. N., ed., *Promisory Notes on the Treasury of Merits: Indulgences in Late Medieval Europe*, Leiden and Boston, Brill, 2006.

Szczur, Stanisław, *Skarbovość papieska w Polsce w latach 1378-1431*, Kraków, Societas Vistulana, 2008.

Taurisano, Innocentius, *Hierarchia Ordinis Praedicatorum*, pt. 1, Roma, 1916.

Tecniche di potere nel tardo medioevo: Regimi comunali e signorie in Italia, ed. Massimo Vallerani, Roma, Viella, 2010.

Thomson, John A.F., *Popes and Princes, 1417-1517: Politics and Polity in the Late Medieval Church*, London, George Allen & Unwin, 1980.

Thuasne, Louis, *Djem-Sultan: fils de Mohammed II, frère de Bayezid II (1459-1495)*, Paris, Ernest Leroux, 1892.

Tierney, Brian, *Origins of Papal Infallibility 1150-1350: A Study on the Concepts of Infallibility, Sovereignty and Tradition in the Middle Ages*, Leiden, Brill, 1972.

——, *The Foundations of the Conciliar Theory: The Contribution of the Medieval Canonists from Gratian to the Great Schism*, 2nd ed., Leiden, New York and Köln, Brill, 1998.

Toews, John B., "Pope Eugenius IV and the Concordat of Vienna (1448). An Interpretation", *Church History*, 34 (1965), pp. 178-194.

Tompa, Frank S., *Cardinal Thomas de Erdeud and His Clan: A genealogical and historical revision*, Pender Island, Huntpaznan, 2001.

Trexler, Richard C., *The Spiritual Power: Republican Florence under Interdict*, Leiden, Brill, 1974.

——, *Public Life in Renaissance Florence*, Ithaca and London, Cornell University Press, 1980.

Tusor, Péter, *The Papal Consistories and Hungary in the 15th-16th centuries: To the history of the Hungarian Royal Patronage and Supremacy*, Budapest and Roma, MTA-PPKE 'Lendület' Church History Research Institute, 2012.

Ullmann, Walter, *The Growth of Papal Government in the Middle Ages: A study in the ideological relation of clerical to lay power*, New York, Barnes and Noble, 1955.

——, "The legal validity of papal electoral acts", *Ephemerides Iuris Canonici*, 12 (1956), pp. 3-35.

Untergehrer, Wolfgang, "'Diligenter se informet et omnia … referat.' Das päpstliche Gesandtschaftswesen als Kommunikationssystem (ca. 1450-1500)", in *Ecclesia als Kommunikationsraum in Mitteleuropa (13.-16. Jahrhundert)*, ed. Eva Doležalová and Robert Šimůnek, München, Oldenbourg, 2011, pp. 13-50.

——, *Die päpstlichen nuntii und legati im Reich (1447-1484): Zu Personal und organisation des kurialen Gesandtenwesens*, PhD Dissertation, München, 2012 (https://edoc.ub.uni-muenchen.de/15862/1/Untergehrer_Wolfgang.pdf).

Urbánek, Rudolf, *České dějiny*, vol. 3, *Věk poděbradský*, pt. 2-4, Praha, Jan Laichter and Academia, 1918-1962.

Vale, Giuseppe, *Itinerario di Paolo Santonino in Carintia, Stiria e Carniola negli anni 1485-1487*, Città del Vaticano, Biblioteca Apostolica Vaticana, 1943.

Van Engen, John, "Multiple Options: The World of the Fifteenth-Century Church", *Church History*, 77 (2008), pp. 257-284.

Vecce, Carlo, "I memoriali ungheresi di Diomede Carafa", *Prospettive settanta*, n.s. 14 (1992), pp. 467-487.

Veszprémy, László, "The state and military affairs in east-central Europe, 1380-*c.* 1520s", in *European Warfare, 1350-1750*, ed. Frank Tallett and D.J.B. Trim, Cambridge, Cambridge University Press, 2010, pp. 96-109.

Vogel, Cyrille, *Introduction aux sources de l'histoire du culte chrétien au moyen âge*, ed. Bernard Botte, Spoleto, Centro italiano di studi sull'alto medioevo, 1981.

Walf, Knut, *Die Entwicklung des päpstlichen Gesandtschaftswesens in dem Zeitabschnitt zwischen Dekretalenrecht und Wiener Kongress (1159-1815)*, München, Huber, 1966.

Wasner, Franz, "Fifteenth-Century Texts on the Ceremonial of the Papal 'Legatus a latere'", *Traditio*, 14 (1958), pp. 295-358.

——, "'Legatus a latere': Addenda varia", *Traditio*, 16 (1960), pp. 405-416.

Watanabe, Morimichi, "Pope Eugenius IV, the Conciliar Movement, and the Primacy of Rome", in *The Church, the Councils, and Reform: The Legacy of the Fifteenth Century*, ed. Gerald Christianson, Thomas M. Izbicki and Christopher M. Bellitto, Washington, D.C., The Catholic University of America Press, 2008, pp. 177-193.

Watt, John A., *The Theory of Papal Monarchy in the Thirteenth Century: The Contribution of the Canonists*, New York, Fordham University Press, 1965.
Weber, Benjamin, *Lutter contre les Turcs: Les formes nouvelles de la croisade pontificale au XVe siècle*, Roma, École Française de Rome, 2013.
——, "L'alun de la croisade? Étapes et difficulté de la mise en place d'un monopole pontifical sur l'alun de Tolfa (1461-1471)", *Cahiers de recherches médiévales et humanistes*, 25 (2013), pp. 597-619.
Weinfurter, Stefan, ed., *Päpstliche Herrschaft im Mittelalter: Funktionsweisen-Strategien-Darstellungsformen*, Ostfildern, Jan Thorbecke, 2012.
Weiss, Roberto, "Lineamenti di una biografia di Giovanni Gigli, collettore papale in Inghilterra e vescovo di Worcester (1434-1498)", *Rivista di storia della chiesa in Italia*, 1 (1947), pp. 379-391.
Whalen, Brett Edward, *The Medieval Papacy*, Basingstoke, Palgrave Macmillan, 2014.
White, Hayden V., "The Gregorian Ideal and Saint Bernard of Clairvaux", *Journal of the History of Ideas*, 21 (1960), pp. 321-348.
Willershausen, Andreas, *Die Päpste von Avignon und der Hundertjährige Krieg: Spätmittelalterliche Diplomatie und kuriale Verhandlungsformen (1337-1378)*, Berlin, De Gruyter, 2014.
Winroth, Anders, *The Making of Gratian's* Decretum, Cambridge, Cambridge University Press, 2000.
Wolff, Helmut, "Päpstliche Legaten auf Reichstagen des 15. Jahrhunderts", in *Reichstage und Kirche*, ed. Erich Meuthen, Göttingen, Vanderhoeck & Ruprecht, 1991, pp. 25-40.
Wynen, Arthur, *Die päpstliche Diplomatie geschichtlich und rechtlich dargestellt*, Freiburg im Breisgau, Herder, 1922.

Zapperi, Roberto, "Caffarelli, Prospero", in *DBI*, vol. 16, Roma, Istituto della Enciclopedia Italiana, 1973, pp. 251-254.
Zey, Claudia and Claudia Märtl, eds, *Aus der Frühzeit europäischer Diplomatie: Zum geistlichen und weltlichen Gesandtschaftswesen vom 12. bis zum 15. Jahrhundert*, Zürich, Chronos, 2008.
Zilynská, Blanka, "Biskup Filibert a české země", in *Jihlava a basilejská kompaktáta*, ed. Dana Nováková, Karel Křesaldo and Eva Nedbalová, Jihlava, Muzeum Vysočiny, 1992, pp. 56-94.

Internet resources

Miranda, Salvador, *The Cardinals of the Holy Roman Church*, http://www.fiu.edu/~mirandas).
MNL Budapest. OL DL, https://archives.hungaricana.hu/en/charters/
Monasterium, http://www.monasterium.net/
Pennington, Kenneth, *Ken Pennington*, http://legalhistorysources.com/
Pennington, Kenneth and Charles Donahue, *Bio-Bibliographical Guide to Medieval and Early Modern Jurists*, http://amesfoundation.law.harvard.edu/BioBibCanonists/HomePage_biobib2.php
Regesta Imperii, http://regesten.regesta-imperii.de/
Repertorium Germanicum & Repertorium Poenitentiariae Germanicum, http://www.romana-repertoria.net/993.html

Index

absolution, 13, 47, 51, 69, 78-87, 98, 134, 193, 211
Accursius, 60
Adhémar of Le Puy, 150
Agnelli, Lodovico, 46
Albert II, King of the Romans, Hungary and Bohemia, 168
Albert of Brandenburg-Ansbach, Grand Master of Teutonic Order, 69, 88
Albert VI, Duke of Austria, 170, 171
Albigensians, 151
Albornoz, Gil, 25
Aleprandis, M. de, 130
Alexander III (Rolando Bandinelli), pope, 18, 63
Alexander VI (Roderigo Borja), pope, 75, 92, 106, 110, 126, 130, 145, 158, 162, 190, 197, 200, 202, 204
Alfonso V, King of Aragon, 159
Altheimer, Konrad, 130
Amelia, C. de, 130
Ammannati Piccolomini, Giacomo, 44, 46, 101, 126, 162, 163, 203, 204
Anastasius, Bishop of Thessaloniki, 56
Ancona, 126, 142
Angelus de Gizalphis, 133
Anne of Foix and Candale, Queen of Hungary and Bohemia, wife of Wladislas II, 124
Apostolic Chamber, 14, 44, 52, 102, 130, 136-147, 152, 203
Apostolic Penitentiary, 11, 13, 68, 69, 75, 77, 79-87, 164
Aquileia, 74, 75, 96, 130
Arabatti, bank, 145
Aragon, 162
Aragona, Beatrice d', Queen of Hungary and Bohemia, wife of Matthias Corvinus, 124, 128, 187
Aragona, Giovanni d', 42, 65, 73, 74, 76, 78, 80, 84, 95, 96, 99, 106, 107, 121, 131, 133, 138, 144, 157, 181, 182, 184, 207
Arcimboldi, Giovanni, 203, 207
Augsburg, 85, 127
Augustinus de Monellis, 133
Austria, 38, 43, 49, 97, 101, 122, 125, 168, 176
Avignon, 168, 202
Avisio, river, 125

Bajezid II, Sultan, 187
Bakóc, Tamás, 47, 92, 100, 123, 126, 133, 134, 163, 164, 192-194, 203, 208
Baldo degli Ubaldi, 18, 58
Balkans, 9, 165
Balue, Jean, 80
Bamberg, 24, 127
Barbazza, Andrea, 18, 28, 40
Barbiche, Bernard, 12
Barbo, Marco, 31, 32, 42-46, 50, 51, 66, 71-74, 76-78, 80-84, 88, 92, 93, 96, 101, 106, 107, 111, 117, 122, 125, 127-130, 132, 133, 135, 138, 141-143, 146, 157, 163, 180, 181, 184, 185, 196, 201-204, 207
Barbo, Pietro, see Paul II
Bardejov, 53, 65
Bartolini, Mariano, 45, 101, 133, 208
Bartoš Písař, Prague scribe, 49
Basel, 127, 197
Basel, Council of (attempt), 197
Basel, Council of, 8, 58, 70, 128, 152, 154, 176, 190, 191, 193, 194, 210
Báta, 134
Bátori, István, 212
Baufremes, Francesco da, 130
Bavaria, 44
Beaufort, Henry, 152

Beckensloer, Johann, Archbishop of Esztergom, 84
Belgrade, 160, 161
Bellemère, Gilles, 26
Benedict XII (Jacques Fournier), pope, 58, 136
Benedictines, 52
benefices, 13, 29, 30, 52, 55, 61, 62, 67-70, 75-77, 80, 82, 84-87, 98, 138, 142, 144, 147, 188, 196, 202
Benešov, 128
Berka of Dubá, Albrecht, 66
Bernard of Clairvaux, 17
Bernard of Montmirat (Abbas antiquus), 18
Bernard of Parma, 18
Bernard of Pavia, 17, 99
Bertachini, Giovanni, 40
Bertrand de Deux, 25
Bessarion, 43, 47, 92, 102, 140-142, 162, 163, 173, 176, 185, 200-202, 204, 206
Biondo, Gaspare, 111
bishops, 7, 13-15, 18, 24, 27, 34, 39, 44, 51, 55, 56, 59, 61-69, 75, 77, 84, 114, 119-121, 123, 133, 135, 136, 138, 150, 174, 189, 195-198, 204, 205, 209, 212
Biskup, Marian, 170
Blet, Pierre, 12
Bohemia, 13, 31, 42, 49, 53, 66, 71, 76, 83, 88, 92-94, 97, 99, 100, 107, 114-117, 127, 136, 144, 149, 150-158, 165, 167, 168, 172-175, 178, 181, 186, 187, 190-195, 197, 205, 209, 210
Bohier, Nicolas, 18, 28, 40, 69
Bologna, 63, 125, 202
Bolzano, 125
Bonfini, Antonio, 49
Boniface VIII (Benedetto Caetani), pope, 18, 24, 55, 57, 61, 112
Borghetto, 125
Borgia, Giovanni, 197
Borja (Borgia), Roderigo, see Alexander VI
Boskovice, Tas (Prothasius) of, Bishop of Olomouc, 48, 173
Bosnia, 161
Boulogne, Gui de, 41
Bourges, 119
Bratislava, 122, 123
Brenner Pass, 125
Bressansone (Brixen), 125
Brittany, 71
Brno, 151
Bruneau, Jean, 18, 28, 40, 98
Brześć Kujawski, 171
Buda, 49, 51, 119, 124, 126, 127, 133, 151, 159, 160, 164-166, 179, 182, 183, 192, 194, 195, 212
Budapest, 87
Bünau, Günther von, 102
Burckard, Johannes, papal master of ceremonies, 41, 44, 47, 104-107, 110, 114, 120, 132, 205
Burgio, Giovanni Antonio Buglio, Baron of, 37, 38, 46, 165, 186, 192, 194
Burgundy, 36, 37, 71, 92, 162, 185, 186, 200, 201
Byzantine Empire, 24

Caffarelli, Prospero, 181-183, 185, 186
Calais, 152
Calixt III (Alonso Borja), pope, 92, 158-161, 170, 174, 200
Camerino, Bartolomeo da, 43, 85, 89
Camisati, Domenico, 144, 207
Campania, 202
Campeggi, Lorenzo, 30, 38, 46, 63, 66, 92, 110-112, 118, 119, 192, 194, 195, 208
canon law, 8-11, 17-30, 37-41, 55-69, 71, 79, 80, 89, 91, 97, 100, 101, 103, 129, 134, 136, 189, 196, 198
Canossa, Lodovico, 38
Canterbury, 138
Capranica, Angelo, 92, 202
Capranica, Domenico, 158
Carafa, Diomede, 128
Carafa, Oliviero, 44, 92, 143, 202
cardinals, 9, 10, 14, 18, 21, 22, 24, 25, 27, 28, 30, 37-40, 44, 46, 52, 58, 70, 71, 73, 100, 102-114, 128, 129, 137-140, 153, 154, 158, 159, 162, 167, 168, 173, 183, 186, 188, 189, 193, 199-208, 214
Cardinals, College of, 8, 10, 14, 24, 99, 103, 104, 106-111, 137-139, 158, 195, 199, 200, 203
Carinthia, 125
Carlisle, 138
Carniola, 125
Carvajal, Bernardin, 47, 70, 102, 107, 109, 132
Carvajal, Juan, 7, 47, 83, 84, 92, 96, 106, 114, 115, 117, 121, 128, 131, 132, 135, 138, 140, 154, 159-162, 170, 173, 180, 189, 191, 192, 206
Casimir IV, King of Poland, 32, 42, 83, 88, 117, 122, 127, 128, 146, 147, 155-157, 170-174, 176, 178-180, 196, 212

Castello, Alberto da, 120
Castiglione, Branda, 151, 152
Castiglione, Giovanni, 160, 206
Castile, 25, 162
Celestine III (Giacinto Bobone), pope, 18, 67, 136
ceremonial, 12, 14, 18, 24, 25, 39, 41, 44, 77, 97-99, 103-124, 146, 165, 187, 188, 190, 204, 205, 213
Cesarini, Giuliano, 152-154, 158, 160, 162, 167
České Budějovice, 155
Chambers, David, 204, 205
chancery, legatine, 24, 34, 48, 49, 94, 129, 131-134, 144, 146, 211
Charles I, King of Spain, 106
Charles the Bold, Duke of Burgundy, 185, 201
Charles, Duke of Münsterberg, 195
Chieregato, Leonello, 46, 129, 130
Christ, 98, 116
Christian, commissary and *auditor* of Ladislaus Geréb, 65
Christopher, burgher of Olomouc, 82
Chur, 86
Cialfi, Angelo, 132, 133
Cibo, Giovanni Battista, see Innocent VIII
Cinthius, cardinal, 67
Cività Castellana, 49
Clemens de Turun, 133
Clement IV (Guy Foucois), pope, 18, 100
Clement V (Bertrand de Got), pope, 57, 137
Clement VI (Pierre Roger), pope, 25
Clement VII (Giulio de'Medici), pope, 123, 195
Coëtivy, Alain de, 92
Cola, Nicholas, 192
Cologne, 41, 127, 145, 189, 196
Colonna, Pompeo, 208
Communellus, B., 133
Compilatio prima, 17
Condulmer, Francesco, 158
confessional letters, 11, 47, 78-80, 93, 134, 143, 185, 211
Constance, 196
Constance, Council of, 70, 151, 193
Coppini, Francesco, 35
Corpus Iuris Civilis 60
Coşeiu (Kusály), 53
Cosmas of Prague, 113
Costa, Jorge da, 202
councils, conciliarism, 8, 9, 27, 58, 59, 154, 191, 195, 199; see also Basel, Constance, Ferrara, Florence, Lateran, Lyons, Pisa, Trent
credentials, 41, 43, 50, 75, 185
Croatia, 49
crusade, 9, 10, 14, 35, 38, 43, 44, 48, 63, 71-73, 78, 79, 83, 90, 91, 97, 118, 122, 134, 139, 141, 144, 147, 149-167, 170-178, 180, 181, 185, 186, 188, 190-193, 202, 203, 209, 212, 214
Czerstede, Brandanus, 86
Czerstede, Johannes, 86

Danube, river, 87, 125, 160
De Vio, Tommaso (Gaetano), 31, 66, 87, 90, 92-95, 108, 119, 122, 123, 131, 133, 208
Decretum Gratiani, 17, 22, 40, 57
Denmark, 92, 93
Despuig, Ausias (de Podio), 73, 74, 76, 77, 80, 95, 138, 143, 144, 181, 207
Dietrich von Moers, Archbishop of Cologne, 190
dispensation, 10, 11, 13, 35, 40, 53, 55, 59, 62, 68, 69, 79-82, 84-87, 96, 194, 196, 211
Dissoncourt, Johannes, 133
Djem, Sultan, 164
Długosz, Jan, Polish chronicler, 48, 117, 146, 171
Domažlice, 153
Dominicans, 33, 193
Dominici, Domenico, 27, 33, 59, 75, 173, 176, 186, 206
Dominici, Giovanni, 151
Dovizi da Bibbiena, Bernardo, 30, 31, 92, 111
Dubrovnik, 161
Durand, Guillaume, 18, 22, 28, 40, 62, 68, 75, 97-99, 113, 119, 120
Duyn, Johannes, 85

election capitulation, 159, 199, 200, 202
England, 25, 31, 35, 41, 63, 66, 92, 110, 118, 119, 130, 152, 162, 164, 169, 170, 202, 211
Enrici, Battista, 145, 206
Erlichshausen, Ludwig von, Grand Master of Teutonic Order, 172
Ernest II of Saxony, Archbishop of Magdeburg, 212
Eschenloer, Peter, chronicler of Wrocław, 32, 33, 48, 116, 117, 128, 155, 175, 180
Estaing, Guillaume-Hugues d', 170

Estouteville, Guillaume d', 138, 144, 158, 185, 200, 201
Esztergom, 128
Euboia, 71
Eugenius IV (Gabriele Condulmer), pope, 8, 31, 58, 152-154, 158, 200
Europe, 7, 10, 15, 40, 49, 72, 73, 89, 91-94, 97, 106, 107, 141, 149, 150, 158, 159, 163, 170, 181, 186, 188, 189, 202, 205, 212-214
Europe, Central, 12-15, 27, 32-34, 38, 42, 45, 46, 48, 51, 71, 73, 78, 92-94, 96, 111, 117, 119, 126, 135, 149, 151, 154, 155, 157-160, 163-165, 167-186, 190-192, 201, 203-206, 214
Europe, Northern, 111
Europe, Western, 168
excommunication, 26, 35, 41, 62, 69, 78-83, 86, 87, 98, 157, 170, 171, 180
Extravagantes communes, 17, 18, 26, 40, 55, 61, 62

Faber, N., 133
Farnese, Alessandro, 30, 107, 108, 208
Fasolo, Angelo, 130
Felix V(Amedeo of Savoy), pope, 8
Ferdinand I, Archduke of Austria, 122, 123
Ferdinand I, King of Naples, 128, 212
Ferrara, Council of, 58
Ferreri, Zaccaria, 38, 69, 70, 89, 210
Ferrero, Antonio, 108, 203
Figueira, Robert C., 20-22, 60, 67, 91, 97
Filipec, Jan, Bishop of Várad, 121, 122, 181, 196, 197, 212
Flavio, Giovanni Battista, 133
Florence, 125
Florence, Council of, 58
Flores, Antonio, 46
Forlì, Antonio da, 142
Fraknói, Vilmos, 51
France, 13, 25, 26, 29, 31, 35, 38, 70, 71, 92, 99, 112, 119, 130, 138, 141, 152, 162, 163, 169, 200-202, 204, 214
Francis I, King of France, 106, 111
Franciscans, 53, 190
Franco, Nicolao, 190
Frankfurt am Main, 152, 160
Frederick III, Holy Roman Emperor, 35, 36, 42, 43, 71, 73, 89, 101, 102, 121, 127, 145, 154, 155, 157, 160, 162, 168, 172, 173, 175, 176, 181-187, 189, 201, 205, 212
Fregoso, Paolo, 202
Fürstenfeld, 78

Gabrielli, Gabriele de', 109
Gambaro, Pietro Andrea, 18, 28, 40, 69, 98
Garatus Laudensis, Martinus, 28
García de Villadiego, Gonzalo, 18, 28, 29, 35, 40, 69, 98, 100, 136
Gauffridus de Bellomonte, 24
Gentile da Spoleto, 70
Georg von Niederaltaich, 53
George of Poděbrady, King of Bohemia, 31, 48, 49, 66, 79, 88, 115, 116, 144, 147, 154-157, 171-178, 180, 195, 210, 212
Georgius de Priolis, 133
Geraldini, Angelo, 34, 46, 145, 197, 207
Geraldus de Bolzanis de Regio, 132
Geréb, Ladislaus, 33, 34, 65, 131, 207, 209, 210
Germany, 13, 25, 31, 35, 38, 41, 45, 46, 54, 59, 63, 66, 70-73, 85, 90, 92-95, 99, 102, 107, 110-112, 122, 125, 127, 130, 133, 138, 141, 143, 144, 149, 151-154, 159, 160, 163, 164, 168, 170, 172, 176, 181, 183, 186, 187, 189, 196, 201, 205, 214
Gherardi da Volterra, Giacomo, 140, 201
Gigli, Giovanni, 130, 211
Gigli, Silvestro de', Bishop of Worcester, 118
Giles of Rome, 57
Ginorus, Johannes, 131
Godin, Guillaume de Pierre, 57
Goffredus of Trani, 18
Göller, Emil, 79
Gonzaga, Francesco, 204
Górka, Uriel, Bishop of Poznań, 84
Grassi, Achile, 38, 147, 208
Grassi, Antonio, 46, 145
Grassi, Paride, papal master of ceremonies, 41, 44, 104-111, 114, 123, 124, 163, 164
Gratian, 17, 18, 59
Gregory VII (Ildebrando di Soana), pope, 9, 20, 21, 67, 75, 136, 189, 208
Gregory IX (Ugolino di Anagni), pope, 18, 55, 61
Griffi, Pietro, 28

Hadrian V (Ottobuono Fieschi), pope, 41
Halberstadt, 63
Heidelberg, 176
Henricus de Segusio (Hostiensis), 18
Henry VII, King of England, 211, 212
Henry VIII, King of England, 63, 106, 118

Henry, Patriarch of Aquileia, 75, 208
heresy, heretics, 53, 58, 80, 83, 88, 150, 151, 153, 157, 158, 178, 180, 186, 190, 192, 195, 197, 212
Hilarius Litoměřický, 180
Hohenstein, Jodocus, 170
Holy Land, 24, 84, 150
Hospitallers, 209
Hug, Johannes, 59
Hugonet, Philibert, 185, 201
Hungary, 13, 24, 25, 27, 38, 41, 42, 45, 46, 48, 49, 51, 53, 63-65, 71-73, 76, 88, 89, 92-94, 96, 97, 99, 100, 107, 112, 117, 121-124, 126-128, 136, 138, 143, 144, 149, 151, 152, 159-161, 163, 165, 168, 172, 173, 175, 181, 183, 185, 187, 190, 192, 193, 203, 205, 209, 211, 214
Hunyadi, John, 172
Hus, Jan, 151, 193
Hussites, 31, 48, 139, 144, 149-158, 167, 174, 177, 178, 190

indulgences, 11, 13, 36, 38, 47, 53, 70, 72, 73, 75, 77-79, 84, 89, 90, 96, 114, 115, 118, 120, 121, 134, 139, 147, 152, 153, 156, 159, 163, 164, 167, 198, 209, 211, 212
Inn, river, 125
Innocent III (Lotario), pope, 18, 22, 67, 68, 113, 149
Innocent IV (Sinibaldo Fieschi), pope, 18, 56
Innocent VIII (Giovanni Battista Cibo), pope, 50, 52, 89, 101, 130, 140, 165, 182, 196, 198, 201, 205, 207, 209, 211
Innsbruck, 118, 125
instructions, 35, 36, 42, 43, 45, 50, 51, 101, 103, 105, 110, 118, 120, 121, 123, 125, 126, 128, 131, 179-181, 187, 194, 198, 204, 209, 210
interdict, 41, 62, 66, 80, 83, 84, 98, 151, 176, 180
Isvalies, Pietro, 44, 47, 65, 78, 82, 92, 93, 110, 124, 125, 127, 133, 138, 143, 192, 208
Italian League, 37
Italy, 25, 58, 92, 118, 125, 126, 157, 163, 168, 197, 202, 212

Jacobus de Boldogasszonyfalva, 131
Jagiellonians, Polish-Lithuanian dynasty, 42
Jamometić, Andrea, 36, 197
Jerusalem, 98, 116
Jihlava, 179
Jiskra z Brandýsa, Jan, 171
Johannes Andreae, 18
Johannes Teutonicus, 18, 63, 68
John (Hungarian), 130, 131
John of Capistrano, 160, 178
John the Baptist, Saint, 98
John XXII (Jaime Duesa), pope, 7, 18, 58, 62, 137
John, Count of St George and Pezinok, 83
John, King of Denmark, 212
Jubilee, 143, 147, 163
judge-delegate, 20, 23, 39, 56, 67, 74, 90
Julius II (Giuliano della Rovere), pope, 46, 59, 76, 102, 108, 110, 201, 202
jurisdiction, legatine, 20, 23, 26, 28-31, 39, 41, 48, 52, 53, 55, 56, 58, 60-66, 70, 74, 76, 97-100, 121, 131, 133, 134
jurisdiction, papal, *iudex omnium*, 13, 23, 55-61, 65, 79, 111, 131, 134, 135, 198

Kalocsa, 52, 145
Kiełbasa, Wincenty, 196
Kirchberg, 86
Koldrer, Silvester, scholar, 53
Kraków, 117, 122, 127, 128, 178
Kubinyi, András, 65
Kutná Hora, 156, 157, 179, 197
Kyer, Clifford Ian, 20, 21, 23-26, 30

Labenter, Henricus, 133
Ladislaus de Cepha, burgher of Buda, 65
Ladislaus Posthumous, King of Hungary and Bohemia, 160, 161, 168, 172
Ladislaus, abbot of Báta, 134
Lando, Girolamo, 31, 32, 34, 96, 116, 134, 147, 155, 161, 170, 171, 173-176, 185, 191, 192, 206, 209
Landshut, 118
Lang, Mattheus, 31, 66, 92, 164, 208
Lapalisse, 119
Lapicide, Johannes, 130
Łaski, Jan, Archbishop of Gniezno, 38
Lateran, Council of (III), 129, 136
Lateran, Council of (IV), 129, 136
Lateran, Council of (V), 59, 193, 194
Lausanne, 8
Le Jeune, Jean, 138
Leo I, pope, 56
Leo IX (Bruno), pope, 21
Leo X (Giovanni de' Medici), pope, 38, 70, 89, 92, 106, 107, 123, 158, 163, 164, 193, 202, 203, 210, 214
Lesage, Georges-L., 12

Liber extra, 17, 18, 22, 26, 40, 55, 61, 62, 67, 68, 74, 91, 97, 113, 136
Liber sextus, 17, 18, 22, 26, 40, 55, 61, 62, 68, 75, 100
Lichfield, 138
Liège, 85, 196
Linz, 122
Lithuania, 70, 89, 210
Livorno, 126
Locher, Henricus, 86
Lolli, Antonio, 118
Lombardy, 24, 41
London, 118
Longueil, Richard Olivier de, 108
Lopecz, Johannes, commissary of Angelo Pecchinoli, 53, 133
Lorenzi, Giovanni, 130, 183
Louis II, King of Hungary and Bohemia, 119, 122, 123, 165, 194, 195
Louis XI, King of France, 162, 185, 201
Louis XII, King of France, 58, 109
Louis, Duke of Bavaria, 118
Low Countries, 202
Luciani, Agostino, 127, 197
Lusatias (Upper and Lower), 49
Lyons, 119
Lyons, Council of (II), 56

Madrid, 190
Mainz, 41, 86, 127, 189, 196
Mair, Martin, 118
Malborghetto, 125
Maleczek, Werner, 12, 45
Mansella, Benedetto, 101
Mansueti, Leonardo, 129, 130
Mantua, 125, 170
Maraschi, Bartolomeo, 35, 43, 45, 46, 78, 89, 93, 101, 126, 131, 145, 157, 164, 192, 197, 198, 204, 205, 207, 212
Marches, 108, 202
Margaret, burgher of Olomouc, 82
Margaret, Saint, 87
Mariano da Siena, 161
Martin V (Oddo Colonna), pope, 8, 151, 152
Mary, Queen of Hungary and Bohemia, wife of Louis II, 122, 123
Massa, Bartolomeo, 130
Matthias Corvinus, King of Hungary, 42, 49-52, 65, 73, 78, 83, 88, 96, 97, 117, 121-124, 127-129, 138, 155-158, 161, 164, 165, 168, 172, 173, 175, 176, 178-187, 190-192, 196, 198, 201, 205, 209, 210, 212
Matucsinai, Gábor, 134
Maximilian, King of the Romans, Holy Roman Emperor, 47, 101, 102, 106, 107, 110, 122, 181, 185-187
Medici, bank, 141
Medici, Giovanni de', see Leo X
Mediterranean, 25
Meissen, 24, 151, 152
Merino, Esteban Gabriel, 38
Meuthen, Erich, 127
Milan, 31, 70, 138
Milei, Johannes de, commissary of Angelo Pecchinoli, 53
Mirandola, 197
Mohács, 165, 166
Monellis, Augustine de, 134
Montefiore, Gentile da, 45, 48, 136
Montepulciano, Fabiano de, 178
Montjeu, Philibert de, 210
Moravia, 49, 53, 150-152, 154, 156, 167, 191, 193
Murad II, Sultan, 154
Muscovy, 70, 89, 210

Nádasdy, Tamás, 131
Namysłów, 117
Naples, 92, 143
Negroponte, 71, 162
Nicholas of Cusa, 45, 54, 85, 92, 127, 138, 154, 160, 169, 170, 178, 189, 191, 206
Nicholas of Modruš, 162
Nicholas V (Tommaso Parentucelli), pope, 8, 154, 169, 170
Norway, 92, 93
notaries, 87, 131, 132
Nowy Sącz, 129
Numai, Alexander, 35, 36, 46, 86, 89, 101, 110, 117, 131, 145, 186, 207
Nuremberg, 127, 152, 153, 182, 184, 186, 201
Nysa, 127
Nyújtódi Székely, Miklós, Bishop of Knin, 179, 180, 184

Ockham, William, 58
Oddi, Francesco, Bishop of Assisi, 131, 160
Olomouc, 33, 51, 79, 156, 179, 193, 196
Opava, 127
Orava, castle in Hungary, 198
Orsini, Giordano, 152
Orsini, Giovanni Battista, 202
Orsini, Latino, 108, 142, 158

Orsini, Orso, 34, 46, 64, 140, 182, 183, 185, 186, 192, 201, 205, 207
Orsini, Roberto Latino, 38, 208
Orte, 49
Otranto, 182
Ottoman Turks, 9, 14, 30, 63, 71, 73, 82, 83, 89, 96, 102, 116, 122, 125, 126, 131, 134, 139, 141, 144, 149, 150, 154, 155, 157-168, 172, 174, 175, 179, 181, 183, 186, 193, 194, 209

Pagnanis, Cesar de, 130
Palacios, Fernando de, 151, 153
Palacký, František, 49
Paleologos, Theodor, 46
Palermo, 67
Pallavicini, Antonio Gentile, 112
papacy, Papal Curia, passim, see also Apostolic Chamber, Apostolic Penitentiary, Papal Chancery, Papal Consistory, Papal Datary, Sacra Romana Rota
Papal Chancery, 34, 42, 43, 50, 71, 94, 131
Papal Consistory, 14, 44-46, 99, 104, 105, 107, 109-111, 114, 119, 185, 187, 200
Papal Datary, 87
Partner, Peter, 25
Passau, 121, 196
Patrimony of St Peter, 202
Patrizi Piccolomini, Agostino, papal master of ceremonies, 41, 44, 47, 104-107, 109, 112, 118, 120-122
Paul II (Pietro Barbo), pope, 27, 33, 48, 93, 155, 157, 158, 161, 162, 171, 176, 177, 200, 201, 203
Pecchinoli, Angelo, 29, 34, 35, 46, 49-54, 65, 66, 75, 89, 94, 95, 126, 127, 131, 133, 145, 164, 181, 185-187, 190, 192, 196-198, 205, 207, 209-211
Pedro de Luna, cardinal (antipope Benedict XIII), 31
Pelegrina, Giovanni da, 130
Pennington, Kenneth, 63
Peraudi, Raymund, 46, 47, 59, 78, 92, 101, 102, 110, 122, 164, 181, 185-187, 207, 208
Perrin, John W., 60
Persico, Tommaso, 128
Perugia, 108, 129, 203
Perusia, Jacobus de, 130
Petrarca, Francesco, 26
Petrovaradin, 160
Petrucci, Francesco, 29, 70, 75, 99
Philip IV, King of France, 57
Philip the Good, Duke of Burgundy, 159
Philippus de Segardis, 133
Pienza, 125
pilgrimage, 80, 84, 134
Piotrków, 171
Pires, Luis, 206
Pisa, Council of (*conciliabulum* 1511), 58, 59, 70
Pius II (Enea Silvio Piccolomini), pope, 10, 27, 31, 32, 35, 58, 102, 154, 155, 161, 162, 170, 171, 173, 174, 191, 200, 201, 206, 209
Pius III (Francesco Todeschini Piccolomini), pope, 47, 85, 93, 118, 125, 132, 146, 156, 178, 186, 200, 201, 207, 211
Platina (Bartolomeo Sacchi), 126, 162
plenitude of power, *plenitudo potestatis*, 9, 10, 13, 26, 55-59, 66, 67, 90, 91
Poitiers, 138
Poland, 13, 32, 38, 42, 44, 48, 70-73, 76, 88, 89, 92-94, 99, 100, 117, 127, 141, 144, 145, 152, 159, 163, 168-172, 175, 181, 185, 193, 205, 210, 211
Polcenigo, Tommaso da, 130
Pomerania, 169
Pontanus, Richardus, 211, 212
Ponte, Antonius de, 211
Ponzano Romano, 51
Porta, Ardicino della, 197, 202
Portugal, 92, 107, 145, 162, 204
Prague, 7, 24, 27, 47, 114, 115, 127, 128, 151, 155, 157, 174, 175, 180, 191, 194, 197, 210
procession, 41, 53, 77, 105-107, 114-117, 120, 124, 191, 203
Prochowice, 117
procuration, 136
Prostějov, 197
Prussia, 169, 170

Rampini, Enrico, Archbishop of Milan, 31
Rangoni, Gabriele, 34, 36, 65, 96, 124, 133, 134, 138, 155, 156, 178, 179, 181, 182, 184, 207
Ransano, Pietro, 49
Ravenna, 141
Reffle von Richtenberg, Heinrich, Grand Master of Teutonic Order, 88
reform, 7-9, 11, 14, 17, 18, 20-22, 48, 52, 75, 87, 127, 153, 189, 190
Regensburg, 24, 47, 93, 118, 125, 156, 160, 169, 170, 178, 186

relics, 87, 116, 120
Rennie, Kriston R., 19, 20
Ricasoli, bank, 145
Richard, Archbishop of Canterbury, 63
Richard, P., 12
Romagnano, Antonio, 132, 211
Roman law, 25, 60, 61, 97
Rome, 9-11, 14, 25, 35-37, 42, 44, 46, 47, 50, 51, 64, 65, 73, 76, 78, 79, 84, 89-91, 95, 97, 99, 101, 102, 104-113, 115, 117-120, 125, 126, 129-131, 138, 140-143, 145, 149, 152-156, 160, 162, 164, 167, 169-171, 173, 175, 179-181, 183, 186-189, 191-194, 196-205, 208, 211, 212, 214
Roselli, Antonio, 18
Rosier, Bernard du, 121
Rovere, Domenico della, 132
Rovere, Giuliano della, see Julius II
Roverella, Lorenzo, 33, 75, 79, 85, 132, 134, 144, 146, 155, 156, 161, 178-180, 186, 206, 207
Rovereto, 125
Rožmberk, Jošt of, Bishop of Wrocław, 175, 209
Rüdesheim, Rudolf of, 27, 33, 35, 118, 144, 146, 155, 156, 171-173, 176-178, 196, 205, 207
Ruess, Karl, 19
Runcio, Domenico, 128
Russia, 92
Ryckel de Leeuwis, Dionysius, 18

Sacra Romana Rota, 111, 112, 134
Salzburg, 138, 196
Sandonnini, Nicolò, 71, 75
Sansoni Riario, Raffaele, 143
Sant'Oreste, 51
Santovito, Andreotto de, 130
Sanudo, Marino, 126
Savelli, Giovanni Battista, 202
Savoy, 71, 132
Saxony, 66
Scandinavia, 127
Schaumberg, Peter von, 206
Schenck, Ludovicus, 86
Schlecht, Tilmann, 135
Schmugge, Ludwig, 11
Schmutz, Richard A., 20, 21, 24
Scotland, 202
Senj, 126
Serbia, 161
Seville, 145
Sforza, Ascanio Maria, 202
Sicily, 67
Siebenborn, 87
Siena, 116, 118, 125
Sigismund I, King of Poland, 38, 69, 70, 89, 210, 211
Sigismund, Count of St George and Pezinok, 83
Sigismund, Duke/Archduke of Austria, 118, 205
Sigismund, Holy Roman Emperor, King of Hungary and Bohemia, 151, 152, 168
Silesia, 31, 48, 49, 116, 127, 128, 180, 197
Sixtus IV (Francesco della Rovere), pope, 34-36, 42, 50, 71, 89, 92, 95, 101, 129, 141, 143, 145, 157, 158, 162, 180-182, 184, 196, 197, 200-203
Sixtus of Tannberg, Bishop of Freising, 85
Slavkov, 53
Slovakia, 53
Smołucha, Janusz, 34, 35, 215
Soriano nel Cimino, 142
Spain, 57, 75, 92, 107, 145, 159, 204, 214
Spoleto, 202
Staré letopisy české Czech chronicle 49
Stefaneschi, Giacomo, 24, 25, 41, 104
Strasbourg, 59
Studt, Birgit, 11, 12
Styria, 78, 125
Swarcz, Georgius, burgher of Košice, 53, 65
Sweden, 92, 93
Swiss Confederation, 99
synods, 14, 55, 189, 190
Szalkai, László, Archbishop of Esztergom, 38, 119, 165, 195
Szatmár, county in Hungary, 66
Szécsi, Dionysius (Dénes), 27, 92, 159, 161, 206
Székesfehérvár, 124, 173
Szydłowiecki, Krzysztof, 122, 123

Tachov, 152
Tartars, 193
Templars, 209
Teutonic Order, 69, 83, 169-174, 176, 196
Theiner, Augustin, 49, 51
Thuróczi, János, 49
Thurzó, Elek, 165
Thurzo, Stanislaus, Bishop of Olomouc, 197
Timur Lenk, 150
tithes, 72, 152, 177
Todeschini Piccolomini, Francesco, see Pius III

Toledo, Francesco da, 32, 116, 155, 162, 163, 170, 171, 174, 175, 191, 192
Tolentić, Luka, Bishop of Šibenik, 36, 37, 42, 46, 75, 185, 186, 200
Tolfa, 44, 161
Tolštejn, castle in Bohemia, 66
Toruń, 146, 169, 171, 172
Trent, 125
Trent, Council of, 39, 63, 66
Trevisan, Lodovico, 92, 158, 161
Treviso, 190
Trier, 41, 87, 127
Tues, Konrad, collector, 145
Tüngen, Nicholas von, 196
Turini, Baldassare, 46, 65, 134, 138, 144, 176, 178, 179
Tuscany, 201

Udine, 125
Unity of Brethren, 54, 193
Untergehrer, Wolfgang, 12, 30, 31, 40, 129, 196, 215
Urban II (Eudes, Oddo), pope, 150
Ústí nad Labem, 152
Utraquists, 7, 31, 114-116, 127, 128, 144, 150, 154, 155, 157, 165, 167, 168, 174, 190, 191, 193-195, 197

Valle, Fantino della, 116, 117, 155, 191
Van Engen, John, 10
Váradi, Péter, Archbishop of Kalocsa and Bács, 145, 197, 198
Varna, 154, 158, 160
Vasily III, Grand Duke of Muscovy, 69
Vayas, Didacus de, 140
Venice, 37, 40, 45, 51, 126, 128, 140, 141, 143
Venzone, 125
Vera, Juan, 92
Verona, 125
Verzelio, Giovanni, 165
Veszprém, 64, 196
Vienna, 49, 51, 102, 114, 119, 125, 127, 140, 141, 173, 189, 191
Visegrád, 128, 198
visitation, 24, 51, 75, 87, 114, 190
Viterbo, Egidio di, 30, 92
Vitéz the Younger, John, 183, 196
Volargne, 125

Walf, Knut, 12
Walter, Hubert, Archbishop of Canterbury, 136
Warham, William, Archbishop of Canterbury, 66
Warmia, 196
Wasner, Franz, 12, 112
Westminster, 66
Wieliczka, 117
Wiener Neustadt, 122, 125, 127, 160
Wilhelmus, priest, 87
Wimars of Erkelenz, Peter, 178
Winroth, Anders, 17
Wladislas II, King of Bohemia and Hungary, 42, 64, 65, 123, 124, 156-158, 179, 191, 192, 198
Wladislas III (I), King of Poland and Hungary, 154
Wolsey, Thomas, 31, 63, 66, 92, 118, 119, 164
Wrocław, 31-33, 48, 116-118, 127, 128, 134, 146, 147, 151, 153, 156, 169, 171, 174-177, 179, 180, 209
Wycliffe, John, 193

York, 138

Zagreb, 126
Židek, Pavel, 210

Printed in Szczecin, Poland
by Booksfactory
November 2017